WENDELL PHILLIPS

Wendell Phillips

WENDELL PHILLIPS

Liberty's Hero

James Brewer Stewart

Louisiana State University Press

Baton Rouge and London

Designer: Diane B. Didier
Typeface: Linotron 202 Trump Mediaeval
Typesetter: G & S Typesetters, Inc.
Printer: Thomson-Shore, Inc.
Binder: John H. Dekker & Sons, Inc.

LIBRARY OF CONGRESS CATALOGING IN PUBLICATION DATA

Stewart, James Brewer.
  Wendell Phillips, liberty's hero.

  Bibliography: p.
  Includes index.
  1. Phillips, Wendell, 1811–1884. 2. Abolitionists—
Massachusetts—Biography. 3. Slavery—United States—
Anti-slavery movements. I. Title.
E449.P56S74 1986   973.7′114′0924 [B]   85-23793
ISBN 0-8071-1257-7

Frontispiece: Wendell Phillips at the age of fifty, engraving by H. W. Smith of Boston. Courtesy Chicago Historical Society, ICHi–12134.

FOR BECKY AND JENNY

Contents

Illustrations

Preface and Acknowledgments

Recent scholarship on the abolitionists has minimized their importance in shaping the issues of their age. Seen as piously removed from partisan affairs, the abolitionists are said to have had an only marginal impact in the North-South political conflict. Perceived as Victorian paternalists, they are declared to have been largely unable to challenge a white supremacist culture. Defined as "possessive individualists," they are considered to have been incapable of recognizing the social costs of "free-labor" industrial civilization. Understood as seekers of religious purity, they are analyzed in psychological terms that show them as more dedicated to self-discovery than to social struggle. In *Wendell Phillips: Liberty's Hero*, the first biography of this towering reform figure in over twenty years, I question or modify each of these interpretations. I do so, however, more often by implication than by direct rebuttal, for I assume that individual biography can not always claim to speak as general history. Moreover, in this book I attempt, above all else, to develop a comprehensive humanistic explanation of Phillips' life and its significance for his age. Hence, I rehearse my scholarly exceptions only when they might not be obvious to specialists or distracting to general readers.

All the same, this work varies from current scholarship by presenting Phillips (and by implication his abolitionist colleagues) as a central figure in the Civil War era. Phillips developed authentic political power as an abolitionist; sought victory in fundamental social conflicts; was a vigorous, consistent racial egalitarian; and appreciated (as a champion of free labor) the harsh social consequences of industrialization. I believe that Phillips' reform commitments can best be understood not through psychology but through a humanistic understanding of his acutely personal sense of history and moral order as these were shaped by private circumstances and public events from childhood to old age. Phillips' motives for reforming seldom led him to self-absorption but, instead, thrust him deeply into political and social conflict.

But in arguing these positions, I do not wish to reassert the "neo-abolitionist" liberal scholarship of the 1960s and early 1970s. Instead, as the title itself implies, this book develops as a central theme Phillips' use of inherited republican traditions in defining his personal identity, sustaining his political consciousness, and directing his public behavior. Although *republicanism* seems to have become a generic term for politics from Machiavelli's time to the IWW's, it was nevertheless, for Phillips, a powerful set of specific family and upper-class Bostonian traditions that stressed liberation as the reward of self-restraint and political liberty as the handmaiden of stern social order. In this respect, the subtitle *Liberty's Hero* itself suggests the lifelong sense of liberation that Phillips discovered for himself and envisioned for the nation after he had himself claimed to be a literal extension of a past that affirmed these republican values. In a closely related sense, the subtitle *Liberty's Hero* also conveys Phillips' deeply held conception of himself as a heroic republican actor, who replicated the inspired leadership of Sam Adams, Oliver Cromwell, and others. Acting on this radically republican sense of himself Phillips challenged his contemporaries to explore their fullest understandings of American freedom. At issue were not only an ideologist's abstractions and a moralist's dreams but also the tangible interests of politicians, entrepreneurs, and planters, as well as of slaves, free blacks, and poor industrial laborers.

And finally, I have tried to display Phillips' private experiences as fully as possible and to develop their significance for his public life. Since this book incorporates a large body of largely unfamiliar Phillips papers (the Crawford Blagden Papers, Harvard University), it explores as has no other biography Phillips' marriage to a mysterious, reclusive invalid and the enormous influence of Ann Greene Phillips on her husband's career. Likewise, these sources reveal Phillips' influential roles within the white abolitionist community and his interactions with blacks as well. In addition this book explains the highly personalized nature of Phillips' rhetoric by connecting such expressions to the moral structure of his private world. And by extending such analyses, it also sets forth the sources of Phillips' eloquence and accounts for his great impact on his audiences.

There are many whom I must thank for helping me with this book. My colleagues at Macalester College, especially Jeff Nash, Peter Rachleff, Calvin Roetzel, Norm Rosenberg, Paul Solon, and the late Ernest Sandeen offered warm friendship along with wise counsel. Generous scholars elsewhere—particularly Eric Foner, Steve Ross, Richard Sewell, Betty Fladeland, Lawrence W. Friedman, James M. McPherson, Aida DiPace Donald, and Richard Curry—also gave unstintingly of their critical insights. Financial assistance from the American Council of Learned Societies, the Newberry Library Fellowship Program, the Mellon Foundation, and the Macalester College Faculty Activities Committee was crucial to my work, as was the help of talented librarians, especially those at Harvard University's Houghton Library and the University Archives, the Massachusetts Historical Society, the Boston Public Library, the American Antiquarian Society, and Macalester College's Weyerhaeuser Library. Sister James Theresa of the College of St. Catherine deserves special mention for providing me a particularly hospitable environment for writing. My talented editor, Judith Bailey, has improved this work at every turn.

Dottie Stewart, as always, contributed her abundant understanding of me and my work to enhance every aspect of this project. I can only reciprocate with deep gratitude and deeper love. Becky and Jenny Stewart, my zestful daughters, often give forth with raucous snoring noises whenever I begin pontificating about Wendell Phillips or any other historical topic. Grateful for their lighthearted lessons in humility, and for much more, I dedicate this work to them.

WENDELL PHILLIPS

ONE

The Aristocrats' Child

The new, brick, Federal-style home, set on Beacon Hill at the corner of Walnut and Beacon streets, gave testimony to its owner's prestige. Its tall lower windows hinted at much taller ceilings within. The home stood a full three stories tall amid its spacious grounds and looked high over the rolling greens of Boston Common, which stretched out across the street. Charles Bulfinch, architect to Boston's wealthiest families, had designed a handsome house. None doubted that John Phillips could afford his new mansion or that he had the social position to put it where he pleased. After all, his grandfather had built a conspicuous mansion on the other end of Beacon Street before the Revolution, and it was still one of Boston's proudest residences. John had obtained his own first fortune by inheritance, his second upon his marriage to Sarah Walley, a member of one of Boston's great old trading families, and the third by giving much-valued legal advice to Boston's mercantile leaders. He then began an illustrious career in the politics of his city and state, and in 1805 John and Sarah Phillips occupied their fine new residence.[1]

Soon, other great families of Boston began to follow them. First came David Sears, who commissioned an elegant Greek Revival mansion in 1806. Then the James Swan family contracted with Bulfinch to design

1. Harold Kirker and James Kirker, *Bulfinch's Boston, 1787–1817* (Boston, 1964), 162–63; Irving Bartlett, *Wendell Phillips: Brahmin Radical* (Boston, 1961).

I

The Phillips family mansion on Beacon Hill was Wendell Phillips' childhood home, 1811–1828. This photograph appeared in the National Association for the Advancement of Colored People, *Wendell Phillips Centenary* (Privately printed, 1911), 3.

three gracious homes on adjoining parcels. By the end of 1807 the distinguished leader of New England's Federalist party, Senator Harrison Gray Otis, had moved in, splendidly. A sightseers' attraction, his home contained eleven bedrooms (each with a fireplace) for children, seven bedrooms for servants, and two enormous bedchambers for the heads of the house. A graceful spiral staircase connected the main foyer to the grand ballroom, and there were ample gardens on three sides of the house. Following this grand arrival came the Appletons, Motleys, Lowells, and still other Otises, each family bringing its crystal glassware and inlaid English furniture. Old Boston families like the Phillipses were now amassing new fortunes and rebuilding their city to suit their needs and tastes. "The great numbers of new and elegant buildings . . . strike the eye with amazement," reflecting, one returning Loyalist wrote, "the rapid manner in which people have been acquiring wealth."[2] In that first new Beacon Hill residence on November 29, 1811, Wendell Phillips was born. His surroundings would mark him forever as an offspring of aristocrats.

John and Sarah Phillips were not overindulgent parents. Still, the more than comfortable circumstances and affectionate family assured Wendell a happy childhood. As the eighth of nine closely spaced children, he had plenty of elder brothers and sisters to befriend and challenge him. There were also solicitous elders close by, notably his paternal grandmother, Margaret Phillips, who visited frequently. Servants tended him too, especially his beloved nurse Polly, for whom Wendell developed so enduring an attachment that years later, after his own marriage and his mother's death, he brought Polly to service in his own home. She was his "second mother," his wife later reminded him.[3] But most of all, John and Sarah Phillips assured Wendell that he was a child of special importance, whose spiritual growth and personal development concerned them deeply.

2. Kirker and Kirker, *Bulfinch's Boston*, plate 12; Samuel Eliot Morison, *Harrison Gray Otis, 1765–1848: Urbane Federalist* (Boston, 1969), 218–26, 223 (quotation).

3. Carlos Martyn, *Wendell Phillips: The Agitator* (New York, 1890), 24, contains a complete list, with dates, of John and Sarah Phillips' children. For John Phillips' mother, see John Phillips to Phoebe Foxcroft Phillips, December 20, 1799, and n.d., both in Crawford Blagden Papers, Houghton Library, Harvard University (hereafter HL); "Memoir of John Phillips," *Boston Monthly Magazine* (November, 1825), 281–92; John Gorham Palfrey, *A Sermon Preached . . . on the Late Hon. John Phillips* (Boston, 1823), 17. On Polly, see Ann Phillips to Wendell Phillips, n.d., Blagden Papers. Many selections from the Blagden Papers have been reprinted in Irving Bartlett, "New Light on Wendell Phillips and the Community of Reform, 1840–1880," *Perspectives in American History*, XII (Cambridge, 1979), 3–251.

Glimpses of Wendell's early life suggest an active, quick-minded child, whose parents encouraged him to be venturesome. The corner of Walnut and Beacon streets introduced Wendell to a neighborhood in which no inquisitive boy could become easily bored. As he followed Beacon Street to the right, he walked over rutted dirt streets through bucolic countryside. One neighbor still put up his own hay; several grazed cows on the Common. Going on slightly farther down the hill (Wendell was now just two hundred yards from his house), he stood on the shore of the Back Bay, where a child could swim, catch things in the water, and clamber about on old pilings. A quick run back over the hill took him to the forty-three grassy acres of the Common, where the pond offered frogs, turtles, and wading. In the winter, there was also sledding near the statehouse over by John Hancock's old barn. Bordering the Common on its far side ran Tremont Street and the beginnings of the bustling city that wealthy families like the Phillipses were rapidly creating out of the leisurely village. New businesses, shipping facilities, and manufacturing concerns expanded rapidly as Boston, involved in a growing nation's economy, increased its size by half during the decade between 1820 and 1830.[4] Had Wendell initially turned left onto Beacon Street from his front door, ten minutes of walking would have taken him past the statehouse and then to State Street, the financial heart of the city, where great merchants and bankers arranged the lucrative investments that underwrote the city's explosive growth.[5]

By 1820 many of these entrepreneurial families had moved in near the Phillipses, and their sons had become Wendell's playmates. Bookish Lothrop Motley grew up to write history, and gregarious Tom Appleton was destined to inherit his father's textile fortune. At ten, however, what mattered to Wendell was the fun he and his two friends had in Lothrop Motley's attic. There Tom Appleton remembered watching while Phillips and Motley would "strut about in any fancy costume they could find, and shout short scraps of poetry and snatches of dialogue at each other." At about that age, Phillips also assisted the precocious Motley with his first attempt at a novel. "It opened," Phillips remembered, "not with 'one solitary horseman,' but two, riding up to an inn in the valley of the Housatonic. Neither of us had ever seen the Housatonic, but it sounded grand and romantic." Both vignettes show Wendell engaged in a friend-

4. Bartlett, *Phillips*, 4–5; Martyn, *Phillips*, 24.
5. Martyn, *Phillips*, 28–29.

ship that allowed him to explore and share his imagination, far removed from stuffy parents. In the usual manner of creative children, Wendell and Lothrop embellished their performances over and over, and Tom Appleton remembered the play acting as "their favorite pastime."[6] John and Sarah did not interfere, preferring to let their son develop on his own what proved to be a lifelong passion for history and the drama he sensed in it.

Tom Appleton, on the other hand, preferred to play outdoors, and Wendell, it appears, was as happy to roughhouse as to act in skits. Tom remembered Wendell as a "manly little fellow," a companion of whom he "was very proud," and judging from his recollections of his own childhood, Appleton was not a boy to keep any friend who balked at hard play. If Lothrop Motley challenged Wendell's creativity, Tom Appleton tested his stamina and sense of class privilege.[7]

As Wendell grew and Boston's economy expanded, friction began to develop between the growing numbers of poor and the upper class. Many of the opulent families on Beacon Hill had moved there to escape the influx of lower-class laborers into their old neighborhoods around Summer and State streets. Behind Beacon Hill, however, near the Charles River, lay a growing black community of artisans and unskilled workers—"Nigger Hill," as the whites called it—which proper families like the Phillipses regarded as "a place of vague horror."[8] By the mid-1820s city officials, acting on citizen complaints, had begun to monitor these "undesirables." In other areas near Wendell's West End neighborhood, population growth and shifts in industrial location also caused boundaries of privacy to rupture and class antagonisms to express themselves. Wealthy residents complained of grog shops, whorehouses and criminal activity.[9]

The children of poor families made increasing use of the Common, and Wendell and other wealthy boys from the Hill resented their presence. Sometimes when blacks appeared, Wendell, Tom Appleton, and others would form into Boston's most privileged neighborhood gang and

6. *Ibid.*
7. *Ibid.*
8. The following two paragraphs are partly based on Thomas Appleton's recollections of his boyhood, "Old Boston," in his *A Sheaf of Papers* (Boston, 1875), 333–51.
9. Roger Lane, *Policing the City: Boston, 1822–1885* (Boston, 1967), 2–25; Andrew R. L. Cayton, "The Fragmentation of 'a Great Family': The Panic of 1819 and the Rise of the Middling Interest in Boston," *Journal of the Early Republic*, IV (June, 1982), 143–67.

attempt to drive them off with volleys of rocks. Failing this, they found themselves tussling with young blacks who refused to be intimidated by self-appointed white "superiors." Wendell's lifelong love of hiking, swimming, and gymnastic sports such as boxing surely began in these rugged friendships and fights. He had also begun acquiring some prejudices about wealth and white skin that he would one day be forced to reconsider.

As high-ranking members of Boston's social elite, Sarah and John Phillips fully expected their sons to succeed them in the "Brahmin aristocracy," as people began to call it. This wish was, in part, their reason for granting Wendell such freedom to associate and explore. They believed he needed to learn early about the society in which he should one day hold power and to acquire quickly the initiative and self-confidence that leadership demanded. At home, moreover, John Phillips took steps to reinforce such goals by introducing Wendell to a principle he would uphold throughout his life—the supreme importance of self-discipline. John insisted, for example, that his sons learn to work with their hands, to develop habits of self-reliance, and Wendell remembered his oft-repeated maxim: "Never ask another to do for you what you can do for yourself; and never ask another to do for you what you would not do for yourself if you could." Acting accordingly, John made his sons learn the rudiments of several artisan crafts (Wendell became especially adept at carpentry) and held them responsible for day-to-day household maintenance.[10]

John Phillips also took care to show his sons examples of the skills leadership in public life demanded. Wendell certainly was present when distinguished family friends like Harrison Gray Otis or Josiah Quincy presided at civic occasions. John Phillips himself was frequently engaged to speak before "several different bodies of men, on various subjects, political, commercial, financial, and philanthropic," where Wendell had plenty of opportunities to observe him. Then too, Wendell could simply vault the fence across the street whenever patriotic occasions such as militia musters, Fourth of July celebrations, or election day festivities took over the Common. Here, in a ceremonial atmosphere, troops would

10. Martyn, *Phillips*, 27; John and Sarah Phillips seem to have been extending parenting experiences of their own upbringings, as discussed in Part 3 of Phillip Greven, *The Protestant Temperament: Patterns of Childrearing, Religious Experience, and the Self in Early America* (New York, 1977), 151–264.

march in full dress to stirring bands, and civic leaders would hold forth eloquently from the reviewing platform.[11]

Evidence suggests that Wendell took these lessons very seriously, even at a young age, and one acquaintance recalled that he "lost no opportunity to hear Edward Everett or Otis talk of policies and politics in Boston." Observing these occasions became to him as "fascinating an occupation" as "visiting the circus is to the country lad who has been performing acrobatic stunts on an old family horse." Many years later, another friend repeated an anecdote that Phillips recounted of himself as a four- or five-year-old, when he used to arrange the parlor chairs in rows, stand before them with a Bible propped in front of him, and address the imaginary audience. When his father inquired as to whether he ever tired of this play, Wendell remembered replying, "No, but it is rather hard on the chairs."[12]

The story, true or not, suggests that in Brahmin families boys were strongly encouraged to think of themselves as public figures, able to command others through force of personality and, by self-expression, to shape the course of events. The story also illustrates how profoundly religion inspired child rearing in pious households like the Phillipses'. While many of Boston's fashionable families were beginning to abandon trinitarian doctrines of "orthodox" Protestantism for Unitarianism, John and Sarah Phillips held to the creed of their Congregationalist parents and vigorously impressed them upon their children. They spoke with an age-old authority confirmed by personal visits, for Wendell's zealously Calvinist grandmother, Margaret Phillips, often resided in her son's home. She kept close track of the family's religious state and continued to make John give strict account of his spiritual standing. At a well-established thirty-four, he still felt constrained to assure his mother that despite his worldly obligations, "I hope to keep my mind on my eternal welfare, agreeably to your kind admonition."[13] Upon her death in 1823, John expressed his sense of loss by recalling to one of Wendell's elder brothers "all of the admonition and advice she has given you. She daily carried you in the arms of faith and prayer for you to the

11. "Memoir of John Phillips," 287; Bartlett, *Phillips*, 6.

12. Mary C. Crawford, *Romantic Days in Old Boston* (Boston, 1922), 152; Martyn, *Phillips*, 27.

13. John Phillips to Margaret Phillips, September 18, 1804 (quotation), November 11, 1811, Margaret Phillips to Phoebe Foxcroft Phillips, December 20, 1799, all in Blagden Papers.

throne of grace." Wendell certainly was no less a recipient than the other children of supplications from this powerful matriarch. His father recalled how "she urged on us all, and frequently, the indispensible importance of preparing for the great change of worlds."[14]

John and Sarah Phillips, too, urged their faith on their children, but with warm persuasion that tempered Grandmother's stern reminders. Few, if any, child-intimidating threats of God's retribution ever echoed through the Phillips household. Later on, Wendell was to assert that he had "learned of my father, long before boyhood ceased," to resist the "yoke of ignorance and superstition" that he always associated with overzealous Puritanism.[15] John Phillips' letters to Wendell's elder brothers clearly confirm his son's recollection. Nor did his parents sense any conflict between their religious urgings and their desires to bring up men who would achieve power and public distinction. They encouraged each son to embrace the Calvinist faith and to live by its creed day to day, insisting that only with divine aid would they acquire the continuous inner discipline so essential for both "an exemplary life" and for salvation. Samuel Phillips, for example, began his Harvard education at sixteen with fatherly reminders to "tend to your arithmatik [sic]," to keep up in Latin and Greek, and to read the Bible daily. John emphasized that secular learning was essential but that "Divine knowledge" was "infinitely more important. The first you must acquire to make yourself useful and comfortable," John instructed. On "the second you must rely, with the aid of Divine Grace, for your well being throughout eternity." He closed the letter with a father's "sincere prayer" that Samuel's life be always "industrious, virtuous and happy." His concerned but loving tone is evident, and he repeated it in other letters to various sons over the years.[16]

Wendell, who resided at home while his father lived, gained his religious instruction in the intimacy of the family setting. There, Sarah Phillips made Christian affection the essence of her son's nurturing, supporting her husband's spiritual authority in Wendell's eyes with the most

14. John Phillips to John Phillips, Jr., March 1, 1823, *ibid.*
15. Phillips quoted in Ralph Korngold, *Two Friends of Man: The Story of William Lloyd Garrison and Wendell Phillips and Their Relationship with Abraham Lincoln* (Boston, 1950), 109.
16. John Phillips to "My Dear Son" (Samuel Phillips), October 17, 1815, John Phillips to "My Dear Son" (John Phillips, Jr.), September 12, 1822, both in Blagden Papers.

compelling of personal appeals. For example, she assured Wendell that he was her favorite child, and she often took him aside for prayers. She also presented him with a Bible, which Phillips kept for the rest of his life and in which, seventy-odd years later, he marked the passages he wished to have read at his funeral. "Be good and do good; this is my whole desire for you," Phillips once explained, was the sum of his mother's injunctions. "Add other things if you may—these are central." Years later, Wendell tellingly described his mother as "having lived in her children, and they almost lived in her." He always, he confessed, felt "best satisfied" with himself "when I see anything in me that reminds me of my mother."[17]

Whatever its specific psychological import, Phillips' statement confirms that Sarah had established a pervasive influence over her son's lifelong development and was successful indeed in transmitting the conviction that both she and God demanded him to achieve self-discipline and to serve some high purpose in the world. She and John took every pain to assure Wendell that evidence of his morally controlled behavior and his expressions of piety elicited their love and approval. They gave him abundant emotional inducements to believe that in matters of eternal significance, as in the day-to-day affairs of life, Phillips family principles, warm parental support, and God's unchanging commands were inextricably bound together. Family and faith, they taught, should compel an unswerving devotion to a fixed internalized code of truth and to the obligation to serve others with distinction. True piety was much more than the handmaiden of a young man's gentlemanly virtues; it was the indispensable prerequisite for family acceptance and a successfully conducted life.

Judged by outward appearances, the Boston Latin School, only a ten-minute walk from home, might not have seemed a very promising place to begin pursuing public success. Nevertheless, Wendell Phillips was enrolled there in 1821 at age eleven. Headmaster Benjamin Apthorp Gould oversaw a classical curriculum and a staff that insisted on its memorization. Some, like Wendell's somewhat older acquaintance Charles Sumner, took easily to long rote assignments of Cicero, Horace, and Tacitus. Others fretted over the tedium of puzzling out "the uninteresting and

17. Martyn, *Phillips* 30; Bartlett, *Phillips*, 9–10; Phillips to Elizabeth Pease, January 31, 1846, William Lloyd Garrison Papers, Antislavery Collection, Boston Public Library (hereafter BPL).

unintelligible rules, notes, exceptions and remarks" that filled their texts.[18] Wendell's later speeches and letters demonstrate that he retained enough from Gould's tutors and his subsequent studies at Harvard to cite ancient history and a variety of classical epigrams easily, but discipline was lax. The boys often did "plenty of talking" and drew pictures as classes went on; Wendell was especially free of restraint in his senior year, when he sat at a desk positioned beyond his master's easy range of vision. Despite the Latin School's deficiencies, however, everyone knew that boys who wished to become "somebody" were enrolling there in increasing numbers. Some said that the Latin School "dandled Harvard College on its knee" since so many of its best graduates simply moved across the Charles River to continue their studies.[19] Other Harvard-bound boys attended Exeter or Andover, two private academies founded by Wendell's kinsmen, but Wendell's family preferred to keep him home.

In 1821 just before Wendell's matriculation, Headmaster Gould decided to start an English department, and Phillips' class was the first required to compose extensively in that language. The broad topics assigned aimed to develop the students' ease and range of discourse on edifying subjects, and they called for opinion, not documented analysis. Fortunately, Phillips preserved some of what he wrote in these personal essays, providing some revealing glimpses of his youthful hopes, ambitions, and convictions.

Once, for example, Wendell thought through the question "What should young men learn from the past?" by insisting that a youth must suffer early, "so that in a future period in his life he might recall those lessons . . . and learn to conduct himself on the perilous path of duty." Those who failed to "gain experience from past misfortune" inevitably squandered the "wisdom and prudence" that could be gained from "lessons so dearly bought," for reversal should teach self-discipline. All humanity, moreover, carried the image of the Creator, Wendell went on, and was the "head and governor" of all God's "visible works." Each person, therefore, had the overriding duty of "elevating" his God-given faculties, in preparation for a destiny of "immortal existence." Hence,

18. James Freeman Clarke, a contemporary of Phillips' at the Latin School, quoted in David Donald, *Charles Sumner and the Coming of the Civil War* (New York, 1960), 9.

19. Edgar Buckingham Papers, Harvard University Archives. Buckingham, secretary of Phillips' 1831 class at Harvard, was also a student at the Latin School when Phillips attended. This valuable memoir gives vivid glimpses of Phillips throughout his youth. Korngold, *Two Friends of Man*, 110.

Phillips continued, people must exercise vigilant self-control over baser urgings, for constant self-regulation liberated an individual to fulfill the Creator's higher designs. For this reason, God did not fashion a human soul "to be subject to animal propensities, to the desires of that body in which it is enclosed." Instead, Phillips declared, the soul was "created to govern and regulate" the wayward impulses of its physical host. "Let us all be careful that we neither benumb our faculties with idleness, [n]or degrade them by applying them to unworthy objects."[20]

Phillips had clearly begun to act out his parents' continuous insistence on self-control, affirming this value to seek the approval of his schoolmasters. Now he had begun to assume that the successful pursuit of adult responsibility meant banishing "idleness" and rejecting "improper or unworthy" aspirations, and he had begun constructing a formulation of methods based on harsh, self-maintained restrictions and highest personal expectations. Years of careful nurture by John and Sarah Phillips had helped to develop a morally exacting young man, anxious to learn well in order to live correctly. As he wrote in another schoolboy essay, since religion initially inspired all that was "noble and sublime" in life, people could find "knowledge of God and His will" revealed through the study of art and literature, as well as through their prayers.[21] Phillips was now constructing specific aspirations, and above all he had begun to see himself as becoming a public figure, one whom others would someday look to as a powerful leader.

His Latin School experiences, however dull otherwise, certainly seemed to indicate that he was blessed with just such precious qualities, physical as well as mental, as were needed to meet these high goals. Already tall and athletic, Phillips was also growing to become handsomely well proportioned; he possessed poise, family position, and "gentleman's" ways and had begun to exemplify to his classmates "beauty, elegant manners and social position."[22] But most of all, Wendell was discovering that he could deliver what everyone acclaimed as unusually beautiful and persuasive speeches. Headmaster Gould required his charges to practice forensics, that skill which Boston's great preachers and statesman had traditionally honed into high art, and at such declamation

20. Wendell Phillips, "Haec Oleim Memimisse Juvabit" (1826), Wendell Phillips Composition Books, Harvard University Archives. Despite the Latin title, the text is rendered in English.
21. Untitled essay (1826), Phillips Composition Books.
22. Buckingham Papers.

Phillips found that he, too, excelled. The gift that belonged to Harrison Gray Otis, Josiah Quincy, and his own father also belonged to him. But the prizes for public address his masters awarded Wendell were indications not only of rare personal ability; they symbolized wider recognition as well. "What first led me to observe him and fix him in my memory," one Latin School classmate remembered, "was his elocution, and I began to look forward to declamation day with interest, mainly on his account."[23] By cultivating Wendell's sense of self-reliance and self-discipline, John and Sarah Phillips had brought up a boy who was able to assume a public pose with natural grace and to arrest the attention of others with his flow of words.

Wendell made no surviving comments on his feelings about discovering this potent talent, but once it was revealed, Phillips' consciousness of the gift did begin to impart a direction to his urgings for achieving self-mastery and public dominion. In an essay considering "the nature of a public life" Phillips wrote clearly of his aspirations while warning that men who desired great power faced great dangers. These could be surmounted only if individuals disciplined themselves, developing their talents to the very highest point. There were always "great rivals" over whom the leader must "excel," he wrote, "implacable enemies to overpower and a fickle mob to conciliate." The person wishing to "possess himself of uncommon attainments, maintain first rank among his classmates, or become a second Cicero" must first learn to exercise constant dominion over himself. "Attention is the key to knowledge," he insisted, "and persevering industry and steady application lead to eminence."[24] The advice Wendell gave his readers in this essay conveyed the assumptions he now was adopting for himself. By achieving mastery over his impulses, Phillips believed he would gain the freedom to obtain fulfillment, power, and eminence. By equating self-control with self-liberation in this manner, he had begun to construct an emotional design for understanding himself and his place in the larger world that would motivate him for a lifetime.

Those who listened to his salutatory address at Latin School commencement exercises could never have predicted the controversial directions in which Phillips' great ambitions would finally lead him. He, of course, had no such inkling either. His speech, delivered in Latin, cov-

23. *Ibid.*
24. Phillips, "On the Nature of Public Life" (1826), Phillips Composition Books.

ered conventional ground, celebrating the search for truth, the wisdom of the ages, and the virtue of prudence. Haughtiness may be read into the notations Phillips penned on the back of his written text, where he denied that this was really his oration at all, since two of his masters had amended it so extensively "that not more than half of it remains as I originally wrote."[25] But whatever his attitude, he certainly seemed to all who watched him a son of whom John Phillips could properly be proud.

The fact was, however, that John Phillips had died four years earlier. His absence from the audience that day represented a force that counted at least as heavily in Wendell Phillips' drive for self-mastery and distinction as did his commanding presence during the boy's first twelve years. John Phillips had died abruptly by heart attack on the evening of May 28, 1823, soon after the passing of his own mother, the only grandmother that Wendell had known. While recovering from one family loss, Wendell had to face a second one, far more grievous and unexpected.[26] It was, no doubt, the terrible shock of his father's death that caused the boy to repress his memory of John Phillips, to whom he seldom referred in subsequent years. "The heart in such a plight forgets," he once consoled a bereaved friend, "but I would not say more, being a poor hand at such thoughts. What griefs I have, I never contend with, but like a coward run away from by forgetting."[27]

Yet the absence of specific recollection had, in itself, a most far-reaching impact. While alive, John Phillips provided incarnate confirmation to Wendell that he was being brought up truthfully and well. At twelve, Wendell was not sufficiently mature to have developed many detached, critical perspectives on this man, suddenly dead, who had been so eminent and so positively involved in the life of his son. John's sudden absence, and the wound of memory that it created, left the boy to grapple alone with all the formidable traditions and imperatives of the Phillips' family. His father had seemed to exemplify them so well, and now he was unavailable to interpret them further. It is little wonder that Wendell, devastated by his grief, began to write that sorrow taught a young man self-discipline and that he yearned for "uncommon attainments" that he could only win through solitary struggle.

25. Phillips, "Salutatory Address" (1827), *ibid.*
26. Bartlett, *Phillips*, 16; John Phillips to John Phillips, Jr., March 1, 1823, Blagden Papers.
27. Phillips to Sidney Howard Gay, n.d. [1847], Sidney Howard Gay Papers, Columbia University Library (hereafter CL).

In Boston, as well as in his own home, John Phillips was widely mourned, and the city's expressions of grief only confirmed Wendell's enormous loss. John Phillips' public contribution had long added honor to his family, whose tradition of distinction stretched back nearly two centuries. John Phillips had entered Harvard at fourteen, and the legal profession four years thereafter in 1788. By 1794, at twenty-four, his practice had become so remunerative, his reputation so highly acclaimed, his oratory so admired that he had been chosen to give the Fourth of July oration on Boston Common, an honor customarily reserved for much longer-established men. His speech, which had become assigned material for two generations of elocution students, had also gained him Sarah Walley's attention and the position of public prosecutor. By 1803 he had entered state government to stay, serving briefly as representative and then until his death as state senator, upholding the Federalist party even as he had opened its elitist structure to more popular participation. The year 1809 had brought selection to the Court of Common Pleas; 1812, appointment to the Corporation of Harvard College; 1820, election to the convention that revised the Massachusetts State Constitution; 1821, elevation as Boston's first mayor to serve under its Articles of Incorporation.[28] The list could go on, but its lesson had always been self-evident to all of John Phillips' sons, Wendell included. Their father's far-reaching accomplishments were actually no more important in their own right than they were as fulfillments of august Phillips traditions.

John Phillips' first ancestors to reside in the New World had arrived with John Winthrop. The Reverend George Phillips had stepped from the *Arabella* in 1630, and thereafter, Phillipses had been in the forefront of their colony's development. Born a gentleman in England and educated at Cambridge, this original patriarch had founded a church in Watertown (later annexed to Boston) and had confirmed his independent spirit by quarreling with Governor Winthrop over religion. Once placated, however, he had helped Winthrop manage the colony during its first decades. His son, the Reverend Samuel Phillips, had been one of Harvard's earliest graduates and, as a distinguished pastor, had upheld his father's dissenting example by being jailed at sixty for voicing "slan-

28. Bartlett, *Phillips*, 10–16; Thomas Wentworth Higginson, *Wendell Phillips* (Boston, 1884), v–vi; Palfrey, *Sermon . . . on John Phillips*, 12–14; Korngold, *Two Friends of Man*, 108–109; David Hackett Fisher, *The Revolution in America— Conservatism* (New York, 1965), 73–74, 271.

derous" opposition to England's efforts to control its Puritan colonists. His two grandsons had made fortunes as merchants, and one had become lieutenant governor. Both had turned to philanthropy as well, donating sums to Harvard and other colleges and adding heavily to the endowments of two academies for younger boys in Exeter, New Hampshire, and Andover, Massachusetts. At Andover, Wendell's father had grown to college age and had begun the climb to eminence that culminated for his son Wendell in fading memories and intimidating paternal precedents, a legacy that the boy must now account for by himself.[29]

John Phillips was buried across the street from his home, in the Common's Granary Burial Ground. If Wendell watched as the casket was put in place, he saw that the leading figures in the state legislature had volunteered as pallbearers. For the rest of the session, every senator and representative would wear crepe on his left arm, symbolizing his grief at losing "the urbanity, integrity and wisdom" of his deceased colleague. Probably Wendell was present, too, a week after the interment as John Gorham Palfrey, minister of the fashionable Brattle Street Unitarian Church, rendered a memorial sermon in his father's honor.[30] Palfrey must have been specifically asked to do this by the many distinguished friends of the Phillipses who worshiped at Brattle Street, for as "orthodox" Congregationalists, the Phillipses themselves were lifelong members of the Old North Church. A larger gesture of respect to bridge the deep schisms between the Unitarians and "Puritans" of Boston could not easily have been imagined.

Certainly Wendell read the obituaries that filled many columns with praise of his father's contributions to his city and state. They lamented the loss of a leader "free from duplicity . . . virulence or rashness," who provided sound guidance "at times of great anxiety and excitement," and they emphasized how the deceased's accomplishments added magnificently to Phillips family traditions of leadership. Finally, they acknowledged the rich benevolence toward his city that John Phillips had exercised in his will "to the full extent of his means, which were very considerable." The $115,000 distributed among medical institutions in Boston, the public library, the Society of Natural History, the Boston

29. "Memoir of John Phillips," 285; Bartlett, *Phillips*, 10–15; Phillips to Samuel L. Blagden, [1883], Blagden Papers (quotation).
30. Palfrey, *Sermon . . . on John Phillips, passim*; George Austin, *The Life and Times of Wendell Phillips* (Boston, 1884), 29.

Maritime Society, the City Music Hall, and various colleges exceeded a tithe of the near million-dollar estate.[31] The sum also suggested the burden of family honor that John Phillips' death now set upon his son. Henceforward, Wendell was to encounter tangible symbols of that honor built, quite literally, into the walls of Boston's public institutions.

Other less concrete reminders of John Phillips, however, quickly confirmed their greater power in shaping Wendell's life. One Sunday, about two years after his father's death, the boy returned home from the Old North Church, where he had listened to a moving sermon on repentance by the great evangelist Lyman Beecher, whose revivals were causing a stir in the city. Beecher's powerful message had urged the "unredeemed" to seize the moment of their own salvation by voluntarily renouncing sin and filling their lives with God's controlling will. Rushing to his room, Phillips threw himself on the floor, begged God to assume mastery over his life and to remove from him all impulses to commit evil. Soon after, at Latin School, Phillips began to hold earnest conversations with his friends about "the trinity, atonement or some other point of orthodox theology."[32]

Certainly, Sarah and John Phillips had consciously directed their son to such a moment of commitment. In such pious households, a conversion experience often marked a significant moment in a son's or daughter's passage from adolescence to adulthood. Yet the necessity of acknowledging his departed father, not to mention strengthening his already close ties with his only remaining parent, Sarah Phillips, clearly added urgency to Wendell's religious upheaval. Apart from any deeper dynamics, Wendell had now embraced the memory of a father and the presence of a mother who together had always held up to him exacting religious obligation as essential for a fulfilled life. Looking back on his experience of conversion many years later, Phillips said revealingly: "From that day to this . . . whenever I have held a thing to be wrong, it has held no temptation. Whenever I have known a thing to be right, it has taken no courage to do it."[33] Wendell's religious conversion at the age of fourteen powerfully reinforced parental lessons taught since childhood. For the rest of his life Phillips would respond to inner forces that constantly urged

31. "Memoir of John Phillips," 286–88; "Inventory of the Estate of John Phillips," undated clipping [1824], Blagden Papers.
32. Martyn, *Phillips*, 41–42; Austin, *Phillips*, 28–29.
33. Phillips to Harriet Beecher Stowe, February [?], 1853, Blagden Papers.

him to confirm his moral superiority and powerful public position, for nothing less would satisfy his ancestors, his parents, or his God.

There are revealing parallels to draw between Wendell's loss of his father and the experiences of the nation at the time of John Phillips' death. Three years after that event, on July 4, 1826, Thomas Jefferson and John Adams both died, and Wendell, like many of his fellow citizens across the nation, saw in this coincidence "a remarkable providence," through which "heaven" had "seemed to set the seal of approbation upon their lives and works."[34] It was natural that John Phillips and these two patriots would die within this three-year span, for all belonged to the same generation, but their predictable passing only spurred the anxieties of a new generation that had now come to maturity as keepers of America's destiny. The founders' departure put the nation's points of origin beyond the new generation's temporal grasp, even as the future presented imponderable difficulties. All that remained were expanding myths and fading memories with which these untested inheritors had to struggle even as they took up the tasks of their own time.[35]

In this figurative but authentic sense, the nation's history and Wendell Phillips' personal narrative had become conjoined in the loss of fathers. In national circles, the "genius" of the founders was extolled for having created a "free republic." In Wendell's case, all tributes to John Phillips only confirmed his belief that his father had redeemed family honor, lived by God's injunctions, and contributed greatly to the uplift of his city and state. Boston bore the impress of his accomplishments in her history and in her buildings just as the city bore those of Sam Adams, James Otis, and John Hancock. Phillips, much later, emphasized his conviction that "Boston boys had reason to be thankful for their birthright. The great memories, noble deeds and sacred places of that town are the poetry of history, and its keenest ripeners of character."[36] His reflections reveal more about his abiding awareness of a heavy personal inheritance than they do about any legacy of John Hancock. In the

34. Martyn, *Phillips*, 41–42.
35. Austin, *Phillips*, 29.
36. The general line of thought in these paragraphs follows George B. Forgie, *Patricide in the House Divided: A Psychoanalytic Interpretation of Lincoln and His Age* (New York, 1980), but is not intended to suggest that my treatment of Phillips' life follows the psychoanalytical explanations propounded therein. The quotation is from Phillips, "The Old South Meeting House," in his *Speeches, Lectures, and Letters: Second Series* (Boston, 1891), 231–43.

decades of sectional conflict ahead, Phillips and the nation would explore the agonizing meanings of their fathers' bequests. In this sense it was fitting that the Boston City Council chose to inter John Phillips in the Common's Granary Burial Ground between headstones that marked the graves of Samuel Adams and James Otis. Wendell walked past the three of them every day on his way to class at the Latin School.[37]

37. Martyn, *Phillips*; 33, Bartlett, *Phillips*, 16.

TWO

The Studies of a Young Apollo

During the 1820s Harvard's administrators strove with a new diligence to prepare their students to enter the Brahmin elite. The wealthy families connected with Boston's economic boom began to underwrite new faculty chairs and the expansion of Harvard's physical facilities, and they sat in increasing numbers on the Board of Overseers. Tuition rose, and upper-class boys from Exeter, Andover, and the Boston Latin School made up an ever-increasing portion of the student body. Early in that decade, President John T. Kirkland introduced a uniform code of dress designed to distinguish Harvard's "young gentlemen" from the ordinary youth of Cambridge. Students went abroad, as regulations stipulated, in full calico gowns that reached the ankle. Indoors, they were required to wear waistcoat and trousers that were either all white or slightly "black mixed." Kirkland further emphasized Harvard's growing social distance from Cambridge by establishing a separate college chapel and eliminating public access to Harvard's library. His successor, Josiah Quincy, continued such policies by closing off Harvard Yard, prohibiting Cambridge residents from using the nearby town common for grazing cattle, and by barring local blacks from the Yard as well.[1]

Harvard's new social direction drew reinforcement, moreover, from

1. Roland Story, *The Forging of an Aristocracy: Harvard and the Boston Upper Class, 1800–1870* (Middletown, Conn., 1980), 3–135.

expanded courses of study. Kirkland believed that gentlemen should acquire physical grace, and so he introduced courses in fencing and gymnastics. Kirkland also felt strongly that gentlemen should possess "polished language and courtly address," and soon the students were declaiming in English as well as Latin and receiving instruction in Spanish and French. They obtained training in rhetoric from Professor Edward Channing, who scorned American speech as vulgar and insisted on the pure "simplicity" of British English. Kirkland and Quincy arranged, too, for the social interaction of undergraduates with their masters and with daughters of prominent Boston families, hoping to introduce the young men to the conventions of polite society.[2] These improvements seemed purposely meant to conform the college to the preferences of the athletic, gregarious, and eloquent Wendell Phillips, who applied to enter in July, 1827. Having passed the day-long entrance examination with ease and knowing that his classmates would include good friends like Motley, Appleton, and Edgar Buckingham, he could hardly have felt more comfortable as a part of the class of 1831.[3]

Certainly, few were better equipped than he with allies and muscles to give back more than he received during the hazing that went on during the first months. Anonymous enemies might disarrange one's entire wardrobe, and "pumpkins, squashes, brick bats and squibs" (water bombs) were hurled through windows by predatory sophomores. Resistance to such trials helped solidify his friendships with other freshmen, as did the defiance that faculty members occasionally suffered from the unruliest of Phillips' classmates. Everyone laughed when classics Professor John S. Popkin (class of 1792, and known as "Old Pop" behind his back) met his hanging effigy face-to-face one day. On another occasion, divinity Professor Palfrey seized an axe and battered down the jammed door of his lecture hall, while his students roared delightedly from within.[4]

Phillips accustomed himself to an unvarying workday that began with compulsory prayers at six. Recitations in Greek and Latin came next, then a cold breakfast followed by more recitations in mathematics and science. Lunch was at one o'clock followed by more work in Greek and Latin. Phillips ate dinner with his classmates at six o'clock and

2. *Ibid.*, 109–35.
3. Bartlett, *Phillips*, 17–18.
4. *Ibid.*, 19–20; Frederick Holland Papers, Harvard University Archives.

finished the day with evening prayers. He found few mysteries in the course of study and probably few moments of intellectual inspiration. Professors required memorized recitations and often announced the previous day those on whom they planned to call.[5] Greek and Latin courses only extended what Phillips had learned from Headmaster Gould, and judging from his neatly drawn pages of exercises, mathematics and geometry must also have come easily. He recalled enjoying mechanics (or physics) and history most of all. Other classes dragged on pointlessly; Phillips spent a semester nodding off as his Spanish instructor droned on about his years as a European revolutionary, for example. "No attempt was made to interest us in our studies," recalled one of Phillips' contemporaries at Harvard. "We were expected to wade through Homer as if the *Iliad* were a bog." Phillips evidently managed to slog along with a comfortable uninterestedness. "He sauntered and studied gently," explained George William Curtis, his good friend of later years. He was not "in the best of his mind . . . a devoted student." Nonetheless, Phillips placed a commendable seventh out of thirty-six in his graduating class.[6]

Phillips encountered the most substantial parts of his education beyond his masters' immediate notice, and one lesson from the Latin School easily carried over. Phillips, who as a boy had once written of "striving for first rank among his school fellows," quickly established himself as a dominant campus leader. He had grown into a strikingly handsome young man. Five feet, eleven inches, in height, he carried his one hundred fifty or so well-muscled pounds with grace, for he rode and fenced skillfully and paid daily visits to the new gymnastic facilities. He had thick, sandy hair and a high forehead. A firm outward extending jaw set off the finely shaped features of his face. "Though I had never seen him before, I was drawn to him by an irresistible attraction" his roommate John Tappan Pierce remembered. "Phillips was really handsome," recalled classmate Edgar Buckingham, "in figure and feature a young Apollo." One can only surmise what conclusions Phillips must have drawn about his looks when his friends insisted that he allow them to measure his body "to see how nearly his proportions come to that ex-

5. Austin, *Phillips*, 35; Donald, *Sumner and the Coming of the War*, 12.
6. Austin, *Phillips*, 35; Lillie Buffum Chace Wyman, *American Chivalry* (Boston, 1913), 3; James Freeman Clarke quoted in Donald, *Sumner and the Coming of the War*, 13; George W. Curtis, *A Memorial of Wendell Phillips from the City of Boston* (Boston, 1884), 37.

ample of Grecian ideas of manly beauty."[7] He was soon initiated into Porcellan, the Gentlemen's Club, and Hasty Pudding, the three most exclusive social clubs. At one time or another he was president of each of them, for he came of a prominent and wealthy family and was a most likable gentleman in the bargain, "the proud leader of the aristocracy" in every respect.[8]

The most telling measure of Phillips' social dominance, however, was his success in winning over the small cluster of southerners at Harvard. These sons of substantial slaveholders often felt like aliens in the gentility of Harvard Yankeedom, and for good reason. A gentleman, in their view, was one who held dominion over inferiors—black slaves and lesser whites who depended on him. Theirs was an ancient view of male dominance within a familial setting, one that most up-to-date Boston youth could not wholly fathom. Yet these southerners sought out Phillips "still more" than did his other admirers, for his masculinity, his mastery of fencing and horsemanship, and his oratorical power reminded them of the "natural aristocracy" they expected to enter upon their return home. Hence they extended their brotherhood to Phillips in whom they sensed a close kinship.[9]

Phillips knew that admirers surrounded him and that he held great power. How this knowledge affected him is a matter of importance that must be approached from several directions. His religious convictions and the influence of Sarah Phillips appear to have remained strong, for he kept his mother's Bible open on his study table, and it is reported that he read it daily. Beside the Bible was the copy of Philip Doddridge's *Expositor* that she had also given him his freshman year. Phillips always appeared alert at morning chapel, but it is not recorded whether he prayed for humility or simply offered gratitude for all his blessings.[10] It is clear, however, that in his junior year he became the target of students who resented the snobbishness of their classmates. Election to the captaincy of the Harvard Washington Corps, the college militia unit, was a major social honor. Students took "great pride in their appearance."

7. Roscoe Conkling Bruce, "The College Career of Wendell Phillips," *Harvard Illustrated Magazine*, XVII (April, 1901), 184; Bartlett, *Phillips*, 20–21; Pierce quoted in Martyn, *Phillips*, 45; Buckingham Papers, Harvard University Archives.
8. Korngold, *Two Friends of Man*, 113; Buckingham Papers; Martyn, *Phillips*, 48.
9. Buckingham Papers. The best extended discussion of southern ideals of leadership is Bertram Wyatt-Brown, *Southern Honor: Ethics and Behavior in the Antebellum South* (New York, 1982).
10. Martyn, *Phillips*, 44–45.

They drilled in the Yard dressed in black coats and white pantaloons, marshaled by officers sporting gold-plated buttons, "feathers, epaulettes and sashes." Phillips, who badly wanted the position, had the backing of his upper-class friends, but the election became a "great struggle," since all those estranged from the Phillips clique voted for someone else. Phillips, in losing, "used some of his fine scorn" on those who had dashed his hopes.[11] The edge of *hauteur* his classmates at the Latin School had noted now seems to have become arrogance.

Yet John Tappan Pierce, who shared rooms with Phillips, and Edgar Buckingham, secretary of Phillips' class and a close friend since the Latin School days, saw more than arrogance in their friend. Both emphasized in their recollections a view of Phillips that many others were to repeat with emphasis over the coming years. Although he was "courted by the wealthy and elegant, whose lives were not correct in all things," Phillips was an uncommonly "sincere, conscientious, devoted friend" to all who sought him out. He possessed something his friends identified as "character." Buckingham described Phillips' evident sense of "responsibility to keep himself pure, upright and good." This quality, Pierce remembered, seemed to keep Phillips "above pretence" or, as Buckingham explained, "without even a word or a thought that the purest might not know or listen to." Always the gentleman, Phillips seemed to be without guile, eliciting the respect and friendship of others. He could always be counted on for understanding and sound advice, Pierce remembered, and his "love of all that was honest" meant that he "always detested a mean action." Phillips seemed, in short, "perfectly transparent . . . no subterfuge, no pretence about him. He was known to all to be just what he seemed."[12] The young man who cut such an impressive public figure was also blessed with a rigid code of honesty that enhanced his constructive way with people.

At Harvard, the term *self-possessed* referred to a gentleman's confident comportment, but as Buckingham and Pierce used it to describe Phillips, it also meant something else. Phillips' "true beauty," in Buckingham's view, came not from his fine looks or proud bearing but "from his kindly, generous manner, his brightness of mind, his perfect purity and whiteness of soul."[13] As his personality matured, Phillips thus seems to have conformed in his own way to the lifelong dictates of his

11. Buckingham Papers.
12. *Ibid*; Pierce quoted in Martyn, *Phillips*, 43–47.
13. Buckingham Papers.

parents. Through the exercise of self-discipline, he was achieving an inner confidence that showed privately in the fixity of his moralism and the spontaneity of his manner, both every bit as appealing as his powerful public stature. Self-control, the essential demand of his upbringing and religious conversion, which enabled him to live by a strict personal code, had now become Phillips' touchstone for projecting himself easily into friendships, where he dominated.

But the theorem first learned in childhood, that freedom derived from self-discipline, also carried far beyond Phillips' social manner and personality. It now shaped his intellectual perspectives and had begun to refine his sense of how he and the world worked together. In another set of his student writings, speech drafts, and expository essays, Phillips vividly conveyed that this influential formulation had begun to shape his views on a myriad of critical questions. A careful analysis reveals the way Phillips' intellect and feelings had begun to interact as he reached adulthood. The beliefs and attitudes that can be seen developing in his college themes were one day to inspire his impulses to reshape America as an abolitionist, and the continuities between Phillips' perspectives as a Harvard conservative and his visions as a radical agitator were as strong as they are striking.

The essays themselves convey an authenticity that invites the historian's trust. As at the Latin School, the assigned topics were broad, and Phillips was required only to state his ideas clearly. Moreover, it is unlikely that he expressed other than his sincere opinions when asked to discuss, for example, the properties of eloquence, the traits of a great leader, or the lessons of history. On all such subjects, Phillips had every reason to feel confident of his thoughts. History had become his passion, consuming his energies and stretching his imagination as never before. The eight volumes of Gibbon's *Decline and Fall of the Roman Empire*; the eight of Hume's *History of England*; the studies of Cromwellian England, the Stuart kings, the French and American revolutions; the writings of Burke, Machiavelli, Locke, and Montesquieu that he borrowed from Harvard's library were by no means all required as assignments.[14] By the standards of that day, Phillips was rapidly turning himself into a historical scholar. In the most revealing of these papers, therefore, Phillips came closer to writing autobiography than he ever would again.

14. Library Records, Harvard University Archives; Bartlett, *Phillips*, 35.

In every such essay, he consistently built his ideas on the all-embracing assumption he had first learned at home and had then addressed openly at the Latin School: that passion must be controlled at all cost, for unrestrained passion could cause personal debasement and endless social destruction, creating the worst imaginable forms of enslavement for individuals and nations. If emotion were channeled by historical traditions and personal restraint, however, it could become a powerful agent for good, promoting progress and permitting individuals to realize their God-given talents. In times of great crisis, Phillips further held, heroic figures could come forward, embracing the traditions of their age, to exert impassioned leadership. Boldly inspired by tradition, these virtuous heroes could seize the crucial moment and act to restore order in society, thereby enhancing the liberties of all.

Phillips not only founded his definitions of eloquence squarely on these assumptions but revealed much of himself in this analysis as well, if only because his own powers as an orator had grown tremendously. He had become a genius at forensics, "possessing the same remarkable eloquence whether in extempore debate or studied declamations." In addition, Phillips had now begun disciplining himself to cultivate his gift; he would copy out into a large notebook (his Commonplace Book as he called it), passages noted in reading that he wished to recall for speeches. The method was his own invention, and he kept at it all his life.[15] In his own day-to-day practice, as in his theories about public speaking, Phillips remained faithful to the formula of his upbringing, making self-discipline the prerequisite for freedom and power in self-expression.

An extemporaneous speaker, he wrote at age twenty, must trust his instincts "to view his subject in every light and form his conclusions in an instant." Yet the speaker's spontaneous insights, in turn, had to be directed by "the most essential requisite" of all—his capacity for "regulating his own thoughts." To frame his words most effectively, the great spontaneous orator must retain control of his moment of inspiration, Phillips insisted, and "follow the same." In closely related essays, Phillips expanded this theory as he considered the nature of oratory and its political implications. "Eloquence is addressed to men, in whom feelings are centered with burning interest," he contended. "It is feeling excited

15. Phillips' method is described in Martyn, *Phillips*, 47, reprinting the recollection of a classmate, the Reverend Dr. Morrison. Phillips, "On Forming Habits of Extemporaneous Speaking. . . ." (1831), Phillips Composition Books, discusses generally how he used this method.

to action by intense, often personal instincts." The more powerful the oratory, "the stronger the *passion* inspiring it" and the more the speaker was compelled to articulate his feelings "in all their fullness and variety." Yet Phillips also expressed his deep fear of social disorder, condemning the demagogue's dexterous efforts to manipulate his listeners' prejudices, and to "enflame their passions" in order to make them "tools for his schemes of aggrandisement." To avoid this danger, eloquence must always be used in the legislative chamber, not on the street corner. In this way, powerful speech would serve the ends of order, remaining *"deliberative,* and addressed to sensible men" who were motivated by "interests," not enslaved by "passions."[16] Phillips could hardly have written more candidly of the ends that he, too, sought when he finally spoke out dramatically against slavery. Eight years later in Faneuil Hall, as he made his first speech as an abolitionist, he would coolly face a most disorderly audience that had just been inflamed by a speaker whom Phillips considered a most disruptive demagogue.

By his senior year, Phillips had concluded that what was true for forensics also applied the world over and determined the rate at which civilization advanced. He so argued in addressing the question of whether civilization had sapped people's natural energies by forcing their conformity to law and tradition. In his answer, an emphatic negative, Phillips scorned the idea of the noble savage. To follow one's natural instincts was to become "self-willed, obstinate and ignorant." The "spirit of the savage is uniformly servile," Phillips insisted, and hence "we see *them* always become submissive," fit only for domination by civilized rulers who understood that true freedom resulted from upholding, not denying, society's customs and laws. Such leaders, in Phillips' opinion, disproved that "civilized life is tame, wanting in impetuosity and energy of character." Without restraints, mankind would quickly "degenerate into a common herd."[17]

Phillips' certainty on these points was only reinforced by the dramatic historical contrasts he discerned between England and France. That Phillips, the son of staunch Federalists, loved England and dis-

16. Phillips, "Habits of Extemporaneous Speaking," "Your Idea of What Makes Writing to Be Poetical, Prose, or Eloquent" (November, 1830), "Whether the Power of Eloquence Is Diminished by the Gradual Progress of Literature and Science" (n.d.), all in Phillips Composition Books.
17. Phillips, "Whether Attachment to Ancient Usages Be a Greater Evil Than a Fondness for Innovation—a Speech" (1831), Phillips Composition Books.

trusted France is hardly surprising. Neither is Phillips' closely related contention that aristocrats, for good or ill, had always possessed the power to shape their societies. Yet the significance of Phillips' analysis passes far beyond the obvious—that here was an aristocrat's contemplation of aristocracy. As Phillips condemned the French nobility for its corrupt passions and extolled the disciplined leadership of England's peers, he envisioned in the interplay of order and passion the moral substructures of his own aspirations. Though unaware that he was doing so, he had begun to articulate the outlines of a compelling republican political ideology.

Predictably enough, Phillips made France's revolution synonymous with bloodlust, the "inevitable result" of giving free reign to passion. In France "mad enthusiasts" had thrown out every device of control, "casting to the wind the wisdom of the ages." Arrestingly, however, Phillips condemned the French aristocracy, not the Jacobins or the "illuminati," as the principal authors of the revolutionary bloodbath. The nobles had artificially set themselves apart from society, he contended, denying all constraints of tradition and obligation. They had begun acting on "base instincts," and in exercising this most dangerous kind of power, they had degenerated into a "haughty set of idlers" who intolerably exploited their "odious privileges." In thus degrading themselves, they naturally had become "objects of popular hatred," had inflamed the "licensciousness [sic] of an ungovernable populace," and had initiated a self-reinforcing cycle of wantonness and revolution. In the end, the French people had collapsed into that state of savagery to which Phillips had already consigned natural man, gladly substituting enslavement by Napoleon for Robespierre's terrorism. The lesson to his own age, thought Phillips, was perfectly clear: people must either submit to the wisdom "of those who have gone before" or "bind posterity in chains which we think it degrading to wear."[18]

Here was a provocative meditation indeed for one who enjoyed such high social standing, possessed such unusual personal skills, and felt so many compulsions to hold power. Phillips had now constructed a powerful foil against which to develop sanctions for his lofty ambitions and demanding temperament. Naturally enough, he found these sanc-

18. *Ibid.*; Phillips, "Whether the Proposed Parliamentary Reform Will Endanger the Monarchic and Aristocratic Portions of the Constitution?" (1831), "A Comparison of Burke and Sir Joshua Reynolds" (1831), both in Phillips Composition Books.

tions in England's history, where he saw no reason to exalt control exclusively, to condemn people's natural inclinations, or to lament the subversion of peaceful progress. In his eyes, England's civilized history of liberty, like France's penchant for enslavement, had been entirely determined by its nobility. England's peers had discovered the ancient truth that their own liberty and creative power depended on embracing the nation's traditions. Thus committed, they had been perfectly equipped, in Phillips' view, to act forcefully on their own initiative in the state's higher interests, for England's was a "natural" aristocracy.

Instead of being sealed off from the body politic and susceptible to self-corruption, England's peers seemed to Phillips to have been "knit with the very vitals of the constitution," completely enmeshed in the nation's history. Their influence, he claimed, had "extended down through all respectable classes," and their power seemed doubly secure, Phillips maintained, because England's nobles had owed their positions to no degenerate hierarchy derived from unmerited birthright. Theirs was instead an aristocracy based on talent (just as Boston's also claimed to be), open to vigorous new men—"the noble spirits of every generation," as Phillips warmly described them—who boasted "personal industry and skill, military success, and the influence of character," who were, in other words, leaders born of a free society with talents liberated through their own self-discipline. Had it not been the English peerage, he rhapsodized, "those many reformers who laid low and deep . . . without bloodshed and almost without commotion" while thwarting the tyrant James II in 1688? And when England had seemed about to be overrun with "atheism and anarchy" during the French Revolution, Phillips imagined, Edmund Burke "arose in his might, and moving among the crowd of inferior spirits, a giant among pigmies, he exposed their arrogant pretensions with all the energy and fire of his mind." He had thundered, Phillips concluded, "and a tumultuous nation was stilled."[19]

Phillips had now discovered his heroes, powerful figures of action from the past who set forth unmistakable examples of distinguished leadership. Burke, Pitt, Wellington, Cromwell, the signers of the Magna Carta, the leaders of the Glorious Revolution—all appeared to Phillips as supremely talented figures rooted in their society, who had struck spontaneously with dramatic power to enforce their passion for orderly

19. Phillips, "Attachment to Ancient Usages," "The Proposed Parliamentary Reform," "Comparison of Burke and Reynolds."

freedom. The fruits of their efforts were to be seen in England's arts, literature, science, and representative government, which Phillips argued were the most advanced and supportive of liberty in the world. "Governments may be violently overturned or peaceably improved," Phillips observed. "In the latter case . . . the peers can stand against any opponent."[20]

These meditations on heroism convey far more than a Harvard Anglophile's belief in Whig history. Clearly, Phillips attributed much of his own class and family position to the English peers, whose wealth, he believed, had been "the evidence of personal industry and skill." He also identified his own great ambitions with their achievements, for their "first aspirings" as "men of talent" had been "to gain for themselves a family and a name." It is not responsible to suggest that Phillips had discovered in Cromwell, Wellington, and the others figures to substitute for his lost father, but it is clear that Phillips had now collapsed the emotional distance between himself and a dramatic past where he could fantasize about his high personal aspirations and his desire to dominate in the most important affairs of his time and also see confirmed his rigid morality of self-restraint. Moreover, he had discovered a way to express his deep attachment to the republican political values of individual liberty and social order that undergirded such visions of history and his unremitting hostility to unregulated power, to "artificial" hierarchy, and to every evidence of unchecked passion in society. In all these respects, the ideological elements that formed the foundation of Phillips' later abolitionism were clearly prefigured. One day Phillips was to make dramatic gestures of his own, seeking to crush the moral anarchy and political disruption that he feared was spreading across the nation, condemning slaveholders and their supporters in the North as corrupted aristocrats and demagogues, much as he had the agents of France's revolution. To the list of patriot-heroes he was already compiling, he would add Elijah Lovejoy, William Lloyd Garrison, Crispus Attucks, and John Brown— great symbols of his own struggles against slavery. In all these respects, Phillips would one day find himself compelled to act on his panoramic vision of history, not just to study it privately and write about it.

Phillips almost admitted to such compulsions in another of his essays, when he compared the contributions of the literary writer to those

20. Phillips, "Attachment to Ancient Usages," "The Proposed Parliamentary Reform," "Comparison of Burke and Reynolds."

of the statesman. The former, he asserted, could gain enduring influence only when writing "as a moralist whose precepts will be pondered and practised" by the public while political leaders rose and fell. A literary figure was successful only when enriching larger cultural traditions and must write "to amuse, to instruct, to ennoble the heart, when his lips are closed forever." Statesmen, however, usually contributed more essentially to the nation. "Without the statesman, society cannot exist," Phillips argued. The demand for literature itself "supposes security and peace" that only the statesman, however short-lived his personal influence, was in a position to secure. The greatest leader of all, in Phillips' view, was that rare genius who could combine the powers of scholar and public leader. "They *were* [so combined] in Burke," he wrote, for Burke "aimed for perfection in each department." With his pen Burke perpetuated "his name in the memory of scholars." With his inspired rhetoric and service, he was "able to gain for his opinions the deference due the statesman."[21]

Phillips was not simply parroting genteel Beacon Hill ideals of learned statesmanship; he was articulating a conception of the scholar as political actor that reached back to older and more potent sources. During America's revolution and long before, publicists and politicians had extolled the ideal of the virtuous patriot-hero, the supremely powerful figure who could lead in times of crisis, principally because he stood above the corruption and intrigue of everyday politics. In England, insurgent writers, suspicious of unchecked power, had long emphasized that an enlightened body of uncorrupted gentlemen, or even a patriot king, must arise to save the nation from licentiousness, elite conspiracy, and the onset of tyranny. During America's revolution, these notions had taken on radical new meanings, and the ideal of the virtuous republican statesman had been born. Figures as diverse as Tom Paine, John Adams, and George Washington had envisioned a harmonious republic created by patriots of great virtue, will, and learning who both inspired and actively represented the highest interests of the people.[22] Phillips had

21. Phillips, "My Library Was Dukedom Large Enough" (1830), Phillips Composition Books.
22. The historical literature on republican ideology is vast. Of particular significance to this treatment of Phillips are Bernard Bailyn, *The Ideological Origins of the American Revolution* (Cambridge, Mass., 1969); Gordon Wood, *The Creation of the American Republic, 1776–1787* (Chapel Hill, 1969); Pauline Maier, *From Resistance to Revolution* (New York, 1972); Cecelia Kenyon, "Radicalism and Republicanism in the American Revolution: An Old-Fashioned Interpretation," *William And Mary*

seized upon this tradition to unite his passionate belief in moralistic history with his never-satisfied need to find inspiring references for directing his life. Republicanism represented a complex body of ideas that the Civil War generation was to revise for a variety of contradictory ends. Southern planters, for example, came to regard their right to hold slaves as essential to their own republican liberty. Northern wage earners, by contrast, were soon to insist that republicanism supported their struggles with factory owners over wages, workdays, and shop conditions. For Phillips, republican axioms were to prove most adaptable to a crusade against slavery; the ideology would supply the historical bedrock for his abolitionism and other radical causes. It would take him decades to explore all the implications of republicanism, but at Harvard, Phillips had already glimpsed its broad outlines, and the revelation of its heroic imperatives was to endure. In his last major speech, delivered over fifty years later (most appropriately, at Harvard), he would elaborate on the duty of the scholar in a republic in just such terms. The true scholar must also be the virtuous, independent statesman who transcended ordinary politics "to stand outside organizations, with no bread to earn, no candidate to elect . . . no object but truth to tear a question open and riddle it with light."[23]

Phillips was able to maintain this remarkable continuity in his thought because he never fell prey to anachronism, the mistake of confusing present and past. Although he often juxtaposed his own time with great events in history, Phillips always knew instinctively that America in the nineteenth century should never be mistaken for Georgian or Cromwellian England. He never found himself trapped in nostalgia and therefore passively withdrawn from or seriously out of touch with contemporary life. On the contrary, Phillips used history as a mythic baseline against which to measure himself and the validity of his social perceptions. History was for him a source of inspiration. Phillips drew extremely moralistic lessons from Burke's England, the Glorious Revolution, and the American struggle for independence, lessons that left him bitterly critical of contemporary practices. Yet he never failed to take account at the same time of the differences between present and past, even while celebrating their inspiring similarities. Consequently,

Quarterly, 3rd ser., XIX (April, 1962), 153–82; Eric Foner, Tom Paine and Revolutionary America (New York, 1976).

23. Phillips, "The Scholar in a Republic," in his Speeches, Second Series, 350.

the past Phillips constructed for himself always made him feel confident, never hesitant, about acting forcefully in the present, and although the validity of his historical judgments could often be questioned, they continuously provided him with a compelling context in which he could act.

Phillips provided a fine example of such thinking in his senior year when he addressed a popular historical issue of that day—whether the modern world was a better civilization than the ancient world had been. His answer showed a revealingly divided mind. The ancients, he asserted, "were by far our superiors" in art and fine literature, fields requiring the expression of individual genius. He also gave the ancients credit for greater advances in science, believing that contemporary investigators simply took up "where they left off." Phillips insisted that a radical point of difference did separate not just the ancient world but all of history from the present "extraordinary age," but he refused to sing the usual "sickening" paeans to humanity's acquisition of enlightened reason. It was true that "ugly old women" were no longer "put to the flame" and that "we have learned to dispute with the pen instead of the sword," but people, he believed, continued to be capable of bigoted ignorance, original sin being what it is. In fact, "the most distinguishing characteristic of the present age," he bluntly asserted, "is that everything is done for the people. Every improvement concerns the many, not the few."[24] He recognized, in short, that many of the oldest supports for elitism were in decay. Most important, he argued, privileged classes had been stripped of their exclusive access to the written word, and now the masses could read and decide for themselves.

The implications of this great change gave him no fear, and he explored them enthusiastically. Nothing had happened over the centuries to improve the moral quality of knowledge, Phillips granted, but when discussion of every subject had begun circulating widely, past and present had separated forever. "The works of learned men" were "no longer published in unknown tongues" and consigned to inaccessible archives. Instead, they were quickly translated, "scattered to every nation and read by all." The implications of this change, Phillips felt, could not be stressed enough. "We have learned to believe that every man has a mind fit (and *able*) to be cultivated," that it is "better for all in a nation to be enlightened, than for a few people to be perfectly learned." Rapid com-

24. Phillips, "The Boasted Superiority of the Present Age" (n.d.), Phillips Composition Books.

munication had transformed knowledge into a democratic commodity, he insisted, and the social implications of this great change had to be recognized. Learning had "fled the colleges and the cloisters" for the street corners and had become "the companion and assistant of us all." Age-old distinctions based on literacy had been swept away. "There is no longer any regular gradation of the rabble, who know nothing, and the disciple who know[s] nothing but what his master tells him." Public education had freed humanity from ignorant enslavement to the privileged few. People were now thinking for themselves, Phillips asserted, creating a "vast change" that had "never entered the conceptions of our ancestors."[25] The prospect clearly excited him. Though a devout believer in tradition and a devotee of Burke, he had no laments to offer for this aspect of the old regime.

Above all, Phillips found exciting prospects in the new forms of communication themselves, which had expanded the public's access to information "almost as much as [had] the invention of printing" and had therefore created a vast new audience. Ephemeral newspapers, reviews, and journals, the "popular character of our literature," now made it possible for a writer to reach the public very quickly. And the change, he insisted, had happened quite recently. "Fifty years ago," a publicist had had to wait interminably before anyone noticed his works, and then they had been read "only by scholars. Now, let him commit his thoughts to the pages of the *Edinburgh Review*," Phillips enthused, "and they are borne into every land," read and discussed by "the learned and the unlearned" alike. The writer who once would have kept his opinions private "now throws his first ardent thought into . . . a pamphlet or an article."[26]

Well-crafted prose might get lost in the process, Phillips granted, and modern Shakespeares were now hard to recognize. But against these liabilities, Phillips believed he saw one all-important gain. The influence of the writer in this "new empire," though short-lived, was extremely broad, far more powerful than it had ever been before. Leaders no longer spoke just to each other, but instead, they molded public opinion and exerted influence that even a Burke could have never foreseen. Anyone sufficiently endowed with talent or will could now address millions, Phillips imagined. One's moment of greatest influence would be brief,

25. *Ibid.*
26. Phillips, "Of the Popular Forms in Which So Much of Modern Literature Is Given to the World. . . ." (n.d.) Phillips Composition Books.

he wrote, and "destined to pass away in a generation," but for great leaders a secure place in posterity should be of "no matter." In times of great national crisis, "when the moment was perhaps critical," when it was time for "the people to act" and "it was necessary that they be instructed," a new hero could arise in a moment. "A light [would] burst from the darkness of his chamber, and like that of Heaven, enlighten the earth."[27] Phillips in this way took a confident posture from the past and never became trapped in it. The new world of democratic information, which Phillips saw himself as entering, seemed to offer him unsurpassed possibilities for inspired leadership. In his later years, as Civil War America's greatest and most radical orator, he would explore every aspect of these presumed opportunities, becoming a self-proclaimed agitator, a politically uncompromised patriot, dedicated to transforming public opinion in the defense of liberty throughout the nation.

Spring and summer of 1831 brought various occasions at Harvard to mark the graduation of Wendell Phillips' class. Class Day was a huge celebration, after which Wendell and his friends threw off their academic robes and raced into the Yard, "running and capering and dancing round and round and round, as if a streak of lightning had been close at our heels," Edgar Buckingham remembered. The young men rolled on the grass "and commenced bawling and singing, each to his own tune." Punch flowed, and Phillips joined in the choruses of the "Harvard Hymn." Formal commencement took place on August 31, and Phillips delivered an oration entitled "Parliamentary Reform and the British Aristocracy," using the occasion to praise his cherished heroes.[28]

To everyone attending, Phillips doubtless seemed an admirable, conservative gentleman. Handsome and gifted in speech, he was certainly bound, like his father, to make a name for himself in Boston's elite. He commanded respect but was also warm, candid, and scrupulously moral with all his friends. Harvard had taught him some lessons that few in the audience could have guessed; at Harvard Phillips had achieved an understanding of the past that reflected his deepest urgings to exercise power and his strongest convictions about control, passion, and freedom. He had acquired the components, as yet unassembled, of a powerful republican ideology distrustful of unchecked power, privileged hierarchy, social disorder, and popular licentiousness. In seeking to fulfill

27. *Ibid.*
28. Buckingham Papers.

the demands of his upbringing, he yearned to emulate the great hero-patriots, those dominating figures who, by crushing disorder with mighty acts, had extended the boundaries of liberty. He fervently believed that the America of his day only multiplied the opportunities for such exceptional men to seize power and mold the nation's future. Phillips departed on commencement day carrying far more than his diploma. He had seen the visions and felt the inspiration that would one day transform his life.

For now, however, Phillips had decided to return to Cambridge in the fall to enroll in law school. To most, it seemed a logical choice. Aristocratic Phillips, as one fellow graduate later wrote, certainly seemed the *"least likely"* member of the class of 1831 "to give his labor and enthusiasm" in a lifetime of "defense of popular rights." Instead, he seemed destined to make law serve the same privileged few in whose neighborhood he had been raised. Another classmate could have had no idea of how seriously he, too, erred when he insisted that "Wendell Phillips in college and Wendell Phillips six years later were entirely different men."[29] The first Wendell Phillips, Brahmin and conservative Harvard graduate of 1831, already possessed all the basic qualities of the second Wendell Phillips, radical agitator, republican abolitionist, and eloquent spokesman for race and class equality.

29. Bartlett, *Phillips*, 25; Martyn, *Phillips*, 46.

THREE

Career Despair and Marriage of Hope

As Wendell Phillips began the study of law, he looked on his choice as the least unattractive of surprisingly few alternatives. Family traditions did not permit him to follow Lothrop Motley and Edmund Quincy as they became gentlemanly writers, living on family wealth. Phillips felt no attraction to the ministry either, unlike his elder brother John Charles, who had graduated from Andover Seminary and now held a pastorate. Perhaps John Charles himself had contributed to his brother's lack of interest, for while Wendell was in college, John Charles, in long letters, had witnessed to the true faith and pleaded with his brother to be "born again in Christ." Often he had exhorted Wendell. "I address you on the supposition that *you know the truth*," he wrote. "I will expect you to answer me as soon as convenient—do not decide hastily, but count the cost well."[1] Wendell, who since the age of fourteen had considered his spiritual estate in good hands, certainly resented his brother's paternalistic sermons, finding in them the sectarian arrogance with which he was soon to charge the orthodox clergy who opposed abolition.

Phillips' eldest brother, Thomas, understood far better than did John Charles the narrow range of vocations that Wendell and many other

1. Bartlett, *Phillips*, 26; John Charles Phillips to Phillips, February 1, December 18, 1830, Blagden Papers.

36

college-educated young men could pursue in the 1830s. He himself had chosen the law, the traditional Phillips profession, and had been practicing with distinction in Boston for a decade. After attending a temperance convention, Thomas urged Wendell to join the movement and put his oratorical skills to practical use, "not only because it is a duty, but . . . because it is getting to be almost the only way in which a young man can recommend himself to the public." Such causes, he observed shrewdly, now seemed "to occupy the places" once held by "political parties and meetings" in launching a young man's career. Wendell, however, was not yet ready to join a movement. Instead, he followed the family path into the legal profession. George William, the brother closest to Wendell in age, was already reading law under private instruction and would soon open his own office.[2] Wendell enrolled at Harvard Law School in 1831.

Phillips found law uninspiring despite the magnetic presence of Joseph Story, the Supreme Court justice who headed the law school. Story, who seemed "incapable of fatigue," usually succeeded in imparting "his own enthusiasm to his pupils." Charles Sumner, for example, Phillips' undergraduate acquaintance, discovered in Story a teacher who inspired like no other, and he studied his cases with monkish concentration. Other classmates prepared for careers of distinction. Benjamin R. Curtis, for example, would sit on the Supreme Court, and George Hilliard would become one of Boston's prominent barristers.[3] But Wendell Phillips, so well situated to begin a similar career, felt no similar response. He studied casually, competently, but without enthusiasm.

Phillips' aimlessness soon began to reveal itself in social reclusiveness. The lion of Harvard's mens' clubs was now shy of social gatherings. Anna Quincy, daughter of Harvard's president, remarked after a chance meeting with Phillips in her parlor that his appearance, though agreeable, was "a mystery, as in general, man delights him not, nor woman either."[4] Yet there is evidence that at least one woman did delight him. At one point he spent nineteen successive evenings in the Tremont Theatre, glassy eyed and riveted to his seat as the beautiful and accomplished English actress Fanny Kemble performed on stage. Here

2. Thomas W. Phillips to Phillips, n.d. [early 1830s], Blagden Papers.
3. Arthur E. Sutherland, *The Law at Harvard: A History of Men and Ideas, 1817–1967* (Cambridge, Mass., 1967), 92–140; Donald, *Sumner and the Coming of the War*, 22–28.
4. Bartlett, *Phillips*, 27–28; Donald, *Sumner and the Coming of the War*, 24.

was a woman Phillips could fantasize about without risking any of the embarrassments possible in Anna Quincy's parlor. He remembered those evenings in the theater in detail, even up to the year before he died; he wrote in 1883 of how he and other students "literally sold whatever they could lay their hands on," including law books, in order to purchase tickets. They saved money for more tickets by walking rather than riding to and from Boston. After the play, they would loiter around the stage door, prepared to cheer when the great lady emerged. Years later, when she played a return engagement in Boston, Phillips again "ran mad . . . with the matchless Fanny, renewing my youth of sixteen years ago."[5]

The crush on Fanny, a natural enough expression of youthful sexual interest, obviously meant more to him than the mock trials before which Story made him give speeches. Pleading the technical points of a contract certainly yielded meager satisfaction to one who had so lovingly extolled Burke and who dreamed of shaping the fates of nations. To gaze instead on Kemble, who dominated and enthralled her audiences through personal magnetism, surely must have heightened Phillips' frustration as he tried to forget his dull studies and mundane prospects. The young man could hardly have drawn fresh support or inspiration from his zealous brother the minister, who had also tried law school. John Charles concluded yet another sermon about God's command to repent and convert with the cheerless lines: "I hope you are giving your attention to the law and find it full of interest—more than I found it—It is well enough for those that like it."[6]

As meditations on heroism were overcome by feelings of inadequacy, Phillips' aimless introspection became ever more evident. In one spare moment, for example, he felt driven, despite a headache, to record a dream in verse, stanza after stanza. He remembered his being ferried in a coffin-boat with a shroud for a sail, steered by a "skeleton helmsman." They sailed across an ocean "teeming with sepulchured [sic] dead," toward "the Islands of Devils," where deceased people whom he had known awaited his arrival:

Hurra, Hurra, the keel cuts the strand
Thus bear away cheerily, quick let us land!

5. Boston *Herald*, October 29, 1883; Phillips to Sidney H. Gay, n.d. [1846], Gay Papers.
6. John Charles Phillips to Phillips, March 31, 1834, Blagden Papers.

How much separation of interest lends
To the parting and meeting of long beloved friends.

According to the poem, he then turned his "glad eyes" toward the dear people with whom he was about to be reunited, only to be awakened by "thunder of cannon," alone again.[7] It was a typical dream, like those prompted in all of us by our deeper griefs. Phillips, however, felt compelled to linger over the experience by recreating it on paper; the self-possession he had always prized so highly was no longer helping him maintain his emotional balance as he tried to assess his future. Law school was taking its toll, and certainly he felt his burdens lighten when finally, in September, 1834, he was awarded his degree.

Phillips decided immediately after graduation to tour Philadelphia and New York City. His trip did suggest a liberated mood, for he had never before traveled outside Boston. Along the way he encountered some living history in the person of Aaron Burr, and another attractive woman, named Mary Elwell. Phillips must have gotten on well with Burr, whom he met in Philadelphia, for the old man graciously offered to show him around the town. Phillips returned the favor soon after when Burr visited Boston, calling for him at the Tremont Hotel and guiding him through the Athenaeum Museum.[8] As for Mary Elwell, who lived in New York, Phillips was smitten enough after meeting her to compose some verse in his Commonplace Book about his infatuation. It concluded on a note of sad separation. "New York, 1834, to Mary Adeline Elwell—EHEU!"[9] Perhaps she had seemed less threatening than had the belle of Cambridge, Anna Quincy. Perhaps, too, Phillips had now developed greater confidence around women of his own age. In any event, Phillips undoubtedly possessed a healthy interest in women as he attained marriageable age. While he felt strongly the imperatives of his class, upbringing, and religious temperament that he repress sexual passion, he was, nevertheless, an extremely attractive single man, handsome, wealthy, educated, and of impeccable lineage. What he desperately lacked was a sense of his life's vocational goals and moral direction, not to mention any confidence in his ability to find them out.

7. Wendell Phillips, Commonplace Book, 613, Garrison Papers, BPL. The poem is reprinted in Bartlett, *Phillips*, 29–30.
8. Martyn, *Phillips*, 52–53; Bartlett, *Phillips*, 30.
9. Phillips, Commonplace Book, 601.

Phillips decided to begin his law practice in Lowell, Massachusetts, some thirty-five miles from Boston. In some ways, the town held promise. The famous Lowell textile mills were located here, impressive symbols of that great transformation in production and labor, the Industrial Revolution, which was already reshaping the economy of New England and the lives of its working people. By harnessing water power to giant looms and jennies to produce cloth bolts, Massachusetts capitalists were turning their state into a major market for slave-grown cotton from the South. The town's economy was expanding, as was its need for legal services, and Phillips' prospects must have looked good. Yet this factory town was hardly Boston, and he surely felt uncertain as, for the first time, he took up residence outside his native city. It is also possible that Phillips came to Lowell because he felt too unsure about his commitment to start his practice with friends and family close at hand. At any rate, by November, 1834, Phillips had begun working with Thomas Hopkinson, a classmate and friend of Charles Sumner's, and had moved to his new quarters. His arrangement with Hopkinson was for a short term, during which Hopkinson was to teach him some of the technicalities of legal practice.[10]

While practicing in Lowell, the great radical-to-be took no interest in the growing social controversies around him. Workers' complaints about conditions in the mechanized mills nearby did not attract his attention, nor did the noisy insistence of a small band of Boston abolitionists that slavery was a terrible sin. Instead, Phillips joined his partner Hopkinson in supporting the career of the rising conservative Whig politician Daniel Webster, whose oratory he had admired since 1828, when he had listened to Webster speak in Faneuil Hall. Webster stood forthrightly for the interests of Lowell's manufacturers and was certainly no friend to the abolitionists. "Mr. Phillips and I have just been saying that we will go heart and soul for him as President," Hopkinson wrote to a friend. Several years later, Hopkinson would even lead a mob against an abolitionist meeting, but in 1834 he seemed to Phillips a proper gentleman, whatever his views on slavery.[11] Their political camaraderie notwithstanding, Phillips and his colleague terminated their arrangement, and spring 1835 found him back in Boston, partnerless and deeply unsure of

10. See Thomas Bender, *Toward an Urban Vision: Ideas and Institutions in Nineteenth-Century America* (Lexington, 1975), 96–129.
11. Bartlett, *Phillips*, 31–32.

himself, in an office he had rented on Court Street near the business district.[12]

Clients proved difficult to come by, and soon Phillips was spending less time with litigants and cases than he did alone or hobnobbing with Sumner and the other attorneys who worked near his office. Already alienated from his chosen profession, he now found himself becoming trapped, ever more obviously, in the embarrassment of mediocrity. By late 1835, after a mere six months of attempting to establish himself, he was already confiding to friends that he was thinking of quitting his practice if things did not improve soon. What he would do next, he did not know, but for now, he could only skirt, in humiliation, the edges of failure.[13]

As his circumstances grew more trying, Phillips attempted to meet them by turning once again to history, the study that in happier times had fired his ambitions, fantasies, and moralistic visions. But now, the heroes from whom he sought inspiration were not old Cromwellians or Edmund Burke but his own ancestors, the great men the burden of whose name he now carried so uncomfortably. Their grand exploits were, of course, all too familiar, but Phillips became consumed in tracing their genealogies, in digging out the minutiae that give family history its most personal meanings. Fascinated with the complexities of unraveling family trees and deciphering heraldic insignia, he took great satisfaction in correcting minor factual errors. Samuel Phillips of Rowley (the son of the first John Phillips) had graduated from Harvard in 1651, not 1650, he discovered. The motto he carefully penned on the flyleaf of the huge folio into which he transcribed his research was "REPENTENS EXEMPLA SUCORUM," a phrase from Cicero meaning "redeem the examples of inspiration."[14] Phillips' choice of motto may well suggest some of the guidance he was seeking. As the major crisis of his adult life settled around him, Phillips struggled against his purposelessness by attempting to renew his sense of mastery over the taxing legacy of his family's patriarchs.

He solicited help from other genealogists, assuring one such expert candidly that "as a young attorney not much employed *professionally*,"

---

12. Lorenzo Sears, *Wendell Phillips: Orator and Agitator* (New York, 1909), 17; Bartlett, *Phillips*, 32.
13. Austin, *Phillips*, 44.
14. Wendell Phillips Genealogical File, Blagden Papers.

he had time aplenty for such projects. His notebooks reveal, too, that he began reading extensively in the histories of New England towns and in the diaries of early Puritans. The plan of research he set out only confirms how all-consuming this enterprise was becoming for him. "Write or go to each town," his detailed instructions read, requesting "the dates of birth and marriage of any individual you want, request an official, *certified* copy." Then he added "N.B. Why not, while about it, record . . . all the children of Samuel [Phillips] of Rowley and Samuel [Phillips] of Salem and the rest?" He discovered, and he noted with pride, that the first John Phillips had been lent the cost of his passage to New England by John Winthrop and that this first patriarch had once defended "a man who had been fined for having an Anabaptist book." Phillips had even dug out the actual petition from the Massachusetts state archives.[15] As he turned over the old sources, however, Phillips gave no hint of what his ancestral encounters were suggesting to him. For the moment, all his investigations indicated was that his self-absorption had drawn him back into the past, where he had once found self-assurance, direction, and promise of fulfillment.

On October 21, 1835, the din of angry voices in the street near his office startled Phillips from his work. The Boston Female Anti-Slavery Society had scheduled a meeting for earlier that day at their headquarters on nearby Washington Street, with controversial British abolitionist George Thompson as the principal speaker. Leading Whig papers had been encouraging "men of property and standing" with "a large stake" in the community (like the Phillipses), to put down this dangerous abolitionist *"rabble."* The day of the meeting, hundreds of handbills were circulated all over the business district, accusing Thompson of being a foreign subversive who merited the "tar kettle." The mob that gathered as the women attempted to meet, upon discovering that Thompson had fled, called for another who they felt deserved their vengeance just as much. William Lloyd Garrison had been angering Boston's whites ever since 1831 with his strident abolitionist newspaper, the *Liberator*. The uproar drew Phillips from his desk and out to the corner of Court and State streets. He arrived just as the mob, several thousand strong, passed by searching for the elusive Garrison who had retired behind the protec-

15. *Ibid.*, Wendell Phillips to John Farmer, April 2, 1836, Wendell Phillips Miscellaneous Letters, New Hampshire Historical Society.

tive walls of the city jail.[16] For perhaps the first time, he glimpsed the turbulent world of active abolitionism, the eventual answer to all his questions about his direction in life.

For the moment, however, as Phillips stood at the intersection, he simply wondered why the mayor did not call out the militia and restore order. Like any scrupulous legalist, he saw the mob as "a very shameful business" and volunteered that he, personally, would "cheerfully take arms [in the militia] in a case like this." The mob's abridgment of civil liberty and domestic order seemed obvious. Phillips would later remember, "I did not understand antislavery then. . . . My eyes were sealed." He knew all about "the Adamses and Otises of 1776, the Mary Dyers and Anne Hutchinsons," but failed to recognize the "Adames and Otises, the Dyers and the Hutchinsons whom I met on the streets in 1835."[17] Contrary to some popular beliefs, Phillips did not witness the Garrison mob and catapult himself into the abolitionists' ranks. Yet the incident did begin a far more complicated process. It gave Phillips something important to discuss soon after with Ann Terry Greene, a vivacious, dedicated member of the Female Anti-Slavery Society, whom he met the following month. From that point on, his life would take a dramatic turn.

One Saturday morning in November, Charles Sumner failed to appear at Phillips' office, despite earlier promises. They had agreed the day before to escort Miss Greene together on a coach ride to nearby Greenfield in the company of a mutual friend, James Alvord, and his fiancée. Sumner, a reader of the *Liberator*, knew that Ann Greene belonged to the Female Anti-Slavery Society, believed in women's rights, and had been trapped in the meeting hall by the Garrison mob the month before. Alvord had assured Sumner and Phillips that Ann Greene was attractive, bright, and plainspoken. Surely she and Phillips could find things to talk about without his help, Sumner thought, as he decided to sleep in.[18] He could hardly have foreseen that within a year Wendell Phillips would shock proper Boston by becoming engaged to this unapologetic abolitionist.

On their ride to and from Greenfield, Ann and Wendell discovered much in common. Both came from families that had added fortunes of

16. John L. Thomas, *The Liberator, William Lloyd Garrison: A Biography* (Boston, 1963), 200–208; Phillips, "The Boston Mob," in his *Speeches, Lectures, and Letters* (Boston, 1863), 213.

17. Phillips, "The Boston Mob," 227.

18. Martyn, *Phillips*, 78; Sears, *Phillips*, 34–35.

their own making to great inherited wealth. Ann's father, Benjamin Greene, had prospered as a merchant before he and his wife both died midway through Ann's childhood, subjecting her, like Phillips, to the early loss of beloved family. Now she lived not far from the Phillips family mansion, in comparable luxury, with her cousin Maria Weston Chapman, wife of financier Henry B. Chapman.[19] Ann Greene was every bit Wendell Phillips' social equal, though she herself remembered thinking otherwise at first. "When I first met Wendell," she was to recall, "I used to think, 'It could never come to pass; such a being as he could never think of me.' I looked upon it as something as strange as a fairy tale." Though vivacious, she had already suffered for years from poor health. Frail and physically self-protective, she must have felt somewhat intimidated as well as attracted by this strikingly handsome, athletic-looking man, but as they rode along, she addressed Phillips without hesitation and left him with one clear impression. If he wanted her to take an interest in him, he had first better take an interest in the cause of the slave. "I talked abolition to him all the time up and all the time there," she recalled.[20] She must have recounted her terror at having been trapped by the mob that October day, while Phillips had been observing from the street corner. And Phillips certainly found her candor refreshing, whatever his opinion of her ideas, for throughout their long marriage Ann Greene was always to tell her husband just this bluntly exactly what she thought. That afternoon she undoubtedly seemed to Phillips an attractive contrast to formal Anna Quincy and a marvelous respite from his anxiety about the purpose of life.

Phillips always claimed that "my wife made an out and out abolitionist of me, and she always preceded me in the adoption of the various causes I have advocated."[21] His recollection is broadly accurate. As they continued to see each other, Greene took care to expose Phillips to the highly charged world of Boston abolitionism. She also drove him closer to the movement simply because Phillips' mother openly disliked Ann Greene's opinions, and Phillips felt compelled to defend them. Yet even after his engagement Phillips took over a year before embracing aboli-

19. William H. Pease and Jane H. Pease, *Bound with Them in Chains: A Biographical History of the Antislavery Movement* (Westport, Conn., 1972), 28–59; Sears, *Phillips*, 34–35; Bartlett, *Phillips*, 33–34.
20. Ann Greene Phillips to Anna Alvord, November 9, 1837, quoted in Martyn, *Phillips*, 87, and without attribution in Korngold, *Two Friends of Man*, 132.
21. Phillips quoted in Korngold, *Two Friends of Man*, 132.

tionism. By itself, Phillips' initial relationship with Ann Greene by no means sealed his lifetime commitment.

Soon after their coach ride Ann Greene began introducing Phillips to Boston's inner circle of white abolitionists, most of whom frequented her own residence in fashionable Chauncy Place. There Phillips met Henry Chapman, who for several years had put his mercantile fortune at the disposal of local abolitionist societies, underwriting the many projects of his striking and dominating wife, Maria. Phillips also discovered that Caroline and Ann Warren Weston were just as aristocratic and no less active than their sister Maria, though less in the limelight. They managed a full-time elementary school (racially integrated, of course) on Boylston Street. Phillips also met a lawyer in whom he must have seen something of himself. Ellis Gray Loring was eight years Phillips' senior and his equal in Beacon Street lineage and wealth, but Loring had gone on from Harvard to help found the New England Anti-Slavery Society, and he now used his legal training to defend black runaways from slavery. He and his wife, Louisa Gilman Loring, were opening their home to fugitives and their bankbook to the editor of the *Liberator*.[22] If, as is likely, Phillips' family had taught him to judge abolitionists as social inferiors, these introductions quickly demonstrated otherwise. Abolitionism was unpopular in Boston, but supporting it did not require one to cast aside the insignia of privilege.

On the evening that Phillips met William Lloyd Garrison, however, the boundaries of class did begin to vanish. Only a movement so socially inclusive as abolitionism could have brought together the son of John Phillips and the son of an alcoholic itinerant who had deserted his family decades before. While Phillips was attending the Latin School, Garrison was working, first as a shoemaker's apprentice, then in a printer's shop. While Phillips was consorting with southern gentlemen at Harvard, Garrison had begun writing for an abolitionist newspaper and had spent six weeks in a Baltimore prison for libeling a slave trader. By the time of Phillips' graduation in 1831, Garrison had come to Boston, settled into a cramped office with ink-spattered windows under the eaves of an old warehouse known as Merchants Hall. There, he composed the first issue of the *Liberator*, flinging out a message against

22. Pease and Pease, *Bound with Them in Chains*, 28–59; Walter Merrill (ed.), *I Will Be Heard! 1822–1835* (Cambridge, Mass., 1970), 550, 443, Vol. I of *The Letters of William Lloyd Garrison*, 5 vols.

slavery that grated on American ears. Slavery was a heaven-provoking sin, Garrison declared. Slaveholders put their souls in dire jeopardy, and the nation itself deserved God's retribution for condoning so heinous a crime. Garrison's demand was for "immediate emancipation," and his opening editorial set the tone for a journalistic career lasting more than thirty years: "I will be as harsh as truth, as uncompromising as justice. . . . Tell a man to moderately rescue his wife from the hands of the ravisher, . . . but urge me not to moderation in a cause like the present. I am in earnest—I will not equivocate—I will not retreat an inch—and I WILL BE HEARD."[23] In the winter of 1835–1836 Phillips probably did not fully understand, let alone share, such radical views, no matter how often he might have heard them. Still, this new circle and its controversial ideas gave him much to think about besides his vocational troubles.

The matters that kept his attention the longest, however, usually involved Ann Greene. Amid his other uncertainties, she represented a powerful point of commitment for Phillips, and he felt himself increasingly drawn to her. The Weston sisters noticed that their cousin had a new admirer, and he impressed them in several respects. When, for example, Phillips lectured at the New Bedford Lyceum in January, 1836, he stayed over at the home of still another abolitionist Weston, Ann Greene's cousin Deborah. She judged her houseguest by exacting standards before reporting, "His lecture before the lyceum this evening was considered very fine," though there was something "slightly *Whiggy* and rather conservative" about his views. Phillips was as yet no firebrand radical, even though he seemed open to learning about the cause. He and Deborah Weston "talked considerable abolitionism," she was pleased to write, and Phillips had even attacked the moderate views on slavery of theologian William Ellery Channing "in very good style. He did better than I expected." Obviously Phillips was now becoming accustomed to Ann Greene and her militant circle. "Intercourse with the abolitionists will, I think, do him good," Weston concluded, and she "liked Phillips' straightforward simplicity." Her succinct conclusion was: "I think Ann Terry has done very well."[24]

The terrible fact was, however, that Ann Greene began doing very poorly. Since June, 1836, her health had been deteriorating dangerously, and no one could diagnose the cause. If her complaints were like those

23. Thomas, *The Liberator*, 7–208.
24. Deborah Weston to Ann Warren Weston, January 22, 1836, Ann Warren Weston Papers, BPL.

that kept her an invalid in later years, then she lost all appetite and fought constant nausea. Violent headaches and sharp pains in her back and arms kept her from sleeping normally, noise made her head throb, and her eyes smarted whenever the shades were raised. Gradually her energy ebbed away, though in mid-September Henry Chapman tried to find hope in her ability to keep down a diet of peaches. By late October the Weston sisters found little to cheer them, for after entertaining a visitor briefly, Ann "took cold and is altogether worse." Ann Weston feared that she would "never get fully well," and indeed the next month brought even further decline. Doctors gave the anguished Chapmans "no hope . . . of poor Ann Terry's recovering," wrote one of the Westons. "She seems entirely debilitated, no constitution, nothing to build on." She was not expected "to live more than a few weeks longer."[25]

Phillips could only stand by in silent agony. When he called at the Chapmans' house, they refused his requests to see Ann. She was far too weak already, they told him, and previous visitors had only taxed her to the point that she might not recover at all. After trying to see her "only once or twice," according to Ann Warren Weston, he evidently became too demoralized to endure another rebuff.[26]

Phillips found his situation intolerable and seemingly beyond his grasp. He was twenty-five and only one of many faceless young attorneys who struggled to meet expenses, even though he had wished for as long as he could remember to achieve the great power and public distinction that his upbringing, ambition, religion, and family honor demanded. Even gifts of eloquence and personal leadership had not saved him from impending obscurity. He knew, moreover, that he loved Ann Greene and that she represented inspiration, stability, and understanding in a world that baffled him. Now she, too, appeared to be slipping beyond his reach, and circumstances seemed to be locking him in. Further inaction would surely lead to complete helplessness, the forfeiture of the ability to affect his situation. When his father had died so suddenly, all he had been able to do was feel an aftermath of shock and bereavement, but as Ann grew worse, Phillips saw at least the opportunity to make an all-important gesture of love before her death. In early December he dropped his inhibition, striking desperately to express his love for Ann Greene

25. Henry Chapman to Maria Weston Chapman, September 14, 1836, Maria Weston Chapman Papers, BPL; Ann W. Weston to Deborah Weston, October 22, November 19, 1836, Weston Papers.
26. Ann W. Weston to Deborah Weston, December 15, 1836, Weston Papers.

and to restore his sense of mastery over his feelings and his purpose in life. The synthesis of passion and control around which, since childhood, he had built so much of his imagination and thought now inspired Phillips to take dramatic action.

Details remain sketchy, but this much is clear. Phillips appeared at the Chapman home in early December, inquired about Ann's health and "fell into great distress" upon "learning how ill Ann was." He confronted Henry B. Chapman, pleading that he be allowed to see her at once. "Ann at this time was at the worst," Ann Weston recounted, and even after Chapman had relented, she refused to see him, believing herself too weak to endure the audience. Phillips continued to press his demand, however, and she finally consented. Then, when he rushed into her sickroom and begged her to marry him, she accepted. "To use Maria's language," Ann Weston reported, "he went upstairs, saw her alone for twenty minutes, and came down *a fiance*." Every day thereafter he visited her, and her health began to improve. "We can't help hoping that she is really getting better," Ann Weston wrote.[27]

Ann's health would continue to fluctuate without explanation throughout her life, but in December, 1836, Phillips had every reason to celebrate his bold decision, for now that Ann was improving, both could feel that her knowledge of his love had renewed her inspiration for living. "Only last year," she recalled, "I thought I should never see another birthday, but must leave *him* in the infancy of our love. Thank God for all His goodness to us, and may He make me more worthy of my Wendell."[28] Had Ann not recovered, Phillips could at least have taken comfort in knowing that she had died fully aware of his love. For the first time in his life, he had felt driven to take spontaneous action to master the chaos he felt around and within him. The axioms that had thus far shaped his identity in so many other respects now confirmed their great redeeming power in the present, and he could anticipate a future that held not uncertainty but the promise of love and understanding.

That Phillips' mother objected to his course of action was also to the good, for he had finally begun to free himself from maternal demands that would otherwise have prevented him from acting at all. Wendell and Sarah Phillips were to reassemble their extremely close relationship after the wedding, but in the meantime Phillips had begun to celebrate

27. *Ibid.*
28. Ann Phillips to Anna Alvord, November 19, 1837, reprinted in Martyn, *Phillips*, 87.

the return of hope and happiness. Three days after his climactic audience with Ann, Phillips returned in triumph from an abolitionist bazaar with a beautiful cameo ring for her, having paid several times its actual value.[29] The profit, he knew, would go to further the work of the antislavery societies. Hence, the gift symbolized at least three things—their mutual love, his sense of liberation and returning self-direction, and their shared recognition that their future was somehow irrevocably tied to abolitionism.

With the engagement, Ann and Wendell began to act out the future symbolized by the ring. The love, playfulness, and freedom they shared during that special time as they traveled to antislavery meetings together are captured wonderfully in the only scrap of their correspondence that survives from that period. Ann wrote him after a trip alone to East Newton, and to the Theological Seminary located there high on a hill, "Give me your hand, my love—is not the weather charming?" As she recreated her walk to the top, she assured him facetiously that she was not planning to study for the ministry, "for though you know I *approve* of a profession [for women], yet I do not intend to follow one. I only *profess* to love you, but no, I make no *professions* or *confessions* touching *that*." Then she made a more substantial confession by far:

> I have *stole* into your chamber today & yesterday *fools rush* in where angels fear to *tread*. . . . I looked in vain for a trace of my beloved. Why did you not leave the print of your footstep on the floor (so easy that) or your creme in the drawer for the slightest thing affection hallows. Tomorrow! how much that little word bears on its bosom for me, for *us* since, we trust it brings us together. 'If heaven a draught of heavenly pleasure spare one cordial in this melancholy vale, tis when a youthful loving' etc. Your *memory must* supply the rest, for it is too *tender* to be *written*. Farewell. thy Ann.

And she added this postscript: "Oh that you were here. I am *all all* alone on a wide, wide sea! What a grand time we should have."[30]

After an engagement of less than a year, they were married on October 12, 1837, in a brief ceremony conducted by Phillips' brother John Charles and attended by the various Westons and Chapmans. Since

29. Lucia Weston to Deborah Weston, December 18, 1836, Weston Papers.
30. Ann Terry Greene to Phillips, n.d. [1836], Blagden Papers.

This paper silhouette is the only likeness of Ann Greene Phillips known to exist. It was first published in Francis Jackson Garrison, *Ann Phillips, Wife of Wendell Phillips: A Memorial Sketch* (Boston, 1886).

Henry and Mary Benson, William Lloyd Garrison's brother and sister-in-law, served as best man and matron of honor, Garrison himself was surely present, adding to the already heavy suggestions of an "abolitionist wedding." John Charles Phillips conducted the service "pretty well," Maria Chapman thought. Ann looked radiantly healthy in a white dress of embroidered muslin, accented with a "pink scarf and belt." Sarah Walley Phillips, however, was deeply troubled by the wedding, and conveyed her distress as her rightful maternal prerogative. Her son was not yet a self-acknowledged abolitionist, but she knew that such people had already influenced him deeply, and Beacon Hill had no place for bluestocking extremists like the Chapmans, let alone a venom-filled printer named Garrison. Sarah Phillips had devoted years of loving motherhood to raising this talented, handsome son, and she feared he was about to squander his prospects, shame his family's name, and above all, violate her love by becoming entangled in disreputable causes. "The old lady Phillips *entre nous*, behaved like a perfect Dragon" at the ceremony, Caroline Weston gossiped.[31]

Sarah Phillips had every reason to behave as she did, for the movement that she so detested arose from sources she found it difficult to understand. Abolitionism was made possible by the portentous developments that New England, like the rest of the nation, had begun to experience in its economy, religion, and politics. It was not possible for a woman like Sarah Phillips to approve a movement whose foremost symbol was a man like Garrison, whom she scorned. Nor could she approve the marriage of her son to another radical, who was urging Wendell to see the bewildering transformations taking place around her through abolitionist's eyes alone.[32]

America did indeed demand new explanations, whether Sarah Phillips liked them or not. Its economy was expanding with unparalleled swiftness as powerful commercial and manufacturing networks linked all sections of the country in tight economic bonds. The large new textile mills in Lowell and the new shoe factories in Lynn bore witness to burgeoning expansion, mechanization, and ever greater regional interdepen-

31. Caroline Weston to Ann W. Weston, October 17, 1837, Weston Papers.
32. The brief overview of the rise of abolitionism that follows comes generally from James Brewer Stewart, *Holy Warriors: The Abolitionists and American Slavery* (New York, 1976), 33–49. For an illuminating analysis of the rise of abolitionism and related movements in a specific locale, see Nancy Hewitt, *Women's Activism and Social Change: Rochester, New York, 1822–1872* (Ithaca, 1984), 1–96.

dence. The fast-growing circulation of newspapers and journals that Wendell Phillips found so fascinating only reinforced the process, as did the new system of mass politics, where two great parties, Whigs and Democrats, built interregional coalitions and recruited voters as never before. In Boston and elsewhere, urban populations swelled with English and Irish immigrants, and the gap between rich and poor widened significantly. Farmers in the west now grew crops for world markets, not for family self-sufficiency, and on southern frontiers, cotton production and slave populations multiplied. Northerners and southerners were suddenly becoming aware of their involvement with each other and increasingly sensitive to the differences between their slave and free societies. American Protestantism, meanwhile, struggled to impart exacting moral direction to the nation as it faced unprecedented social dislocations caused by these developments. Great preachers like Phillips' old favorite, Lyman Beecher, called upon Americans to repent, to seek God's inspiration, and to live a new life of holiness that would replace what was perceived as degenerating morality with a new era of Christian harmony. Great revivals swept through New England and the Midwest calling thousands to dedicate their lives to combating sin in their own hearts and arresting the chaos overtaking their "fallen" nation. To such pious souls only personal dedication seemed to stand between an America mired in corruption and God's all-consuming judgment.

It was in such feelings that abolitionism had its beginning, for to New Englanders and Midwesterners it might suddenly seem obvious that the primal source of the nation's pollution lay in the plantations of the South. There, all powerful masters seemed to defy the injunctions of Heaven itself, depriving their slaves of the Bible, sanctified marriage, and the fruits of their own labor. Lacking all Christian restraint, slaveholders seemed free to follow their licentious, exploitative instincts to the fullest, reversing God's own moral order by ruling arrogantly in his place over his own human creations. It began to seem a Christian's God-given duty to alert the slaveholder and the nation at large to this greatest of moral perils. Religiously inspired young men and women all over the North began making soul-rending conversion to the slaves' cause and demanding immediate emancipation. By 1833 the American Anti-Slavery Society, located in New York City, presided over a growing confederation of groups that covered the North from Illinois eastward.

People like Garrison, the Westons, the Chapmans, and Ann Greene Phillips had come to possess a vision of a harmonious, biracial America.

They proposed to liberate over two million slaves, worth many more millions of dollars, who were owned by the nation's most cohesive and powerful political elite. They would seek to do so by moral suasion, agitating with pamphlets, meetings, and petitions to purge all the nation, the North no less than the South, of its apathy and degeneracy and to eradicate two centuries of racism, "colorphobia," they called it. The people that Phillips now counted as friends certainly entertained utopian hopes, but such high expectations were necessary motivation for attacking so large and powerful a system and for trying to imagine, as abolitionists did, how it must actually feel to live as a slave. It took great conviction to demand that impartial law repeal the slaveholders' arbitrary power, that a just society based on self-disciplined free labor supersede the coercion of the whip, and that morally self-sustaining nuclear families displace the chaotic passions unleashed from the slave quarters. It was little wonder that they agreed wholeheartedly with Garrison's opening salvo in the *Liberator*, "On this subject, I do not wish to think, speak or write with moderation."

These, then, were the people and doctrines that marriage now brought so close to Phillips' life. In many ways, the abolitionists' hatred of slavery's licentiousness paralleled his own rigid moralism, his detestation of unchecked power and passion, and his republican conviction that social order was the incontestable precondition of freedom. As he and Ann began to honeymoon in Framingham ("very cosily," according to Caroline Weston), ringing phrases like Garrison's were probably far from Wendell's thoughts.[33] He could take satisfaction, though, that order and direction had begun to return to his life, for the choice of a conventional vocation now had become secondary to the greater question of a commitment to abolitionism itself.

33. Caroline Weston to Ann W. Weston, October 17, 1837, Weston Papers.

FOUR

The Second Wendell Phillips

A considerable portion of the interest from his father's holdings had begun coming to Wendell Phillips when he reached the age of twenty-one, and he knew that when his mother died he would receive a large share of the family estate. Furthermore, the Greene family fortune nearly matched John Phillips', for when orphaned, Ann and her brothers had each inherited $93,000 dollars. At the time of her marriage, Ann was already one of the wealthiest young heiresses in Boston's memory. Moreover, people were beginning to request Phillips as a paid lyceum speaker, and a tour now and then through the coastal or backcountry towns of Massachusetts could net him money enough to cover several months of household expenses.[1] Phillips now enjoyed more latitude than ever as he began to examine his feelings about abolitionism. As practiced by Ann Phillips, Garrison, and the others, the cause demanded a kind of whole-souled commitment that Phillips could no more induce than he could have induced a conversion when his brother John Charles had exhorted him so gratuitously about his need for rebirth.

He hesitated, in part because he knew that he had already strained his mother's affections by marrying Ann, and he felt concerned lest he demand too much. "She differed with me utterly on the matter of slavery," Phillips explained later on, and "grieved a good deal" about what

1. Bartlett, *Phillips*, 131.

she saw as a "waste of my time." His brother George also gave Phillips a blunt reminder about traditional family views on racial matters, writing in August, 1836, about the rescue of two presumed fugitives by some courageous Boston blacks: "The idea that the niggers, in open day, carried off from the Supreme Court room two prisoners has something so laughable in it one can hardly appreciate the insult. . . . The nig is uppermost now for sure."² George showed no hesitation at offending a brother who was smitten with an abolitionist, and his remark gave Phillips still another reason for approaching the movement cautiously.

He appeared only on the fringes of abolitionist gatherings at first, while recording objections to slavery in his Commonplace Book. Soon after his engagement, for example, he wrote privately against the Bible's literal justifications of slavery by arguing that the institution was nevertheless "against the spirit of Christianity." People must therefore "waken to duty" and promote abolition. Duty, in turn, took Phillips to the annual meeting of the Massachusetts Anti-Slavery Society, held in a large horse barn during January, 1837. Managers of Boston's meeting halls, fearing riots, had refused to rent to so controversial a group. The minutes record Phillips' silence, but he heard others testify against slavery in this strange setting as he surveyed the unusual variety of participants.

First came Amos Dresser, a white, middle-class theology student who recounted his story of being publicly whipped by angry slaveholders in Nashville, Tennessee. He had been caught with abolitionist pamphlets intended for local distribution in his bag. Then arose a Mr. Johnson, a slave from the plantation South, who described in a thick dialect the brutalities he had witnessed there. Finally came Harvard attorney Ellis Gray Loring, who offered a resolution that true allegiance to country, liberty, and God required that "every man openly espouse the anti-slavery cause." Any membership so diverse clearly had a place for another Boston gentleman, and although there is no record of Phillips' reaction, four days afterward Ann Weston reported that he was "becoming quite an abolitionist." In the next few months, he continued, silently, to attend the meetings.³

In March, 1837, at the quarterly meeting of the Massachusetts Anti-Slavery Society, Phillips broke his silence to make remarks that filled

2. Phillips to Pease, January 31, 1846, Garrison Papers, BPL; George Phillips to Wendell Phillips, n.d. [1836], Blagden Papers.
3. *Liberator*, February 4, March 15, 1837; Ann W. Weston to Deborah Weston, January 30, 1837, Weston Papers.

columns. The abolitionists had gathered in Lynn, Massachusetts, amid controversies set off by their recently begun petition campaign. In prior years, abolitionists' petitions to the government had provided vital pressure for legislation that had emancipated slaves throughout the British Empire. The same tactic had been useful in the United States during the eighteenth century when the North had abolished slavery. Now abolitionists had been busy again, circulating petitions to Congress to prohibit the admission of new slave states, to abolish slavery in Washington, D.C., and to enact other laws unfavorable to planters' interests. By mid-1837 Congress had been flooded with such requests, and legislative debates on slavery grew even more intemperate. Fearing sectional disruption in politics, Whig and Democratic leaders from North and South contrived a rule of procedure that prohibited all debate on antislavery petitions. When received, they had to be silently and automatically tabled. Passed in 1836 and in force until 1844, this famous gag rule only spurred the abolitionist campaign. Many northerners resented this clear abridgment of their political rights and signed petitions more willingly than ever. John Quincy Adams, the former president, now a Massachusetts representative, began his own crusade to rescind the rule. "Old Man Eloquent," as some now called him, thrust antislavery topics into House debate at every opportunity, defying party leaders who attempted to censure him and provoking debates that seethed with sectional hostility.[4]

Intertwined as it was with the abridgment of American civil liberties, the gag-rule issue fit well with the cautious frame of mind Phillips brought to the Lynn meeting. To oppose the rule one need not make complete cause with the abolitionists. Phillips therefore put forward a resolution praising Adams as a distinguished citizen, "the champion of the fundamental principles of the Constitution." He then defined the restriction he placed on his views. "I will not wander from my subject to slavery," he said. "It is our own rights which are at issue." Phillips warned that the gag rule was leading whites, not blacks, to a general constitutional crisis when "the time-honored rights which had been fought for on British ground" would have to be defended again. The problems of slavery demanded discussion, not gag rules, he insisted, for silence would only hasten the final overthrow of free speech and the rise

4. The best discussion of these general trends is still Russel B. Nye, *Fettered Freedom: Civil Liberties and the Slavery Controversy* (Ann Arbor, 1949).

of "a mighty slave-holding state to overshadow and mildew our free institutions." This was the closest Phillips came to condemning slavery.[5]

Garrison reported that Phillips' remarks "surprised and charmed the audience" and that they marked his "complete adhesion to the movement and his abandonment of legitimate worldly ambition." After Phillips had finished, abolitionists congratulated him with warm embraces.[6] But actually, sectionally inclined Congressmen in the North had also begun making remarks like these, and none of them would have considered becoming a full-fledged abolitionist. The Wendell Phillips who had deplored the Garrison mob on legalistic grounds in 1835 remained unchanged. He had surely amplified his views and was no friend to slavery, but he had not altered his basic assumptions.

Nor did Phillips, contrary to myth, selflessly and consciously spurn his evident destiny as Massachusetts' next Daniel Webster when he finally declared himself an abolitionist. To be sure, the Phillips family tradition exalted political power but exclusively as high-minded legislative service motivated by patrician ideals of deference and honor. Such political attitudes had died with John Phillips' generation. The new, bare-knuckled style of mass politics grated hard on the Phillips' sensibilities. "We have been to the Capitol once or twice," George Phillips reported to Wendell from Washington, D.C., in 1836. "The House looks like thunder. No take-off on the stage could go beyond it—Here all is talking and laughing . . . walking about and standing in little knots, writing letters and doing nothing. Some poor fellow with a fool's cap sheet is hammering away, gesticulating with all vehemence with no soul to look at him." The Senate seemed less disreputable but equally pointless. "If all the Senators appear like our own, I see no honor in it," George Phillips assured his brother. "Their body reminded me of a College Society—The same little spirit—the same attention to trifles—apparently the same and even more regard to the affect [sic] on the gallery around."[7]

Amusing the gallery with trifles or hammering away unheeded surely did not appeal to an orator who had dreamed so long of emulating Burke and Cicero. Phillips would feel compelled to reshape mass politics precisely because he felt himself so far above and so alienated from the

5. Phillips, "The Right of Petition," in his *Speeches, Second Series*, 1–5.

6. Francis Jackson Garrison and Wendell Phillips Garrison, *William Lloyd Garrison, 1805–1879* (4 vols.; New York, 1885–89), II, 128–30.

7. George Phillips to Phillips, May 7, 1836, Blagden Papers.

process itself. As his father had before him, he believed that one must transcend ambition for petty office in order to serve the community's highest good, and he had expressed just such assumptions when he praised England's aristocrat-heroes. Accordingly, he had also supported Daniel Webster and now John Quincy Adams as statesmen who spurned the hucksterism of campaigning and the slavery of party drill in order to serve the nobler ends of freedom and social order. Once he even revealed that simple disinterest, "accidental abstinence" as he called it, had kept him from the ballot box for years, even before his abolitionist principles so dictated.[8] For all these reasons, Phillips could never have considered a career as an antislavery-minded elected official, although, at the same time, such attitudes left him profoundly distressed with the pettiness and corruption of political life and terribly anxious to see it reformed. Nevertheless, his classmates would still have recognized him as the "first" Wendell Phillips, the Harvard conservative.

Suddenly, however, everything seemed to change. On November 7, 1837, in the Mississippi River town of Alton, Illinois, a mob gathered around a warehouse. Inside, an armed Elijah P. Lovejoy guarded his printing press from an inevitable attack. An endlessly stubborn abolitionist editor, Lovejoy had consistently refused to be scared off, though mobs had destroyed his presses and threatened his life during the previous three weeks. Now the mob put torches to the building, and Lovejoy rushed out, gun in hand. He crumpled, dead, as the bullets hit him.[9] The angry men who gathered around the body could have had no idea that this murder was about to bring to life an abolitionist far more powerful than Lovejoy had been. In this most celebrated abolitionist martyrdom, Phillips finally found the inspiration for his own rebirth. When news of Lovejoy's death reached Boston in early December, the "second" Wendell Phillips was born. He would always remember this event as the primary source of inspiration for his radical commitment: "The gun which was aimed at the breast of Lovejoy brought me to my feet. I can never forget the agony of that moment."[10]

Faneuil Hall was filled to capacity on December 7 for the Lovejoy protest meeting arranged by the prominent minister and antislavery moderate William Ellery Channing. The event was heavily publicized, and

8. *Liberator*, February 20, 1857.
9. The best analysis of Lovejoy's life and of the Alton mob is Merton Dillon, *Elijah Lovejoy, Abolitionist Editor* (Urbana, 1961).
10. *National Anti-Slavery Standard*, April 27, May 25, 1867.

evidence suggests that Phillips had been asked to speak. By his own testimony, however, Phillips made clear that he was not aware of this invitation. "I had just been married and was living in Framingham," he recalled emphatically, "and did not know of the proposed meeting when I came to Boston that morning."[11] Even with foreknowledge, however, the spontaneous course of the meeting would have made it impossible for him to have used a prepared speech, had he had one ready.

Channing had envisioned a meeting that would condemn all violence, Lovejoy's recourse to arms as well as his killers', but the abolitionists insisted on vindicating their newest martyr and condemning his murderers. Rumors of mobs had also attracted numerous "gentlemen of high standing" known for their proslavery views and plenty of lower-class antiabolitionists, ready for violence if it were to be directed at the knot of abolitionists, Phillips among them, who sat near the middle of the hall. In this volatile setting, no formal agenda was likely to hold sway for long.[12]

The meeting began, as Channing had hoped, with the reading of his resolution condemning "lawless force" on all sides. First Channing himself, then attorney George Hilliard spoke in favor of the resolution as the audience grew impatient. Still, as one witness remembered, "everything so far was decorous." Abruptly, however, a "harsh, discordant voice" from the gallery interrupted, demanding recognition. Everyone saw that it was James T. Austin, attorney general of Massachusetts, and as Phillips listened, the official charged with enforcing impartial law in the commonwealth put his office and his personal reputation on the side of Lovejoy's killers.

Austin angrily asserted that the mob had been perfectly right to kill Lovejoy. People had repeatedly warned Lovejoy not to print his incendiary newspaper, especially since Alton was located only a few miles from the slave state of Missouri, and Lovejoy's mad persistence had threatened domestic peace even in his own city. The mob was justified in acting to prevent anarchy, Austin continued sarcastically, just as good Bostonians would be if some insane "man of philanthropic feeling" attempted to

11. Phillips to James Freeman Clarke, January 11, 1883, James Freeman Clarke Papers, HL.

12. *Liberator*, December 15, 1837; Bartlett, *Phillips*, 47–51; William P. Phillips, *The Freedom Speech of Wendell Phillips* (Boston, 1890); Martyn, *Phillips*, 86–101, provide documentation for the events of the Lovejoy meeting, except as noted specifically.

open a cage of ferocious animals to prey upon the city's population. Besides, he insisted, the Alton mob had behaved no differently than had Boston's own revolutionary ancestors. If Lovejoy had a right to publish, then George III had an equal right to tax his own colonies. Like John Hancock and Sam Adams, Lovejoy's killers had been forced to take the law into their own control, as "*an orderly mob,*" to purge their city of "the disgusting instruments of their degradation."[13]

People hooted, applauded, cursed, and shook their fists while Austin's harangue went on. As Phillips understood them, Austin's words were turning America's history of freedom into moral chaos by celebrating mob rule, slavery, and murder, and the audience was responding to Austin's coarse language by degenerating into a similar state of anarchy. Disorder, the social force Phillips hated most, seemed to be rising around him as he sat in Faneuil Hall, Boston's shrine of political liberty and free speech. Hurriedly, Phillips asked Amos Phelps, an abolitionist sitting next to him, "Who is to answer Austin?" Phelps replied, "No one. Come up, then, and answer him yourself." As the shouting grew louder and the gavel pounded uselessly, Phillips pushed his way, unannounced, to the platform. It was little wonder that he was to maintain, looking back on his life, that "events, rather than my own will," had selected his path for him.[14]

Yet Phillips had been preparing for years, albeit unknowingly, for this very moment. Through his study of history, he had learned to express his detestation of unlicensed power and ungoverned passion, his fear that they spawned disorder and led straight to tyranny. He had also come to emotional terms with his family's demands through his identification with great patriot-heroes, virtuous defenders of tradition, who had arisen and seized power in order to restore the people's liberties, banishing corruption with their mighty acts. Now he saw himself, like Cromwell, Pitt, or Edmund Burke, about to stand forth alone to restore freedom by crushing the intolerable anarchy building around him. Again, he had nearly obliterated his emotional distance from the past, but now he would not just write about heroism. He would seek to exemplify it, seizing control in a moment of crisis as the scholar-activist Burke had done. Foul perversion had been made of Boston's republican traditions, degrading Hancock, James Otis, and most of all, his own father, John

13. *Liberator*, December 15, 1837.
14. Phillips to Clarke, January 11, 1883, Clarke Papers; Phillips to Salmon P. Chase, July 23, 1865, Salmon P. Chase Papers, Historical Society of Pennsylvania.

Phillips, and all the other great Phillipses whose history he had rediscovered in the genealogies. Austin had debased their memory, transforming them into rioters and killers. Phillips would redeem them all, and Elijah Lovejoy too, as heroes of orderly liberty, and by so doing, he would also redeem himself from his vocational indecision.

For the rest of his life, Phillips believed that he had glimpsed in this moment exactly what lay behind all this degeneracy, whether in far away Alton or surrounding him in Faneuil Hall. It was a republican's nightmare, the unchecked power of a system of human relations, founded in tyranny, that spread disruption across the nation—slavery. Here, he would later explain, was "an abnormal element which nobody had counted in. No check, no balance had been provided" to stem its chaotic influences. He remembered suddenly becoming "conscious that I was in the presence of a power whose motto was victory or death," recognizing "for the first time" the "death grapple" into which he "had unthinkingly been drawn."[15]

At last, Phillips felt he knew what he was supposed to do and what he must tell the unruly crowd. The highest emotional sanctions of his upbringing, religion, and family honor supported him as he walked with gentlemanly ease to the podium. Standing there, he looked to the portraits of Hancock, Otis, and Sam Adams, the heroes buried next to his father on the Common, which stared back across the crowd from their places on the far wall. He always claimed that it was to them, not the audience, that he really spoke.[16] The "second" Wendell Phillips now stood ready to address the people of Boston.

The setting was fitted perfectly to the expensively tailored young gentleman standing impassively on the podium, a stunning contrast to the ranting Austin. Phillips appeared entirely self-possessed, and as he began speaking, his voice sounded both commanding and somehow softly indignant. He seemed relaxed, his gestures moderate and easy, even as his tone conveyed cold anger. Just as he had described in his Harvard essay on public address, he had "formed his thoughts at an instant" and he now began retracing them one by one. In both thought and execution, Phillips' speech conveyed a compelling synthesis of iron control and deep passion, the same emotional design that had supported his development since childhood. As he laid public claim to his calling,

15. *National Anti-Slavery Standard*, May 25, 1867.
16. George W. Smalley, "Memoir of Wendell Phillips," *Harper's Magazine* (June, 1894), 133–41.

Phillips had discovered the highest purpose he could imagine for his gift of eloquence.

He was surprised, Phillips began, to hear Austin, the voice of law in Massachusetts, speak so enthusiastically of mobs. He was even more disturbed at the applause Austin had "received within these walls" dedicated to patriotic liberty. To compare the actions of "the mob at Alton, the drunken murderers of Lovejoy," with the inspired resistance of "those patriot fathers" was "an insult to their memory" and a perversion of truth. "The glorious mantle of Revolutionary precedent could never be thrown over the mobs of our day," Phillips declared, for the Sons of Liberty had embodied order. They had struck "for their rights as secured by the laws," taking up arms not to overturn but "to sustain the law and the constitution." The vital contrast between Alton's murderers and Boston's patriots was this: "The men of the Revolution went for right as secured by law. The rioters of today go for their own wills, right or wrong." Pointing to the portraits of Adams, Hancock, and Otis, Phillips spoke of his own reaction upon hearing Austin compare Lovejoy's killers to these great patriots: "I thought those pictured lips would have broken into voice to rebuke the recreant American—the slanderer of the dead. . . . In the sentiments he has uttered, on soil consecrated by the prayers of Puritans and the blood of patriots, the earth should have yawned and swallowed him up." Repelled or exhilarated by Phillips' vivid fusion of history and the present, the audience exploded with cheers and angry cries. As chaos reigned, Phillips stood aloof and relaxed on the platform, the picture of aristocratic ease and self-possession.[17]

When order was finally restored, Phillips continued with an impassioned defense of Lovejoy's recourse to arms, denying that his violent act was in any sense disruptive or illegal. "He did not cry anarchy, and let slip the dogs of civil war, careless of the horror that would follow." Instead, Phillips emphasized, Lovejoy and his few defenders represented the only forces of restraint left in Alton, where magistrates, mayor, and militia had all capitulated to the mob. "Anarchy did not settle down on that devoted city until Lovejoy breathed his last," Phillips insisted. "Till then, law, in his person, sustained itself against all its foes."[18]

Finally, Phillips declared, Lovejoy had attempted much more than the defense of his own liberty, for in his action he had revealed himself as a

17. Phillips, "The Murder of Lovejoy," in his *Speeches*, 2–10.
18. *Ibid.*

man of supreme will, a republican hero who had sought to liberate Alton itself from tyranny. "The crisis had come," said Phillips, "it was time to assert the laws." Someone had to take bold steps to show the people "the priceless value of their freedom of the press, to bring back and set right their confused ideas." Lovejoy had "looked out on a community staggering like a drunken man" and had concluded rightly that the people had become "deaf to argument." So he had raised his revolver hoping desperately that "they might be stunned into sobriety. Insulted law called for it," Phillips declared, for Lovejoy had clearly seen, just as the patriots of 1776 had seen, "the necessity of resistance." Had the year been 1776, not 1837, none would have dared to charge Joseph Warren with imprudence, as Austin had charged Lovejoy; no one would have said of him that "he died as a fool dieth."[19]

When Phillips concluded, the meeting ended quickly, for no one elected to follow him to the podium. Having overcome the cacophony of the crowd and restored order to Faneuil Hall with his words, he found himself embracing a new vocation that answered all imperatives of family, religion, and his own ambitions for power and distinction. Claiming Ann Phillips' vision as his own, he could feel himself a living extension of the heroic history with which he identified so strongly. The disordered world around him now contained the promise of its own redemption, for he could see himself using his voice to become for his time what Burke and Patrick Henry had been for theirs, a great spokesman for republican liberty, a forceful restorer of public virtue and the harmony of a lawful society. His "world of dreams" had been scattered, just as he later remembered, but it was a new vision that had pushed it aside. As Ann Phillips rejoiced and Sarah Phillips despaired, he now joined completely with the "heroes" of his own time. Soon after the speech, Ann Phillips remembered, Wendell closed his Court Street law office forever "and gave himself, heart and soul, to the cause of abolition."[20]

Phillips quickly came to power in Massachusetts abolitionism. By 1838 he had been appointed general agent of the Massachusetts Anti-Slavery Society, and the Boston Anti-Slavery Society had elected him its president. Local antislavery societies constantly invited him to speak, forcing him to refuse more than he accepted. By early 1839 he stood in

19. *Ibid.*
20. Lillie Buffum Chace Wyman, "Reminiscence of Wendell Phillips," *New England Magazine* (February, 1903), 730.

the forefront of Boston's abolitionist leadership, returning to Faneuil Hall with Garrison and Edmund Quincy, son of Harvard's president, for a debate on the abolition of slavery in the District of Columbia. Several of the speakers (but not Phillips) gestured dramatically toward the portraits on the back wall as they made their most eloquent statements.[21]

Even as the movement gained converts and Phillips' influence increased, however, the American Anti-Slavery Society began to fall apart. Deep conflicts over principles and personalities developed around Phillips' irrepressible friend William Lloyd Garrison, who attacked orthodox churches with inquisitorial zeal. Worse, he openly repudiated the Sabbath, the authority of ministers, and the literal reading of Scripture. Moreover, he espoused nonresistance, denying the moral power of human government and declaring obedience to God alone. After he endorsed womens' rights and invited women to share equal power in the antislavery societies, many—including such feminist abolitionists as Maria Chapman, Lucretia Mott, Lydia Maria Child, Abby Kelley, and Elizabeth Cady Stanton—did just that. Garrison also attracted followers who seemed to many as exotic as his ideas. Charles Calistius Burleigh, for instance, dressed like the prophet Jeremiah, and Henry C. Wright wrote publicly about his dreams. To test his nonresistance principles, Samuel J. May once slept unarmed, locked in a cell with a homicidal maniac. Parker Pillsbury, Stephen S. Foster, and Nathaniel Rogers, a trio of harsh-spoken New Hampshire folk, disrupted church services with impromptu denunciations of proslavery religion. Somehow, all of them got on with Garrison's aristocratic Boston confederates and became the Phillipses' dearest friends, but the meetings of the antislavery societies grew ever more rancorous.

This flowering of isms reflected the abolitionists' general hostility to conventional authority and their broadening impulse to seek utopian alternatives. Abolitionists, who detested the master's Godless power over his bondsmen, began to judge all personal relationships and institutions by the same standards. Churches, political parties, marriage, and the internal workings of the antislavery societies themselves suddenly became open to exhaustive scrutiny for elements of slavery in its broadest sense. For Garrison and some of his Boston-based followers, perfectionism, nonresistance, and feminism were obvious correlations of abolitionism. In addition, such abolitionists felt certain that their recent

21. *Liberator*, January 29, 1839; Garrison and Garrrison, *Garrison*, II, 274.

experiences justified these drastic conclusions. They had been mobbed by their neighbors, spurned by the churches, and repressed by both political parties. A nation so mired in infamy, North as well as South, surely needed a peaceful revolutionizing of values before its institutions would change.[22]

Other abolitionists, though no less suspicious of "Godless" power, looked on all this with squeamish disgust and counterattacked. Their leaders were generally orthodox evangelicals who believed that the Bible and the churches were the greatest of all instruments for spiritual emancipation. Arthur and Lewis Tappan, Joshua Leavitt, Henry B. Stanton, James G. Birney, and others considered *Garrisonian* a synonym for *heretical*. Concerning women's rights, some quoted Paul's letters and stood for male dominance, but all were certain that the issue would not be a popular addition to abolitionist doctrine. In fact every Garrisonian belief seemed to them to undermine some God-sanctioned institution or social relationship, at a time when abolitionism needed to build on the public's growing concern over civil liberties. The movement faced critical times, they argued, because Texas, a huge slave republic, was applying to enter the Union. Many northerners feared this prospect, but they needed to be politically mobilized even perhaps in a separate abolitionist party. Mad Garrisonianism would only make abolitionism repellant to the new supporters so desperately needed to reverse the nation's slide into slavocracy.[23]

Phillips gave his wholehearted support to Garrison, and their acquaintance quickly grew into closest friendship. Garrison was always much more than a friend to Phillips; he was the peerless saint who had made Phillips' self-liberating discovery of his new vocation possible in

22. The best analyses of the factions and social subgroups within abolitionism and of the splits between them are Aileen Kraditor, *Means and Ends in American Abolition: Garrison and His Critics on Strategy and Tactics, 1834–1850* (New York, 1969); Lawrence J. Friedman, *Gregarious Saints: Self and Community in American Abolitionism, 1830–1870* (New York, 1982), 11–126. These two works take opposite views of the internal dynamics of the abolitionist movement and the reasons for the schism that took place. Both views have merit and are not mutually exclusive. Important perspectives on the abolitionists' long-term relationships with each other and with institutions are developed in John R. McKivigan, *The War Against Proslavery Religion: Abolitionism and the Northern Churches, 1830–1865* (Ithaca, 1984).

23. See, in addition to the works cited in the previous note, Stewart, *Holy Warriors*, 51–73, for a general discussion of these developments. For a perceptive and somewhat conflicting view, see Ronald Walters, *The Antislavery Appeal: American Abolitionism After 1830* (Baltimore, 1976), 3–36; Lewis Perry, *Radical Abolitionism: Anarchy and the Government of God in Antislavery Thought* (Ithaca, 1973), 18–294.

the first place. Phillips saw Garrison as abolitionism's great pioneer, the inspired visionary who had dispersed the clouds of ignorance and apathy that had hidden slavery for so long, opening vistas of freedom for two million enslaved blacks and offering to white reformers like himself new lives of transcendent moral purpose. "How can we ever thank him for clearing the atmosphere to which he has lifted us?" Phillips once asked an audience of abolitionists. Because of Garrison's bold vision, they too had "broken the shackles of party, thrown down the walls of sect, trampled on the prejudices of their land and time" in order to seek life's highest meanings. "Life, what a weariness it is," Phillips exclaimed, "with its drudgery of education; its little cares of today, all to be lived over again; its rising, eating, lying down—only to continue the monotonous routine. Thank God that he has inspired any one of us to awaken from wearing these dull and rotting weeds—revealed to us the joy of self devotion—taught us how we intensify life by laying it as a willing offering on the altar of some great cause." Phillips and all abolitionists had "been redeemed into full manhood" because of Garrison. "My friends," he assured his listeners, "if we never free a slave, at least we have freed ourselves in our efforts to emancipate our brother men."[24] Lovejoy had provided the moment of Phillips' conversion, but Garrison was his personal liberator, the hero who had freed Phillips to live out the conversion's implications. For Phillips, as for so many abolitionists, slave emancipation and self-emancipation had become fully conjoined, and therefore he responded angrily whenever adversaries accused Garrison of atheism. Soon Garrison's opponents began advising one another to "keep a healthy look out" for Phillips, too, as the factional quarrels intensified.[25]

Phillips himself soon began adding to the controversy. When, for instance, the Massachusetts Anti-Slavery Society met in early 1838, he made an unsuccessful effort to have Garrison's editorially independent *Liberator* declared the official newspaper of the society. October found Phillips in Worcester, decrying attempts by Henry B. Stanton and Beriah Green to commit abolitionists to voting for antislavery candidates. Soon after, he consulted with Garrison about founding a monthly periodical for promoting female equality within the movement.[26]

24. *Liberator*, January 24, 1851.
25. Alanson St. Clair to Amos Phelps, January 30, 1839, Amos Phelps Papers, BPL.
26. Garrison and Garrison, *Garrison*, II, 240–42, 245–46; *Proceedings of the Sev-*

As these skirmishes became brawls, Phillips began to elaborate his own views on the issues. Since a woman was no less sincere about abolishing slavery than a man, "why is she not entitled to utter her indignation anywhere, everywhere, and most of all in antislavery committee rooms and platforms?" he queried conservative Arthur Tappan. (Ann Phillips might have asked the question herself.) With equal vehemence, he rejected separate political action. At the January, 1839, Massachusetts Anti-Slavery Society meeting, Henry B. Stanton and other anti-Garrisonians introduced resolutions binding abolitionists to vote for "pure" political candidates, Phillips arose and "tore Stanton to bits," condemning compulsory voting and the proposed third party as fatal measures. Both, he emphasized, would pollute a moral cause with corrupting political compromise enslaving abolitionists to the requirements of party discipline. If Stanton had his way, abolitionism was doomed, he warned, to "an unhallowed grave."[27]

Beneath these surface debates on policy Phillips believed he discerned a much deeper issue, one involving the fundamental morality of the abolitionists as a community. The fellowship of abolitionism must itself remain pure, he insisted, for otherwise each person in the movement would forfeit all power to emancipate others, and the abolitionists, like the slaves, would again face thralldom. Once more, Phillips inextricably combined the imperatives of black and white emancipation, writing that "the real cause of this opposition" to Garrison arose from the "fundamental principle upon which the *Liberator* has been conducted. That rights are more valuable than forms; that truth is a better guide than prescription . . . that all forms of human device are worse than useless when they stand in Truth's way." The anti-Garrisonians' greatest disservice to the movement lay not in their misguided ideas about politics and Garrison's religion but in their self-corrupted moral natures. Garrison's foes had allowed themselves to become inwardly blighted by "the pride of settled opinion, love of lifeless forms," and "undue attachment of sect," he insisted. Phillips' radical temperament forced him to demand, then, a movement made up of only those who

---

enth *Annual Meeting of the Massachusetts Anti-Slavery Society* (Boston, 1838), ii–iii.

27. Phillips to Arthur Tappan, reprinted in Crawford, *Romantic Days*, 158; Ann W. Weston to Deborah Weston, March 3, 1839, Weston Papers; *Liberator*, February 20, 1839.

were "frank, fearless, and straight-hearted" in their devotion to "the great truths of human rights," free of those who had stifled their own moral instincts with devotion to self-serving formulas. He was convinced that natural "harmony and brotherly kindness" within the abolitionist fellowship would only continue to dissolve as long as it contained the anti-Garrisonians, "because the hearts of some have become cold," their "fire of enthusiasm ha[s] died away."[28]

The movement's purity must be restored at once, Phillips declared, and recreants purged. Those who remained true to Garrison would then find "their hearts . . . grappled together as if by hooks of steel," joined in a redeemed community that would again be morally capable of overthrowing slavery. A victory over slavery, he argued, "would be a victory over pride, over self-interest, over avarice, over lust, over all the prejudices and bad passions of the human breast." Such a triumph would be possible only if abolitionists, too, rid themselves of these great sins and spoke again for "omnipotent truth." After all, he concluded, the "human conscience [was] the fulcrum," and "the truth, the lever" to "uprear the universe."[29]

In 1840 the anti-Garrisonians finally seceded from the American Anti-Slavery Society to form new organizations and attempt third-party politics. From that time on, Phillips enjoyed the exclusive company of "saints," whose moral sense of God's truth completely supported his own. As he battled to secure the purity of the antislavery societies, Philips had actually discovered a new religion, abolitionism itself, which offered him opportunities to use his rhetorical gifts that a conventional pastorate could never have equaled. It provided him with a far more compelling creed than had his Congregational heritage, and it even furnished a comprehensive rebuttal to his sermonizing brother John Charles.

Although Phillips hailed Garrison as his savior, he never became Garrison's disciple in doctrine. The religion of abolitionism actually had few compulsory articles of faith beyond belief in immediate emancipation. Early in 1838, for example, Phillips rejected Garrison's religious perfectionism, insisting that human nature had yet to improve since Adam's time, and refused to endorse the Non-Resistance Society that Garrison, Edmund Quincy, Henry Wright, and the Chapmans had organized. Phillips, of course, believed that God smiled on all who rose up in

28. *Liberator*, January 11, 1839.
29. *Ibid.*, January 11, May 21, 1839.

defense of inalienable rights. Garrisonians insisted that they maintained a "broad platform" in their meetings so that abolitionists (excluding the anti-Garrisonians, of course) could debate their ideas freely, and
Phillips enjoyed this crucial freedom to differ with his colleagues. Like
so much else in abolitionism, freedom of self-expression confirmed that
the fellowship itself was liberated from narrow dogma.[30] For Phillips, the
broad platform meant something else as well. From the very first, he had
seen the problem of slavery in America somewhat differently from his
many associates, and freedom of speech guaranteed his opportunity to
develop this vision.

Most abolitionists spoke of slavery in the prophetic language of
Jeremiah and Jesus, warning of sin and the holy retribution awaiting an
apostate nation. Slavery in the South reeked of heaven-defying perversion, and a "moral revolution" was required to bring about a whole-
souled apocalyptic recognition throughout the nation of its vast com-
plicity in this terrible sin. Phillips, by contrast, spoke of slavery in the
political language of republican ideology. His was, to be sure, a language
charged with a moral and religious fervor that no Garrisonian could help
but applaud, and it accorded with perfectionist thinking at many points.
Yet Phillips was far less immediately concerned than were most of his
colleagues with redeeming souls for Christ and decrying the nation's
standing in the sight of God. Instead, Phillips hated slavery as an institution that was preeminently social and political. His criticisms invariably stressed its destructive moral impact on all of American political culture, religion, of course, included. He most certainly regarded the
actual enslavement of black humanity as a gross perversion of Christian
ethics, but beyond this, as he emphasized throughout his Lovejoy speech,
he feared that the power of slavery was running rampant through all the
nation's institutions, that the institution was increasing its strength by
spreading violence, social degradation, and political tyranny. He always
remembered the Lovejoy meeting as a revelation to him of the per-
vasiveness of slavery's influence, an "abnormal element, which nobody
had counted in." Slavery "sends out poisonous branches over the fair
land, and corrupts the very air we breathe," he emphasized in 1837. The
South "cannot be corrupt, and we sound."[31] In Phillips' view, slavery

30. Kraditor, *Means and Ends*, 118–41; Perry, *Radical Abolitionism*, 55–92; Garrison and Garrison, *Garrison*, II, 228–29; *National Anti-Slavery Standard*, May 25,
1867.
31. Phillips, "The Right of Petition," 5; "Murder of Lovejoy," 5.

must be abolished because, by heinously exploiting blacks, the southern planters were also orchestrating the no less monstrous enslavement of all Americans everywhere, in their churches, their politics, and their own moral choices about day-to-day living. Phillips meant this belief as a powerful Christian metaphor but understood it even more deeply as a terrible and pressing political fact. Garrison, the Christian nonresistant, prophesied divine retribution. Phillips, the radical republican, armed himself with words, seeking to gather power and obliterate tyranny wherever he found it.

Phillips emphasized these republican perspectives to the near exclusion of all others when he spoke during the later 1830s. He warned abolitionists that "slavery saps our own strength and blinds our foresight," so that Americans were "no longer aware of its deadly influence on the body politic." People therefore must rise up against "the tyranny of a many headed monster" uncaged by the South, which snuffed out life and liberty as it pleased. The "despotism of the Sultan" seemed benignly predictable by comparison, he remarked. To combat such a juggernaut, Americans must rediscover not only God's commandments but also the unfinished tasks of republican history. In "order to establish the rights of the slave, we must first establish our own," he wrote in 1839. "The patriot as well as the abolitionist" must become energetically "concerned in this struggle" to "finish what our fathers left unfinished when they declared all men free and equal."[32]

Hailing the abolitionists' Christian inspiration, Phillips insisted that such moral insight obliged them all the more to press for massive changes in politics and law. The abolitionists' mission, as he described it in 1839, was to write the Declaration of Independence into the statute books, "to enlarge the canvas of law, till it shall cover all men, both black and white. . . . when, in 1780, our fathers hung up the shield of this declaration, in their [Massachusetts] constitution, they did not make it broad enough."[33] Abolitionists must rouse the people to demand impartial legislation, vigorously enforced, that would protect them by crushing their enslavers. To this end, Phillips now dreamed of sponsoring powerful codes, as yet unwritten, that would erase all distinctions of color. Only when the law became color-blind would civil liberty, political freedom, and economic self-determination begin to reign in Massachusetts as well as in Virginia.

32. *Liberator*, January 29, May 30, 1839.
33. *Ibid.*

In Massachusetts, Phillips granted, abolitionists did enjoy freedoms of speech and assembly unknown in the South. Yet, indicating how far behind him he had left his legal conservatism by 1839, Phillips insisted that the liberties of Massachusetts' citizens derived from the state's own republican traditions as established by "her Sedgewicks, her Quincys, her Otises and her other leaders of the revolution," and the United States Constitution did nothing to support them.[34] By 1839, in fact, Phillips had begun suspecting quite the reverse, and he viewed with deepening hostility the constitutional structures that bound the North to the slave states. If abolitionist agitators imperiled the Union, he declared that year, "I say . . . let the Union go. . . . Perish the Union when its cement must be the blood of the slave. . . . If the temple of liberty must be built, like those of Mexican idols, out of human skulls," the sooner it was toppled the better. In the aftermath of disunion, northerners would be able to translate the ideal of republicanism from "a dream to a reality" and could reform their governments to "spread blessings over the white man and the colored" alike.[35]

Such egalitarianism, though no less sweeping and utopian than any other abolitionist's, nevertheless kept Phillips well grounded in the republican values that suffused the political culture of his age. No matter how vehemently most Americans disagreed with his ideas, they well understood and highly valued the terms he used. They, no less than Phillips, distrusted the corrupting effects of unchecked power on traditional American freedom. In fact, they had already begun rallying in recent elections to protect republican liberties from a variety of unrelated enemies—the "tyranny" of Andrew Jackson, the "money power" of financiers and the Bank of the United States, the "secret influence" of the Masonic Order, the "unnatural hierarchy" of Catholicism, and so on. Northern working classes employed other versions of republicanism to convey their rising hostility to mechanized labor, and southern whites used their own interpretation to voice suspicions about conspiring Yankee "consolidators."[36]

34. *Ibid.*
35. *Ibid.*
36. Stimulating recent explorations of republican themes in American political culture can be found in Michael F. Holt, *The Political Crisis of the 1850s* (New York, 1978); Sean Wilentz, "On Class and Power in Jacksonian America," *Reviews in American History*, X (December, 1982), 45–63; Sean Wilentz, *Chants Democratic: New York City and the Rise of the American Working Class, 1788–1850* (New York, 1984), 23–107, 172–219, 299–325; Foner, *Tom Paine*; Daniel Walker Howe, *The Po-*

In this critical respect, Phillips began acting as a highly conscious political figure, a self-created republican patriot-hero who eagerly sought
victory in conflicts over fundamental questions of power and privilege.
Having abandoned his conservative legalism, he now urged a revolution
in law to banish from America all racial hierarchy. Hence, he always directed the Garrisonians, as a movement, toward open conflict with
America's dominant political parties and economic interests. Abolitionists certainly harbored self-absorbed desires to remain untainted by
the impure world outside their movement, but Phillips' leadership and
his ideology sought also to inspire an overriding imperative to remake
America, not retreat from it.[37]

February, 1839, brought Phillips his first opportunity to enlarge the
canvas of law by sponsoring a petition to the Massachusetts legislature
drawn up by the women abolitionists of Lynn. It urged the repeal of state
laws that upheld racial discrimination, for although adult black males
could vote in Massachusetts, schools and many other facilities remained
segregated, and state law prohibited interracial marriage. The public was
particularly outraged at the presumed encouragement of miscegenation
in the abolitionists' petition. At a Senate hearing Sarah Barker, a black
woman, in the company of twenty or so black and white abolitionists,
presented the document. They and Phillips, who spoke as her advocate
in the same hall in which his father had once presided, were treated with
contempt.[38]

Soon after, Phillips delivered a speech in Boston's Marlboro Chapel,
where he castigated the legislature for denying the petition. His remarks
were not recorded, but according to Ann Warren Weston, "He tore the
legislature all to pieces, then ground them to atoms, then strewed them
upon the water, and condemned [Governor Levi] Lincoln as only fit for
the representative of scurrilous, licentious profligates." One legislator
in particular, an old family friend named Minot Thayer, complained bitterly in private to Phillips about his "severe and unjust sarcasm against
my character." Phillips, according to Thayer, had declared that "I was

---

litical Culture of the American Whigs (New York, 1978); Robert Shalhope, "Republicanism in Early American History," William and Mary Quarterly, 3rd. ser., XXXIX
(February, 1982), 334–56.

· 37. Friedman, Gregarious Saints, believes introspection to be the dominant mood
of abolitionism.

38. Ann W. Weston to Deborah Weston, March 11, 1839, Weston Papers; Bartlett,
Phillips, 53.

only worthy of representing a community of *brutes*, that I polluted the carpet upon which I spit, . . . and that unless my constituents ousted me, . . . they ought not enjoy the privileges of citizens."[39]

In all likelihood, Phillips had said these things. He quickly became notorious for studding his speeches with scathing personal language, provoking controversy throughout his career. He once explained his motives this way: "If to criticize freely the actions of public men be ruthless or intolerant, how is history to be written?" In other words, Phillips believed himself to be a vigilant sentinel of liberty and justified his harsh words as necessary to alert the people to the corruption of politicians and legislators. When "a man puts on the robes of office, his acts become the property of the nation," Phillips contended, "and every man, on fitting occasion, may summon him to the bar of public opinion." In developing this justification, Phillips was invoking yet another old republican formula, which had always stressed the power that virtuous censors exercised when calling forth public resistance to legislative tyranny and corruption.[40] In his own mind, therefore, his use of invective armed him with political power, for it allowed him to subject all governmental action to the public's critical scrutiny. Clearly, however, he had also begun to discover in this personalized style of attack a way to express his urgent demands for moral order and some of his personal anger as well. Phillips had begun to contribute his scathing rhetoric to a lifetime of struggle to make Boston and Massachusetts into models of egalitarian government for people of all races.

Phillips' verbal assault on the legislature opened a campaign by abolitionists that led, several years later, to the repeal of Massachusetts laws against interracial marriage. It also confirmed his apostasy from Beacon Hill. Chapmans, Quincys, and Westons of course provided friends of his own class, but he now began encountering entirely new segments of society, including, for the first time, the working class and the poor. Venturing into seacoast and manufacturing towns like Taunton, Lynn, Worcester, and Scituate, and even onto "Nigger Hill," he drummed up donations for abolitionism by meeting the farmers, artisans, shopkeepers, and day laborers who were the rank and file of Bay State abolitionism. These were revealing encounters that made him most uncom-

39. Minot Thayer to Phillips, March 12, 1839, Blagden Papers.
40. *Liberator*, September 11, 1846. For analysis of heroic themes in early American political thought, see Maier, *From Resistance to Revolution*; Bernard Bailyn, *The Origins of American Politics* (New York, 1968).

fortable about his privileged circumstances. They led him to believe that poverty, unlike southern slavery, was not the result of arbitrary power and that class inequality among free laborers actually reinforced the republican abolitionist principles he now believed in so deeply.

Phillips confessed that he "hardly dared stand by the side" of these working-class abolitionists who made their living "by drudgery and daily toil, and by the sweat of their brow." He wondered, "Who are we that we should pressure to rank ourselves with those that are marshaled in that host? What have *we* done? What sacrifice have *we* made? Where the luxury that *we* have surrendered?" Phillips had a valid insight. It was certainly easier to be a rich abolitionist than a working-class one. Yet Phillips also envisioned abolitionism as a harmonious body of saints, a churchly assembly that conducted its internal relationships by the same values that it sought to enforce throughout America. At this very time, in fact, he was struggling to oust Garrison's enemies, hoping to restore a fellowship that knew no "artificial" distinctions of gender, religion, or politics. These hard-working abolitionists, Phillips therefore decided, only confirmed that the movement did indeed transcend all human differences, all class distinctions among them. In fact, in view of their meager incomes, the support these poor people gave toward emancipating the slave made them the greatest Christians of all, for they "lived in the religion of the present . . . while the pulpit was busying itself . . . with forms of sin that had been buried in the graves of 1800 years." Phillips even concluded that by overcoming their economic hardships through morally ennobling work and activism freely undertaken, poorer abolitionists had attained a greater empathy with the slave than he himself ever could. They "poured their all into the treasury of the common cause," Phillips remarked, "while others were pampered with luxury and never felt for their brothers in bonds as bound with them."[41] This supposed insight of the poorer abolitionist, more than anything else, convinced Phillips that economic disadvantage was by no means necessarily degrading. After all, unlike chattel slaves, these fishermen, shoemakers, and farmers were allowed to use their God-given skills to advance their own fortunes, develop moral discernment, improve their local communities, and work freely for the liberation of their fellow humans. Their freedom was the truest measure of a republican citizenry.

In decades to come, many people in the North were to grow increas-

41. *Liberator*, April 19, 1839.

ingly disturbed about similar distinctions that they perceived between their progressive, orderly, free-labor civilization and the turbulent, regressive society of the slave South. From 1845 onward, as slavery gained political and economic strength by expanding into western territories, northerners began demanding an end to it, invoking the slogan of "free soil, free labor, and free men." For all its extremism, Phillips' emphatic republican conviction about the moral superiority of an America universally dedicated to self-employment spoke directly to the primary values of the North's rapidly expanding middle-class political culture.[42] Henceforth, his demands and many of the North's shared political creeds would remain significantly attuned to each other. Although often considered a pariah and sometimes exercising only marginal influence, Wendell Phillips would always have much of substance with which to agitate as the Civil War slowly drew closer.

42. See Eric Foner, *Free Soil, Free Labor, Free Men: The Ideology of the Republican Party Before the Civil War* (New York, 1970).

FIVE

Europe and Essex Street

Ann Phillips remained in good health, "looking nicely," for the first year of their marriage. She and Wendell lived in Boston during the fall and winter of 1838 and spent the summer at the Phillipses' seaside estate in Nahant, near Lynn. Ann delighted in her husband's growth as an abolitionist, remarking that she had "learned little" since their marriage, "while Wendell, only two years older seems to know a world more." She mentioned nothing about the continuing friction between her and Sarah Phillips, who still resented Ann's abolitionism, especially her delight in frightening "ministers' wives about the county half to death, talking on the woman question." Soon, however, Ann curtailed such activities as she began complaining once again of shooting pains and violent nausea, although she suffered no terrible crisis this time. Baffled doctors suggested a tour abroad as a way to recuperate. Phillips hastened to resign his positions in the antislavery societies and prepared for a trip that would mark the end of Ann's public life. Ten years later he was to recall that "our last life was in England—perpetual leech chamber since—so no wonder we talk a great deal of all we saw and felt and the great kindnesses we received there."[1]

They sailed from New York City on June 10, 1839, carrying commis-

1. Ann Phillips to Alvord, November 9, 1837, reprinted in Martyn, *Phillips*, 87; Ann W. Weston to Aunt Mary [Weston], July 9, 1838, Weston Papers; Phillips to Pease, February 9, 1850, Garrison Papers, BPL.

sions as delegates from the Massachusetts Anti-Slavery Society to the World Anti-Slavery Convention, scheduled to meet in London the following year. Factions of quarreling Americans were sparring to capture English support, and the Phillipses were chosen to advance the Garrisonian cause. They mapped out an itinerary that would bring them first to London, then through France to Rome where they would winter before returning to England for the convention. Their pleasant ocean crossing promised a happy tour. Ann "never missed a meal" and was seasick only twice. The couple played shuffleboard, watched for porpoises, and mixed with an "interesting" if "motley set" of "Southerners . . . surveyors, French wanderers, East Indian middies, Irish nothings, rugged John Bulls, tradesmen's wives . . . and an old general of seventy with a wife of twenty-five." Aboard ship, Wendell also wrote the first of many loving and detailed letters to his mother. Contrary to her hopes, he did not diminish his commitment to abolitionism during his time abroad. As will be seen, European experiences only deepened and expanded his convictions. Yet in these letters Phillips also assured Sarah that he wanted as much as ever to be counted as her close and loving son.[2]

The Phillipses landed in London, and Wendell was seized with historical ecstasy: "We passed through an ancient gate, weather beaten, marked with 1687 and the name of ill-fated James 2d," he reported to Sarah. "Tell John he cannot imagine how forcibly it shatters one, these places covered so deep with the memories of the past, haunted by the great days gone by." Here was genealogy, set in ancient pavements and building stones.[3] Yet contemporary England proved just as fascinating. Prominent British abolitionists greeted them, and several became enduring friends. Richard Webb, a Dubliner, was a leader in British abolitionism and friendly toward Garrison. Sprightly Elizabeth Pease, a wealthy woman who came from Quaker stock, helped underwrite the American Anti-Slavery Society, and Ann and Wendell judged her a "very intelligent and interesting woman." She took charge of the young Americans' social calendar, one high point of which was a visit to George Thompson's house.[4]

2. Phillips to Sarah Walley Phillips, June 24, 1839, and see other letters of Phillips to his mother, 1839–41, all in Blagden Papers.
3. Phillips to Sarah W. Phillips, June 30, 1839, *ibid.*
4. Douglas C. Riach, "Richard Davis Webb and Antislavery in Ireland," in Lewis Perry and Michael Fellman (eds.), *Antislavery Reconsidered: New Perspectives on the Abolitionists* (Baton Rouge, 1979), 149–67; Louis Ruchames (ed.), *A House Dividing Against Itself, 1836–1840* (Cambridge, Mass., 1971), 326–27, Vol. II of *The Letters of*

Here they met the great abolitionist-orator whose tour of New England had inspired the Boston mob witnessed by the Phillipses in 1835. American abolitionists counted Thompson a hero, and Phillips had already written him, giving a Garrisonian view of developments in America. Thompson conversed warmly with the Phillipses and presented to Ann several articles as contributions to sell at the Boston Anti-Slavery Bazaar. Enjoying such prominent contacts as Thompson, the Phillipses remained in London through August, and as the summer passed, Elizabeth Pease and Ann sometimes shopped for hours at a stretch, leading Wendell to believe that his wife's health had "gained steadily." Encouraged, they embarked in September for France, with Rome as a final destination.[5]

As they toured the continent, Wendell Phillips sometimes betrayed his New England provincialism, as when he decided that "there was nothing interesting in these French cities . . . of perpetual cafes and tobacco shops . . . none of that busy look old and New England has." Yet his responses to foreign cultures were usually more complicated than this. The service of Holy Communion he observed in Marseilles, for example, both repelled and inspired him. The statuary and the priests seemed grotesque and superstitious, but the liturgy had a power of "awful reverence" that "surpassed description." French civilization certainly permitted him to expand his sense of history's dramatic possibilities, for he visited the homes of Voltaire and Rousseau and the church where John Calvin had preached. "I sat and stood in the pulpit where he might have stood," Phillips reported. Later, in Frankfurt, Germany, he continued such investigations, examining a pair of Martin Luther's slippers and lingering over a Gutenberg Bible.[6] Rome, of course, added so richly to his catalogue of historical sites that he felt that "there was no describing" such scenes—"To see monuments on which Paul's eye had rested, or the place over which Peter had been crucified—Rome is the shrine of the world," he rhapsodized. Wendell and Ann explored the palace of the Caesars, the Pantheon, the Colliseum, Trajan's Column, and

---

William Lloyd Garrison, 5 vols.; Wendell and Ann Phillips to Maria Weston Chapman, July 30, 1839, Chapman Papers.

5. Phillips, "Letter to George Thompson," in his *Speeches, Second Series*, 15–19; Phillips to Sarah W. Phillips, July 26, 1839, Blagden Papers; Wendell and Ann Phillips to Maria W. Chapman, July 30, 1839, Chapman Papers.

6. Phillips to Sarah W. Phillips, December 18, 1839, Blagden Papers; Phillips to Mary Grew, reprinted in Martyn, *Phillips*, 140–41.

the Vatican's great art. "It seems useless to catalogue interesting objects, so numerous are they here," he exclaimed to his mother.[7] Phillips had always superimposed history imaginatively on his sense of the present; now on daily walks he encountered constant evidence of historical eras layered one upon the other.

As their travels progressed, Phillips grew increasingly disturbed by the "powerful contrasts" he encountered between "wealth beyond that of fairy tales, and poverty, bare and starved at its side." The misery that Phillips believed "bad laws and bad religion alike" had fastened on the bulk of Europe's population violated all his Yankee assumptions about how a free society ought to work. It "saddens one here at every step," he informed Garrison. "In our country, the same contrasts exist, but they are not as yet so sharply drawn as here. The moral stagnation and death . . . only makes us value more highly the stirring arena at home."[8] Faced with such terrible poverty, Phillips could not rest comfortably with evasive thoughts of American superiority. He felt compelled to develop some deeper social judgments. All true Christians, he now decided, must recognize the limits of self-interested individualism and agree that owning property automatically entailed *"responsibility for the right use of what God has given."* The wealthy must be held to account for their impact on society by the "needy brother," who, Phillips was now convinced, held a title to the bread of life every bit "as sacred as the owner's own." The rich should therefore expect their property rights to be "infringed upon . . . whenever the owner allows the siren voice of his own tastes to drown out the cries of another's necessities."[9] Phillips had certainly not embraced class conflict, but he had discovered an abiding fear of the power of wealth to generate social disorder. To him it now seemed obvious that the theoretical freedom of unenslaved laborers had agonizing limits, though not (ominously) "as yet" in America. Always a champion of free-labor individualism, Phillips had been driven to conclude that the poor, though technically not enslaved, could not be expected to remain silent when struggling against insurmountable obstacles. Faced with utter hopelessness, they should not be expected to regard other people's deeds of ownership as inviolable documents. Phillips' own

7. Phillips to Sarah W. Phillips, January 2, 1840, Blagden Papers; Phillips to an unnamed correspondent, January 5, 1840, reprinted in Martyn, *Phillips*, 127–28.
8. Phillips to William Lloyd Garrison, April 12, 1841, reprinted in *Liberator*, May 6, 1841.
9. *Ibid.*

crusade against American corporate power lay a quarter century in the future, but the roots of that commitment originated in these much earlier meditations on poverty in Europe.

Then there was the problem of race relations in Europe, or better, as Phillips judged it, the disturbing absence of such a problem. Even as "refinement" stood "face to face with barbarism," it appeared to him that black people all across Europe were treated as social equals. When the black Garrisonian Charles L. Remond first came to London, for example, Phillips noticed that aristocratic reformers treated him with great respect. As Phillips strolled the most exclusive street of Paris, moreover, he saw "fashionably-dressed white and colored persons walking together" without arousing anyone's notice, whereas in Boston such scenes had already prompted controversy, even riot. In Catholic ceremonies, blacks were welcomed not just as parishioners but as clerics. Phillips noted one black priest "who mingled freely with those about him, and he was not stared at as a monster when he entered the frowning portals of the Propaganda College at Rome."[10] At home, Phillips knew, blacks were not welcome at the Old South Church.

In all these respects Phillips allowed his exposure to European customs to make him far more aware than before of racial injustice and increasingly sensitive to problems of poverty and class. "I am sure of one thing," he affirmed as his sojourn ended, "I would like to have the same minds made awake and deeply interested in *every* cause, no matter what its complexion, which helps to relieve and elevate humanity." As he struggled to make clear judgments from his impressions, he felt obliged to seek "the abolition of every thing that adds one particle of weight to the unavoidable burden of humanity, or makes any distinction, possible to be avoided, in the comfort and station of any human being."[11] Phillips had left Boston a deeply engaged abolitionist. He was to return with a much-expanded and heightened suspicion of tyrannous power, which he now defined in economic as well as racial terms.

In May, 1840, Wendell and Ann returned to London, eager to discharge their duties at the World Anti-Slavery Convention. Now they felt more at home, for they met the aristocratic leaders of British abolitionism, Viscount Morpeth, Baron Brougham, and Thomas Clarkson, among others. "I tattle on all this to show you how far from *vulgar* the *Liber-*

---

10. *Ibid.*; Phillips quoted in *Liberator*, August 13, 1841.
11. Phillips to John Collins, June 16, 1841, Garrison Papers, BPL.

ator would be, ma, in London," Phillips chided his mother, suggesting that he moved easily among authentic nobility whose titles dwarfed the social pretensions of Beacon Hill.[12] The Phillipses also met a man who was hardly considered a blue blood, the famous Daniel O'Connell, renowned leader of the successful drive for Irish Catholic representation in Parliament, who now worked for repeal of the political union that tied Ireland to England. Phillips listened to this great orator profess his cause and marked approvingly O'Connell's public refusal to accept a contribution from an American slaveholder.[13] Among Catholics as well as Protestants, Phillips was developing contacts that he would maintain for decades. Once home, Phillips would quickly explore the possibility of creating a common cause between Boston's abolitionists, the Irish of that city, and abolitionists in the British Isles.

The World Anti-Slavery Convention itself turned out to be a disappointment. On June 12 delegates from many western nations—including Garrisonian friends Lucretia Mott, Elizabeth Cady Stanton, John Collins, and George Bradburn—crowded into Freemason Hall. Garrison's foes were there too, led by James G. Birney. Back in the United States earlier that spring, the factions had finally split, leaving Garrison's confederates in control of the American Anti-Slavery Society. Now both groups struggled for English support, and to that end, Birney challenged the credentials of Ann Phillips and the other female delegates. She, Stanton, Mott, and others were forced to join the other ladies in a curtained section of the hall until the men decided the issue. Outraged, Ann scrawled a note to Wendell on the back of the official program: "Please to maintain the floor—no matter what they do," and (according to tradition) told him, "Wendell, don't shilly-shally!" So, when it was moved that the women not be seated, Phillips countered with an amendment to admit all delegates regardless of gender. After furious debate, Phillips' amendment was crushingly defeated, the Garrisonians soon lost interest in the proceedings, and Garrison himself, arriving late, boycotted the conference. For the rest of the convention, Phillips occupied himself learning about British efforts to weaken the American slave economy by growing cheap cotton in India with free labor.[14]

12. Phillips to Sarah W. Phillips, July 24, 1840, Blagden Papers.
13. Phillips, "Daniel O'Connell," in his *Speeches, Second Series,* 408.
14. Ann Phillips to Phillips, June 12, 1840, Blagden Papers; Lucretia Mott to Maria Weston Chapman, July 29, 1840, Chapman Papers; Samuel J. May to Phillips, June 13, 1840, Samuel J. May Papers, BPL; Phillips, "Cotton, the Cornerstone of Slavery," in his *Speeches, Second Series,* 13–15.

The convention also dealt the Phillipses a much more serious disappointment, for the excitement of the event undid all of Ann's recovery. Although by this time they were homesick and although Sarah Phillips disapproved of their long absence, Wendell and Ann saw no choice but to stay longer on the "hated continent," hoping desperately that Germany's spas would hold curative powers for Ann. "Nothing but the strongest conviction of duty" could have led them to this decision, Wendell tried to reassure Sarah. "You know how much I have always felt we owed our good mother . . . more than all others can ever repay."[15] If such words placated Mother Phillips, the treatments in Frankfurt and Heidelberg did nothing for Ann. Afterward, the Swiss Alps bored Wendell, and spring, 1841, found them in Naples, hoping vainly that the warm weather would make Ann feel better. Clearly, something much more serious and chronic than either of them could have foreseen was afflicting her, but staying longer would be of no help. She had now remained seriously ill for over nine months. "Nothing brings home so vividly to Ann as the sight of an occasional colored man on the street," Wendell wrote, as he prepared Garrison for their arrival in Boston. "So we are ready to return to our posts, in nothing changed."[16]

Actually, much had changed. Wendell and Ann Phillips now had to confront the dismaying possibility that her lingering illness might make her a permanent invalid. At the same time, Wendell's examination of race and class relations had given him considerably more radical convictions than before. Clearly, as he revealed to Garrison, Phillips had managed to gain a deeper, more mature perspective on his original abolitionist commitment as he traveled about the continent. He had been wondering for some time, he revealed, whether he had acted too impetuously that day in Faneuil Hall, "taking steps that the judgment of age would regret—with being hurried by the enthusiasm of the moment." His answer, of course, was a heartfelt reaffirmation of his original action. "I am rejoiced to say that every hour of such thought convinced me more and more of the overwhelming claim our cause has on the lifetime devotion of each of us." In July, 1841, after two agonizing weeks of ill-

15. Pease to Maria W. Chapman, November 17, 1840, Chapman Papers; Phillips to Pease, May 15, 1841, Garrison Papers, BPL; Phillips to Sarah W. Phillips, July 24, 1840, Blagden Papers.

16. Phillips to William L. Garrison, April 12, 1841, reprinted in *Liberator*, May 6, 1841.

ness at sea for Ann, they disembarked.[17] Wendell Phillips was returning more expansively radical than ever while Ann was rapidly sinking into complete invalidism.

They summered in 1841 with Wendell's family in Nahant, and the situation was uneasy for everyone. If Sarah Phillips had prayed for Europe to temper her son's fanaticism, just the reverse had happened. He was eager to speak at antislavery meetings again, and everyone grew testy during long evening arguments when Sarah, Wendell, Ann, and other family members "would dispute away on the great questions." Whenever they touched on abolition or women's rights, Ann and Wendell grew resentful of high-toned Thomas and George Phillips, who seemed to treat them like "heretics and almost infidels." Everyone resorted to chess and backgammon in hopes of avoiding unpleasantness, but when Wendell went "abolitionizing" for two or three days, Ann became miserable. "I do not feel right in this atmosphere," she lamented angrily to Elizabeth Pease, "and like Rip Van Winkle I am ready to exclaim 'I am not myself. I am somebody else—that's me, yonder.'" Little wonder, therefore, that Wendell and Ann soon sought housing of their own.[18]

The house at 26 Essex Street was an inheritance from Ann's father. Small shops surrounded it, and the neighborhood was nearly "deserted of residences." Mr. LeFavour's Millinery occupied a storefront on the first floor directly beneath Wendell's second-floor study. The building, constructed of "time stained" red brick, was small, with a dining room and kitchen occupying the first floor, Wendell's study and maid's room on the second, and adjoining bedrooms on the third. A narrow porch with a wrought iron railing on the second floor allowed a person to stand over the entryway and observe the street below.[19] Wendell and Ann Phillips moved in during September, 1841, for the house and its nondescript location perfectly expressed their estrangement from Beacon Hill and their desire for isolation. Perhaps, too, these modest circumstances made Wendell feel less uncomfortable about his wealth. There was no room for entertaining; the house was only large enough for a single servant and for the two of them.

17. *Ibid.*; Phillips to Richard D. Webb, July 27, 1841, Garrison Papers, BPL.
18. Ann Phillips to Pease, September 17, 1841, Garrison Papers, BPL.
19. Richard J. Hinton, "Wendell Phillips: A Reminiscent Study," *Arena* (July, 1895), 230; Higginson, *Phillips*, viii. Crawford, *Romantic Days*, 181, contains a photograph of 26 Essex Street.

Even before they moved in, Ann's health again slipped badly, and as the old symptoms returned, she retreated to her room and began to respond defensively to her illness. Others soon began avoiding her. "Since I have become ill, the world has held quite a different aspect for me," she informed Elizabeth Pease. "Many that I thought friends have fallen off, and many have misunderstood the nature of my state of health, so much that there is no pleasure in communicating with them." As the couple set up housekeeping, Maria Chapman expressed "fear that it will go hard with Ann," and her anxieties proved correct. Before long, Ann informed Elizabeth Pease that she was confined entirely to her room, where Wendell would read to her in semidarkness or transcribe her correspondence as she dictated it. Referring to herself, Ann reported, "she sees no company, makes no calls, looks forward to spring and birds when she will be a bit freer." Good health, she noted, "was as hard to regain as lost virtue."[20]

Her grim jest slowly became a permanent fact. Wendell Phillips was once asked what he meant by his customary reply to inquiries that Ann's health was as usual. He meant, he explained, that Ann was strong enough to watch the traffic on Essex Street from her bedroom window and to tend her flowers on the sill. Occasionally, she could leave her room, but never for more than an hour, and she always had meals in bed. Often, however, her health would collapse, and she would be forced to spend long periods "almost entirely pulled down from even her usual low state by some more trying illness than common." *Prostrated* was his term for her condition at its worst. The *hospital* was Ann's word for 26 Essex Street during such times.[21]

Ann often voiced angry frustration over her condition: "I have had such a dreadful winter, so sick that life is a burden to me," she wrote on one occasion. "I do not know what to do. I am tired of suffering. I have no faith in anything [to cure me]." At other times, she felt terrible guilt because of the burden she placed on her active husband: "I grow sicker every year, Wendell lovelier, I more desponding, he always cheery. . . . For his sake, I would like to live." All too often, her morale dissolved, overwhelmed by "too many thoughts—too many tears—too many cares." By 1842 the vivacious girl who had written so charmingly to her

20. Maria W. Chapman to Deborah Weston, November [?], 1841, Ann Phillips to Pease, July 3, September 17, 1841, both in Weston Papers, BPL.
21. Phillips to Pease, January 31, 1847, February 19, 1850, both in Garrison Papers, BPL; Ann Phillips to Phillips, n.d. [1860], Blagden Papers.

fiancé about her hike up Andover Hill had forsaken the outside world. Wendell, for his part, sometimes tried to give this devastating reversal its best construction, remarking that "it was as if she had acquired some brightness and force in those days, which has stayed by and borne her up all these years."[22]

No one ever learned the cause of Ann's sickness, and it is impossible to diagnose precisely now. Except for an invalid's pallor and a slightly stooped carriage, she appeared normal enough, though she was small, "thin as pharoah's [sic] kine," by her own description, and spoke in a lilting, girlish voice. Edmund Quincy, one of the Phillips' closest friends, saw Ann rarely and was therefore surprised by her strong appearance in 1846. She "looked better than I ever saw her, which was very few times in my life," he wrote, although he was assured that Ann was "very ill." Quincy offered his own diagnosis, the one that many others also accepted and that, as he knew, infuriated Wendell and Ann: "It is one of those mysterious complaints in which the organic . . . is mixed up with a good deal that is imaginary. But that is a dead secret," he emphasized to Richard D. Webb, "for neither of them would ever forgive such a suggestion. The end of it," he predicted, "will be . . . long life."[23]

Quincy was right, for on his deathbed in 1884, Wendell Phillips was to agonize over what would become of Ann. As to Quincy's medical assessment, it is as good as any. Upper-class women of this era were particularly vulnerable to protracted "feminine complaints" that had cultural as well as physical causes. Doctors ascribed these symptoms to hysteria, neurasthenia, or defective nerves, and they generally prescribed bedrest. The women themselves sometimes grew fascinated with these illnesses and with their manifestations and treatment as well. Some of Ann's closer correspondents shared this tendency and supported her preoccupation with sickness by writing her about their own discomforts. Perhaps, too, a modern medical consultant is correct in suggesting that Ann's illness originated in rheumatism or rheumatic fever.[24] Whatever

22. Ann Phillips to Pease, February 24, 1845, January 31, 1846, Phillips to Pease, February 19, 1850, both in Garrison Papers, BPL; Wyman, "Reminiscence of Phillips," 728.
23. Wyman, "Reminiscence of Phillips," 728–29; Edmund Quincy to Webb, July 14, 1846, Edmund Quincy–Richard D. Webb Papers, BPL.
24. For samples of such letters to Ann, see those of Helen Benson Garrison, July 22, 1850, Mary G. Chapman, July 25, 1842, Caroline Weston, March 9, 1844, and Deborah Weston, August 21, 1857, and see a medical description of Ann's symptoms in Dr. Henry Bowditch to M. Louis, June 14, 1839, all in Blagden Papers. The suggestion that

its origin, the disease caused Ann Phillips a lifetime of anguish. Moreover, it forced Wendell to face the incontrovertible fact that until his own death, Ann's illness would dominate his daily life as no other force could.

It is tempting to search for evidence of Wendell Phillips' frustration, and occasionally some can be found, for time and again the demands of Ann's illness forced him to forgo speaking engagements and important meetings and to override his reforming activities. Occasionally, he put his work first, prompting Ann to complain that he was so busy "that we seem to have no time to think of health." When he was thwarted, he sometimes became peevish at Ann's complaints and wished that he could learn greater patience. Certainly, the atmosphere of sickrooms and water-cure spas made him feel restive. Once, for example, in 1846 Wendell Phillips left Ann in Boston in order to "revel at Nahant" alone. "How comfortable it is," he sighed, "to get rid of these impedimentia."[25] Yet the evidence of his frustration is rare and never reaches a deeper level. Without any open resistance, he took up the lifetime obligations of Ann's illness, and their relationship quickly began to mature into one of love, understanding, and fulfillment.

This assertion on its face seems improbable. Wendell Phillips—handsome, athletic, enamored at one time of Fanny Kemble—embodied masculine vitality. Now he was partner in a marriage where sexual fulfillment was almost certainly rare, maybe impossible. Whatever the exact circumstances, their physical relationship certainly demanded restraint, and they were to remain childless. Moreover, the illness of the very person who had helped him in his painful struggle to find his vocation prevented him from pursuing that task wholeheartedly. Finally, Phillips, who had always possessed social grace and great personal warmth, now lived reclusively in a place "plain and bare, without and within," as one Boston abolitionist described it.[26] Nothing, indeed, could seem to have been more repressive than the isolated world within 26 Essex Street.

The evidence, happily, supports an absolutely opposite conclusion, and ironically, considering her dislike of Ann, it was Sarah Phillips who

---

Ann Phillips suffered from rheumatism or from the effects of rheumatic fever is offered in Bartlett, "New Light on Phillips," 37.

25. Ann Phillips to Pease, February 24, 1845, Garrison Papers, BPL; Phillips to Ann Phillips, n.d. [1874], Blagden Papers; Phillips to Sidney H. Gay, September 15, 1846, Gay Papers.

26. Higginson, *Phillips*, viii.

was most responsible for Wendell's successful adjustment. It was she who had exercised the dominant force in his upbringing, especially after her husband died. Wendell received from her his religious instruction, and after his marriage, he had been eager to remain accountable to her and to prove that he was as attached to her as he had ever been, sending her warmly reassuring letters from Europe. He had, moreover, returned with Ann to Nahant, his family's gathering place, seeking his mother's reconciliation and approval. More than twenty years after her passing, Sarah remained an indelible force, a memory powerfully shaping Wendell's conscious thoughts. "If there be any truth in spiritualism," he once wrote Ann, "I think my mother may be my guardian angel—the thought of her comes to me so often, and at such singular times. It ought to make me better—perhaps it will." Ann Phillips certainly could appreciate, as she wrote, that Sarah "was everything to Wendell."[27]

Sarah Phillips had taught her son to believe, above all, that he must discipline his inner feelings so that his conscience could direct him to higher tasks. His spiritual fulfillment, she had emphasized, depended first on his practicing vigorous self-restraint. Since childhood, he had deferred to this powerful woman who had insisted so completely on his obedience and whom he loved without reservation. In later years, therefore, he was always to find himself attracted to others much like her in personality. Strong-minded feminist abolitionists like Maria Weston Chapman, Abby Kelley Foster, Mary Stearns, Lydia Maria Child, and Elizabeth Pease became his closest friends, and he even lauded women such as these as the inspiration for his own abolitionist commitment. "Let me thank the women who came here twenty years ago for all that they have taught me," he declared at the ceremony commemorating the Boston riot of 1835. By their heroism on that occasion, he claimed (inaccurately), they "had opened my eyes, and I thank them for that annointing." Phillips reflected his instinctive deference to females when he maintained that since women exercised so great an influence over America's morals, they must be granted full civil rights. Voting and legislative involvement, he often argued, would help check their pervasive social power. Phillips claimed that he drew special inspiration from the women's rights meetings he attended, and certainly he spoke of its leaders with genuine awe. "Never," he once declared, had he seen "a more intelligent

27. Wendell and Ann Phillips to Pease, January 31, 1846, Garrison Papers, BPL; Phillips to Ann Phillips, December 10, 1867, Blagden Papers.

or cultivated audience [or] more ability guided by better taste on a platform" than at gatherings of feminists.[28]

Responding to Sarah's pervasive influence, Wendell Phillips almost invariably felt disposed to submit to powerful women, and in Ann, of
course, he had discovered the most complete embodiment of such power.
Sarah had also taught her son that his attainment of life's spiritual rewards depended on his constant restraint of passion. Phillips was therefore far better prepared than even he suspected to bow to the sexual
repression and routine sacrifices demanded by Ann's illness. By so adjusting, he opened the possibility of higher fulfillment for them both.
Wendell Phillips therefore did not "cope" with Ann's affliction. Instead,
he worked with her to integrate it into an unusual but indisputably successful marriage. Their strong relationship, in turn, actually nourished
his public career instead of restricting it. Wendell Phillips once summed
up his view of his marriage in a letter to Elizabeth Pease: "Ann is . . . so
much my motive and prompter of every good thing that I fear, should I
lose her, there'd be nothing left of me worth your loving." And to Ann
herself he wrote, using the third person, "I am not worthy to button her
old black shoes. She is my motive and inspiration. He owes her everything."[29] Wendell had long been given to saying precisely such things
about his own mother.

Inside 26 Essex Street, Wendell Phillips became Ann's nurse. His nurturing perhaps substituted for conventional sexuality as their primary
form of physical communication, for he massaged her back, shoulders,
and limbs whenever she was in pain. Each day he arose early "to tuck
my baby up and warm her clothes in the morning." And at night, Wendell checked on Ann constantly, tending to her aches and comforting
her, always lighting a match for the lamp as he passed from his darkened
bedroom to hers. Abby Kelley Foster recalled counting twenty dead
matches when she paid him an early visit, and Dr. David Thayer, whom
the Phillipses consulted, once counted fifteen. Wendell took every meal
at Ann's bedside, shopped carefully for her favorite foods, and read to her
whenever she wished, becoming her only source of information. "I
should not get along at all," she confessed, "so great is my darkness were

28. Phillips, "The Boston Mob," 226–27; Phillips, "Woman's Rights and Woman's
Duties," and "Suffrage for Women," both in his *Speeches, Second Series*, 128–38,
110–27; Phillips to Pease, March 9, 1851, Garrison Papers, BPL.

29. Phillips to Pease, November 3, 1845, Antislavery Collection, BPL; Phillips to
Ann Phillips, March 24, 1867, Blagden Papers.

it not for Wendell to tell me that the world is still going on."[30] Even during trips to health spas, Wendell's role did not change. He analyzed her symptoms, monitored her progress, and assisted in treatments whenever he could. When Ann grew depressed by her failure to recuperate, Wendell offered optimism. "I am determined to think that she is only now going back in order to get better the faster, bye and bye. . . . Ann herself has not much hope—*but I have*," he typically affirmed.[31]

By becoming Ann's nurse, Wendell assumed an unaggressive role, while she became ever more dependent on him. "I can do nothing without you," she told him; "I have so much more on my mind than I am able to attend to, that I cannot act with discretion." In short, their relationship reduced them both, but especially Ann, to a dependency that resonated with nurturing language. Wendell, of course, was more likely to adopt the tone than was Ann, but such language did flow freely in both directions. Wendell, for example, invented a score of diminutives for Ann, who became his "little Char," "baby," "baby Char," "*little Bird*," "Poor Puss," "Baby Beauty," "little twee," "little dud-dud," among many others. Ann gave Wendell fewer names, but used them no less frequently; he was her "Bessie" (a name he also used for Ann), her "little darling child," or by far most often, "Gra." Wendell, in addition, addressed Ann in childish forms of the third person. "Baby Beauty," he wrote her in 1857, "I think as Gra grows older he hates all the more to leave her. . . . Slept as usual. But had no little *feelums* in the morning— no baby to pet me—no little Char to sweeten my breakfast —poor Gra." Ann's letters reciprocated in this vein, as when she fretted apologetically about Wendell's skimpy traveling wardrobe: "So you see poor little Bessie will worry for fear her Gra is not comfortable. . . . I know you will forgive your little Bessie Char, whose headache is too much to write more."[32] Illness had forced the Phillipses to substitute the submissive

30. Phillips to Ann Phillips, n.d., Blagden Papers; Martyn, *Phillips*, 197; Wyman, "Reminiscence of Phillips," 728; Wendell and Ann Phillips to Pease, November 25, 1841, Garrison Papers, BPL.

31. See Phillips to May, September 1, 1853, Samuel J. May–J. Miller McKim Papers, Cornell University Library; Phillips to Sidney H. Gay, October 7, 1845, April 3, [1853], Gay Papers; Phillips to Helen B. Garrison, July 19, August 24, 1852, Blagden Papers; Phillips to Elizabeth Pease, November 21, 1852, Garrison Papers, BPL (quotation).

32. Ann Phillips to Phillips, January 15, [1858], November 21, 1854, Phillips to Ann Phillips, November [?], 1867, all in Blagden Papers. Any casual perusal of the Phillips correspondence contained in the Blagden Papers will quickly confirm this list of names and add more.

sentiments of the nursery for the more aggressive language of a conventional relationship. Lacking usual marital outlets, they developed an alternative superstructure of words for expressing affection, concern, and trust. The adaptation, though unusual, served them particularly well for over forty years.

When the situation is viewed in this light, it is easier to understand why visitors claimed never to find 26 Essex Street dull or depressing and to believe Wendell's and Ann's assertions that they savored life in their domestic setting. Nurturing, as Wendell Phillips practiced it, gave their home a cheerful atmosphere to which Ann referred fondly as "little, noisy, sunny, dusty, cosy, dirty Essex Street." Usually Essex Street and Ann Phillips remained so closely linked in Wendell Phillips' thinking that he was hardly able to distinguish between them. "I have just purchased some *bowls* that I long to bring home, [which] are light and small, just the thing for *baby's* nose and *hands*," he once wrote her. "That little finger has *always* from the first and *now* brings me home. Gra longs for his little chamber, the work table, his 'little place' & his Char." They loved to converse on light subjects in French and to talk seriously about abolitionism, but in conversation, as in many other parts of their relationship, Wendell left the initiative to Ann. "Silence would reign at Essex Street unless I broke it," she once remarked.[33]

But Wendell, finally, controlled the atmosphere of the household, just as his nurturing responsibilities demanded. He purchased fresh flowers to cheer Ann's room and did all the marketing. A terribly particular shopper, he would, for example, habitually buy two boxes of strawberries when he only needed one, so that the very best from each could be picked out for Ann. He also selected potatoes of nearly identical sizes simply because this symmetry pleased her. When he believed that Ann's health or peace of mind were being threatened, he became extremely combative and angry. For example, he hired organ grinders to play daily outside Ann's window, and she loved the music, but a neighbor complained in 1858 that the concerts disturbed the fragile health of a seriously ill relative and asked Phillips to restrict them. For nearly a year, Phillips refused to compromise until threats of police action forced a grudging settlement. Another time, Wendell drew the wrath of his brothers and sisters when he haughtily demanded that he and Ann be allowed

33. Ann Phillips to Helen B. Garrison, August 20, 1847, Garrison Papers, BPL; Phillips to Ann Phillips, March 30, 1867, Blagden Papers; Martyn, *Phillips*, 197.

to occupy the family vacation residence in Nahant by themselves. Trips to the florist, painstaking inspection of produce stands, squabbles over organ grinders, and vacations—all were essential to show Ann that he wished to make her surroundings as reassuring as possible. In all these ways, Wendell Phillips also helped to guarantee that 26 Essex Street, though often a somber hospital, also encouraged his and Ann's spontaneous sharing of laughter and affection. He always claimed that "there is more sun and fun in Essex Street than anywhere else in Boston."[34]

Because of this supportive setting, Ann and Wendell Phillips were able to expand their relationship by allowing others to share in it. In the fall of 1849, they took a major step in this direction by adopting vigorous eleven-year-old Phoebe Garnaut, the orphaned daughter of one of Ann's many nurses. Until she grew older, Phoebe represented an enormous responsibility for Ann, regardless of Wendell's whereabouts. Yet Ann felt particularly able to understand this young girl and to raise her well, for Ann herself, of course, had lost her parents at just Phoebe's age. Phoebe became Ann's closest companion when Wendell was away and soon Phoebe too was referring to Wendell as "Dear Bessie Gra" and admonishing him to "take care of yourself and come home safe to your loving daughter . . . [and] come home soon or the chocolates will be all gone." She lived with them, except for her time at boarding school, until her own marriage in 1864.[35]

Less intimately but hardly with less investment of emotion, Wendell and Ann assumed responsibility for sponsoring Wendell Phillips Garrison. William Lloyd Garrison had named his second son after Wendell Phillips, who, with Ann, then took his responsibility for this namesake very seriously, paying his way through Harvard and giving him warm support throughout childhood and adolescence. Wendell Phillips Garrison was one of few to feel welcome entering 26 Essex Street without an appointment. "If there was ever a person who could lay claim to double parentage, I think it must be allowed that I am he," Wendell Garrison once confided to Ann.[36] Though childless, the Phillipses as-

34. For the organ-grinder and Nahant controversies, see the correspondence (1858–59) between Wendell Phillips, A. C. Baldwin, and E. E. Baldwin and see Phillips to Miriam Blagden, March 5, 1850, Miriam Blagden to Phillips, March 9, 1850, Margaret Blagden to Phillips, March 9, 1850, all in Blagden Papers.
35. Phoebe Garnaut to Phillips, n.d., and December 4, 1855, Ann Phillips to Phillips, n.d. [1860], all in Blagden Papers.
36. Bartlett, *Phillips*, 280; Wendell Phillips Garrison to Ann Phillips, July 21, 1858, Blagden Papers. See also Phillips to Pease, November 21, 1852, Garrison Papers, BPL;

sembled their own version of a successful and loving family, thereby attesting once more to the vitality of their own relationship.

Because of these common endeavors and exchanges of obligation, Ann and Wendell Phillips slowly became able to explore the limits of personal independence to a very surprising extent, and both learned to develop their lives alone to enrich what they shared together. Marriage supported each partner as a completely developed individual. Their decision in 1854 that Wendell should leave Essex Street for weeks of touring lectures marked a momentous passage across this threshold. With this step, Wendell finally accepted the enormously difficult fact that Ann's illness was permanent. Never again did they try a health spa. Instead, they agreed that Wendell must begin to pursue his vocation as a nationally recognized public speaker, especially now that train travel, the telegraph, and the stenographic reporting of speeches had so greatly expanded his mobility and potential audience. Ann agreed to confront her illness without her husband, and Wendell agreed to suppress his need to nurse her at every turn. For both, it was a decision requiring great courage and mutual trust, and the consequences were no less remarkable. Ann Phillips discovered that she could greatly expand her boundaries of self-sufficiency, while Wendell gained fame as the greatest, most controversial public speaker of his day. Each found joy in the other's achievements, sharing their feelings with admirable honesty.

There were times of great strain for Ann when her husband was away. Overcome with loneliness and suffering, she would plead with Wendell to return: "Do not let anybody persuade you to do *any thing* for them if you are able to come [home] Monday. Don't fail, for I know I shall feel too sick to be without you." Sometimes panic seized her when his letters stopped coming or when she learned he had been sick. At such times, she sent off frantic telegrams: "Is Wendell Phillips in Chicago? Is he well? Answer by telegraph!" To spare her these moments, Wendell tried to post notes from every train station and hotel, some only a few words long, often amounting to fifteen a week.[37]

Wendell and Ann Phillips to Wendell P. Garrison, September 1, 1860, William Lloyd Garrison Papers, Sophia Smith Collection, Smith College Library (hereafter SCL); William L. Garrison to Phillips, October 15, 1857, Wendell and Ann Phillips to Wendell P. Garrison, January 1, 1861, both in Blagden Papers; Wendell Phillips to William L. Garrison, September 17, 1855, Oswald Garrison Villard Papers, HL.

37. Ann Phillips to Phillips, n.d. [1860], Ann Phillips to C. Durfee, secretary of the lyceum (a telegram), March 9, 1858, and see Phillips to Ann Phillips, many brief letters, all in Blagden Papers.

More often than complaining, Ann mixed reassurance with candid statements about her condition, for without both, her husband would have felt guilty and misled. She needed to remind herself as well as Wendell, moreover, that she could manage without him. "I felt very sorry that I should set out and cry before you left, but I could not help it. I felt so sick and disheartened," she wrote in 1860. "I am glad for yr. sake that you have gone away, for I think the change of scene and not hearing my complaints will do you good. . . . I hope things will brighten, & that you will gain a great deal by this jaunt." She also gave full voice to her resentment at his absence, for such outbursts were just as essential as her support in maintaining their understanding. Unless she felt free to complain, there would clearly be no lecturing at all. "Goodbye dear," she snapped in 1872. "Would you please explain to me why you prefer lecturing to anything else in the world? Why can't you be happy doing something else?"[38]

Wendell always chose nurture and sympathetic longing as the motifs for his responding letters. The following example echoes dozens of others: "Gra can't help writing you just one line to say how much he is feeling for little dud-dud left all alone. I hope you'll get through the week easier than you expected. Gra try to behave better next winter." At other times, he expressed his deep desire to be comforted by Ann and to return at once to 26 Essex Street: "Little Baby grows sweeter and dearer every day," he once wrote. "I was lying down before lecture . . . and thought 'if now home I could get 15 minutes sleep & baby would watch to wake me'—I could not trust *anyone else*—She never misses anything that Gra needs—Dear precious Char, light and comfort of my life—Precious—Good-Bye." Clearly, anger had no place in his part of their correspondence, and he took pains to erase all suggestion of it, quickly asking "Char's pardon" whenever he acted pettish or peevish, or spoke with sharpness. "Gra," he soothed her, "loves Char dearly . . . never means anything, and is sorry instantly."[39] When Wendell wrote Ann he maintained emotional boundaries that she was free to ignore. Yet this dialogue, overall, resonated with candor and emotional power. Though they have merit, psychological theories of neurosis and repression fail to explain fully how the Phillipses actually maintained their vibrant rela-

38. Ann Phillips to Phillips, n.d. [1860], January 11, 1872, both in Blagden Papers.
39. Phillips to "Andy Tandy" [Ann Phillips], n.d., Phillips to Ann Phillips, March 7, 1868, both in Blagden Papers. The final series of quotations is taken from undated letters of the 1860s and 1870s, Phillips to Ann Phillips, all in Blagden Papers.

tionship. Commonsense terms such as *understanding* and hard mutual effort reveal at least as much.[40]

The many humorous and rewarding moments shared by the Phillipses in their correspondence augment this positive view of their life together. Wendell, for instance, always attempted to make Ann a vicarious participant in his tourings by writing delightfully about his adventures, as when he filled six pages with vivid descriptions of his stay in an "obstreperous hotel":

> Men are taking exercise at midnight and all day overhead—horrible boys grinding up and down stairs, slamming doors all day, such unaccountable noises that I go to my door to look out, just for curiosity & really decided once to ask what was going on over my head. . . . Nothing like a small country inn for uproar. . . . The man upstairs seems now to be taking up a bureau & dropping it in the middle of the room & then jumping on top of it—the boy has hustled up a girl to play with noisier than himself. . . . Hurrah! A nervous woman has just come out and choked off the boy & girl nuisance—Blessings on her![41]

He also complained good-naturedly to Ann about crying babies, bad food, and fleabites. Once, he wrote of the "queer interesting newspaper boy—an English orphan," whom he had befriended on the train and who, thanks to his efforts, was about to be adopted. Orphans, of course, always interested Ann. So did bizarre fashions, as Wendell knew when he wrote to her of a lady he saw on a train. She wore a ridiculously oversized bonnet made of garish "sage green cashmere" and attached to a huge "floating cape, fourteen inches deep." Wendell drew a sketch of it

40. My disinterest in psychohistory is partly dictated by the nature of Phillips' writings on his personal life. They are not deeply meditative and can best be understood, I think, by using common sense and empathy. When documents convey a greater range of introspection by the subject of a biography, the value of psychohistory is indisputable. See for example, Lewis Perry, *Childhood, Marriage and Reform: Henry C. Wright* (Chicago, 1980). When documents are not appropriate and the approach is attempted anyway, the failings of the method are apparent. See, for example, Michael Rogin, *Fathers and Children: Andrew Jackson and the Subjugation of the American Indian* (New York, 1975). The limits and strengths of the approach as applied to abolitionism as a whole are best exemplified in Lawrence Friedman, *Gregarious Saints*. I comment more extensively on these matters in James Brewer Stewart, "Young Turks and Old Turkeys: Abolitionists, Historians, and Aging Processes," *Reviews in American History*, XI (June, 1983) 226–32.

41. Phillips to Ann Phillips, n.d. [1867], Blagden Papers.

for Ann, labeled "Just the one for Bess." He loved to surprise her with enclosures, and once he sent a menu from a Dubuque, Iowa, hotel, in which he had circled "all the things I *ate*, for my health's sake, and put admiration marks next to those I longed for, but abstained from for your blessed baby's sake." (They bantered much about Wendell's appetite.)[42] Another time, Ann opened his letter and out fell something absolutely preposterous. Wendell's note explained: "I enclose a precious relic—a veritable bit of Gra's *toenail*. It will remind you of his cutting yours & it is quite as good a vehicle of sentiment as a lock of hair. You need not tell of it, as nobody will understand it but Char and Gra."[43] The object was suddenly not preposterous at all, but a symbol of their love and laughing closeness.

Ann, though usually too weak to write extensively, sometimes gave back as much teasing as Wendell gave her: "I have a note from dear Edmund [Quincy] beginning *Dearest* Countess. I *may* let you see it. Think of that. *You* don't call me *Countess*! What care I for you!" She also insisted, over Wendell's amused protests, that she was "THE HEAD" of 26 Essex Street, and therefore had the right to nag him about his clothes and eating habits. More important, she also accepted Wendell's serious invitations for involvement, becoming a candid critic of his abolitionist activities. He gave her many opportunities, furnishing her descriptions of the meetings he attended, the people he talked with, and his views. For instance, she particularly disapproved of his consorting with antislavery politicians like Joshua R. Giddings and Salmon P. Chase, saying of the latter, "Such a free soiler as he does more *harm to anti-slavery* than Pierce, Douglas & Co." She bridled whenever she felt that Wendell acted too hesitantly. "Yr. delicacy about Sumner strikes me as ridiculous," she wrote in 1868. During the Civil War, Ann learned that Phillips had spoken favorably about compensating planters for emancipating their slaves and protested indignantly: "It is not right to bribe people to do right. Do think of these things. Do try to satisfy me . . . do let us abolitionists stick to anti-slavery. Leave worldly measures to worldly men."[44]

42. Phillips to Ann Phillips, two letters, n.d., and a third, dated internally as 1867, *ibid.*
43. Phillips to Ann Phillips, April 10, 1872, *ibid.*
44. For typical letters in which Phillips shared serious information about his public activities, see Phillips to Ann Phillips, December 5, 1859, March 31, 1862, March 8, 1868. The quotations of Ann Phillips are found in Ann Phillips to Phillips, December 5, 1856, March 1, 1860, March 20, 1862, all in Blagden Papers.

Clearly, these were the sentiments of one who assumed an absolute right to speak as her husband's equal. After all, Ann knew that it was her sacrifice that made it possible for Wendell to travel and speak in the first place. In a much more profound sense, their successful, challenging marriage was what sustained Wendell Phillips throughout his many decades of tireless reforming. He knew that this was so even as early as 1842. That year he confided to a friend with candor and complete accuracy, "A sick wife though she may be, I owe the little I am and do almost wholly to her mature and guardian spirit."[45]

45. Phillips to Webb, June 29, 1842, Garrison Papers, BPL.

SIX

Race, Class, and New England Abolitionists

Three weeks after returning from Europe in the summer of 1841, Wendell Phillips became happily engaged in civil disobedience, joining abolitionists in New York, Philadelphia, and Boston to resist segregation in the transportation systems. He told gatherings of abolitionists about the freedom he had witnessed blacks enjoying in "backward" Europe, and he rode in Negro cars, defying railroad company rules. In these cars he began to understand for the first time some of the day-to-day humiliation facing black people in Massachusetts, and what he learned affronted him.[1]

Riding on the Eastern Railway in September, 1841, Phillips sat dressed in gentleman's waistcoat and top hat with a black Garrisonian, a printer's assistant named William Nell. The car was dirty, smelly, and dark, thanks in part to the grimy little windows, which were nailed shut. The conductor behaved churlishly toward Phillips, for he was consorting with a "nigger." Bred a gentleman, Phillips felt particularly sensitive to insults and from his privileged position actually empathized more completely than did most whites with blacks who endured these degradations. Others who resisted—including David Ruggles, a redoubtable

1. *Liberator*, August 13, 1841; *National Anti-Slavery Standard*, September 23, 1841; Carleton Mabee, *Black Freedom: The Nonviolent Abolitionists from 1830 Through the Civil War* (New York, 1970), 91–127.

black artisan who regularly invaded "whites only" cars—were therefore gentlemen too, regardless of their social origin or race.[2] For Phillips, social equality between the races offered the truest test of a republican state, uniting rich and poor as well as black and white. And conversely, hierarchies of racial discrimination constituted as great a danger to the North's body politic as did southern bondage itself. To draw battle lines against slavery in the nation of necessity meant passing laws to erase caste lines in Massachusetts. Social designs that would endure for a lifetime thus drew Phillips into integration struggles during the 1840s, and in this respect, Radical Reconstruction began for him then, in Boston, not in the South in 1867. After the Civil War, when legalized bondage but not black subjugation had ended, Phillips would always insist, "We have abolished the slave, but the master remains."[3]

In February, 1841, Phillips spoke against segregation at the state legislature, emphasizing that those he represented (a petitioning group of black and white abolitionists) were not acting as sectional agitators but simply as Massachusetts citizens. Privately owned railroads received "special privileges and franchises" from the state, he argued. The state, therefore, had the right and the duty to make these enterprises treat all citizens as equals. "These corporations are public servants," Phillips maintained, "and therefore bound to serve in accordance with the laws of the commonwealth," which had been designed "to secure the rights of all the people." The Jim Crow cars constituted a violation of black people's citizenship as well as a "direct insult" to their persons, and "this community, Mr. Chairman, is not one whose theory tolerates privileged classes." Were shabbily dressed whites suddenly forced into segregated seats, Phillips observed, public outrage would stop the practice at once. Legal equality recognized no limitations of class; it should permit no racial ones either, and to prevent the inequity of segregation, he contended, the legislature needed only to enforce the principles upon which Massachusetts' law had first been founded. "We ask not for the creation of new law," he emphasized. "We ask the legislature to say *what is law*." Since law, according to Phillips, must insure the public's good above all else, legislators should override the private choices of the segregationists. Otherwise, the state was assisting in the destruction of the

2. *National Anti-Slavery Standard*, July 4, September 23, 1841; Oliver Johnson to Phillips, September 12, 1841, Blagden Papers.
3. See, for example, *National Anti-Slavery Standard*, February 3, 1866.

republican liberty of everyone in Massachusetts, black and white, rich and poor.[4]

The legislature failed to respond to Phillips' arguments, and railroads continued to discriminate for several years before succumbing to abolitionist pressure. As Phillips had made clear during this contest, however, he now equated racial equality with the public's good and insisted that positive law must prevent an individual's discriminatory use of private property. To a greater extent than some other Garrisonians, Phillips had seized the power of the state, not the conscience of a converted public alone, to secure freedom for all races and classes.

By 1846 abolitionists had again embroiled Boston in racial controversy, this time over segregated public schools, and Phillips began to apply his legal axioms to state facilities as well as to privately owned ones. For nearly a decade, Boston's blacks had petitioned to end segregation in the schools. Finally they decided on more drastic steps and began removing their children from classes. Suddenly city authorities showed new concern, and the Boston School Committee agreed to study the matter, but over the protests of its two Garrisonian members, Edmund Jackson and Henry Bowditch, concluded that segregation allowed safer, better education for both races. Boston's city solicitor, Peleg Chandler, endorsed their position and Horace Mann, secretary of the Massachusetts Board of Education, kept discreet silence as he searched for a compromise.[5] Phillips lashed out at them all in articles in the *Liberator*.

"It is a good sign," he remarked sarcastically, that the School Committee found it necessary to call in public officials like Mann and Chandler "to share the infamy with them. The post of persecuting the colored children . . . becomes too hot for them to maintain it alone." The commissioners were "small men," Phillips charged, and Solicitor Chandler brought shame upon his office by supporting an "odious system" as a "tool of a few narrow-minded and prejudiced men." Mann's "timid silence" was also a fair barometer of white Boston's "paltry moral vision," Phillips continued. A year later, when Mann's annual report failed to condemn segregation, Phillips renewed his attack, speaking, as usual, in what he considered the harsh, personal language of a vigilant republican censor. Referring to the School Committee, he explained to

4. *Liberator*, February 16, 1842.
5. Mabee, *Black Freedom*, 167–68.

Edmund Quincy, "Their report and their conduct deserve scathing—which is the only thing that will reach them."[6]

Phillips' vituperation did not lead to a quick victory over the School Committee. Finally, however, in the 1850s a series of court battles and legislative maneuvers led by Charles Sumner, among others, did result in the passage of a statewide school desegregation law. In this long struggle, as in the railway boycotts, white Garrisonians like Phillips had cooperated effectively with Boston's most militant blacks, many of whom were barbers, artisans, and day laborers. Their interracial organization had, for some moments at least, obliterated the boundaries of class as well as caste, just as Phillips' republicanism so often required. Black activists for their part appreciated the help of well-heeled white sympathizers like Phillips just as much as he admired their tenacious love of freedom. Thus, when the state antisegregation law finally passed in 1855, John T. Hilton, William Nell, and other black leaders arranged a celebration at which Phillips and Garrison were invited to be the only white speakers.[7] The honor certainly confirmed the premises that supported Phillips' commitment to legislated racial equality, for through agitation, a renegade aristocrat like himself and working-class blacks like Hilton had bridged dangerously wide social distances. As a result, so had Boston's school children, white as well as black, and education had improved for them all now that they sat in class together. So, as Phillips judged it, had the republican health of Boston's body politic improved. He therefore had many good reasons to regard abolitionism as a combative, socially inclusive, and fully egalitarian racial movement, which recognized no distinctions of color or station.

Nevertheless, when Phillips joined the inner circle of Boston's abolitionists in wealthy Maria Weston Chapman's drawing rooms, black artisans such as John Hinton or William Nell seldom appeared. Black abolitionists found the "Boston clique," as everyone called them, a patronizing, overprivileged lot, and Phillips ranked high in the group. In the early 1840s, for instance, many of Phillips' friends praised the great new fugitive-slave-turned-abolitionist Frederick Douglass as their own

6. *Liberator*, August 28, 1846, May 25, 1853; Phillips to Quincy, August 8, 1846, Edmund Quincy Papers, Massachusetts Historical Society (hereafter MHS). For Phillips' attack on Mann, see the *Liberator*, December 24, 1847, February 4, 1848.

7. Mabee, *Black Freedom*, 170–81; James Oliver Horton and Lois E. Horton, *Black Bostonians: Black Life and Community Struggle in the Antebellum North* (New York, 1979), 67–96; John Daniels, *In Freedom's Birthplace* (Boston, 1914), 449.

wonderful invention, but when Douglass struck off on his own and began an independent newspaper, innuendos and racist gossip began to circulate in cliquish circles. In their dealings with blacks, white abolitionists were often given to paternalism and sentimentality. Blacks
tended to react by drawing away into self-help groups of their own during the 1840s and 1850s, while white Garrisonians showed a declining
sensitivity to the marginality of blacks in their movement.[8]

Despite these trends, Phillips' day-to-day relationships with blacks
generally helped to diminish racial estrangement even as it grew within
abolitionism generally. At first glance, to be sure, Phillips presented
himself as a formidable aristocrat to people of all colors, and he was certainly capable of snobbery whenever he felt socially threatened. Yet he
also carried into personal race relations the same sincerity and openness
that his college friends had found so likable, and he never gave evidence
of the conspicuous racism that affected some of his white colleagues. As
a patrician egalitarian whose heroic self-conceptions gave him great personal confidence, he exerted instead an extremely strong, unusually
positive impact on his black associates, as Frederick Douglass once eloquently testified. Douglass, certainly no servile deferrer to whites,
wrote Phillips in 1846 that he felt "great inferiority to yourself." He
hastened to explain that this shocking comment actually bespoke a
trust in and respect for the self-possessed Phillips that bordered on awe.
"Do not scold me for this. I tell you the truth when I say I have for you
such grateful regard and admiration that I cannot bring myself to approach you familiarly." Phillips, Douglass confessed, had "been to me a
brother," imparting so much "good counsel that I feel more like a
disciple to you than a familiar friend." His praise recalls that of Edgar
Buckingham and John Tappan Pierce, Phillips' old college classmates.
Phillips, in turn, attributed to Douglass during this time all the quali-

8. The documentation of racism among white abolitionists and in northern
middle-class white society in general used to be a cottage industry for historians.
Now it is a major enterprise. The most balanced, useful works on these subjects
include George M. Fredrickson, *The Black Image in the White Mind: The Debate
on Afro-American Character and Destiny* (New York, 1971); William H. Pease and
Jane H. Pease, *They Who Would Be Free: The Black Search for Freedom, 1830–1861*
(New York, 1974); and R. J. M. Blackett, *Building an Antislavery Wall: Black Americans in the Atlantic Abolitionist Movement* (Baton Rouge, 1983). Friedman, *Gregarious Saints*, 161–95, underrates the element of personal and political egalitarianism in
white abolitionism, but discusses the subject in revealing depth. If Phillips is in any
way representative of larger cultural trends, the fashionable indictment of white male
Victorian racism should be reconsidered.

ties of his own gentlemanly style. "Language, taste, fancy eloquence, vigor of thoughts, good sound common sense are all his," Phillips insisted. "He never thinks of his color, and we never do." Although this statement contradicts its own claim to an absence of racial consciousness and carries stong overtones of Beacon Hill superiority, there is no reason to doubt Phillips' sincerity.[9]

No other black abolitionist addressed Phillips as candidly as did Douglass. William Nell, William Wells Brown, and Charles L. Remond, other prominent black Garrisonians, generally approached him as a fair-minded co-worker, and he managed private matters for all of them when they traveled on abolitionist business. As a general agent of the American Anti-Slavery Society, moreover, Phillips usually arranged speaking itineraries and set salaries for all agents, black and white. In discharging these responsibilities, Phillips treated all his colleagues alike, and as a consequence, the tenor of their business letters to him was always friendly, candid, and trusting, regardless of the writer's race.[10]

Phillips was also able to criticize his black colleagues, however, and to behave like a patronizing Brahmin, too. One of his closest associates, Charles L. Remond, struck him as falsely conceited, and Phillips felt that this fault "injures him for sober, matter-of-fact, useful home toil." Remond's "foolish ways" sometimes led him to behave like a "wayward child," in Phillips' opinion; he dressed gaudily and tried to imitate Douglass. But however patronizing, these were Phillips' judgments on another's taste and comportment, not statements based on the color of Remond's skin. As Phillips also made clear, he deemed Remond's service to abolitionism as "very valuable & his position and testimony true and consistent." On another occasion, he had harsh words for J. W. C. Pennington, a black anti-Garrisonian who was, in Phillips' opinion, "self-seeking, trimming, and utterly unreliable." But again, these were personal judgments, and Phillips usually assumed the worst about foes of Garrison, whatever their race. Indeed, when Douglass, whom he regarded so highly, defected to the new organization's Liberty party,

9. Frederick Douglass to Phillips, March 28, 1846, Blagden Papers; Phillips to Pease, February 24, 1845, and see Phillips to Webb, August 12, 1842, and to Pease, February 24, 1845, all in the Garrison Papers, BPL.
10. See the files for William Nell, William Wells Brown, Charles L. Remond, and William and Ellen Craft and compare the files of white agents Edward N. Davis, Parker Pillsbury, Stephen and Abby K. Foster, and Arnold Buffum, all in the Blagden Papers.

Phillips criticized the move with great disdain, but never implied any racist generalizations.[11]

Above all, Phillips never reciprocated the open bigotry tinged with class arrogance that Maria Weston Chapman and Edmund Quincy sometimes conveyed in their letters to him. Quincy, especially, could wallow in racial crudity. When, for example, a local black criticized his speaking style, Quincy penned the following response "for the Liberator if W.P. approve":

> E.Q. returns his grateful acknowledgements to his coloured correspondent & assures him that his advice is taken in good part & will be followed as far as possible. He begs to know whether his (his coloured friend's) mother knows he is out? He would respectfully inquire of him, "How's yer marm?" Whether he can truthfully exclaim "O! Crikey don't I love my mother?" He would say that he thinks him (his col'd friend) some pumpkins he does. And that he thinks he is a nigger living in Lynn. That a nigger quite capable of getting this up lives there he (E.Q.) has on the authority of —— Pike, Esq. He also thinks that his col'd friend was assisted by a wench living about as far towards the South Shore. You didn't suck in this child, this time. No, Sirrr, No Sirreee—horsefly![12]

Phillips did not approve, and the letter never appeared in the Liberator.

Black activists seem to have trusted Phillips enough to complain forthrightly to him about the insensitivity they encountered from others in the white movement, assuming that Phillips would take their dissent to heart, not reply with defensive admonitions. In 1859, for example, Phillips was listed on a roster of white male speakers who were to pay tribute to the insurrectionist John Brown. Agnes Mary Grant, a black editor from New York City, wrote Phillips bitterly about this exclusionary decision: "Why is it that White Men are forever making speeches and glorifying themselves," while eloquent blacks "with their bursting hearts and grand utterances are kept in the background in this so falsely

11. Phillips to Pease, October [?], 1844, February 24, 1845, January 31, August 29, 1847, February 19, 1850, all in Garrison Papers, BPL., contain Phillips' observations on Remond and Douglass. Phillips to Sidney H. Gay, February 19, [1853], Gay Papers, contains Phillips' reference to Pennington.

12. See, for example, Maria W. Chapman to Phillips, June 26, [1846]; Quincy to Phillips, June 19, 1847, both in Blagden Papers.

called Free North, as much socially and politically proscribed, almost, as their enslaved Bretheren [*sic*]?" It was a telling indictment, and it was addressed to someone Grant thought would understand and share her complaint. How Maria Chapman or Edmund Quincy might have replied to Agnes Mary Grant makes interesting speculation. Phillips, Grant knew, had an exemplary reputation among blacks, as Douglass acknowledged well into 1852, writing that Phillips had "said more cheering words to me, and in vindication of my race, than any man now living." Grant, then, could find some satisfaction in knowing that Phillips was likely to take her anger seriously.[13]

Douglass' compliment was warmly justified. No white exceeded Phillips in supporting black pride and traditions. In the 1850s he began to deliver two widely repeated speeches, each of which celebrated a black revolutionary and integrated the history of the black struggle into a biracial drama of republicanism. When, for example, he spoke of Crispus Attucks, the black patriot who fell at the Boston Massacre in 1770, Phillips placed him "in the forefront of the men that dared," the figure who was "the emblem of Revolutionary violence at its dawn." As Phillips treated him, Attucks became an earlier Lovejoy, a black hero enrolled with Sam Adams and James Otis, "who had liberated *white* colonists from British slavery." Characteristically juxtaposing past with present, Phillips would next identify the black abolitionists of his own day as Attucks' worthy successors, for they, too, struggled to disenthrall all Americans, but whites especially, from racism and apathy.[14]

Toussaint L'Ouverture, Phillips' second great revolutionary black exemplar, had liberated Haiti from French rule in the 1790s. As Phillips explained him, Toussaint was a black genius who had created a great Negro republic out of the chaos and disruption of slavery. Toussaint, Phillips declared, had been a more able Cromwell than Cromwell himself, a self-taught scholar-activist in the mold of Edmund Burke, who had forged demoralized slaves into a "thunderbolt" that had repulsed the best of European armies. "Haiti, from the ruins of her colonial dependence has become a civilized state," he declared, "a very jewel of antislavery testimony and evidence." The story of Toussaint's insurrec-

13. Agnes Mary Grant to Phillips, December 9, 1859, Blagden Papers. For more on the occasion Grant referred to, see Benjamin Quarles (ed.), *Blacks on John Brown* (Champaign-Urbana, 1972), 1–31; Frederick Douglass, *Autobiography*, quoted in Bartlett, "New Light on Phillips," 109 n.

14. Phillips, "Crispus Attucks," in his *Speeches, Second Series*, 66–72.

tion was "the finest chapter in the history of the race," proving beyond all question the capacity of the black race for self-government. No one should hold up the black race to "pity or contempt," he emphasized, for heroes like Toussaint and Attucks confirmed that all blacks were "entitled to a place, side by side with the Saxon."[15]

Phillips, obviously, was not impressed with the "scientific" treatises on white racial superiority that began to appear during his day and had little sympathy for those who believed that blacks were naturally loyal, good humored, imitative, spiritual, and docile. Harriet Beecher Stowe filled *Uncle Tom's Cabin* with such characterizations and Phillips dismissed her book as "mere sentimental excitement." Some of Phillips' close associates of the 1850s, notably Theodore Parker and Thomas Wentworth Higginson considered slaves too degraded to strike for freedom on their own. Phillips, by contrast, measured the black race, slave or free, by his stern but racially inclusive standards of republican history, where what counted most was courage, an instinctive love of liberty, and an inspiration to strike boldly against tyranny. By such criteria, "negro blood, instead of standing at the bottom of the list, is entitled . . . to a place as near our own as any other blood known in history." Sometimes he even claimed that blacks were superior to whites. "Your Anglo-Saxon blood—it is water," he once told a white audience. In America's mythology and history, just as in the schoolrooms and train cars of Massachusetts, Phillips insisted that black people take a dignified and equal place, and his demand set him apart from paternalistic white reformers or those who trafficked in romantic racialism.[16]

Most revealing of all, Phillips was able to maintain his egalitarian racial postures under very trying personal circumstances. In his most private dealings with black people, he encountered situations where paternalism would have been, for many whites, the only response imag-

15. Phillips, "Toussaint L'Overture," in his *Speeches*, 468–94; *Liberator*, July 8, 1859; *National Anti-Slavery Standard*, July 16, 1859.

16. My references here are to Ronald Takaki, "The Black Child-Savage in Antebellum America," in Gary B. Nash and Richard Weiss (eds.), *The Great Fear: Race and the Mind in America* (New York, 1970), 29–35; Jeffrey Rossbach, *Ambivalent Conspirators: John Brown, the Secret Six and a Theory of Slave Violence* (Philadelphia, 1982), 182–210; Richard Slotkin, *The Fatal Environment: The Myth of the Frontier in the Age of Industrialization, 1800–1890* (New York, 1985), 227–78; Friedman, *Gregarious Saints*, 160–95. On *Uncle Tom's Cabin*, see Phillips to Pease, November 22, 1852, August 7, 1854, Garrison Papers, BPL. Phillips' other statements come from Phillips, "Toussaint L'Ouverture," 469; *Liberator*, June 6, 1850.

inable. Phillips was, after all, well known throughout the North for his wealth and his willingness to befriend the oppressed. Obscure blacks facing desperate circumstances therefore turned to him for money and often sought his direct intervention. Invariably, he responded with great compassion and generosity, remaining sensitive to his supplicants' feelings as well as to their needs. He betrayed no symptoms of moral self-congratulation and acted in confidentiality whenever he could. There can be no question that he handed out large sums in small amounts to blacks as well as whites in order to ease his conscience, for he admitted that his great wealth could make him feel terrible guilt, especially when he thought of his poorer co-workers. Yet unlike Gerrit Smith or Lewis Tappan, two other abolitionists who could match his fortune, Phillips never tried to ease his discomfort by organizing paternalistic charities or by advertising his largess. None more than Phillips violated the stereotype of the stiflingly moralistic Victorian philanthropist.

The case of Anthony Burns, for example, involved a fugitive slave whom Phillips unsuccessfully defended after his arrest in Boston in 1854 and who was returned to bondage in North Carolina. He wrote to Phillips in near-illiterate desperation, asking him to "dow all you can for me." Phillips responded by managing to arrange Burns's release and his subsequent matriculation at Oberlin College. Two years later, his spelling and handwriting much improved, Burns again wrote Phillips, this time sharing his hopes to become educated; the following year he sought Phillips' advice about beginning a life in politics. "No one is better able to instruct me in this point of view than you," Burns assured him.[17]

John Oliver, by contrast, was already at Oberlin when misadventure struck. He had run up debts, his wife had threatened to desert him, and he faced the Ohio winter without boots or a warm coat. Twice Phillips sent him money and carefully answered his questions about where he might best set up a business in New England. In the postwar years, this same John Oliver repaid his benefactor by sending Phillips news of racial conditions in Virginia, where he had become a government official and political activist. By this time, Phillips had become editor of the *National Anti-Slavery Standard* and had good use for such firsthand reporting.[18]

Phillips' constructive approach to interracial charity was sometimes

17. Anthony Burns to Phillips, n.d. [1854], August 2, 1856, August 29, 1857, all in Blagden Papers.
18. John Oliver to Phillips, January 1, August 21, 1857, July 6, 1866, all *ibid.*

as obvious to whites as it was to blacks. In 1860 one William Walker wrote to Phillips in desperation. A white who opposed slavery but who nevertheless found himself the executor of a southerner's estate, Walker had taken temporary custody of a sixteen-year-old slave who was a part of the inheritance. Could Phillips help to find an apprenticeship for this young man? No one else seemed able to assist. Walker's second letter to Phillips suggests the quality of Phillips' first response: "I thank you so much for the interest you manifest on behalf of this boy: This feeling, this principle which characterize[s] your life I do not find among abolitionists . . . generally. They care much about the slave and nothing about him when he is free."[19] Phillips' meetings with the Boston clique were largely lily white, but the wrought iron fence around Maria Chapman's mansion could not circumscribe his positive racial influence within the abolitionist community.

There were other cases like these, but two in particular illustrate Phillips' unusually constructive approaches to interracial philanthropy. The first incident, involving a boy named Bernardo, also offers a rare glimpse of the grass-roots abolitionist community in one of its best moments. In 1852 Phillips began to sponsor Bernardo, an illegitimate young boy of mixed parentage, described euphemistically as being of Cuban background. Bernardo was seriously ill, and Phillips saw to his adoption, paid his expenses, and brought him gifts. Bernardo wrote Phillips only once, for he was ashamed of his poor penmanship, caused by the wracking cough that made his hand shake badly. Bernardo's adoptive parent, Mrs. F. H. Drake, "resolved to give him a mother's care & kindness," and made it a point to "devote my time to his comfort and enjoyment" by reading and talking with him whenever the boy wished. Soon Phillips' friends, Abby Kelley and Stephen Foster, began to visit Bernardo too, bringing presents of fruit, but Bernardo remarked that "no boy could have had a kinder friend" than Phillips. Bernardo died in November, 1856. Another of Phillips' abolitionist colleagues, Edward N. Davis, delivered the funeral sermon at no charge, and many people donated money for the headstone. "Not a word about repentance or condemnation" was mentioned in the service, only "kind and Christian recognition" of Bernardo's "pure life and character" as a "more than ordinary lad." Antislavery friends from all around attended the funeral.[20] Phillips

19. William E. Walker to Phillips, April 10, April 21, 1860, both *ibid.*
20. Isaac Mayo to Phillips, November 8, 1852, G. H. Small to Phillips, November 30, 1852, Mary Raymond to Phillips, February 22, 1853, Bernardo to Phillips, August

and the other openhearted people who had given their help had also demonstrated that the abolitionist community could be loving and inclusive.

A case that certainly tested Phillips' racial sensibilities to their limits and revealed his enormous aristocratic self-confidence involved black, pregnant, unmarried Susan Randall, a stranger who turned to Phillips in desperation in 1858. A traveling entertainer, Carl Formes, had put her "in great trouble," Randall explained, but refused to accept paternal responsibility. Randall was destitute when she wrote to Phillips from Hartford, Connecticut, six months advanced in her pregnancy and afraid to turn to her mother. Formes was now playing Boston, and Randall begged Phillips to find him and make him live up to "what it is his duty to do for me." She also enclosed a medical certificate attesting to her pregnancy. Hers was a desperate and courageous act, and Phillips showed great sensitivity to her plight. Duty, as this self-possessed gentleman understood it, meant something besides sermonizing charity. Responding like a reliable business agent, he first reconfirmed Randall's identity and medical condition by writing to her doctor in Hartford. Then he found Carl Formes and made him agree to support Randall during her pregnancy, delivery, and recovery, obtaining each payment directly from Formes and sending it on to her. He also doubtless complied with Randall's other request, telling Formes never to mention this matter to anyone else. Each month Phillips sent Randall the money, and she acknowledged with small notes of thanks. In late March, 1859, she bore a son, and shortly thereafter Formes's obligation ended. "I shall soon be able to earn my living again," Randall wrote Phillips in her final letter. "I can never forget your kindness to me as a stranger, for you can never know the relief your kindness gave my mind at the time. I wish it were in my power . . . in any way, to express my thanks."[21]

Many years after the war, Phillips received a letter from a certain Mary Desmond, who had once visited at 26 Essex Street. In reminiscing, she remarked of "how little the world or newspapers know of the daily, nay hourly acts of charity that is performed . . . to every proeple [sic] of every nation" in the Phillips household. She remembered that indigents

---

3, 1856 (quotation); F. H. Drake to Phillips, September 8 (quotation), October 2, 12, November 17 (quotation), 1856, all *ibid*.

21. Susan P. Randall to Phillips, December 15, 1858 (quotation), Phillips to Dr. G. B. Hawley (draft), December 22, 1848, Hawley to Phillips, December 23, 1858, Randall to Phillips, January 9, February 13, March 14, April 26 (quotation), 1859, all *ibid*.

traveled "constantly . . . upstairs to dear Mrs. Phillips' sick room" and that Phillips had once interrupted his shaving to run next door for money to give to someone in need. Ann Phillips and her husband considered charity a privilege of the privileged, a means for solving the ever-present dilemma of possessing wealth while championing the poor, black or white. In charity, as in desegregation struggles, dealings with abolitionists, and speeches on great black heroes, Wendell Phillips expanded the boundaries of reform by obliterating distinctions of race. The exacting standards he demanded for the nation were, in truth, the ones he tried his best to live by himself.[22]

Blacks, however, were not the only disadvantaged people to whom Phillips made overtures in the 1840s. As he battled racial segregation, he also attempted to breach the growing hostility between Boston's lower-class Irish Catholics and the city's Protestant majority. Starting in the late 1830s, new Irish Catholic immigrants began entering Boston's work force in substantial numbers. They posed the first serious ethnic and class challenge to Boston's Anglo-American majority and its governing elite. They were mostly poor laborers, anxious to preserve their cultural heritage even as they laid strong claims to American citizenship. Hence, they organized Irish fraternal clubs, embraced the Democratic party, devoted much attention to their local priests and parishes, and viewed the dominant Protestant culture of Boston with deep suspicion. Yet abolitionism, especially as Phillips understood it, claimed to embrace all people, irrespective of class or place of origin, and the Irish, he assumed, should be no exception. If Boston was to evolve as a republican city, the Irish must contribute to the city's governance from their own traditions of freedom while submerging their peculiar identity in the greater crusade against slavery. In England, after all, Phillips had heard the great Daniel O'Connell lash out against slavery as the antithesis of all that Irish Catholic patriots should hold dear. Moreover, from revolutionary days onward Protestant Americans had held the English in contempt for their enslavement of brave Ireland, and Phillips shared heartily in this tradition. Now, as the Irish migration sparked new ethnic and class tensions, Phillips led other Boston abolitionists in trying to unite the cause

22. Mary Desmond [Chalmers] to Phillips, July 25, 1876, *ibid.* Examples of Phillips' charity to whites are numerous. See, for example, Thomas Cashman to Phillips, January 16, August 13, 1856, July 22, 1857, from the Westboro Massachusetts State Reform School, Blagden Papers. Phillips to May, December 4, 1842, May-McKim Papers, contains a revealing series of inquiries by Phillips about a potential recipient of his charity.

of Ireland's independence from England with that of black emancipation. As he did so, the ethnic and class limits of his own egalitarianism began to emerge.[23]

In the beginning, Phillips felt excited at the prospect of welcoming Boston's Irish into the Massachusetts Anti-Slavery Society. In December, 1841, the black Garrisonian Charles Remond came home from England carrying a petition containing sixty thousand signatures of Irishmen who urged their American brethren to cooperate with the abolitionists. Many abolitionists, in turn, began to endorse Irish home rule, and Garrison reprinted O'Connell's speeches on the subject in the *Liberator*. A great meeting was arranged in Faneuil Hall to seal this new alliance, and Phillips gave the main address, lauding O'Connell as a republican patriot and Irish Americans as his political kinsmen: "I trust in the love of liberty which every Irishman brings to the country of his adoption," Phillips declared. "Shall his countrymen trust that [slaveowner's] hand with political power, which O'Connell deemed it a pollution to touch?" Ireland was "the land of agitators and agitation," Phillips continued. "We may well learn a lesson from her in the battle for human rights." The following year, Phillips again pursued this theme in Faneuil Hall and again to a mixed audience of Protestant abolitionists and Irish Catholic immigrants. He scoffed at the idea of "prejudice against Catholics among the abolitionists," proposing "three cheers for Pope Gregory XVI—and may they ring gloriously from these arches of liberty's home! . . . Prejudice against the Negro—a genuine Irishman has none!"[24]

Phillips' last comments suggest the difficulties that arose soon after Remond's petition arrived, for Irish Bostonians felt threatened by the association with Protestant extremists being forced on them by O'Connell and others in the faraway homeland. From their perspective, abolitionists seemed to be disturbing the domestic order in their new country, and they considered themselves proper patriots. Besides, these immigrants felt no obligation to befriend Boston blacks, often their competitors in the labor market. On the other end of the race and class spectrum, meanwhile, white Garrisonians could not hide their aggressive Protestantism, their affluence, or their contempt for immigrant

23. See Gilbert Osofsky, "Abolitionists, Irish Immigrants, and the Dilemma of Romantic Nationalism," *American Historical Review*, LXXIX (June, 1975), 889–912, for the best study of abolitionist-Irish relations.
24. *Liberator*, February 4, 1842, November 24, 1843.

working-class culture from critical Irish scrutiny. Ill will soon began to surface on all sides, for American Catholic leaders began to question the authenticity of the petition, and the bishop of New York declared that people in Ireland had no business telling Irish Americans what reform movements to join. O'Connell, a keen politician, responded by backtracking, and abolitionists began to accuse him of cowardice. By the end of 1843 the Irish American–abolitionist alliance had collapsed.[25]

When O'Connell refused to vouch for the petition, Phillips' optimism sank. Back in March, 1842, he had felt hopeful that "Dan'l will speak out and speak right on this matter," and he urged that O'Connell "send us a startling, scortching [sic], bitter, inspiring, pointed" rebuke for his Irish-American detractors. But by late June, Phillips grew "red hot" over O'Connell's vacillation, writing: "Fool! How little he knows his interests on this side of the water!" O'Connell, bought with the "southern gold" of Irish-American slaveholders, had become the pawn of "scheming politicians," and abolitionists should "despise his little soul." A year later, when O'Connell again swung toward antislavery, Phillips praised him once more.[26] By this time his attempt to unite with Boston's immigrants in an international crusade against southern slavery and British tyranny had failed completely. Barriers of class, ethnicity, and religion had proven too large for either side to overcome.

Phillips, of course, felt that he had acted in good faith toward his Irish neighbors, for he was a sincere supporter of home rule. Yet his glimpses of these immigrants certainly did not increase his respect for Irish culture or remind him of the Protestant working-class abolitionists that he so admired. Instead, Irish social behavior repelled him, as he admitted bluntly after speaking at one of their meetings. "Never shall I do it again," he swore, for his "mouth tasted bad for days after." It was "so unlike an abolition meeting," he reported, "filled with mean politics, demagogical, earthily worldly." Then too, Ann Phillips certainly reinforced her husband's reaction with her own prejudices. Once, for example, she became furious at him for appearing before Irish Catholic audiences, declaring, "Wendell, I cannot be left for you to lecture to Catholics. I cannot be left for Irish. . . . You promised me you would not

25. Osofsky, "Abolitionists and Irish Immigrants," 889–912.

26. Phillips to Webb, March 30, 1842, Phillips to Richard Allen, March 30, 1842, Phillips to Webb, June 29, 1842, all in Garrison Papers, BPL; *Liberator*, November 24, 1843.

anymore. . . . I am sorry to write so, but I cannot bear it."[27] The immigrants certainly noticed Phillips' biases and came to distrust him, especially after he assailed another of their favorites, Father Theobald Matthew, an Irish temperance leader who toured the United States in 1849. When Matthew failed to condemn slavery, Phillips excoriated him.[28] Still, as Ann Phillips' comments also suggest, Phillips never gave in completely to his distaste for Irish culture and politics, though he and the Irish certainly remained at odds, especially when lower-class mobs disturbed abolitionist meetings. Yet after the war when Phillips entered the labor movement, Daniel O'Connell regained his place among Phillips' rhetorical pantheon of great patriots.

Phillips' republican interpretations of class and cultural conflicts account for his ambivalence toward the Irish, for though he found their culture crude, his distaste for it left him less deeply prejudiced than one might first suspect. Phillips certainly considered Irish Americans degraded, but not innately inferior. The source of their corruption, as Phillips saw it, resided with their leaders, not with the people themselves. It was an opinion he made very clear during the petition debacle. The "poor people who flung up their hats and shouted" at the Irish repeal meetings, "were true metal in right hands, fit for great things," he wrote in 1842. The problem, he believed, was that they had been victimized by priests and politicos, "interested men and bar-room demagogues," who manipulated their "sincere enthusiasms" for selfish ends. Abolitionism, a bastion of republican independence, by contrast, "kisses no man's toe." In Phillips' view, the problem with Boston's Irish was that "we cannot get between them and their leaders."[29]

His was, to be sure, a terribly elitist judgment, comporting perfectly with his privileged background. Phillips deeply believed in the tradition of rebellion among blacks, but he felt sure that the American Irish were incapable of being liberated into middle-class respectability by any other than saviors like himself. Consequently, Phillips could not respect the Irish as a group possessing its own cultural integrity and pursuing its legitimate interests. They, in turn, certainly could not welcome him as a true comrade-in-arms. After the Civil War when their rights of personal economic freedom became the issues at hand, Phillips would reach out

27. Phillips to Webb, March 30, 1842, June 29, 1842, Garrison Papers, BPL; Ann Phillips to Phillips, February 17, 1869 (quotation), n.d. [1867], both in Blagden Papers.
28. *Liberator*, August 24, 31, 1849.
29. Phillips to Allen, March 30, 1842, Garrison Papers, BPL.

to them again. Until that time, however, Phillips and the North's Irish Catholic working class would remain largely estranged. As racial barriers diminished in Phillips' abolitionism, class and ethnic limits became increasingly well defined.

As the decade of the 1840s opened, Phillips further clarified his ideas on race, class, and ethnicity by addressing two other issues that lay at the heart of all these concerns—private property and the moral significance of work itself. The occasion to do so arose early in the 1840s when some of Phillips' colleagues ventured beyond abolitionism to consider the general problem of poverty. Two Garrisonians in particular, John A. Collins and Adin Ballou, led the way, each concluding that economic suffering could be eliminated if people would only overhaul society's mechanisms governing the acquisition of wealth. Collins made his discoveries in England, where he became a disciple of utopian socialist Robert Owen; by 1844 he had founded a colony in upstate New York where property was held in common. Ballou, a Christian anarchist, transformed his farm in Milford, Connecticut, into the Hopedale Community, where he sought to end competitiveness by exposing his followers to spiritualism, phrenology, temperance, cold water cures, and pacifism. Phillips joined Garrison, Quincy, and most other abolitionists in rejecting the validity of such experiments. Phillips admired Collins for his "wholehearted zeal," but he was certain that "his community . . . would be more of an utter failure than its principles, merely, would lead one to suspect, and that is saying a good deal." The same fate, he was equally certain, awaited Ballou's experiment.[30] Soon Collins and Ballou abandoned organized abolitionism, for they had rejected one of the movement's most sacred tenets—that a free society depended, most of all, on the sanctity of every person's social and economic individuality.

Herein lay Phillips' deepest objection to their projects, as he explained quite bluntly, declaring that every scheme like Ballou's or Collins' "*kills individual development.*" Within utopian communities he discerned the same unnatural power to tyrannize that made slavery, racial segregation, and the Irish Catholic hierarchy so objectionable to him. Inevitably, he wrote, "a few leaders grow expert and clever—the rest lose the advantage of that discipline and become mere tools." By depriving people

30. Phillips to Pease, April [?], 1844, August 29, 1847, both in Garrison Papers, BPL. For communitarian impulses within abolitionism, see John L. Thomas, "Antislavery and Utopia," in Martin Duberman (ed.), *The Antislavery Vanguard: New Essays on the Abolitionists* (Princeton, 1965), 240–70.

of their economic independence, socialism thus became the antithesis of freedom, "the double-reinforced essence of aristocracy," little better for the individual's self-fulfillment than enslavement to a southern master.[31]

Soon after offering those sentiments privately, he elaborated on them in public. Speaking before the 1847 meeting of the Massachusetts Anti-Slavery Society, he noted that the utopians were not alone in asserting that northern workers were enslaved by low wages. Apologists for southern slavery were making similar claims. In rebuttal he denied that "the laborers of the North and the slaves of the South" could ever be placed "on the same level." With so few exceptions as to make them meaningless, "I believe that the term wages slavery would be utterly unintelligible to an audience of laboring people, as applied to themselves." Phillips thought it absurd to equate slave labor with free, for he maintained that northern workers could alter unfavorable conditions with votes, but slaves could not. Slaves had no escape from the lash, but, he declared, when capital abused free laborers, "the economy will make them capitalists." Did "the crowded competition of cities reduce their wages?" he asked. "They have only to stay home, devoted to other pursuits, and soon diminished supply [of labor] will bring the remedy." In the Old World class enslavement was undeniable, but in the United States, Phillips insisted, all would be completely well with free laborers if the government sold off its public lands, stopped wasting money on military expenditure, and stimulated the free market by legislating female equality. Beyond these measures, Phillips stressed above all that free workers themselves could always practice "self-denial, temperance, education, and moral and religious character" so as to elevate their individual positions. In this sense, he declared, poverty itself could represent a personal challenge to succeed that was certainly not available to either the utopians or the southern masters' slaves. Instead, either the lash or some socialistic codebook subjected personal strivings to coercive external manipulation. Apart from the reformer's efforts to promote these individualistic traits, all hope for political changes, in Phillips' view, would be "vain and futile."[32] Freedom, in this most essential sense, meant moral and economic self-ownership, the antithesis of enslavement to any higher human authority.

31. Phillips to Pease, April [?], 1844, August 29, 1847, both in Garrison Papers, BPL.
32. *Liberator*, July 9, 1847.

To be sure, only someone independently wealthy could sincerely suggest that workers find "other pursuits" until the market corrected their wages. Clearly, he assumed that the shocking gulf he had witnessed between rich and poor in Europe bore no resemblance to American life. For all its naïveté, Phillips' confidence in the justness of the marketplace was shared by most Americans of his era. This axiom, moreover, also lay at the heart of his republican egalitarianism, for he insisted above all else that no person of any race or religion should be impeded from realizing all that talent and ambition would allow. Hence in considering the proper position of blacks, Phillips held simply that all fetters of caste and enslavement must be stricken from them and that the laws of the state must be made to enforce this liberation. The abolitionist, too, must be blind to distinctions of color. By contrast, Phillips incorrectly regarded the Irish as dupes who remained in brutish ignorance because of manipulating priests, bishops, and ward bosses. They, unlike the blacks, seemed to have no John Hiltons or William Nells to inspire and lead them to freedom. Phillips failed to see that the Irish, like the blacks, chose their leaders and defined their interests by the standards of their own communities and that they rejected as Protestant arrogance Phillips' elitist insistence on enforcing his own universalized ideas of liberty. Black leaders and communities could endorse many of Phillips' values simply because these values coincided with their own. Phillips' egalitarian individualism prevented him from perceiving this crucial difference in position between the two groups. Little wonder that blacks hailed him as a liberator before the Civil War, while Irish-American laborers viewed him with such marked hostility.[33]

Yet Phillips ultimately proved no conventional apologist for the free market. It is true that he had already seen the most advanced features of capitalism's rapidly mechanizing manufacturing sector, having practiced law in the factory town of Lowell. In addition, his family's summer estate in Nahant was just outside Lynn, where formerly independent artisans were being made to produce shoes on assembly lines. In the 1840s, however, workers in these places had not as yet begun to protest

33. For the ablest discussion of abolitionist economic thinking, see Jonathan Glickstein, "'Poverty Is Not Slavery': The Abolitionists and the Labor Market," in Lewis Perry and Michael Fellman (eds.), *Antislavery Reconsidered: New Perspectives on the Abolitionists* (Baton Rouge, 1979), 195–218. See also Foner, *Free Soil, Free Labor, Free Men*; Foner, "Abolitionists and the Labor Movement in Antebellum America," in Christine Bolt and Seymour Dresher, *Antislavery, Religion, and Reform: Essays in Memory of Roger Anstey* (Folkstone, Eng., 1980), 254–71.

openly that their jobs were growing more burdensome and their economic independence less certain. The more disturbing implications of factory civilization for republican liberty still remained hidden for those who, like Wendell Phillips, were not forced to awaken each workday to the screech of the factory whistle.[34] When, however, workers began to declare that industrial labor threatened their individual freedom and economic initiative, none defended their interests more vocally than did Phillips. Before the Civil War, Phillips' radicalism was genuine but racially and socially inclusive, never class-based or culturally pluralistic in its focus. He believed that a corrupted South had spawned a great slave power and that it, not a "monied monopoly," gnawed at the vitals of the body politic. His duty, as an abolitionist, therefore, was to smash that power forever.

34. For working-class whites' ambivalent response to abolitionists and their free-labor economic theory, see Paul Faler, *Mechanics and Manufacturers in the Early Industrial Revolution: Lynn, Massachusetts, 1780–1860* (Albany, 1981), 199–200, 211–14. Evidently, artisans and mechanics themselves rejected the wage slavery analogy with chattel servitude during the 1840s and 1850s but resented the abolitionists' economic ties to factory ownership and their paternalistic approach to working-class culture. For other views on this subject, see Alan Dawley, *Class and Community: The Industrial Revolution in Lynn, Massachusetts* (Cambridge, Mass., 1976), 65, 101, 194–99; Wilentz, *Chants Democratic*, 74, 263–64, 382.

SEVEN

Disunionism and Politics

In May, 1842, Lydia Maria Child wrote to Wendell Phillips from New York City announcing that she wished to resign as editor of the *National Anti-Slavery Standard*, the official newspaper of the American Anti-Slavery Society. "Taste, principle and philosophy," she explained, no longer permitted her to "prepare such hyena soup with brimstone seasoning, as suits many of our friends." Disbelieving that "such dishes were a benefit to our cause," she lamented that the society had not even one publication "that would not disgust or repel minds even slightly acquainted with our principles." The most pungent spice in the "hyena soup," in her opinion, was Phillips' proposal to dissolve the Union.[1]

Three months before Child's letter, Phillips had declared in a Faneuil Hall speech that the North was "the real slave-*holder* of America, and that the Constitution of 1787 was the [South] Carolinians' charter of safety." The following month, he had proposed that petitions be circulated "asking Congress to take measures for the immediate dissolution of the Union," for it was the duty of every Christian "to withdraw from a government which upholds indignity." Lydia Maria Child was certainly as dedicated an abolitionist as was Wendell Phillips, but she believed in "plain speaking . . . mixed with kindness, and zeal tempered with discretion" as the way to attract new converts. Phillips, on the con-

---

1. Lydia Maria Child to Phillips, May 3, 1842, Blagden Papers.

trary, insisted that "the only man who can benefit the cause is he who comes to it self-impelled . . . his eye fixed on God, careless of effects or success." By early 1843 at Phillips' urging, the Massachusetts Anti-Slavery Society "dissolved the union by a handsome vote," as Edmund Quincy reported.[2] The following year, after considerable debate, the American Anti-Slavery Society did likewise. Long before this, however, Lydia Maria Child had resigned and with many others had fled Garrison's camp.

Their departure little bothered Phillips, for soon religious perfectionists began rallying to his call, led by the New Hampshire contingent of Abigail Kelley, Stephen S. Foster, Nathaniel P. Rogers and Parker Pillsbury. With Garrison, Henry C. Wright, and the rest of the Boston clique, they eagerly renounced the Constitution in order to disenthrall themselves from political corruption, persuaded by the moral logic of personally separating from a proslavery Union as they had from proslavery churches.[3] To this end, Phillips could arraign America's churches as loudly and biblically as the most fervent anticlerical, professing "little faith" in orthodox denominations and growing excited when lay people severed connections with them on abolitionist grounds. "I love these manifestations of independent purpose of mind," he once exclaimed. But unlike Garrison and most other perfectionist-minded converts to disunionism, Phillips remained convinced, as a Protestant, of humanity's innate capacity for sin. Referring to Garrison's antichurch and antisabbatarian crusades, for instance, Phillips confessed that "these *theological* reforms have but a secondary interest to me." Moreover, when it came time to enroll in Garrison's Non-Resistance Society, Phillips abstained. He had little sympathy when Foster, Wright, Garrison, and others called for abolitionists to shun all slave-produced products in the name of personal purity. "If we do," he jibed, "what shall we do next—dig our fields with our fingers, for *iron* shovels come from mines where oppression reigns?" Disunion, unlike boycotts, was, in Phillips' view, a morally exacting political demand for emancipation from a government controlled by slavery. "There is a 4 July 1776 to men as well as to nations," he remarked once to Charles Sumner while explaining why he

2. *Ibid.; Liberator*, February 4, March 11, January 28, 1842; Quincy to Webb, February 21, 1843, Garrison Papers, BPL.
3. The best discussions of abolitionist disunionism are Aileen Kraditor, *Means and Ends*, 118–78 passim; Perry, *Radical Abolitionism*, 55–92, 158–88.

refused to support the Constitution. "I speak for changing the laws, all the time washing my hands of them."[4] Throughout the 1840s, Phillips worked for abolitionist victory in politics while hoping to transcend the corruption he judged as endemic to the electoral process. It was a visionary's task, filled with frustration, and even many abolitionists, not to mention ordinary citizens, dismissed him as pursuing hallucinations. But as he pressed on, Phillips also brought the influence of radical abolitionism to bear in the deepening sectional conflicts of the 1840s.

The Liberty party, which Phillips so despised, first prompted him to reject the Constitution, for he hated those "apostates" even more now that they had organized as an independent party with James G. Birney for their presidential candidate. From 1840 onward, these abolitionists urged the electorate to emerge from its corrupt allegiance to the Whig and Democratic parties and to vote instead for candidates pledged to ending slavery. In Massachusetts especially, the Liberty party established a strong organization and exerted an indisputable influence in state elections, seizing the political initiative in the larger abolitionist movement. Phillips reacted in an equally political vein, espousing disunion and announcing in 1841 that the third party represented a hopeless experiment. Even if it won the presidency (which was impossible), such a victory would be meaningless, he insisted, for "how little is done, after all, when a man is chosen to swear his support to a proslavery constitution."[5] Phillips maintained instead that true abolitionists must rid themselves "not merely of *old* parties, but of parties themselves . . . reaching beyond the ballot box" to challenge the proslavery structure of government itself. Certainly, he added, they must not content themselves with tallying meaningless scores in electoral charades where the rules always made slavery the winner. Besides, third-party abolitionists inevitably degraded themselves and squandered their moral power by seeking political station, Phillips warned. "From such thoughts and prospects [as holding office] our hero resolves to compromise with the world," leaving the slave in chains. "Stamp always and ever the plan of

4. Phillips to Charles Sumner, February 17, 1845, Charles Sumner Papers, HL; Phillips to John Jay, Jr., June 6, 1842, Jay Family Papers, CL; Phillips to Pease, November 25, 1841, February 2, 1848, Phillips to Webb, June 29, 1842, all in Garrison Papers, BPL; *Non-Resistant* (January, 1839).
5. Reinhard O. Johnson, "The Liberty Party in Massachusetts, 1840–1848: Antislavery Third Party Politics in the Bay State," *Civil War History*, XXVII (September, 1982), 236–65; *Liberator*, December 31, 1841 (quotation), January 28, 1842.

the third party with the seal of your reprobation," Phillips instructed the Pennsylvania Anti-Slavery Society in late 1841. Heeding his own advice, Phillips counterattacked, presenting disunionist resolutions at antislavery meetings, only to have them soundly rejected.[6] Most Garrisonians were not yet ready to savor hyena soup.

It was black George Latimer, not white Wendell Phillips, who finally persuaded most Garrisonians to vote for disunion. Latimer was arrested in Boston in October, 1842, as a fugitive, despite protests that he had purchased his freedom years earlier. Massachusetts Chief Justice Lemuel Shaw cited the 1793 Fugitive Slave Law and its constitutional precedents and denied every writ for Latimer's release filed by abolitionist attorney Henry Bowditch. Later, Shaw explained that he felt as sorry as anyone else for Latimer, but that his oath to the United States Constitution had obliged him to remand the captive to slavery. When it became clear that no legal maneuver would work, abolitionists purchased Latimer's freedom outright, a precedent not likely to deter other slave catchers.[7] Wendell Phillips was furious. He charged that the power of slavery, incarnated in Lemuel Shaw, had committed a grave assault on the Massachusetts body politic. Although Phillips was at the time struggling to overturn segregation and advance local liberty for all, the chaotic spirit of slavery had intervened, cloaked in constitutional writ, to throttle republicanism in Boston.

In early November, as Latimer sat in his cell, Phillips attended a tumultuous protest meeting in Faneuil Hall. Tension ran high, for many Irishmen, who resented the abolitionists' class biases and racial views, were present. The crowd shouted abuse when Charles L. Remond attempted to speak, drowning him out with cries of "down with the darkey—sell the nigger." Next, Edmund Quincy introduced resolutions condemning the Fugitive Slave Law but was overcome by shouts of "We're white . . . lie! lie!" Joshua Leavitt, representing the Liberty party, was also hooted down. The scene reminded Phillips of the Lovejoy meeting of 1837.[8] Riot again stifled free speech, but even worse, a black citi-

---

6. *Liberator*, December 31, 1841; January 28, March 11, 1842.
7. The best discussions of the Latimer case and the legal issues it raised are William M. Wiecek, "Latimer: Lawyers, Abolitionists, and the Problem of Unjust Laws," in Perry and Fellman (eds.), *Antislavery Reconsidered*, 196–219; Thomas D. Morris, *Free Men All: The Personal Liberty Laws of the North, 1780–1861* (Baltimore, 1974), 94–130; Robert M. Cover, *Justice Accused: Antislavery and the Judicial Process* (New Haven, 1975), 168–74, 266–67, and *passim*.
8. *Liberator*, October 28, November 4, 11, 18, 1842.

zen now sat in the city jail, kept there by the same United States Constitution for which the crowd in Faneuil Hall howled approval. When Phillips finally spoke, it was in deepest anger to indict the crowd as a corrupted tool of the planter class, shackled to slavery by its reverence for the federal Constitution.

Who was really responsible for Latimer's plight, Phillips asked his audience? Not the jailer, the sheriff, or even the slave catcher. "No. They are *but your tools*. You are the guilty ones." The people of Boston "bolt and bar that poor man's dungeon," Phillips declared; "I know that I am addressing the white slaves of the North." Hissing filled the hall, and Phillips responded: "Yes, you dare to hiss me, of course. But you dare not break up the chains which bind you . . . to slavery. Shake your chains," he jeered. "You have not the courage to break them." He condemned the crowd as fools who could not "bear free speech," and he told them to go home. "Faneuil Hall," he said, "has no place for slavish hearts." Boston stood clearly revealed by Latimer's abductors as "chained down by the iron limits of the United States Constitution," with its "bloody clause," the Fugitive Slave Law. No true Bostonian would allow "such a constitution to live for an hour," Phillips declared, recording his "testimony against this pollution of our native city." Phillips was certain that Shaw's decision confirmed beyond question the political truth of disunion.[9] Certainly the resolution that he and Quincy put before the meeting expressed this conviction: "Massachusetts is, and of right ought to be a free and Independent state. . . . she cannot allow her soil to be polluted with the footprints of slavery without trampling on her Bill of Rights, and subjecting herself to infamy. . . . She is solemnly bound to give succor and protection to all who may escape the prison of bondage, and flee to her for safety."[10]

Phillips had now seized upon "No union with slaveholders" as a motto for angry political warfare. In this instance, Justice Shaw should have ripped off the "mask" of judicial duty, which he had used to hide his true feelings about Latimer. He should have acted on conscience by defying the Constitution and resigning, Phillips insisted. As he subsequently argued in the *Liberator*, the 1793 law was perfectly constitutional, and therefore Shaw could have defied it only if he also defied the fundamental political document that gave it legal standing. Then, at least, justice in the commonwealth would not have been undermined by

9. *Ibid.*, November 22, 1842.
10. *Ibid.*, November 4, 1842.

him personally. "Our conflict with Judge Shaw," Phillips explained, "is that when liberty lay bleeding, when the overbearing insolence of the Slave Power had thrown down, in the usurped name of the Constitution, all individual freedom, he betrayed . . . the honor of Massachusetts." As in his Boston desegregation struggles, Phillips had once again embraced civil disobedience while appealing to higher codes of freedom, specifically, the Constitution and Bill of Rights of the Commonwealth of Massachusetts. Disunion represented to him not simply a token of personal purity but a stringent demand that the state actually secede to preserve its republican liberty and its allegiance to its own laws.[11]

Upon hearing Phillips' doctrine, Massachusetts' conservative Whigs struck back angrily through the Boston *Courier* and the Boston *Atlas*, in which they attacked him for his "blackguardism and shameless abuse" of so reputable a man as Justice Shaw. Phillips, in turn, supported a petition demanding that the Massachusetts legislature amend the federal Constitution to free the state entirely from any obligation to uphold slavery. The petition attracted sixty thousand signatures, demonstrating that whatever their opinions of Phillips' disunionism, a healthy number of Massachusetts citizens harbored no desire to regard themselves as pawns of the slave power. Meanwhile, Phillips privately lobbied state senators for the most stringent bill possible, arguing before the legislature that disunion, not amendment, was the only effective remedy.[12]

In late March, 1843, the legislature responded by passing a new Personal Liberty Law, a significant departure from the laws of other northern states regarding slavery. It prohibited Massachusetts justices from accepting jurisdiction under the 1793 Fugitive Slave Law and barred state officials from abetting the arrest of presumed escapees. Garrison hailed the new law as "tantamount to an act of emancipation for all slaves who shall escape from the South." Though it was not disunion, the law was sufficiently antislavery to increase anxiety among the "cotton aristocrats" whose textile fortunes controlled the Whig party and fed the industrial revolution in Massachusetts. The Boston *Advertiser* echoed "Cotton Whig" politicians such as Daniel Webster, Robert C. Winthrop, and Edward Everett, lamenting that the legislature passed any bill at all.[13] To them, as to Phillips, the cry of "No Union with Slaveholders"

11. *Ibid.*, November 18, 1842.
12. Phillips to George Boutwell, March 17, 1843, Phillips to T. Hood, March 20, 1843, Garrison Papers, BPL; Morris, *Free Men All*, 114–15.
13. Morris, *Free Men All*, 115; Kinley Brauer, *Cotton Versus Conscience: Massa-*

suggested as much about southern markets and direct dealings with powerful slaveholders as about abstract questions of morality.

In the aftermath of the Latimer case, the Massachusetts and the American Anti-Slavery Societies quickly ratified disunion. Phillips, who had initially adopted the doctrine to assail the Liberty party and fight off slave catchers, now was obliged to justify this position in substance as a tenet of abolitionist orthodoxy. The Liberty party gave him his chance, for among its supporters were talented legal minds such as Alvan Stewart, William Goodell, and Lysander Spooner, known since as "radical constitutionalists." All of them published convincing pamphlets in the 1840s that argued, contrary to Phillips' views, that slavery was illegal under the federal Constitution. Since that document was based on the "natural law" of freedom, they held that all statutes in favor of slavery were by definition unconstitutional. Judges and sheriffs must therefore abrogate such laws as part of their routine duties, and voters must rally behind Liberty party candidates who swore to uphold this true version of the Constitution. All these writers also rejected Phillips' legal positivism, that is, his claim that slavery was protected by laws that, though wholly immoral, were perfectly constitutional and so must be interpreted literally.[14] Phillips responded to these challenges in 1844 and 1845 by composing two large pamphlets of his own. The first, *The Constitution, a Proslavery Document*, established the Garrisonian legal theory that would hold sway until the end of the Civil War. The second was entitled *Can an Abolitionist Vote or Hold Office Under the Constitution?* It distinguished Garrisonian formulas of direct political action from those of the Liberty party.

When he had first called for disunion, Phillips had appealed to common sense. Any fool, he thought, could see that the Constitution upheld slavery in its three-fifths slave representation clause, its provision for a fugitive slave law, and its grant to Congress of the power to quell insurrection. Now, as he felt pressed to substantiate these claims, he turned as usual to history, this time in search of villains. He found them in abundance in James Madison's records of the 1787 Philadelphia debates among the Founding Fathers, which furnished a wealth of documentation for his suspicions. These "quite valuable" records, regarded

___

chusetts *Whig Politics and Southern Expansion, 1843–1848* (Lexington, 1967), 55–113; William M. Wiecek, *Sources of Antislavery Constitutionalism in America, 1760–1848* (Ithaca, 1977), 228–48; *Liberator*, April 7, 1843.

14. Wiecek, *Antislavery Constitutionalism*, 203–27, 249–75.

by Americans, Phillips correctly observed, as *"Political Scripture,"* confirmed to his complete satisfaction that the Fathers had indeed consciously incorporated protection for slavery into their Constitution.

The Constitution, a Proslavery Document presents a compendium of evidence, drawn together by Phillips to reveal "how, with deliberate purpose, our fathers bartered honesty for gain, and became partners with tyrants, that they might profit from their tyranny." In support of this claim, Phillips quoted such eminent jurists as John Marshall, James Kent, James Iredell, and Joseph Story, whose writings confirmed slavery's prominence in the Constitution. Massachusetts, however, lived under a charter of state-level freedom, Phillips stressed, and this point became crucial to his entire argument. Slavery had already become moribund there, in his opinion, when the state had drawn up its own constitution in 1780, prior to entering the federal union. From the first this charter had been untainted by slavery, and Massachusetts citizens could now appeal to its republican codes in order to oppose the tyranny of federal statute. The only path to justice, he concluded by this reasoning, ran "over the [Federal] Constitution, trampling it under foot," not around it to try "to evade its meaning" by appeals to natural law. Phillips, in short, had assumed the posture of a narrow legal literalist in order to become as much a secessionist on behalf of his state as any slaveholding "fire-eater"; he used the southern constitutionalists' own best arguments for completely contrary ends. One such extremist, a friend of John C. Calhoun's, appreciated this fact, wryly observing that the *Constitution, a Proslavery Document* was an "able pamphlet [that] . . . we might circulate to great advantage, excluding a few paragraphs."[15]

Unlike Calhoun, the Liberty party did evade the Constitution's meaning, according to Phillips, and with dangerous results, for its theory encouraged officials to defy specific statutes and thus to court the breakdown of law and order. Liberty party supporters failed to realize that immoral laws were no less binding on public servants than were moral ones. As a believer in original sin, Phillips emphasized that he was not inclined to trust individual sheriffs and justices to choose rightly which

15. John A. Campbell to John C. Calhoun, November 20, 1847, in J. Franklin Jameson, (ed.), *The Correspondence of John C. Calhoun*, Vol II of the *Annual Report of the American Historical Association, 1899* (Washington, D.C., 1900), 1143; Phillips, *The Constitution, a Proslavery Document; or, Selections from the Madison Papers* (New York, 1844), *passim*. See also Phillips, *Review of Lysander Spooner's Essay on the Unconstitutionality of Slavery. . . .* (Boston, 1847).

to overturn. The Liberty party had thus taken "the first steps toward anarchy," Phillips warned, and as a republican apostle of social and legal order, he would have none of it.[16] For just the same reasons, moreover, Phillips also argued that the Liberty party courted social disaster when claiming that slavery could be voted and legislated into extinction. All they would actually gain, he warned, would be a greater measure of tyranny and degradation for all Americans. Instead, he held that government must be regarded as "a voluntary association of individuals" that he, and each person, must join or reject "as duty dictates." Therefore, since the majority of Americans currently upheld a proslavery federal government, Phillips took the position that he must only "obey those laws which seem to me good—and . . . submit to all the penalties which my disobedience to the rest brings to me." In short, by renouncing the Constitution, Phillips willingly submitted to the penalty of forfeiting his right to vote.[17]

Phillips had not the remotest intention of diminishing his citizenship when he denied his allegiance to the Constitution, as he emphasized when Charles Sumner once charged him with abandoning his political claims. "What right have you to set up a govt. and *force* me to pay taxes, and then tell me I must leave the country or be guilty of all the sins *you* incorporate into your Govt., I confess I cannot see," Phillips retorted. "The God who made the land is *my* God as well as yours."[18] He had, he declared, simply submitted to the penalty of not voting because to do otherwise was to obey the slave power's law. At the same time, Phillips argued that the decision not to vote actually magnified an abolitionist's political power, expanding one's sphere of citizenship instead of diminishing it. Instead of enslaving themselves to the Union and to a corrupted political party as the Liberty men had done, disunionists had actually seized much broader power to influence all of American political culture. As fully active republican agitators, he argued, they put their uncompromised efforts, not just some "tainted" ballots, behind the drive for black emancipation. "I must exert . . . influence through *right* means," he insisted to Sumner. "Mark the difference between

16. Phillips, *Review of Spooner*, 10–18.
17. Phillips, *Can an Abolitionist Vote or Hold Office Under the United States Constitution?* (New York, 1845), 26 and *passim*.
18. Phillips to Sumner, February 17, 1845, Sumner Papers; Sumner to Phillips, February 4, 1845, Blagden Papers.

speaking and voting or taking office. I will use any and all my influence for the reform of Govt. . . . but I will neither steal, nor rob, nor murder to support the constitution or qualify myself for office."[19]

It was a theory that Phillips tailored perfectly to suit his self-conceived role of a virtuous public censor who yearned to wield political power. Perfectionists, too, embraced it as their own, for his axioms expressed a moral combativeness and hostility to existing institutions, which were shared by Garrison, the Fosters, Henry C. Wright, and others. They could no more than Phillips tolerate the terrible ambiguity of the United States Constitution concerning slavery.[20] Yet Phillips continued to insist most explicitly that disunionism's chief goal, despite its heavy perfectionist Christian overtones, was political change, not religious utopianism, and he declared that the Garrisonian's first "object is not to make everyone a Christian or a philosopher, but to induce everyone to aid in the abolition of slavery." By focusing so broad and powerful an influence on parties and their leaders, Phillips sincerely believed, abolitionists would surely "accomplish our object long before the nation is converted into saints." Other Garrisonians certainly found hope in this self-assured estimate, whatever their religious positions, and they gladly took Phillips' view as their own. Even Charles C. Burleigh, whose religion was perfectionism incarnate, once stated that "no more effective vote is ever cast in its bearing upon politics [than] from lips denouncing the constitution." Edmund Quincy, a zealous nonresistant, also agreed wholeheartedly with Phillips that "the abolitionist who stands aside from the Government . . . does not renounce, but multiplies his political influence."[21]

Despite this sweeping promise of ultimate political victory, recruits to the disunionist banner always proved rare. Yet the greatest utility of Phillips' doctrines had little to do with their popularity, for they spoke most effectively to already-converted Garrisonians who had long desired sainthood but who wanted no less desperately to transform the nation's politics. Members of the American Anti-Slavery Society had al-

19. Phillips to Sumner, February 17, 1845, Sumner Papers.
20. For an effective treatment of the founding fathers' actual dealings with slavery, see David B. Davis, *The Problem of Slavery in the Age of Revolution, 1770–1823* (New Haven, 1974).
21. See Foner, *Tom Paine*, 107–44; Staughton Lynd, *The Intellectual Origins of American Radicalism* (New York, 1968); Phillips, "The Philosophy of the Abolition Movement," in his *Speeches*, 120; *National Anti-Slavery Standard*, reprinted in the Concord (N.H.) *Herald of Freedom*, September 6, 1844; *Liberator*, June 3, 1853.

ways regarded themselves as a sacred community, free from the taint of the sinful world, and disunion certainly amplified this feeling. Just as important, the doctrine furnished Garrisonians with a militant challenge to "timid" officeholders, "misguided" Liberty party leaders, and "manipulated" voters, especially when Phillips propounded it so eloquently. For all its hyperbole, the cry of "No union with slaveholders" thus gave the American Anti-Slavery Society a strong sense of group sanctity and powerful assurances of political pertinence during two decades of sectional tumult.[22]

After swearing allegiance to disunionism, the Boston clique, though always close, began to congregate more often at Maria Weston Chapman's house, only a five-minute walk from the homes of Garrison, Francis Jackson, the Weston sisters, and Wendell Phillips. Edmund Quincy also appeared there constantly, for he lived in nearby Dedham. These were what Phillips called the elite "few of us" who met informally to manage "by a little collaboration" the affairs of the American and Massachusetts Anti-Slavery Societies. As Phillips had urged since the late 1830s, they had actually become a "world in themselves and in each other," as one clique member described their association. The group also encompassed Henry C. Wright, the Fosters, Samuel May, Jr., Samuel J. May, Sidney H. Gay, Parker Pillsbury, and Nathaniel Rogers, who were less influential because they traveled as agents, lived out of town, or were not by background wealthy Bostonians.[23]

Everyone in the clique acknowledged Garrison as the primary source of inspiration, a role that suited him perfectly.[24] Phillips continued to consider him the embodiment of moral wisdom, and the Garrisons reciprocated by naming their second son Wendell Phillips Garrison. The Phillipses helped the Garrisons through times of financial need, and Garrison, in turn, felt that there was none more sympathetic than Wen-

22. For the pulls of perfectionism and politics in the clique, see Friedman, *Gregarious Saints*, 225–52. I differ in emphasis with Friedman and I am more skeptical of Walters' *Antislavery Appeal*, 3–19, 111–46, wherein it is argued that very little of substance separated abolitionists in general and Garrisonians in particular from the dominant elements of American political culture.

23. Phillips to Francis Jackson, January [?], 1847, Garrison Papers, BPL; Friedman, *Gregarious Saints*, 43–67.

24. See, for Garrison's leadership role, James Brewer Stewart, "Garrison Again and Again and Again," *Reviews in American History*, IV (December, 1976), 539–45; Bertram Wyatt-Brown, "William Lloyd Garrison and Antislavery Unity: A Reappraisal," *Civil War History*, XIII (March, 1967), 5–24; Friedman, *Gregarious Saints*, 48–52.

dell Phillips "to whom I can more freely unbosom myself, in any emergency."[25] Both William and Helen Garrison were attentive to Ann and sympathetic to her ills. Privately and at antislavery gatherings, the two leaders constantly praised and defended one another. "I owe you, dear Garrison, more than you would let me express—and my mother and my wife except[ed], more than to any other one," Phillips assured his mentor. "Since within the sphere of your influence, I trust I have lived a better man."[26]

Yet Phillips and Garrison were never jovial companions. Phillips developed much warmer associations with two of Boston's wealthiest abolitionists, Maria Weston Chapman and Edmund Quincy. His collaboration with Chapman bordered on conspiracy. Seeing each other almost daily, they seldom wrote, but Phillips filled his letters with paraphrases of her opinions. Chapman was recognized as abolitionism's *grand dame*, and Liberty party detractor Lewis Tappan once called her "a talented woman with the disposition of a fiend" who managed Phillips, Garrison, and the rest "as easily as she could 'untie a garter.'" The clique's social impressario, she arranged antislavery fairs and bazaars, and Phillips, always eager to exert his leadership, became her gentlemanly equivalent. By his own admission he drew up nearly two-thirds of the resolutions introduced at antislavery society meetings, "for every body so hates writing resolutions." He also handled the details of the antislavery bureaucracy, oversaw the editorship of the *National Anti-Slavery Standard*, and set the agenda for annual meetings.[27]

25. Phillips to Pease, March 9, 1851, Garrison Papers, BPL; William L. Garrison to Phillips, October 15, 1857 (quotation), January 1, 1851, both in Blagden Papers. See also William L. Garrison to Phillips, September 9, 1855, Villard Papers; Wendell and Ann Phillips to William L. Garrison, Jr., September 1, 1860, Garrison Papers, SCL.

26. William L. Garrison to Ann Phillips, January 1, 1851, Helen B. Garrison to Ann Phillips, August 8, 1846, August 2, 1851, July 18, 1848, William L. Garrison to Phillips, August 9, 1847, all in Blagden Papers; *Liberator*, February 17, 1847; Phillips to William L. Garrison, January 6, 1846 (quotation), William Lloyd Garrison Papers, BPL.

27. Tappan quoted in Pease and Pease, *Bound with Them in Chains*, 29; Phillips to Maria W. Chapman, August 2, 1848, August [?], 1846, and n.d., Phillips to Pease, January 3, 1848 (quotation), Maria W. Chapman to Ann and Wendell Phillips, October 22, 1843, August 10, 1845, all in Blagden Papers; Phillips to Maria W. Chapman, July 21, 1846 (copy), Phillips to Sidney H. Gay, March 29, August 12, 1846, April [?], August [?], 1847, all in Gay Papers; Phillips to J. M. McKim, October 3, 1844, December 5, 1847, Phillips to May, April 20, 1849, all in May-McKim Papers. See also, in general, the correspondence folders for Abby K. Foster, Edward D. Hudson, Parker Pillsbury, and Stephen S. Foster in Blagden Papers.

Phillips willingly shared this leadership position with Edmund Quincy, his most intimate friend. Nearly identical in age and background, these two, friends since Harvard days, even resembled each other physically. Once, an English visitor spied them strolling down Park Street and remarked that they were the only Americans he had seen that actually "looked like gentlemen." Quincy was haughty, a dilettante who exuded Federalist polish. With him, Phillips could relax and act like his Brahmin self. They became a fraternity of two and played at being aristocrats by writing flowery letters in mock Sir Walter Scott style, turning Latin phrases and endowing one another with honorific titles. Phillips became "the high noble Lord, Wendell, Earl Arundel," and Quincy dubbed Ann "the Countess." Phillips addressed Quincy as "Edmund, By Divine Providence Bishop of Norfolk," or as "the Unworthy Scion of the Gens Quinctia." Sometimes the charade sparked hilarity, as once when Phillips was startled by a noise behind him in his library. He turned to look and there stood Quincy, unannounced, decked out "in a costume of George II's time—cocked hat, buttons, sack coat and all," clutching a gold-headed cane and wearing "a gold lace vest to his knees— lace ruffles—lace neckband—rings and a silver-mounted rapier." Phillips saluted him as "Sir Charles Grandison" before collapsing in laughter.[28] Quincy's talents, like his tastes, complemented Phillips', for he loved to write but was not a confident speaker. Therefore, he contributed articles to the *National Anti-Slavery Standard* and the *Liberator* but left the speechifying to Phillips. Together they filled hundreds of pages with gossip, trivia, and decisions made *in camera* about the management of the antislavery societies.[29]

Reinforced in these ways by his fellow aristocrats, Phillips saw no inconsistency whatever in personally dominating the movement that he believed was so egalitarian. But Phillips' high-handedness seldom caused resentments, for just as at Harvard, Phillips' colleagues deferred to his candor and gentlemanly understanding. He became the Boston clique's

28. For examples of "aristocratic letters," see Quincy to Phillips, October 10, 1849, and n.d. [1846], both in Blagden Papers; Phillips to Quincy, August 21, 1848, Quincy Papers. This incident is recounted in Phillips to Sidney H. Gay, March [?], 1847, Gay Papers. For a good study of Quincy, see Robert V. Sparks, "Abolition in Silver Slippers: A Biography of Edmund Quincy" (Ph.D. dissertation, Boston University, 1978).

29. See generally the Quincy correspondence file, Blagden Papers; and the Phillips correspondence file, Quincy Papers.

social facilitator, and even the most obstreperous reformers usually responded to his genial, frank leadership. The church-disrupting excesses of Stephen Foster and Parker Pillsbury never bothered him greatly, for instance, and both of these harsh-voiced ultras became his devoted lifetime supporters. Outspoken Abby Kelley Foster, Stephen's wife, another Phillips loyalist, grew particularly close to Wendell and Ann after the Civil War. All these volatile people considered Phillips a reliable friend who understood their grievances and truly respected their differing opinions. Phillips, in turn, dismissed their raucous anticlericalism as *"highly illogical"* but loved them for their "sweet, devoted, heart-on-fire" commitment to the slave. He could, he once confessed, only admire "the holy indignation, tapering off into pitiless sternness," of saints like Pillsbury and the Fosters. His only misgiving about them was the tendency he saw in them toward a narrow-minded lack of humor. All too often they would "miss the joke and only flare up at what they deem[ed] irreligion."[30]

Humor, as Phillips soon discovered, was his all-important lubricant for keeping relations among sensitive colleagues smoothly under his control. He dispensed it abundantly, filling his letters with bad puns, worse poems, and even satires on the Garrisonians' personal quirks, especially when he was answering an angry or depressed colleague. "I had not had time till now to answer your very funny and cheery letter," Lydia Maria Child responded to one such message. "I thank you from my heart. I am ashamed of my despondency and will trouble my friends no more with it."[31] Another demanding associate, Sidney Howard Gay, well-born editor of the *National Anti-Slavery Standard* during much of the 1840s and 1850s, was overly sensitive, a whiner who provoked fights and then sulked. He incessantly sought reassurance from Phillips that the clique did not think ill of him. Phillips used lighthearted banter on him too, sending him ridiculous poems along with gentle lectures about learning not to be so thin-skinned. Gay invariably came around: "God

30. On these relationships, see the Stephen S. Foster, Abby K. Foster, and Parker Pillsbury correspondence files, Blagden Papers. Also consult the Wendell Phillips correspondence file in the Abby K. and Stephen S. Foster Papers, American Antiquarian Society (hereafter AAS). For quoted material, see Phillips to Pease, June 29, August 12, 1842, Garrison Papers, BPL; Phillips to Child, March 7, 1842, in Eleanor Lewis (ed.), "Letters of Wendell Phillips to Lydia Maria Child," *New England Magazine*, V (June, 1892), 130–32; Phillips to Sidney H. Gay, March 16, 1853, Gay Papers.
31. Child to Phillips, March 7, 1842, Blagden Papers. For the letter to which Child referred, see Lewis (ed.), "Letters of Phillips," 130–32.

bless you, my dear Wendell, for the best friend that ever a man was blessed withal." In the meantime, Phillips carefully defused resentments Gay had stirred up among other clique members.[32]

A close friendship grew between Phillips and Gay as this therapeutic relationship ran its course. Phillips, made patient and considerate of others' feelings by Ann's illness, became Gay's father confessor and an affable confidant to Gay's wife, Elizabeth, as well.[33] In this way, Phillips' aristocratic nature generally fostered good will, not resentment, within the Boston clique, as he himself appreciated. Once, an unfriendly journalist referred to him as "the oily Phillips," and Phillips proudly adopted the sobriquet as an accurate label for his role. "A quiet, moderate, halfway sort of sim-sam fellow" is the way he once laughingly described himself, and he was always proud of his gentlemanly displays of indifference when others tried to provoke him. "I can truly say," he once wrote Gay, "I thank God that he made me . . . so that I can shake my head defyingly, and [in] utmost carelessness, even at intended insult, since if there be anything about it worth remembering, time will give me means for proving it was passed by only because it was despised. I'm very generous, AHEM!"[34]

Only once before the Civil War did a colleague openly rebel against Phillips' social dominance, and that was Nathaniel P. Rogers, every bit as bright, articulate, and scintillating a personality as was Phillips. The latter once described him as "good Rogers, kind Rogers, whom I love and admire, and his sweet wife and his seven children also."[35] Rogers took up religious anarchism in the mid-1840s, however, and began to assault all authority—church, state, capitalism, and worst of all, the authority of the Boston clique. Rogers came to believe that true abolitionism required throwing out all controlling mechanisms in favor of spontaneous gatherings without agenda, resolutions, budget, executive committee,

32. Phillips to Sidney H. Gay, March 9, 29, 1846, Gay Papers; Sidney H. Gay to Phillips, July 18, 1846, Blagden Papers; Phillips to Maria W. Chapman, July 6, 1845, Chapman Papers. For an example of the sort of doggerel Phillips wrote to Gay, see Phillips to Sidney H. Gay, April [?], 1847, Gay Papers.
33. Phillips to Sidney H. Gay, July 29, 1846, March [?], 1849, March 26, 1853, Phillips to "Lizzie" Neale, February [?], 1845; Phillips to Elizabeth Neale Gay, February 25, 1845, all in Gay Papers.
34. Phillips to Sidney H. Gay, July 29, 1846, September [?], 1847, Gay Papers; Phillips, "1831 Class Reunion Questionnaire," [1846], Harvard University Archives.
35. Phillips to Child, March 7, 1842, in Lewis (ed.), "Letters of Phillips to Child," 131.

or any organization whatever. Quarrels that addressed these issues soon boiled up over the ownership of the abolitionist newspaper Rogers edited, and schism followed. Rogers had support in the New England hills and in Cape Cod, where abolitionists were countrified, poor, and anticlerical, and thus when he accused the Boston clique of abusing power, he struck a responsive chord. Phillips soon lost patience with "dear Rogers, as he has always been," and took steps with his New Hampshire allies Foster, Kelley, and Pillsbury to purge this dangerous individual.[36] As the patrician republican understood it, abolitionism exemplified equality and law, not anarchy. Phillips held no brief for class-conscious militants. To him, the quarrel reeked with illegitimate jealousy, for Rogers sought to become "the nucleus around which all disaffection to the Massachusetts clique will rally." His supporters were social misfits "half educated, impertinent and too misguided to see that if we were aristocratic, we wouldn't employ poor folks." (Phillips never stated his free-labor beliefs more bluntly or snobbishly than this.) Phillips felt that the Rogers crowd counted themselves cheated because "the Boston clique live in the city—in broad cloth and have, some of us, been to college." In his view, they were simply too self-serving to understand that ability, not class, actually determined the pecking order in the abolitionist movement. Maria Weston Chapman "has influence not because her gown is silk," Phillips insisted, "but because her head is strong and her hand willing." As Phillips helped to usher Rogers out of abolitionism, he insured once again that free-labor ideas and class solidarity, enforced by sometimes imperious bluebloods like himself, would always define the American Anti-Slavery Society.[37]

During his wars with the clique, Rogers registered an additional complaint, charging that Garrisonian disunionists were "purblind with politics. They do not throw political dust, but they kick it up and love to be in it. They do not hold office or vote, but they love to hover about the polls, to watch the balloting of others, and about the state houses, where they can enjoy the turmoil of legislation." A bit before Rogers issued

36. Perry, *Radical Abolitionism*, 123–28; Ann and Wendell Phillips to Pease, February 24, 1845 (quotation), Garrison Papers, BPL; Stephen S. Foster to Phillips, January 1, 1845, Parker Pillsbury to Phillips, December 27, 1844, January 8, 1845, Abby Kelley to Phillips, September 23, 1845, all in Blagden Papers.

37. Phillips to Webb, May 25, 1845, Garrison Papers, BPL. Friedman, *Gregarious Saints*, 59–61, treats the Rogers affair exclusively as a family quarrel within the clique, without attending to its class and political overtones. Perry, *Radical Abolitionism*, 123–28, is better balanced.

this criticism, Phillips confirmed its validity in his own case, candidly writing Elizabeth Pease, "I acknowledge that politics is a sore temptation, to me at least."[38] Clearly, the rapidly growing national conflict over slavery was what quickened Phillips' interest and Rogers' criticism. By 1846 the slave state Texas had been annexed and admitted to the Union, President James K. Polk had opened military hostilities with Mexico, and free-soil opposition to the slave powers' occupation of new territory had begun to spread in the North.

In Massachusetts politics quickly began to sectionalize. Phillips' old friend Charles Sumner moved to the forefront of a "Conscience Whig" insurgency, which demanded that the party's "Cotton Whig" leadership join its outcry against the further expansion of slavery. Winthrop, Webster, and Everett responded for the party at first by making anti-Texas statements, while assuring their southern Whig allies that they meant not a word of them. Soon a serious factional breach between Conscience and Cotton Whigs opened in Massachusetts and other northern states. Even before the war with Mexico had started, the Liberty party had added significantly to such tensions by drawing enough antislavery votes away from the Whigs' Henry Clay to help Democrat James K. Polk into the presidency in 1844. Now, as American troops marched across Mexico, the two-party system began its slow evolution toward Civil War, and Wendell Phillips took steps that contributed significantly to the process. At the same time he discovered complexities in this changing political world that were frustratingly difficult for him to understand.

In some respects, Phillips' stark disunionism took on an unexpected pertinence as conflict grew over Texas. By 1844 free-state politicians and their constituents began to echo what Phillips had been saying for several years: that slavery was taking an ominous hold on American values and institutions. Phillips therefore marked the advent of this extreme rhetoric enthusiastically, writing to Elizabeth Pease in 1846 that "men who would have whispered disunion with white lips a year ago now love to talk about it. Many leading men will talk as we were laughed at for talking a while ago." In some respects, Phillips actually understated the trend. As early as 1843, for instance, twelve northern congressmen, led by John Quincy Adams, Joshua Giddings, and John A. Briggs (soon to become the governor of Massachusetts), had declared that annexation of

38. Concord *Herald of Freedom*, July 2, 1845; Phillips to Pease, October [?], 1844, Garrison Papers, BPL.

Texas would call the Union's legal basis into question. The Massachusetts and Ohio state legislatures passed similar resolutions two years later, and Giddings then openly made opposition to the Mexican War based on disunionism the platform of his congressional reelection campaign. In their own ways, all these political figures were articulating feelings most familiar to abolitionists, which carried them beyond conventional legal axioms and party discipline. They, like the Garrisonians, were deeply worried about republican freedom, especially when their own political allegiances tied them so tightly to slaveholders.[39] In this most important respect, Phillips' ideas and those of dissenting northern politicians began to coalesce as sectional politics intensified.

From the first, however, Phillips also found important differences separating him from seasoned politicians like Adams, Briggs, or Giddings. These men, he knew, actually held no sympathy for his full-blown disunionism. Their rhetorical gestures certainly acknowledged the vexing problems the Constitution had always presented for antislavery politicians, but nothing more. All of them, moreover, would certainly have judged it folly to turn their backs on the slave power and their own careers by renouncing their oaths and leaving Congress, as Sumner, for one, bluntly told Phillips in 1845 as he, Palfrey, Charles Francis Adams, and other Conscience Whigs struggled to seize power in Massachusetts. Phillips, nevertheless, always charged that these politicians were repeating the Liberty party's "fatal mistake" of supporting the Constitution, that none of them had even endorsed immediate emancipation, and that their moral timidity and compromised positions deserved only scorn. Once, for example, he pictured Palfrey as having "his feet entangled in the network of that covenant with death he has chosen to support. On the other side towers Calhoun, armed with his battle axe, nerved with hope of saving his own plantation. How unequal the contest!"[40]

None of these insurgents heeded any of Phillips' warnings. Instead, they viewed politics as a rewarding challenge, built great careers, and were joined along the way by other giants of the Republican party such as William Seward, Salmon P. Chase, Benjamin Wade, and Abraham Lin-

39. Phillips to Pease, January 25, 1846, Garrison Papers, BPL. James Brewer Stewart, "The Aims and Impact of Garrisonian Abolitionism, 1840–1860," *Civil War History*, XV (September, 1969), 198–209. Holt, *Political Crisis of the 1850s, passim*, is the most comprehensive synthesis of the impact of republican ideology on party structures as related to questions of slavery.
40. Sumner to Phillips, February 4, 1845, Blagden Papers; *Liberator*, June 9, 1848.

coln. Phillips, as we have seen, felt strongly drawn to politics for quite contrary reasons, which set him at odds with these new political insurgents. While they mobilized voters, he righteously decried the shabbiness of elections and insisted, as a republican moralist, that government simply conform to his demand that it serve the highest good. In short, Phillips wanted to influence sectional politics because the ideas traded there always challenged or echoed his own, but he greatly distrusted and envied these talented office-seekers, flawed in doctrine, who sought office instead of virtue, but who had nevertheless begun to define the national conflict over slavery. As the Mexican War escalated sectional tensions, Phillips thus faced the terrible problem of securing a dominating influence over this ever larger but ever more remotely conducted contest.

Even as early as 1842, Phillips acknowledged this critical shift in sectional momentum, writing that because of the gag-rule controversy in Congress, "we are making abolitionists by the hundreds—or rather circumstances are making them for us." He also discussed this development before audiences of abolitionists, emphasizing that "we, sir, are not nor ever have been the disunionists, nor are we in any degree responsible for the present agitation on the subject." Popular antislavery feeling, he declared, "grows out of the thing itself—the opposing principles of liberty and slavery being united in one government." Those responsible therefore were politicians and the larger forces that shaped their choices, not the abolitionists: "They who put the gunpowder under the Capitol provide for blowing it up."[41] By 1846 the gunpowder was no longer the gag-rule, but the free-soil issue and the famous Wilmot Proviso that northern politicians attached to it. This legislation, first proposed in 1846, would bar slavery's expansion into any territory taken in the war with Mexico. Whenever it appeared in Congress, representatives became sectionalists, voters grew excited, and cracks began to show in façades of party unity. Then as polarization spread, Phillips wanted to feel assurance that he and his co-workers were determining its outcome, while preserving their unique mission from the corruptions of electoral politics.

By the mid-1840s Phillips was developing a position that reduced the deep ambivalence caused by these conflicting desires. His efforts stimu-

41. Phillips to Allen, March 30, 1842, Garrison Papers, BPL. *Liberator*, July 11, 1851.

lated his own sense of moral purity and reassured him of his political importance. He began to ignore his first recognition that sectionalism grew from "the thing itself" and began to tell his colleagues that they, the abolitionist disunionists, were really the ones responsible for Congress's turmoil over slavery. By developing this position, as will be seen, Phillips fell prey to inconsistencies that would plague him with political frustration. Nevertheless, starting in the early 1840s, he insisted that the abolitionists need only continue to follow the path of God-given duty, for the final impact of their faithful agitations would be a political crisis that would destroy the slave power forever. "Men ask how we expect to dissolve the Union," he once remarked. "I expect to have it dissolved for me." Abolitionists would speed the day simply "by weighing our Union—by taking down its high pretensions—by letting the gas out of the balloon that has been blown up by the fuming pretensions of many aspirants for office."[42]

As cause-and-effect political analysis, these ideas had serious weaknesses that would bother Phillips no end, but as a theory of agitation for a censorious republican, they contained a bounty of possibilities. Henceforward Phillips defended this position by simply insisting (contrary to the facts) that antislavery politics did not exist until Garrisonians began them. "Ever since the nation started on its way, there has been slavery," he stated in 1846, but none had objected to the institution until abolitionists dragged it into public view. "We have awakened the nation," Phillips exulted, "we have awakened the world." The fruits of these first victories had now appeared in politics, he asserted, for abolitionist agitators had proven that the American system of governance reacted solely to public opinion. Parties themselves were "like snakes," he explained. "The tail moves the head." Party leaders, therefore, were simply the creations of their constituents, whom abolitionists had aroused with their clarion moral cries. Referring to conflicts over slavery emanating from Washington, Phillips once observed: "We cannot make crises. We can only prepare for them" by employing the abolitionists' "only weapon . . . an appeal to the conscience against slavery as a sin." Now, he asserted, thanks to the Garrisonians, people were prepared to see what the Mexican War actually revealed—slavery's death grip on all of American life. Common citizens, therefore, were responding to the abolitionists' preachments by voicing "not the old cry of Liberty *and* Union, but Lib-

42. *Liberator*, October 19, 1846, February 20, 1857.

erty with or *without* Union—Liberty at any rate." The heads of the political snakes, the party leaders, had reacted to this change in public
opinion by adopting antislavery views of their own, Phillips claimed,
thus creating even more political strife. Abolitionists therefore must
struggle mightily to hold these men to strictest moral account, all the
more to dictate their behavior. In this way, Phillips declared, ultimate
political power would continue to belong to the Garrisonians.

The antislavery politician still upheld the Constitution's "bloody
covenant," Phillips warned, and always attempted to "conceal half his
principles to carry the other half." Every elected official sought immediate approval above all else and was therefore always "looking back over
his shoulder to see how many would follow." This need for a constituency, Phillips emphasized, was another crucial point in the political process where Garrisonians must always exert great power. Whenever the
legislator shot a backward glance, he should always see vigilant Garrisonians whose object was "duty, not success," and who would "wait, no
matter how many desert," for truth to prevail, monitoring his behavior
and exposing its flaws to his constituents. Abolitionists must strive
to "turn the thoughts of the rank and file of the party . . . to the rotten-
ness of their platform, and urge them to force their leaders to express
some opinion on them." Thus, while Phillips convinced himself that his
work had actually inspired the sectional conflict, he simultaneously denounced as corrupt the very same party leaders that he claimed as the
abolitionists' (and therefore his own) creations. His was certainly an
antipolitical style of politics that no officeholder, not even the intensely
moralistic Sumner, could ever fathom.[43]

Although laced with self-justification, Phillips' political theorems
did have valid applications. He claimed correctly, for example, that disunionist doctrine provided an important counterweight to southerners'
threats of secession, which northerners otherwise answered only with
defensive appeals to law and compromise. "If, as the South has contended, secession is a constitutional right," Phillips declared bluntly in
1848, "well, we will commend the poisoned chalice to her lips." He believed with some logic that disunion constituted a slogan well suited to

43. *Ibid.*, January 8, 1847, October 19, 1849, October 14, June 24, 1853, May 16,
1845. Joshua Giddings, whose eldest daughter was a Garrisonian, seemed to understand the disunionists' political style better than did other elected officials. See Douglas A. Gamble, "Joshua Giddings and the Ohio Abolitionists: A Study in Radical Politics," *Ohio History*, XXIX (November, 1979), 36–56, for a revealing insight into this
matter.

disturb the complacent Yankee voter. It held up "a mirror to the national mind," Phillips explained in 1848, showing it "its own deformity as judged by an absolute rule of right." When politicians spoke of slavery, theirs were the "hackneyed" words of "mere expedience," and "conscience sleeps under such a call," but let the cry ring out for disunion, and the torpid political atmosphere grew turbulent; "it startles a man to thought . . . and thunders in his ear, *Thou art the slaveholder.* After that, let him vote, if he can, much good it may do him!"[44] Disunionist rhetoric, especially when rendered in Phillips' elegant tones, added an undeniably rich extremism to the North's political voice. Sectional politicians, no matter how militant, always seemed moderate to their constituents compared to such unabashed fanatics. From the southern perspective, however, it became increasingly difficult to distinguish between New York Senator William Seward and Boston disunionist Wendell Phillips. Both, after all, spoke of "irrepressible conflicts."

The conflicts that attracted Phillips' immediate interest, however, took place in Massachusetts, not in Washington. By 1845 and 1846 Conscience Whigs had grown increasingly bold as they continued their struggles with their party's Cotton Whig rulers. In response, the Boston clique followed Phillips' political strategies. They launched a broad effort of informal support and agitation, endorsing no candidates but kicking up "political dust" wherever they could on behalf of Sumner and his allies. Quincy and Garrison, for example, hounded the Cotton Whigs in the *Liberator*, and Phillips joined Garrison at anti-Texas rallies organized statewide by the Conscience Whig insurgents. Garrison agreed to serve as an elected delegate to another such meeting and was "rapturously applauded" after delivering his disunionist opinions. Phillips, in turn, began noting Bostonians' increasing tolerance for "*strong* talk." Soon after, Charles Sumner delivered an ornate anti–Mexican War speech, for which Phillips congratulated him, and when the Conscience Whigs finally created a large committee to organize anti-Texas feeling in Massachusetts, Phillips was nearly the first to join. Garrisonians and Conscience Whigs together announced a huge nonpartisan meeting at Faneuil Hall, and Phillips shared the platform with Sumner, Palfrey, and John Quincy Adams.[45]

44. *Liberator*, March 2, January 14, 1848.
45. Brauer, *Cotton Versus Conscience*, 115–245, provides an overall review of this struggle. See also *Liberator*, September 26, October 9, 1845, October 2, 23, 30,

Heartened by the coalition's prospects, Phillips felt certain this meeting had been "a good thing." Besides "dragging forward . . . some who
were all ready, but didn't know it and now talk as we do," it also gave him
incentive, early the next year, to foster more political conflict just as the
split between Cotton and Conscience Whigs became unbridgeable,
thanks to John G. Palfrey. In January, 1847, Palfrey, now a United States
representative, utterly defied his party's leaders by refusing to support
Robert C. Winthrop's election as Speaker of the House. Elated by Palfrey's bold deed, Phillips wrote to him warmly, "Could I, conscien-
ciously[sic], throw a ballot, I would spend one the 1st of May & have . . .
the pleasure of voting for a man who nails his colors to the mast." But
true to his theory, Phillips praised Palfrey's heroism in several speeches
instead of voting for him, and he turned the hated Robert C. Winthrop
into one of his favorite objects of rhetorical abuse.[46] Phillips clearly
found such political combat exciting and certainly felt that he was aid-
ing Palfrey's faction over Winthrop's as guardian of Massachusetts' republicanism. As he had already made clear in his discussion of tactics,
disunionism certainly required no self-denying ordinance against direct
political action.

All the while, however, Phillips actually hoped that voters in large
numbers would begin to enroll as disunionists by openly refusing the
ballot and by joining the American Anti-Slavery Society. Consequently,
he ceaselessly urged the abolitionists to move forward, combating with
moral weapons a slave system "that stretches its influence into every
department of life . . . so fearful that no length of time can lessen its
horrors." To attract new supporters, Garrisonians must continue to defy
the churches "in the spirit of Christ," preach disunion in the name of
"true patriotism," and avoid the barest hint of political compromise.
Often he would plot the course of history, demonstrating that slavery
had grown like a cancer since 1787, reviving from near extinction to absolute national dominion. The Union itself, he reminded them, was the
cause of this development, proving forever the folly of the Founding Fathers' attempts to "contain slavery within its *Constitutional limits.*"

1846; Sumner to Phillips, August 19, 1845, Blagden Papers; Phillips to Sumner, August 17, 1845, Sumner Papers.
   46. Frank O. Gatell, *John Gorham Palfrey and the New England Conscience*
(Cambridge, Mass., 1965), 140–42; *Liberator*, January 28, May 9, 1848; Phillips to
John G. Palfrey, December 9, 1847, John Gorham Palfrey Papers, HL.

Had the nation, today, any "better or bolder men" than Franklin, Washington, or John Jay, Phillips asked? "Why try over again an experiment already tried under the best of . . . auspices which has failed?" Yet this was what Liberty men and Conscience Whigs proposed to do. The timid politicians' promises to restrain slavery by applying the Wilmot Proviso must be exposed to the electorate as worthless, "precisely equivalent to damming up the Mississippi with bulrushes." Such language and such doctrines, Phillips hoped, would inspire his fellow abolitionists to foster political upheaval through grass-roots efforts to recruit more disunionists. In the same meetings where he spoke so fervently, he also spearheaded a campaign to organize one hundred separate abolitionist conventions, which would expand Garrisonian influence across New England, achieving many political conversions to a doctrine based on an utter contempt for parties, voters, and the federal Union.[47] Somehow, according to Phillips, abolitionists now had to succeed in making their notably unpopular creed attractive, without sacrificing principles.

Unmindful of the impossibility of achieving such a goal, Phillips pushed forward, sharing the rostrum in Faneuil Hall with Sumner and John Quincy Adams as crowds gathered to protest the seizure of a fugitive, known only as Joe. Late in 1846, a New Orleans ship captain had simply kidnapped this unfortunate and packed him off to slavery. The resolutions before the meeting condemned such illegal acts. Phillips spoke strongly against them because he felt the outrage made a compelling popular case for disunion but not because the act was illegal. It was not the unjustness of Joe's captivity but the unjustness of slavery itself that concerned Phillips. No slave, he declared, should ever be returned from Boston under any circumstances. Instead of debating legal niceties, Bostonians ought "to remember James Otis' time . . . when people did not *look* the soldiers out of the city" but took immediate steps "*to dissolve the political* bonds. Now is the time for another Fourth of July to roll out similar words to those that were rolled out in 1776," he challenged his listeners. "I know how little truth there is in the anti-slavery professions we hear around us."[48] The political impact of words like these cannot be measured empirically though it is certain that few fresh recruits flocked to Phillips' standard. Nevertheless, as he intensified his attacks on Webster, Winthrop, and the Founding Fathers, none doubted

47. *Liberator;* May 10, 1845, February 4, June 6, 9, 1848.
48. *Ibid.,* October 4, 1846.

that Phillips' activities were surely promoting sectional polarization in Massachusetts politics.[49]

Having begun with such unrealistic hopes of attracting a multitude of new converts, Phillips soon became dismayed by disunionism's stunning unpopularity. Large defections hit the Garrisonian societies once the rank and file heard the disunionist message. Income plummeted, the organization shrank, and Phillips' "Hundred Convention Movement" died aborning. Even diehard Garrisonians grew demoralized, and the agents and editors whom Phillips directed told him bluntly what was wrong. Dynamic Abby Kelley, for example, on the circuit in western Massachusetts in 1844, reported that she found "frequent cause to blush at the laziness and inefficiency of the old organization. . . . The people hardly know of the Liberator." Four years later, editor Sidney Gay of the *National Anti-Slavery Standard* apologized for sounding like a pessimistic "croaker,"

> but still I know that antislavery as represented by the old org[anization] is without any visible influence, & with but little outside of Mass., E[astern] Pa., & to a slight degree in Ohio. . . . I know we want money, which we can get if we try, but we don't try. I know the *Standard*, which should be the chief antislavery paper of the country, has no more influence than some little country Liberty paper. . . . Don't wonder that I get worried out and tired out at last, with a position that seems almost useless.[50]

Northern disunionism was still hyena soup on voters' palates in the 1840s, as it had been on Lydia Maria Child's. Besides, organizing new antislavery societies in factory towns and back country hamlets was a far harder task than projecting heroic cadences before respectable audiences in Faneuil Hall and required skills lacking among college-educated urbanites who lived in brick houses. Only Kelley, Foster, and Pillsbury, poorer folk themselves, enjoyed any long-term success or satisfaction as grass-roots agents of disunion.

That the Liberty party was better at such organizing was evident from their growing vote totals.[51] The party's success galled Phillips; he

49. *Ibid.*, January 8, 1847, and see May 8, 1845.
50. Abby K. Foster to Phillips, February 5, 1844, Sidney H. Gay to Phillips, January 19, 1848, both in Blagden Papers.
51. See Johnson, "The Liberty Party in Massachusetts"; James Brewer Stewart, *Joshua R. Giddings and the Tactics of Radical Politics* (Cleveland, 1970), 84–102.

was dismayed that the hated party's "apostates" always seemed to capitalize on the "pure" Garrisonians' best efforts. Stephen Foster, writing from Ohio in 1846, railed to Phillips that the Liberty party "took such ever lasting pains to deceive our converts and beguile them into their ranks." From outstate Massachusetts and New Hampshire, Edward D. Hudson and Abby Kelley reported likewise. Pillsbury tried to stop these trends in 1846, requesting money and reinforcements from Phillips while lamenting that "the enemy are sowing the *tares* of the New Organization and *tear*-ing our movement to pieces for the ballot box of the third party."[52]

Phillips, worried and frustrated, responded to these entreaties by setting up new editorial help for Gay at the *Standard* and pleading for funds. He also tried to shore up disunionism by inviting antislavery Whigs to ally with Garrisonians against their common enemy, the Liberty party. Giddings, for instance, received a letter from Phillips in 1847, imploring him to attend the annual meeting of the Massachusetts Anti-Slavery Society. "We know still better and deeper than any man can, what an impulse and voice you would give to the anti-slavery feelings of New England," Phillips urged the congressman.[53] Though Phillips still considered all politicians flawed, he began to distinguish between antislavery leaders from major parties, like Giddings, and the morally bankrupted compromisers who ran the Liberty party. The former he judged as "brave and noble," for they threw off the trammels of party allegiance to act "with audacity" against slavery. Unlike the Liberty party recreants, they were at least advancing toward true abolitionism. Phillips also insisted that such leaders actually validated his claim that political parties behaved like snakes.[54] For all their self-evident contradictions, Phillips' political judgments were also entirely self-reinforcing.

Yet nothing Phillips attempted could bring disunionist supporters. For all the strong talk that had excited him, he had to admit disheartening results. "As fast as we . . . make abolitionists, the new converts run

52. Stephen S. Foster to Phillips, September 14, 1846, Edward D. Hudson to Phillips, October 9, 1846, Kelley to Phillips, May 5, 1843, April 20, 1844, Pillsbury to Phillips, December 29, 1844, all in Blagden Papers.
53. Phillips to Sidney H. Gay, May [?], 1846, November 5, 1847, March [?], 1849, Gay Papers; Phillips to May, April 20, 1849, May-McKim Papers; Phillips to Joshua Giddings, January 16, 1847, Joshua R. Giddings Papers, Ohio State Historical Society. See Gamble, "Giddings and the Ohio Abolitionists," for more on this political interplay.
54. *Liberator*, June 6, 9, 1848.

right to the Liberty Party," he wrote to Elizabeth Pease. He now felt disunion to be "so high a standard, so great a sacrifice [that] few make it. Meanwhile the Liberty Party grows." It was most "disheartening to see that every blow we strike falls in some degree against ourselves." Phillips had begun to discover that the frustrations of disunionist politics lay in precisely those qualities that were its greatest strengths. The inconsistencies he had permitted himself in his theories now returned to blight his hopes, for he held that Garrisonian agitators drove the slavery conflict forward by shaping public opinion. Yet he also recognized the contrary fact that Washington, not Faneuil Hall, now determined the political crisis over free soil and defined the issues for the voters. He had celebrated extremist disunionism as an uncompromised moral position that only the exceptional could occupy, and yet he also expected voters in significant numbers to repair to his standard. In short, Phillips' conflicting desires for both power and moral purity never permitted him to live realistically with a simple truth: sectionally minded people wished, most of all, to affect their nation's policies at the ballot box and had no desire whatever to cast aside the Constitution. The more compellingly the Garrisonians spoke against the proslavery Union, in fact, the less willing antislavery voters would actually be to forfeit their franchise. It was far more likely that they would vote for the first available Liberty man or Free-Soiler. His was a sufficiently compelling rationale for inspiring abolitionists to keep disunion in the public eye, but in actual elections Phillips' theory left him with no political satisfaction at all. At best, he could take solace in his Calvinist moralism and his Brahmin disgust for electioneering. Human nature always sought "some short cut, some royal way to heaven, some thing else than plain, hard duty," he wrote Elizabeth Pease. "And if you add to this that an American idolizes the ballot box . . . you will easily understand the result."[55]

By 1848 Phillips therefore found himself forced to seek political solace elsewhere. That year, most of the Liberty party merged with dissident Whigs like Sumner and Giddings and insurgent Democrats led by Martin Van Buren to form the Free-Soil party. Van Buren, a great Jacksonian politician and former antiabolitionist, headed a ticket with Charles Francis Adams that demanded "free soil and free labor" and declared the need for emancipation but remained silent on the doctrine of immediatism. Phillips gloated over these Liberty party concessions to expedi-

55. Phillips to Pease, October [?], 1844, Garrison Papers, BPL.

ence and thought their support of Van Buren was "the richest of all rich things," for it proved once more the wisdom of disunionism, as he assured Elizabeth Pease. Still, by 1849 he was again warning that the American Anti-Slavery Society courted bankruptcy, for the Free-Soilers' appeals to antislavery voters had "mildewed" disunionist harvests once again, putting "just enough of namby-pamby Antislavery into the common papers to take off the edge of the people's interest in ours. . . . Meantime we are in debt," he wrote to Samuel J. May. "Not a biscuit in the larder—on the contrary, many biscuits eaten and not paid for."[56] Nathaniel P. Rogers would have been amused to hear that penury, not anarchy, had made Phillips into a "no organization abolitionist."

By their own reckoning, not Phillips' certainly, the Free-Soil party did well in the 1848 canvass. They elected a dozen congressmen, tipped the balance in the presidential contest to the Whigs' Zachary Taylor, and sent tremors through every level of the two great parties. In 1849 and 1850 the political system headed toward sectional deadlock as Congress debated about what should be done with territory taken from Mexico. In the deepening political crisis, Mrs. F. H. Drake (Bernardo's future guardian) wrote Phillips to ask a very serious question: What had the disunionist abolitionists actually accomplished since the early 1840s? Phillips answered with an eloquent expression of commitment that allowed him to explain away all his political ambivalence and sense of failure.

"Set the world on fire," Phillips first responded triumphantly. Garrisonians had "driven frightened slaveholders to Mexico to get land and help" for their beleaguered system. They had "broken two or three great sects to pieces" and had "confounded both political parties." But next Phillips found himself forced to take a longer view. "We are too apt to be in a hurry and look for some immediate result," he counseled. Abolitionists, whose enormous task was the "re-education of a whole people," must be patient with small gains. In any case, said Phillips, abandoning politics altogether, direct results were not the proper standard by which to judge the Garrisonians' success. What counted most was the wisdom that reformers themselves derived from the struggle. Abolitionists in this respect had been "repaid tenfold" for their labor simply by discovering for themselves "how little dependence can be placed on the pro-

56. Phillips to Pease, January 1, 1847, *ibid.*; Phillips to Sidney H. Gay, August 26, 1848, Gay Papers; Phillips to May, April 20, 1848, May-McKim Papers.

fessed piety about us—how rotten the church is—how hard-hearted and tyrannical society is . . . and what a thorough need there is of higher moral education." And then he told Mrs. Drake of the greatest accomplishment of all. "Which of us ever dreamed . . . what selfish lives we were leading," he asked, " 'till the slave plucked the bandage from our eyes —& showed us our feet resting on his neck?" Contradictory political theory aside, this is what Phillips' disunionist politics most often came down to: "We must look upon ourselves as enlisted in God's host *for life, for life.*" [57] Agitation reconfirmed the self-purifying discovery of evil and the lifetime duty to engage and subdue it. Garrisonian politics ultimately made a person into a sanctified and militant party of one. In Phillips' case, it led him back to Faneuil Hall where, in the company of his beloved clique, he would again speak out against the Constitution and hope, somehow, to force a great reckoning with slavery.

57. Phillips to Mrs. F. H. Drake, October 11, 1849 (typescript), Garrison Papers, BPL.

EIGHT

Whigs and Slave Hunters

In March, 1850, Wendell Phillips consigned his senator to the lowest circle of hell: "If, in the lowest deep, there be a lower deep for profligate statesmen, let all former apostates stand aside and leave it vacant. Hell, from beneath, is moved for thee at thy coming."[1] Thus did Phillips greet Daniel Webster's famous Seventh of March Speech in the United States Senate defending the Compromise of 1850. This legislation sought to preserve political balance between North and South and to bury slavery questions forever. When it passed, California was admitted as a free state, and in the remaining territory taken from Mexico, slavery questions were left for later resolution by state-level plebiscite termed "popular sovereignty." To placate the North, slave trading, but not slavery, was prohibited in the District of Columbia, while to recompense the South, Congress greatly strengthened the 1793 Fugitive Slave Law. Now federal commissioners, not state judges, would process fugitive cases, and whites like Phillips who assisted fugitives risked severe penalties. Those accused of escaping were deprived of the right to jury trials, the protection of writs, and the opportunity to testify, and without these protections legally free blacks as well as authentic escapees were threatened with possible seizure and shipment south. Yet Webster, the senator from Massachusetts, had voted for these measures and urged Americans to sup-

1. *Liberator*, March 22, 1850.

port them. By his actions he transformed himself, in Wendell Phillips' eyes, into an incarnation of every element corrupting America's body politic.

Since 1837, as we have seen, Phillips had identified himself with the heroic abolitionist, the Lovejoy or Garrison who acted with passionate inspiration to disenthrall the Republic from the disruptive tyranny of slavery. Now, in Webster, Phillips discerned their antithesis, the flesh-and-blood embodiment of slavery's triumph disguised as compromise. Webster had been enslaved by slavery, Phillips decided, and, though extremely powerful, had become morally depraved and politically emasculated. As Massachusetts Cotton Whigs held testimonial dinners in Webster's honor for his having saved the Union, Phillips turned the senator into a compelling rhetorical symbol of the South's corrupting power. It was Phillips' first step in a campaign to shatter the new shackles he felt slavery had riveted on his state and nation. Moreover, as he formulated this terrifying image of Webster, he also gave voice to far more personal sources of his hatred of slavery and its supporters.

Two weeks after Webster had spoken, Phillips began a series of counterattacks. Joining with antislavery leaders of all persuasions, he helped to organize a mammoth protest meeting in Faneuil Hall, which he then addressed with a particularly condemnatory speech. He also filled a special issue of the *Liberator* with a searing review of Webster's Seventh of March Address.[2] Although a host of Massachusetts luminaries, led by Ralph Waldo Emerson, Samuel Gridley Howe, John Greenleaf Whittier, and Theodore Parker also condemned their "fallen" senator, Phillips allowed Webster to predominate in his rhetoric as had no figure since Elijah Lovejoy's death.

Phillips had much more personal reasons than the Compromise of 1850 for launching his savage attacks against Webster. First of all, Webster certainly reminded Phillips of his own unhappy past, those painful years of compromise and misdirection he had endured before embracing abolitionism. To his shame, Phillips could not forget that he had admired Webster so greatly at that time as to wish his election as president. Furthermore, Phillips resented Webster as his greatest competitor for forensic dominion in Massachusetts, for their messages and self-assigned political roles were acknowledged by all as moral opposites.

2. *Ibid.*; Phillips and Samuel Gridley Howe to Sumner, March 21, 1850, Sumner Papers; Phillips and Howe to Richard Henry Dana, March 21, 1850, Richard Henry Dana Papers, MHS.

Phillips, the republican "hero," guarded his independence and flaunted his moral purity. Webster, the unionist "statesman," was also the political insider who took retainers from great textile merchants and spoke as the servant of State Street bankers. Little wonder, then, that Phillips felt so impelled to overwhelm this formidable rival who spoke so majestically for slavery as the senator from "republican" Massachusetts.

From platforms throughout Boston, Phillips endlessly proclaimed that, but for Webster, the crisis of 1850 would have resulted in northern victory, not a slaveholder's triumph disguised as compromise. "All the virtue of the North [was] aroused, and needed but a *man* as a leader to dare all and do all." The moment called for an inspired hero who could wrest moral order from the political chaos slavery had created, a new Lovejoy or Patrick Henry. But instead the eunuch Webster had stepped forth, "cold, tame, passionless, politic," a leader whose instincts for liberty had been corrupted beyond arousal, for all his life he had "been bowing down to the Slave Power," hoping "to secure the Presidency." Webster, in sum, had extinguished within himself all feeling for the republican traditions of his state and had taken on the most degraded characteristics of the tyrants who ruled him, Phillips charged. He had supposed "that he was living in old feudal times, when . . . a statesman was essential power in himself," just as the plantation master assumed when ordering his black chattel. So driven had Webster been to satisfy his "great temptation" for high office that he had become entirely "willing to sacrifice his manhood" and had thus given up the honor of his state and section.[3]

No other figure, Phillips next asserted, had ever commanded more potential power than Webster had seemed to in 1850, even as slavery and freedom met in deadly confrontation. "He stood like a Hebrew prophet between living and dead," able by simply upholding "the cross of common truth" to sweep away "the black dishonor of two hundred years." Instead, Webster's corrupted character let his will melt before the temptation of self-serving politics, leaving him incapable of the manliness needed for taking heroic action: "He gave himself up into the lap of the Delilah of slavery, for the mere promise of a nomination and the greatest hour of the age was thrown away." Webster, like Lucifer, had fallen from "the very battlements of heaven" to the coldest depths of hell, asserted

3. *Liberator*, March 22, 1850; Phillips, "Public Opinion," "The Surrender of Sims," and "Idols," all in his *Speeches*, 39–40, 49, 63, 251, 255.

Phillips, where he ultimately found himself incapable of feeling any real emotions at all. His raw passion for office had so extinguished his moral sensibility that he regarded slavery with "judicial coldness" and preserved a "wary and decorous impartiality between Liberty and Despotism." Hence, the senator had remained aloof "in the director's room of the Merchants Bank," preoccupied with his quest for meaningless power, while slavery, unchecked, continued its barbarizing march across the nation.[4]

Phillips' description of Webster's villainy stressed not cerebral conspiracy but the victimization of free America by selfish passions so strong in their impact that they reduced citizens to powerlessness and their elected leaders to impotence. In Phillips' opinion, Webster constituted a far more dangerous and infinitely less admirable figure than the forthright John C. Calhoun, "the pure, manly, uncompromising advocate of slavery; the Hector of a Troy fated to fall." Calhoun at least had preserved his political virility by defending a principle, no matter how perverted. Worse still, in Phillips' view, the public seemed to perceive Webster as the exemplar of a high-minded patriotism to be emulated; they did not seem to recognize the moral self-pollution that actually motivated his actions. "The men we honor, and the maxims we lay down in measuring our favorites, show the level and morals of the time," Phillips warned, and to one so terribly hero-conscious, it certainly seemed "a grave thing when a state puts a man among her jewels." Little wonder, then, that Phillips saw it as his compelling duty to expose Webster's truly debased nature as the falsest hero of all, the antithesis of the self-disciplined republican, the man who had permitted his basest instincts to overwhelm him.[5]

Time and again Faneuil Hall audiences heard Phillips urge rebellion against Webster and all that shaped his perverted character. At the least, he declared, the senator must be made to "learn to respect the intelligence of New England, which knows at least when it has been betrayed." He must be shown that the people of New England had "studied too faithfully in the school" of their republican fathers to tolerate his leadership further. "Let the axe sever forever the tender cord that bound him to

4. *Liberator*, March 22, 1850; Phillips, "Public Opinion," 39–40, 49, "The Surrender of Sims," 67–69, "Idols," 251, 255.
5. *Liberator*, March 22, 1850; Phillips, "Public Opinion," 39–40, 49, "The Surrender of Sims," 63, "Idols," 251, 255.

the hearts of Massachusetts." As Phillips explained it, the need for purging Webster from the body politic could not be greater, for America represented freedom's last battleground. "There are no more continents or worlds to be revealed," he emphasized, "no more retreats beyond the sea, no more discoveries, no more hopes. Here the mighty work is to be fulfilled, or never, by this race of mortals." Massachusetts's citizens must therefore fully avenge themselves on Webster, Phillips declared, for "*you* are the instruments, fellow citizens, by whom these bright auspices are to be accomplished." Webster should never again be permitted to claim the loyalties of "the *man* who looks on the sufferings of good men in other times, the *descendant* of Pilgrims, who cherishes the memory of his father, the *patriot* who feels an honest glow at the majesty of the system of which he is a member." Unfeeling tyranny would reign henceforth in Boston and America, unless the people rose in an act of self-purification to expel this "pestiferous leader" and to crush the slaveholders who owned his soul.[6]

In assailing Webster so bitterly, Phillips sincerely believed that no personal motive drove him. "It is not as Daniel Webster that I criticize him, but it is as the Massachusetts Senator." As always, he considered himself but a patriotic censor who exposed official misdeeds and public corruption. Yet these denials, and indeed, Phillips' arraignments themselves, including unabashed attacks on Webster's masculinity, conveyed a much deeper moral outrage than he could ever recognize. As we have seen, Phillips had grown up convinced that he must develop his own creative powers through rigorous inner control. He had then put this axiom at the center of his sense of history, his abolitionism, his free-labor economic and social values, and his formulations of republican liberty and heroism. In his marriage, too, the theory had yielded rich personal rewards, for he had learned long before 1850 that his strength as Ann's lover and husband depended in the last analysis on his enduring patience and self-control. Webster, however, seemed a living denial of Phillips' psychic makeup; he embodied a perverted reversal of Phillips' animating truth and therefore represented a terrible personal threat that must be rendered impotent. Behind the senator stood the truly emasculating power that utterly denied all those life-saving values—slavery itself, which demanded dominion over one's political choices, one's labor, and even one's most intimate relationships. Only by destroying Webster and

6. *Liberator*, March 29, 1850.

his guiding spirit, slavery, could Phillips attempt to crush the disordered moral system that he sensed all around him. "The rights which we remorselessly sacrificed, when they were the rights of colored men only, have become fully avenged on us," he declared in 1850, "and this question of slavery has become the question of the age here" in Boston.[7] In Webster, Phillips had finally found a symbolic rhetorical vehicle for venting his deepest detestations of chattel slavery and its offspring social chaos and for affirming his most basic understanding of his own self-worth. Little wonder that he consigned the senator to hell's lowest circle and became as completely committed to destroying Webster as he was to overturning the Fugitive Slave Law.

In light of such an explosion of feeling following Webster's compromise, it was understandable that Phillips felt almost as if he were starting his abolitionist career all over. Mobs suddenly seemed as commonplace as they had been in the mid-1830s, as he found out in New York when he attended the annual meeting of the American Anti-Slavery Society. After two days of riotous interruption by lower-class Irish Catholic Democrats, the abolitionists had been forced to retreat to the Reverend Henry Ward Beecher's church to conclude deliberations. Later that same year, Phillips' recollection of mobs received a further sharpening when English abolitionist George Thompson, target of the 1835 mob, once again visited Boston. Phillips attended a joyous reunion with this old friend, "like all times of deep fealty . . . mingled with mirth and profound emotion," but then the mobs returned.[8] Garrison had planned a meeting at Faneuil Hall to welcome Thompson, but Webster's supporters filled the seats, greeting every speaker, especially Phillips, with ceaseless abuse. Finally the police arrived, declared the meeting out of control, and dispersed everyone. Shortly thereafter, Phillips responded defiantly, declaring that such disruption constituted "the last spasm of defeated Whiggery—Webster Whiggery," for the growing public outrage at the Whigs' devotion to slavery would insure their political destruction. "This rent in the mantle [of the Union] all the Websters in the mill cannot weave up," he jeered. "Perpetuate slavery amid a race such as ours!—Impossible!"[9]

Phillips drew this resounding encouragement from the quick devel-

7. *Ibid.*, July 26, 1850, October 14, 1853.
8. *Ibid.*, May 17, 24, 30, August 30, 1850.
9. Phillips to Pease, January [?], 1851, Garrison Papers, BPL; *Liberator*, November 22, 1850; Phillips, "Welcome to George Thompson," *Speeches, Second Series*, 28–39.

opment of widespread resistance in Boston to the new Fugitive Slave Law. A protest meeting against it, held in October, 1850, brought Phillips together with Frederick Douglass, now a Liberty party supporter; former Conscience Whigs who had become Free-Soilers; and two militants-without-portfolio, Theodore Parker and Thomas Wentworth Higginson. Pastors of unaffiliated "free churches," these two had emerged as leaders of a second generation of abolitionists by abandoning conventional Unitarianism for much more aggressive sectional beliefs. Parker, in particular, had become Phillips' close confidant, having moved in 1847 to quarters very close to 26 Essex Street. He and Phillips shared a contempt for abstract theology, denominational religion, and the United States Constitution. Following this gathering, a vigilance committee was formed, charged with organizing an insurgency that would make the Fugitive Slave Law unenforceable in Boston. Phillips and Parker gained appointment to its executive committee, and the larger group soon enrolled over two hundred members, all pledged to disobey the law and to aid fugitives at every opportunity.[10]

At first, the committee worked well. In December, 1850, when agents of a Georgia slaveholder appeared with warrants to arrest two escapees, William and Ellen Craft, committee members harassed them on the streets until they gave up and went home. Then, in February, 1851, a fugitive known as Shadrach (actually Frederic Wilkins) was arrested, and Boston's black militants acted on their own, seizing the fugitive and heading off toward the town of Leominster as bystanders cheered. Shadrach spent the night in the home of the same Mrs. F. H. Drake who later took care of Phillips' ward Bernardo. In Washington, meanwhile, President Millard Fillmore angrily noted this defiance and sent special instructions to his attorney general to prosecute resisters vigorously.[11]

Phillips cared little for Fillmore's directives, for of course he regarded Shadrach's rescuers as perfectly law-abiding citizens. The Fugitive Slave Law, he wrote, had spread terrible alarm throughout the black community, and such resistance was the only means for harassed citizens to protect freedom and to reassure the fearful when tyranny crowded in. After all, nearly a hundred people had fled the city after Shadrach had been seized, Phillips was informed, and one woman in her seventies had asked

10. *Liberator*, October 18, 1850; Vigilance Committee Records, Garrison Papers, BPL.

11. Bartlett, *Phillips*, 152–53.

his advice about where to find safety. Phillips, who judged it "horrible to see the distress of families torn apart" by fear of federal marshals, therefore agreed wholeheartedly when Garrison insisted that Shadrach's rescuers "were not animated by a lawless spirit, but by a deep and commendable sympathy for an outraged man. . . . 'Resistance to tyrants is obedience to God.'"[12] Regarding himself, as always, as an agent of order and justice, Phillips felt instinctively drawn to the role of conspirational insurgent in a city where Webster and his cohorts plotted evil. Imagining the federal marshals as Redcoats, himself as a latter-day Son of Liberty, and Boston as a historic battleground for freedom, he wrote enthusiastically to Elizabeth Pease:

> The long evening sessions—debates about secret escapes—plans to evade where we can't resist—the door watched that no spy may enter—the whispering consultations of the morning—some putting property out of their hands, planning to incur penalties, and planning also that, in case of connection, the Government may get nothing from them—the doing, and answering no questions—intimates forbearing to ask the knowledge which it may be dangerous to have—all remind me of those foreign scenes which have hitherto been known to us, transatlantic republicans, only in books.[13]

In this way, Phillips' vivid historical imagination permitted him to compensate for his burning anger at Daniel Webster's domination of Massachusetts politics and his helpless frustration with Washington's leaders for declaring peace in the conflict over slavery. "We are straining every nerve to save Massachusetts from the infamy of letting even one man go back to bondage," he wrote with intensity to Liberty party leader Gerrit Smith in March, 1851.[14] By acting on such feelings, at least he could believe that he was retrieving the initiative for the abolitionists in Massachusetts and redeeming his city from the evil wrought by Webster and his friends.

The moment of hope was brief, however, crushed by the violent ar-

---

12. Phillips to Pease, March 9, 1851, Garrison Papers, BPL; Horton and Horton, *Black Bostonians*, 115–25; *Liberator*, February 21, 1851.
13. Phillips to Pease, March 9, 1851, Garrison Papers, BPL.
14. Phillips to Gerrit Smith, March 22, 1851, Gerrit Smith-Miller Family Papers, Syracuse University Library.

rest and successful return to slavery of Thomas Sims, in April, 1851. Sims, an escapee from Georgia, had resisted furiously, wounding one of his captors with a knife before being taken by marshals to the United States Courthouse. But there was to be no repeat of Shadrach's escape, for city officials remembered President Fillmore's orders and soon 150 policemen ringed the courthouse. Only people authorized by the federal marshal, a determined Francis Tukey, were permitted in the building. Inside, six guards watched the doors to the room where Sims was held, and six more kept surveillance over the prisoner himself. Finally and most dramatically, Tukey decided to encircle the courthouse with a great iron chain, suspended three feet above the ground, to control the crowd outside. To everyone sympathetic to Sims's plight, the chain perfectly symbolized the manacles that the slave power had clamped so viciously upon liberty in Massachusetts. Meanwhile, antislavery lawyers began bewildering legal maneuvers by filing for a writ of *habeas corpus* for Sims's release with Federal Commissioner George T. Curtis as well as with State Supreme Court Justice Lemuel Shaw. Both magistrates, however, refused to entertain arguments questioning the constitutionality of the Fugitive Slave Law and therefore refused to issue the writ. On April 11, Curtis declared that on the grounds of extradition, Sims must be returned to slavery.[15]

All the while, the vigilance committee could agree on nothing. Higginson concocted a plan to have Sims leap from the third floor of the courthouse, which failed when Marshal Tukey had iron bars installed in the windows. No one assented, furthermore, either to Phillips' idea of bribing the captain of the ship hired to transport Sims to Georgia or to Parker's plan of boarding the vessel and seizing the captive. Higginson, frustrated, complained bitterly of the "want of preparation on our part for this revolutionary work. . . . This is especially true of reformers," who do "what seems right to themselves but without reference to others."[16]

Despite the abolitionists' disorganization, officials feared violence, and so, as long as Sims remained in the courthouse, they refused to let protestors meet in Faneuil Hall or in the statehouse yard. "The city and

15. Austin Bearse, *Reminiscences of Fugitive Slave Days in Boston* (Boston, 1880), 24–34; Bartlett, *Phillips*, 155–58.
16. Thomas Wentworth Higginson, *Cheerful Yesterdays* (Boston, 1896), 143; Ann W. Weston to Deborah Weston, May 15, 1851, Weston Papers; Thomas Wentworth Higginson, Journal, April 13, 1851, Thomas Wentworth Higginson Papers, HL.

State have betrayed us and joined the enemy," Phillips announced to the angry throng finally gathered on Boston Common. He demanded not a "discussion of opinion" but a "plan of action," insisting that "Yankee ingenuity" could devise a way to "drive a four wheeled wagon load of slaves through any law which drunken legislators can make." Laws enforced by bayonets and armed soldiers "cannot stand, ought not stand, will not stand long," he insisted, claiming that he rejoiced "in all this insolent array of force." Any black threatened by a federal marshal, said Phillips, "should feel justified by using law of God and man in shooting that officer." Such violence, he emphasized, was perfectly proper because every black citizen now lived without legal protection, "remitted back to his natural rights." Since whites still enjoyed civil liberty, however, they must attempt to stop the extradition of Sims with massive nonviolent resistance only. Phillips urged them to "crowd the streets and surround the court house," physically preventing Sims's extradition. It would be a "damning disgrace to Massachusetts" if Sims were returned to slavery "without every village enroute rising *en masse* to block the wheels of government."[17]

Unimpeded by Phillips' efforts, the wheels of government did move forward. Early in the dawn of April 13, Boston police, sabers unsheathed, escorted Sims to the Boston wharf. As he was put aboard ship, vigilance committee members could only look on, crying shame and singing an abolitionist hymn. Six days later in Savannah, Georgia, Sims endured a public whipping, while Cotton Whigs in Boston and unionists everywhere savored their triumph, and the hated Webster openly mocked the abolitionists as a vanquished foe.[18] In speech after speech, Phillips vented his burning hatred of those who it seemed ruled so licentiously in offices once held by his father.

Speaking from local platforms in 1851 and 1852, he denounced his conservative foes, the "peddling hucksters of State and Milk Streets," who owed him "full atonement for the foul dishonor they have brought upon the city of my birth." Where his ancestors had presided, corruption now ruled—in the mayor's office, in the statehouse, and in the banks and exchange halls of the business district. Phillips registered his "deep and indignant protest" against the "cowardly and lying policy" of the police and against the mayor's "deliberate and wanton violation of the laws of

17. *Liberator*, April 11, 1851.
18. Boston *Advertiser*, April 15, 1851.

the commonwealth" in "selling a free man into bondage that State Street and Milk Street might make money." Massachusetts judges had displayed "personal cowardice, pitiful subservience, utter lack of official dignity and entire disregard for their official oaths." Behind this debased behavior, Phillips charged, stood corrupt Cotton Whig financiers, clutching their "bursting ledgers" and unraveling the moral fabric of the commonwealth's political economy, having long ago forgotten "that a man is worth more than a bank vault." Orchestrating them all, of course, was the archvillain Daniel Webster, "recreant New Englander," who pledged to "silence this slave generation" even as he yielded "the interests and honor of Massachusetts and New England" to his masters in the South. In remanding Sims, Boston's officials had become tyrants, according to Phillips, and the city's social and economic wellsprings had been polluted by slavery. Only the abolitionists remained to nurture the spirit of order and freedom, having "exhausted every device, besieged every tribunal, implored the interference of every department, to obtain the bare execution of the laws of the Commonwealth, knowing the value of true law and real order." They had, in other words, attempted to repeat in Boston what Phillips always believed that Lovejoy had tried so valiantly to do in Alton, and now they, like that earlier martyr, must declare that it was "better, far better, that human laws be trampled under foot and the order of society broken every day . . . than one man should be sent back to slavery."[19] Choking with frustration and transfixed by a violence-filled vision of the past, Phillips nevertheless continued to ask that whites practice legal resistance only, but now he also spoke with a stridency that even he had never voiced before.

Yet even as he continued to cry out for orderly obstruction, a shrill endorsement of white abolitionist violence was unmistakable in Phillips' rhetoric. If whites must remain nonviolent themselves, he declared at the Massachusetts Anti-Slavery Society meeting in 1851, they must also begin "launching a new measure" by actively supporting blacks who took up arms, either against their masters or against the federal marshals. Whites, he counseled, should remain peaceable and certainly must never manipulate black fugitives for the purpose of "manufacturing antislavery sustainment . . . the game sickens me when the counters are living men." Unlike many of his co-workers, Phillips despised the tactic

19. Phillips, "Surrender of Sims" and "Sims Anniversary," both in his *Speeches,* 55–70, 74–90.

of encouraging fugitive slave incidents as a means for agitating for abolition, but whites must support blacks who drew guns in self-defense, even to the point that, were a fugitive actually to shoot Lemuel Shaw or George T. Curtis, white abolitionists must protect the black from arrest. Such a death might actually "have a wholesome effect," Phillips said. "*Sic Semper Tyrannis*," he exclaimed with a fury hot even for him, "so may it ever be with slavehunters!" But even as Phillips' bloodthirsty words reflected his deeper anger, his ambivalence toward the actual use of guns and counterinsurgents also displayed itself. "Mark me," he next qualified, "I do not *advise* anyone to take the life of his fellow," but he declared that he could now only sneer at those who shed tears over *Uncle Tom's Cabin*, with its sentimental portrayals of submissive and loyal slaves. "Your nerves are very sensitive," he jibed at such readers; "see that your consciences are as sensitive. . . . would that those tears could . . . crystalize into principle, out of which the weapon of antislavery patience, perseverence and self-sacrifice is to be wrought."[20] Thenceforward, until John Brown finally broke the pattern, Phillips found his thoughts alternating wildly between visions of bloodshed and fears of social chaos. Even as he preached now-traditional Garrisonian disunion, he began advising whites to prepare for an emancipation achieved by slave insurrection. Speculating publicly, he theorized that armed black resistance soon might spread such terror throughout the nation that politicians would finally be forced "to grapple with the problem of slavery." More likely, though, open revolt would finally tear slavery apart. At some "critical juncture in our national affairs," he prophesied, blacks would feel inspired to rise, for his study of history had revealed to him that "emancipation . . . is the child of convulsion." Phillips admitted that he quailed at the "dreadful . . . scenes of blood through which a rebellious slave population must march to their rights," but 150 years of slavery were far "more sickening" to his moral senses than the carnage of revolt itself. "Tell me," he once challenged his listeners, "if Waterloo or Thermopylae can claim one tear from the eye of even the tenderest spirit . . . compared with the daily system of hell amidst the most civilized and democratic people on the face of the earth!"[21]

Phillips, of course, had always endorsed acts of violence after the fact when they were accomplished by those like Toussaint L'Ouverture who

20. Phillips, "Sims Anniversary," 89.
21. *Ibid.*, 73, 93.

served the high cause of liberty. The ambivalence he displayed about actually seeing force employed had equally deep roots, however. He had strongly defended Lovejoy's recourse to guns, but he had also claimed for years that abolitionists must shape politics through public opinion, not arms, and must meet unjust laws with nonviolent protests. As an order-loving republican, Phillips possessed an instinctual hatred of social disorder, which kept him insisting that abolitionists remain peaceful prophets. In the same year that he first called for insurrection, for example, he also emphasized his view of abolitionism as the "all-talk party," whose efforts guaranteed that the "age of bullets is over," that "the age of the thinking man has come." Phillips therefore was able to regard his aims as peaceful, his effect on political culture as calming; he vowed that with the "aid of God, every man I can reach I will set *thinking* on the subject of slavery" and insisted, "The age of the reading man has come." He was still able to promise, "I will try to imbue every newspaper with Garrisonianism." As the North's most compelling platform warrior began celebrating insurrection, he did so only by assuring himself at the same time that his actions helped his cause to progress peacefully.[22]

Phillips' hesitant, confused, but ever-growing advocacy of violence contributed to a general trend in abolitionism, which grew as fugitive slave incidents multiplied. Angry Syracuse abolitionists wrested an escapee from federal marshals in 1851, and the same year, a slaveholder seeking a fugitive ventured into Christiana, Pennsylvania, where resisters shot and killed him. In Boston, meantime, new voices like Higginson's and Parker's added mightily to the atmosphere of militance. Higginson, for instance, began organizing disunionist conventions where rhetoric no less uninhibited than Phillips' set the mood. At one such gathering, Garrison publicly burned a copy of the United States Constitution and, following that, a copy of the Fugitive Slave Law. As the fascination with violence grew, the Boston clique found that it was being pulled in conflicting directions by its members' attraction to both warfare and peace. For more than a decade, their belief in nonviolence had bound them together as a spiritual community that saw itself as generating the spontaneous fellowship implicit in doctrines of "moral suasion," perfectionism, and nonresistance. Phillips, Garrison, Quincy, the

22. *Liberator*, January 28, 1852; Phillips, "Public Opinion," 50.

Fosters, and the rest endlessly defended their cherished political doctrines of peaceful agitation against the supposedly coercive expediency
of the third-party abolitionists. Now, as their own frustrations drove
them toward embracing force, clique members understandably felt reluctant to violate the time-sanctioned creeds that had for so long sustained their common fellowship. When Phillips asserted that the "age of
bullets" was over, he was reassuring his eager Garrisonian listeners, no
less than himself, that moral suasion and harmonious Christian fellowship remained their uncompromised ideals. Then, supported by such
words, he also invited his dear friends to join him in the rhetoric of violence as fully as their instincts permitted.

No less persuasive for all his personal ambivalence, Phillips rehearsed
all these themes many times during the early 1850s, as Garrisonians
girded themselves against the slave power's renewed aggression. Today
he is especially remembered for these speeches, which have earned him
a reputation as abolitionism's most systematic philosopher.[23] His actual
motives, however, were hardly philosophical. He knew that his friends,
like himself, had become "weary of this moral suasion, and sigh for
something tangible, some power they can feel." Demoralized Garrisonians, distracted by thoughts of violence and their own evident powerlessness, listened attentively whenever Phillips declared with such eloquent sincerity that despite the darkness of the hour, moral suasion
was certain of ultimate victory. "The gem forms unseen. . . . the great
change in the nation's opinion is the same," he assured them. "Look
back over twenty years," he invited, and "see the great change." Once,
the nation's leaders had shut their eyes to slavery. Now, thanks to the
abolitionists, "they have been made to talk. The great parties of the
country have been broken to pieces and crumbled. . . . Real liberty is
gaining the ascendant—and the part we have to act in all this great
drama is . . . to uphold *our* ascending, until we shall see it culminate in
the highest heaven over our heads!" All this would surely come to pass,
said Phillips, because the abolitionist movement, as Garrison had invented it, constituted "the most sagacious adaptation of means to ends,

23. See Richard Hofstadter, "Wendell Phillips: The Patrician as Agitator," in his
The American Political Tradition and the Men Who Made It (New York, 1948),
137–63; Robert D. Marcus, "Wendell Phillips and American Institutions," *Journal of
American History*, LVI (June, 1969), 39–56, for stimulating developments of this
theme, which vary significantly from the viewpoint presented here.

the strictest self-discipline, the most thorough research . . . such as no other cause of the kind in this country or England has ever offered."[24]

Phillips, to be sure, felt just as reassured as his audience as he warmed to these grand themes. He justified moral suasion with a republican theory that allowed him to exalt the agitator as the preeminent American patriot-statesman; it was a perfect apology for his own self-conceived role. Moreover, his ideas certainly furnished much-needed encouragement to Boston abolitionists, who had just seen their most desperate efforts crushed at the orders of Webster and Fillmore. "In an age such as ours," emphasized Phillips, "the so-called statesman has far less influence than many little men," like the Garrisonians, "who are silently nurturing the regeneration of public opinion. . . . Now, Webster counts but one!" The printing presses and the nation's literate citizens, "the thinking masses," not its supposed leaders, actually dictated the direction of society, creating "a government of news and morning papers." Because of this development, Phillips asserted, moral suasion abolitionists had actually come to control the nation's conflicts over slavery, for over the years, their constant agitation had slowly caused a deepening popular revulsion against the peculiar institution. Typically, he illustrated this assertion with a simile. "The beginning of great changes is like the rise of the Mississippi. The child must stoop and gather away the pebbles to find it. But soon it swells broader and broader, until it bears on its bosom the navies of a mighty republic, fills the gulf and divides the continent."[25]

This vast assertion was actually an extension of familiar political claims Phillips had been making for disunion since the early 1840s. Now, however, to confirm it he was able to invoke for his Garrisonian hearers over two decades of their own shared history, citing satisfying evidence of their ever-growing national influence. What, he asked, had "first quickened the zeal and strengthened the hands" of John Quincy Adams and Joshua Giddings during the gag-rule struggles of the late 1830s? What had shipwrecked Daniel Webster's presidential hopes throughout the 1840s? What, indeed, had set the North's lawyers at each other's throats over "the citizenship of the colored man and the . . . antislavery character of the constitution"? When Charles Sumner, Robert Rantoul, William Seward, and the rest gave sectional speeches in Con-

24. Phillips, "Public Opinion," 39–42, "Philosophy of the Abolition Movement," 105–106.
25. Phillips, "Public Opinion," 36–37.

gress, "how little . . . they present which was not familiar for years in our anti-slavery meetings." The cause of all these portentous successes, was, of course, the Garrisonians' steady progress in shaping the debate on slavery. As further evidence, Phillips also claimed that the same Free-Soil politicians who abused the Garrisonians in public were actually quite "willing to confess, privately, that our movement produced theirs, and that its continued existence is the bread of their life." Phillips asked, "Who converted these men and their distinguished associates? Who taught the *Christian Register* and the Daily *Advertiser* [well-known Boston antiabolitionist papers] that there is such a thing as a slave or a slaveholder in the land?" All these powerful elements were "converted by simple denunciation," Phillips exclaimed, "by the 'reckless,' 'routing,' 'bigoted,' 'fanatic' Garrison, who never troubled himself about facts, nor stopped to argue with an opponent, but straight away knocked him down." By this time, Phillips had his audiences laughing with self-congratulation, refreshed in their devotion to moral suasion, to their memories of shared struggle, and to one another.[26]

Then, typically, Phillips pressed one final claim; he made a case for the Garrisonians as the saviors not just of the slave but of all that was liberating in America's governance, economy, and social morality. As a believer in original sin, who greatly distrusted all unsupervised power, he emphatically stressed that both government and society always tended toward apathy and tyranny. It was therefore essential that "prophets like Garrison" be ever active to "stir the monotony of wealth" and "reawaken the people to great ideas that are constantly fading from their minds." Abolitionism, as Phillips explained it, thus gave essential refreshment to the republican spirit of American political culture. "Every government is always growing corrupt," Phillips insisted, and every officer in it was, "by the necessity of his position, an apostate . . . an enemy of the people, of necessity, because the moment he joins the government, he gravitates against that proper agitation that is the life of the republic." The greatest Garrisonian mission of all was therefore to castigate the politician's actions and to trample on his tyrannous laws, resisting the state's slide into corruption by showing the people how to drive their representatives from power.[27]

Politics therefore were terribly important for Garrisonians, Phillips

26. Phillips, "The Philosophy of the Abolition Movement," 90–116.
27. Phillips, "Public Opinion," 53.

said, but not for "the mere scramble for loaves and fishes" that happened in elections. Politics were important, instead, "as the bridge that shall span the chasm between Faneuil Hall and the United States Senate . . . [and] the man who walks over it must carry with him every principle that he has made the roof echo with in Faneuil Hall—he must drop nothing along the way." It was a most crucial abolitionist objective to erase altogether the distance that elected officials invariably tried to open between themselves and the political culture from which they had sprung. His was a classic statement of republican theory: those elected must be made to perform as the people's direct attorneys, and if they failed in acting thus, the people must turn them out or must oppose extralegally the tyranny that inevitably resulted. Politicians were by nature manipulative "hucksters," Phillips further insisted. They "whisper at home what they would be afraid to have heard in Washington, say at Washington what they would be afraid to have heard at home, and are politically dead when the two places meet and compare notes." In such a political world, the abolitionist agitator alone kept alive that "reckless enthusiasm of the revolutionary days," when republican government had actually legislated the moral vision of an aroused people. The abolitionists, he maintained, must therefore never flag in their efforts to uphold and renew that great tradition. Their "quarrel with parties and policies" must "never cease" until liberating abolitionist values shaped political behavior everywhere—"not one thing at Christiana [where the slave catcher had been shot] and another at Washington . . . not one thing at an anti-slavery meeting to gain confidence, and another thing in November to gain votes—but everywhere, at all times, and in all capacities—radical, defiant, aggressive, trampling all slave laws, and either openly denying the legality of slavery . . . or repudiating the government as a covenant with death and an agreement with hell."[28] Never did Phillips speak more directly from his own egalitarian values or from his overriding compulsion to reshape American politics to his stern moral codes.

There was even more than this to inspire hope among Garrisonians, Phillips insisted as he finished his disquisition on philosophy. He spoke of "a silver lining" that would guarantee abolitionism's greatest success, even if the movement failed to sustain moral politics or even to free the slave. Again Phillips invoked an old republican concept, the idea of a

28. *Liberator*, June 24, 1853.

"moral economy," arguing that even if all else failed, abolitionist agitation would nevertheless renew the ethical underpinnings of the nation's capitalist system and the value of day-to-day labor. Through their "uninterrupted agitation," abolitionists would keep life-giving moral truths circulating freely throughout America's body politic, he declared, so as "not to let liberty be smothered in material prosperity." The nation was growing in wealth and size, Phillips told his friends. But as its Cotton Whigs and slaveholders attested, the moral underpinnings of its economy had long ago begun to collapse. Moral suasion alone possessed the power to "save the freedom of the white race from being melted down into luxury, or buried in the gold of its own success." Garrisonian agitators, Phillips explained, preserved and promoted republican values that harmonized material progress and the nation's spiritual growth. Without such inspiration, distracted Americans would spend their energies completely in pursuit of dollars, markets, and daily bread, never stopping to realize that their labors bore only the fruits of tyranny and apathy.[29]

So ended Phillips' wide-ranging justifications, in which he invoked some of the most powerful themes of America's republican tradition—a distrust of unchecked power, a celebration of social harmony in a moral society, a justification for popular resistance to tyranny, and a defense of an ethical free-market system that supported the highest good. Even as he inspired demoralized colleagues with such compelling formulations, Phillips swept away his own disillusionment, denied his angry confusion, and directed his frustration back into the larger society. There, his own role of agitator nonpareil, as he himself had just justified it so inspirationally, always awaited.

In the early 1850s, Massachusetts politics developed complexities that might have made any Garrisonian grateful for not voting. Temperance and antislavery sent Whigs, Democrats, and Free-Soilers into byzantine bargaining and conflict, out of which emerged a Democratic–Free-Soil coalition that put Charles Sumner into the Senate seat vacated by the hated Webster. Phillips, elated, sent Sumner a warm note of congratulation but, two months thereafter, showed himself willing to risk his relationship with his old friend by putting it to a republican agitator's political test. Once Sumner had assumed his duties, Garrisonians

29. *Ibid.*, and for variations on these themes, see May 27, August 1, 1852, February 13, 22, 1853.

immediately sent him a petition demanding the release of two antislavery heroes, Daniel Drayton and William Sayres, who had been convicted and jailed for their attempt to smuggle slaves out of Washington, D.C. Sumner moved cautiously, knowing that noisy petitioning would only diminish his chances of securing a presidential pardon. Phillips, however, joined Garrison in attacking Sumner's slowness, and the senator protested with hurt puzzlement in a private letter.[30]

Phillips attempted to reassure Sumner of his friendship and of his "entire confidence" in Sumner's motives. Yet he also left no doubt that his friend's ascent to national office had changed his view of their relationship significantly. Sumner was unjustified in complaining about Garrison's criticisms, Phillips told him, for the disagreement was "*your fault, not his.*" Furthermore, Sumner's inaction on the petition was "more than a fault—tis a blunder . . . impolitic and wrong." Phillips promised to continue trusting him "at least till the end of the summer and [to] listen then to his explanation." He made it clear that he still valued Sumner personally as highly as ever, but he reminded Sumner that he had now become Phillips' senator, a public servant and a point of political influence. From now on, the agitator would treat him as the "philosophy of abolitionism" demanded, putting political need ahead of personal affection. The two continued to exchange letters in which comradeship mixed awkwardly with criticism until the outbreak of the Civil War revived a more congenial spirit.[31]

Phillips had little to do but write such nagging letters and try to fight boredom in the summer of 1852. He was marooned in Florence, Massachusetts, near Northampton, the site of Dr. Munde's Water Cure Establishment, a placid change from the pace of the vigilance committee. Ann had suddenly become so ill that she was doubled up in pain and had to be carried on a litter. She and Wendell rented a private railroad car for the trip from Boston, hoping again to find some remedy for her affliction. They stayed on for more than a year, including two full summers, but at the end, Ann had become no better. In the meantime, she subjected herself to the rigors of hydropathy, wrapped in wet sheets, submerged in tubs of water, and encased in mud packs. Dr. Munde, trained in Europe, applied mineral water "made comfortable by artificial heat,"

---

30. Donald, *Sumner and the Coming of the War,* 200–201; *Liberator,* March 19, 1852; Sumner to Phillips, April 16, 1852, Blagden Papers.
31. Phillips to Sumner, April 27, 1852, Sumner Papers.

and the treatments went on incessantly. "We dabble so much in the water that my hands begin to be *webbed* and I detect occasionally a high *quack* in Ann," Wendell joked.[32]

Although Dr. Munde's facilities included a gymnasium and a bowling alley, Phillips quickly grew restless. He browsed in the Florence general store, slept until ten, and became a sidewalk superintendent for a local construction project. Since the only horse available refused to trot properly, he resorted to aimless puttering. "Yesterday, I picked up all the scraps of paper in the garden and today the stage was late. . . . Our cat caught a mouse Saturday evening." Abolitionist matters occasionally broke this monotony, as when Webster died in October, 1852. Phillips composed an obituary that praised his antagonist's oratory and legal skills but also asserted that the senator had succeeded only in "saying common things uncommonly well." Phillips concluded, "If the Fugitive Slave Law could have died with him, he would have indeed slept in blessings." Phillips fled from boredom by dashing off to nearby Williams College; he met the "bluest of the blue Connecticut orthodoxy up there" and disturbed the conservative atmosphere with a speech that praised the radical agitator as the guardian of American democracy. He also repaired to Boston several times to give inspirational talks on abolitionist philosophy and returned from one such trip in November, 1852, with Phoebe Garnaut, his and Ann's adopted daughter, who was on vacation from boarding school.[33] Phoebe, bright and energetic, lightened the Phillips' spare moments and Wendell passed the time helping her with her Latin and French. Edmund Quincy, knowing that his friend was at loose ends, drove up from Dedham for a visit and found that Wendell had also resumed his duties as Ann's nurse, spending many hours each day in her darkened room. Though Ann remained as before, twisted by pain and too weak to walk, Quincy's first concern was that Wendell was damaging his own health by cloistering himself so completely. "It does seem," he wrote a friend, "that God had given him his great powers for something better."[34]

From his vantage point in Florence, Phillips' general view suggested few constructive uses for his time, and he brooded over the victories of

32. Handbill for Dr. Munde's Water Cure Establishment in Blagden Papers; Phillips to Wendell P. Garrison, n.d. [1852 or 1853], Garrison Papers, SCL.
33. Phillips to Helen B. Garrison, July 19, August 24, 1852, Phillips to Pease, November 21, 1852, Garrison Papers, BPL; *Liberator*, December 16, 1852.
34. Quincy to Webb, January 13, 1853, Quincy-Webb Papers.

slavery since 1850. "Webster's friends rule Boston," he wrote Elizabeth Pease in November, 1852, "and revenge themselves on everything called antislavery." In the presidential election that year Phillips welcomed the "annihilation" of Webster's Whig party, but Democrat Franklin Pierce entered the White House with a huge national mandate to enforce the Compromise of 1850. "We gain ground daily," he reassured himself by assuring Pease, for the Whig defeat might lead to "the formation, very soon, of two great parties, Northern and Southern, and the beginning of the end." His prediction happened to be stunningly accurate, but whether "the end" meant black insurrection, peaceful disunion, civil war, or yet another sectional compromise, no one at that time, certainly not Phillips, could possibly have foreseen.[35]

Phillips could, however, see the necessity of attacking Horace Mann, the former state commissioner of education, who was now a Free-Soil congressman. Undoubtedly the boredom of Florence helped sustain Phillips' combativeness in the long newspaper squabble that broke out between them in early 1853, as did Phillips' certainty that fundamental issues were at stake. The two hotly debated the Constitution, specifically Phillips' charge that Mann's oath of office made him an active accessory to upholding the Fugitive Slave Law. Both grew angry, and Mann revealed that he had long resented Phillips' abuse of his 1846 school board report condoning segregation. Mutual friends intervened, and Theodore Parker lectured Phillips that the quarrel "will do you no good and much harm and weaken you both."[36] Despite the evidence of frayed tempers, Phillips' savage attack on Mann also revealed political thinking that was as sophisticated for an abolitionist as it was utopian.

Phillips explained his motives in a letter to Sumner, written as the controversy with Mann dragged on. Earlier, Sumner had complained again about Phillips' criticisms, and Phillips replied that Sumner must remember the Garrisonian axiom that "our agitation . . . keeps yours alive in the rank and file." When "carping editors, country ministers and priests" read Sumner's speeches in favor of legislation based on an antislavery interpretation of the Constitution, Phillips explained, such people immediately wondered why the Garrisonian "did not have the sense to think of *such* solid arguments." In short, Sumner's doctrines offered the electorate convincing approaches to resisting slavery, but

35. Phillips to Pease, November 21, 1852, Garrison Papers, BPL.
36. Theodore Parker to Phillips, n.d. [March, 1853], Blagden Papers. See also Phillips to May, and to McKim, [March], 1853, May-McKim Papers.

these approaches were flawed by their failure to embrace disunion. Worse still, Sumner's pronouncements carried great political weight with voters. "You are are read by millions and shape their conduct," he reminded the senator. The total effect of Sumner's widely known doctrines was thus to convince people that "all is safe if the [Fugitive Slave] law [alone] is repealed," and this belief persuaded them, "by easy steps," to "submit contentedly to the usurpation" itself. "Your readers," Phillips stressed, "will often apply what you mean of yourself in *one* capacity to their *whole life* and being."[37] In this way, Phillips feared, Sumner's doctrines might encourage people to accommodate themselves to the ever-increasing demands of tyrants and corrupters.

This point, in fact, was the fundamental issue in Phillips' quarrel with Horace Mann as well. Phillips was convinced that Mann, by treating Garrisonian disunionism with open scorn, had sought to discredit abolitionism among his grass-roots constituents. Mann, in other words, was encouraging his electorate to make that subtle acceptance of ever-expanding tyranny that Phillips had just explained to Sumner. Especially in light of the Sims affair, Phillips considered such conduct despicable and decided that Mann needed to be taught to respect the disunionists. "Mann rode a high horse, thought little of his foes and thought he would ramble those vulgar Garrisonians in the mud. I'll teach him," Phillips vowed to Quincy, "that Garrisonians never go out, even on the most gala occasions, without their 'pockets full of rocks.'" Clearly he regarded this fight as a "test question" of his doctrines, where winning meant maintaining political respect in the public eye. "If I floor him," Phillips wrote, "no man will relish disputing my positions." When the quarrel finally abated, Phillips, predictably enough, declared it a political victory for abolitionism. The exchange, in his opinion, had "forced from *him* [Mann] a promise to reveal his *real* opinion of the slave clause. If politics can flash these startling torches full in the face of a proud and confident people," then voters would begin "to press to their hearts a cause which is fated, through the government or over it, to have its way." Phillips considered this "politics of unspeakable value" and a substantial vindication of his role as public censor.[38]

37. Phillips to Sumner, March 7, 1853, Sumner Papers.
38. Phillips to Quincy, January 22, 1853, Quincy Papers; *Liberator*, June 24, 1853. The entire Mann-Phillips quarrel can be followed in the *Liberator* issues of February and March, 1853. See also Phillips to Lysander Spooner, March 25, 1853, Lysander Spooner Papers, BPL.

As it turned out Phillips soon needed all the political militancy he and his colleagues could generate. In September, 1853, he and Ann finally returned home from Florence to a friendly greeting. Garrison, Quincy, and the Westons welcomed them with a bronze statue, worth over a hundred dollars, that portrayed a female slave holding two white children.[39] As winter came, however, politics soon disturbed the placid atmosphere, and by February, 1854, people in angry gatherings were discussing Senator Stephen A. Douglas' new bill to organize the Kansas and Nebraska territories. Douglas proposed to repeal the Missouri Compromise line of 36 degrees, 30 minutes, which had prohibited slavery in these areas and to let the settlers decide the question by popular sovereignty. Slavery, in effect, would have large new territories opened for possible expansion. Even as these debates intensified, three federal marshals from Virginia walked the streets of Boston searching for a well-built, thirty-year-old escapee. Near midnight on May 24, 1854, they seized Anthony Burns and wrestled him into the courthouse. Ann Phillips' distraught letter to her cousins in Weymouth, the Westons, conveyed the angry dismay that swept through the Boston clique as the news broke. "So, for mercy's sake both of you come into town and give your advice and counsel. . . . if this man is allowed to go back there *is no antislavery* in Mass[achusetts]—We may as well disband at once if our meetings and papers are *all talk.*"[40]

Wanting no repetition of the Sims debacle, Ann Phillips clearly saw the abolitionists' difficulty. There were dissidents aplenty in the city, ready to take up Burns's cause, but getting so fractious a group to agree on a plan of action would not be easy. While the marshals had stalked Burns, abolitionists and women suffragists had been checking into local hotels by the hundreds for this was "anniversary week" in Boston, when several reform organizations held their annual meetings. Talk, as Ann Phillips feared, soon began. Wendell Phillips rushed off to meet with wrathful but indecisive vigilance committee members, who appointed him to a smaller executive committee along with Parker, Higginson, and Samuel Gridley Howe. Phillips and Higginson divided over the latter's eagerness to obtain weapons and storm the courthouse. Eager to act this time, Higginson hastened to purchase axes and drum up volunteers.

39. *Liberator*, January 20, 1854.
40. Ann Phillips to Ann W. Weston and Deborah Weston, [May], 1854, Weston Papers.

Phillips, meantime, tried to gain peaceable access to the courthouse to offer legal assistance to Burns. His and Higginson's contrasting choices marked well the differences between a self-appointed guerrilla warrior and a republican agitator who still hated disorder most of all. When he was refused admittance, Phillips appealed in person to Boston's fugitive slave commissioner, Judge Edward G. Loring, for written permission to see the prisoner. Loring gave him a letter but remarked to Phillips in passing that Burns probably would be going back to slavery, convincing Phillips that Loring, who was commissioned to adjudicate Burns's case, had prejudged the outcome without even hearing evidence or argument. Loring, Phillips believed, was flaunting his immoral allegiance to slave-holding tyranny.[41]

Deeply discouraged, Phillips returned to the courthouse and met the black captive Burns, who clearly showed the terror of his ordeal. Deeply moved by one who was so "trembling, ignorant, confused, astounded, friendless, not knowing what to say or where to look," Phillips persuaded him to accept legal assistance and arranged for Richard Henry Dana, a Free-Soiler, to represent him. Believing Loring to be fatally biased, Phillips assumed that such efforts were foredoomed but went ahead nevertheless, if only to reassure the powerless, abused Burns.[42]

That afternoon, May 25, city officials doubled the guards surrounding the courthouse and girded for that evening's widely advertised protest meeting. By seven o'clock huge crowds had already overflowed from the central auditorium into the anterooms of Faneuil Hall, and Phillips hastily conferred with the executive committee. As the meeting was about to start, Higginson broached his plan for freeing Burns by force, believing that he had the committee's unanimous support. By then, however, Phillips had already left this gathering to address the crowd in the main hall, so Higginson had not, in fact, consulted him. Later, Phillips was to write Higginson, "That you did not tell me and thus give me a chance to help you instead of making a fool of myself in Faneuil Hall, I'll never forgive you."[43]

Phillips found himself in an excruciating situation, sure that Loring

41. Bartlett, *Phillips*, 173–84; Tilden Edelstein, *Strange Enthusiasm: A Life of Thomas Wentworth Higginson* (New York, 1970), 155–74, provides a general basis for this paragraph and for the narrative of the Burns affair in the following paragraphs. See also Ann W. Weston to "Dear Folks," May 30, 1854, Weston Papers.

42. Phillips, "The Removal of Judge Loring" in his *Speeches*, 185–86 and *passim*.

43. Edelstein, *Strange Enthusiasm*, 160–65; Phillips to Thomas Wentworth Higginson, June 14, 1854, Higginson Papers.

Telegraphic Despatch.

Slavery Triumphant !!

FREEDOM KNEELS TO PIRACY !!!!

Boston, Friday Morning, 10 o'clock, A. M.

Commissioner **LORING !!** has ordered **BURNS** to be given up, and the Military are now out in full force to **PROTECT** the **VILLIANY** of **SLAVE GOVERNMENT !!** and sustain a band of **INHUMAN KIDNAPPERS** on soil consecrated to **FREEDOM** by the Blood of our Fathers !!!!!

" O Lord, God, to whom vengeance belongeth ; O God, to whom vengeance belongeth, show thyself.

" Lord, how long shall the wicked, how long shall the wicked triumph ? "

Southbridge, June 2, 11 o'clock, A. M.

Abolitionists used handbills like this one, dated 1854, to rouse Bostonians against the Fugitive Slave Law.

had already privately condemned Burns and unaware that Higginson and fifteen armed men were awaiting a signal to attack the courthouse. Again he found himself thrown back on appeals to the crowd that they mass in an orderly assembly around the courthouse and use their presence to prevent the soldiers from taking Burns away. It was the same impotent advice he had given just before Thomas Sims had been marched off to slavery. "My resolution is," he told the audience, "that I will try to behave in this case, so that we will wipe away the stain of Thomas Sims, so that no kidnapper shall dare to show his face in Boston. Make your resolution as I do," Phillips implored. "See that man [Burns] for yourselves and never lose sight of him, so long as his feet rest on Massachusetts soil. Who says aye to that?" His speech, like Parker's that followed, was hotly passionate. "Their words marched on as 'armed *battalia*,'" one member of the audience remembered. Neither speaker urged violence, but by the time Parker concluded, the crowd was becoming a mob that cried out for action. Phillips returned to his feet, and projecting his most stentorian platform voice, he demanded a restoration of order while pleading that five hundred well-disciplined volunteers join him in surrounding the courthouse. It would be a "fatal step," he argued vehemently, were the meeting to dissolve into a "tumultuous, aimless, purposeless mob."[44]

At that precise moment, Higginson's agent, standing in the crowd, cried out a prearranged signal that blacks had just begun "storming the Court House."[45] The audience, having become the mob Phillips had warned against, rushed out, and he found himself nearly alone in the rapidly emptying hall. He did not follow after but, disheartened, joined Edmund Quincy and Phoebe Garnaut for the walk back to Essex Street. Once again, as in the Sims affair, the republican who exalted order felt he had been overwhelmed by the fearful passions he had so often ascribed to slavery.

The next day, Phillips learned that Higginson's violent experiment had been defeated, too. When the crowd had rushed from Faneuil Hall, Higginson's men had used this distraction to attack the courthouse but had failed. They had killed a guard, however, and President Franklin Pierce reacted quickly, sending a telegram to Boston's federal marshals. "Your conduct has been approved," it read. "The law must be enforced."

44. *Liberator*, June 2, 1854.
45. *Ibid.*

Two fresh companies of Marines soon arrived to bolster the garrison at the courthouse. Phillips, fearing personal reprisals for the death of the guard, sent Phoebe Garnaut and the Phillips' maid, Polly, to a neighbor's house for the night. Ann, however, refused to leave home, even though some of her own loved ones now found themselves behaving like fugitives in their militarily occupied city.[46]

Defeated at every turn, Phillips found himself reduced to helpless speechmaking and to sitting in the courtroom while Loring moved Burns's trial to its conclusion. Outside, troops continued to pour into Boston. Abolitionists claimed that there were twenty-two companies, more than a thousand soldiers, stationed in the city, carrying live ammunition. From Phillips' perspective, it became difficult to decide where was the more brutal violation of liberty—in Loring's courtroom or in the streets of his beloved city. The alternative choices merged, however, when, after four days of trial, Loring ordered Burns back to slavery and the militia formed up in front of the courthouse to execute the order.

Nearly fifty thousand people jammed into the street leading from the courthouse to the wharf, where a ship awaited Anthony Burns. The police, unable to disperse the crowd, contained it on the sidewalks by standing on the curbs in close ranks, side by side, with their arms interlocked. Marines, meanwhile, formed into a mounted cortege, and deputy marshals assembled on foot around Burns. They attempted to manacle him but thought again when Burns swore that he would fight if they tried it. Then Phillips appeared with Parker and Dana to wish him farewell, promising that they would continue to seek his freedom. The procession began moving forward to loud cries of "Shame! Shame!" Flagstaffs on public buildings carried the Stars and Stripes at half mast or upside down, shopkeepers draped their storefronts in black, and people hung out of upper windows, jeering and spitting at the passing soldiers. As the armed procession crossed Commercial Street, the crowd surged through the police cordon toward Burns, and the Marines charged with swords drawn, seriously wounding several people. With order restored, the troops broke into raucous choruses of "Carry Me Back to Old Virginny" as they moved Burns onto the ship. In striking contrast to the terrorized state in which Phillips had first found him, Burns now comported himself with insulted dignity. Phillips understood that he had met a remarkable man and that he had become deeply attached to An-

46. Ann W. Weston to "Dear Folks," May 30, 1854, Weston Papers.

thony Burns the person, not just to his cause. The realization added even more to the terrible despondency that was now beginning to overcome him with defeat.

Phillips plunged into a period of deep depression in the aftermath of the Burns affair. His pride in his self-control and his hatred of sentimentality rarely allowed him to reveal in his letters more than the outlines of his feelings. Finally, though, he shared some of the abiding anger and remorse with his old friend Elizabeth Pease in faraway England. That he waited nearly two months before writing to her suggests the depths of Phillips' anguish and also the difficulty he had in expressing his emotions while keeping them firmly in hand. "'Twas the saddest week I ever passed," he assured her. Though friends had insisted that the Burns outrage would make many converts for abolitionism, Phillips admitted he had been unable "to think of the general cause." Instead, his mind had remained transfixed by his own personal failure to help Burns, even as this fugitive had "cast his case on our consciences and placed his fate in our hands. I could not forget the man in the idea." For the next eight weeks, he informed Pease, he had struggled to control his preoccupation with Anthony Burns, "to think more of the 2,000,000 [slaves] and less of the individual," but even this attempt to quiet his guilty memories did not relieve his depression. Worse still, he feared that Burns's recapture really did not matter to most people. "Like Uncle Tom's Cabin and all such shams," its public impact was proving "far less and general than thoughtless folk anticipated." Abolition might "gain a few hundred," he granted, "but the mass settles down very little different than before." With this admission, abolitionism's confident philosopher glimpsed the terrifying prospect that there was no sure, steady advance in public opinion after all, and if this was actually so, why agitate? Why contribute great oratory to the cause? Why try to inspire the dwindling fellowship of the American Anti-Slavery Society? Why assume that Yankees cared for, or even remembered, their revolutionary legacies of republican freedom? Suddenly Phillips found his most fundamental assumptions and goals opened to an endless questioning that implied its own refutation.[47]

Yet he continued his unusually confessional letter, looking next to the nation at large, and felt his despondency intensify. "Indeed, the Government has [been] taken into the hands of the Slave Power completely,"

47. Phillips to Pease, August 7, 1854, Garrison Papers, BPL.

he lamented to Pease. The political bridge between Washington and Faneuil Hall that he had described so eloquently had, he feared, collapsed. Perhaps it had never existed. "In *national* politics we are beaten," he lamented. "There is no hope." After devouring Kansas and Nebraska, the slave power would soon annex Cuba and Mexico, for in America, he reminded Pease, "events hurry forward with amazing rapidity." He foresaw in his gloom the erection of a "vast slave empire, united with Brazil, darkening the whole West. The horizon was never so dark," he wrote. "Our union, all confess, must sever on this question—It is now, with 9/10, only a question of time." To his horror, the full fruits of moral suasion might well be total dominion by the slave power over the entire western hemisphere.[48]

This dismaying thought drove Phillips' focus inward and brought him face-to-face with his gravest misgivings of all. Perhaps, he feared, he had misunderstood his own deepest spiritual resource, history itself. "How much we have to unlearn as life advances," he admitted to Pease. "History and biography, and more specially the history of philosophy must be written over again as soon as men really grow liberal toward each other, discard the concept of *tolerance*—which itself *implies* . . . a right to be otherwise—and see every man's *right* to have his own opinion." The range of disturbing personal and political implications raised by the Burns tragedy now made Phillips wonder whether he had ever understood history correctly in the first place. Perhaps he had been reading the misguided words of narrow, ignorant thinkers who had no idea of what true liberty really meant.[49]

Phillips could affirm only one thing to Elizabeth Pease as he closed this tortured letter, and that was the inspiration of Ann Phillips. Slavery's conquests did not extend inside 26 Essex Street, Phillips realized, or sully the character of the dear person he lived with there. Despite Ann's disheartening health, she remained, he wrote, "in most excellent and cheerful spirits—interested keenly in all good things." Ann, he continued, is "so much my motive and prompter in every good thing" that "I sometimes tell her . . . that I fear, should I lose her, there'd be nothing left of me worth your loving."[50] Ann, as he was finally revealing, provided him with his last spiritual resources. Fortunately, they were also

48. *Ibid.*
49. *Ibid.*
50. *Ibid.*

his best ones. As it turned out, it was her act of crucial support that gave Phillips the strength to slough off his terrible misgivings and renew his sense of commitment by expanding it.

Just after Phillips wrote so despondingly to Elizabeth Pease, he and Ann made a most fateful decision. They finally accepted the awful fact, which Dr. Munde's Water Cure had reconfirmed, that Ann would never get well.[51] This courageous step not only marked a new departure in their relationship but opened the most significant phase of Wendell Phillips' career as well. There would be no more wasted months at health spas; they would vacation each summer, but for pleasure only. Ann would learn to stay at home without him for weeks at a time, attended by Polly and Phoebe only. She would manage her pain without the help of her nurse-lover, the person who understood her as no other could. He would set out to become a nationally prominent public speaker by touring far from Essex Street, where he could encounter a listening public of unprecedented size. A sprawling grid of track now linked Boston to the rising cities of the Ohio Valley and the Great Lakes Basin, and in three weeks time, Wendell could speak to tens of thousands. Stenographic reports would, in turn, allow newspapers to reprint his spoken words *verbatim* the following day. He was about to burst from the confines of Tremont Temple, Faneuil Hall, and the routine meetings and publications of the antislavery societies, seeking to become America's "second Cicero," just as he had dreamed since his youth. As in his marriage and choice of vocation, Phillips again resolved a terrible spiritual crisis by taking on a formidable new challenge, and again Ann was his primary inspiration and support—this time at great sacrifice to herself.

On November 20, 1854, Phillips set out on his first "abolitionizing trip," as Ann soon called them. He was to make dozens of them during the next quarter century. The list of those who would join Phillips at the podium at his various stops included Horace Greeley, editor of the New York *Tribune*; Salmon P. Chase, Ohio's new Free-Soil party senator; Antoinette Brown, the dynamic feminist, Cassius M. Clay, a hard-bitten political abolitionist from Kentucky; Ralph Waldo Emerson, the transcendentalist sage; and Joshua R. Giddings, one of the most radical anti-

51. One month after the letter to Pease, Oliver Johnson wrote to Phillips to discuss arrangements for a speaking tour that would necessitate his first extended trip away from Ann, a trip he would not have made without gaining her consent. See Johnson to Phillips, September 7, 1854, Blagden Papers.

slavery politicians ever to sit in the House of Representatives.[52] Phillips would make major stops in Utica, Rochester, Syracuse, Detroit, Cleveland, and Cincinnati, before finishing with three days in Philadelphia. The impressive variety of his fellow speakers and the wide-ranging itinerary suggested the extent of the audience that Phillips now sought.

The moment he had left 26 Essex Street, Ann began fretting that he had forgotten his brush, comb, and other personal items. "I hope you have got socks and bonnets enough, but I'm afraid not," she wrote him the next day. "I see so many in your drawers. So you see little Bessie will worry for fear that her Gra is not comfortable."[53] In later letters Ann would often write of her pain and loneliness to her traveling husband, but her first letter sent him off fully loved and much appreciated. A few days later, Ann received a small measure of the recognition she so clearly deserved in the form of a letter from Samuel J. May, who was a good friend and also one of Wendell's local tour sponsors. He knew what a great sacrifice Wendell's trip meant for Ann, and so he told her how much he appreciated her for "letting him come away for so long." Besides, he added, only half in jest, "we have it on high authority . . . that you prepare his lectures for him, so we are under still greater obligation to you."[54]

Before Phillips had departed, however, he had taken steps to resolve the two most important legacies of the Burns affair. The first involved his last promise to Anthony Burns himself, which Phillips redeemed by helping to purchase Burns's freedom. Later, of course, Phillips was to sponsor and advise Burns when he was a student at Oberlin College. The second legacy concerned Edward G. Loring, against whom Phillips launched a personal crusade, demanding his removal from the bench on the grounds that he had proven unfit to administer the law in Massachusetts. It was a task that required three years of testifying, petitioning, and general public hounding, but finally, in 1857, Phillips was to have the satisfaction of reading that the governor of Massachusetts had relieved Edward G. Loring of his duties.[55]

52. Johnson to Phillips, September 7, 1854, Blagden Papers.
53. Ann Phillips to Phillips, November 21, 1854, and see November 29, December 5, 1854, all in Blagden Papers.
54. May to Ann Phillips, November 27, 1854, *ibid.*
55. Phillips, "The Removal of Judge Loring," 154–213.

NINE

The Orator and the Insurrectionist

"I regard you as providentially raised up to be the James Otis of the new revolution," wrote William Lloyd Garrison to Phillips in 1857. The year before, Thomas Wentworth Higginson had also offered him the same challenging thought: "Some prophetic character must emerge as the new crisis culminates. . . . Your life has been merely preliminary to the work that is coming for you."[1] The Kansas-Nebraska Act opened this new crisis, and in its aftermath Wendell Phillips began to fulfill this prophetic role that he too, of course, had long yearned to attain. After Stephen A. Douglas' bill became law, parties slowly collapsed, the nation lurched toward catastrophe, and Wendell Phillips secured a formidable reputation as the North's most compelling sectional orator. Through forensics, not disunionist politics, Phillips finally began gathering the national power he had always wanted, even as he forced the radical voice of abolitionism into debates that led to Civil War.

The Kansas-Nebraska Act set off a sectional footrace to the territories and triggered a disruptive train of events. Free-state and southern settlers became locked in guerrilla combat as they struggled to control the territories. Meanwhile, former Whigs, former Democrats, and Free-Soilers endorsed the Wilmot Proviso and coalesced to form a huge new sec-

1. William L. Garrison to Phillips, October 15, 1857, Thomas W. Higginson to Phillips, November 18, 1856, both in Blagden Papers.

tional party that called itself Republican. The Whig party fragmented, and the Democrats began splitting along sectional lines. In the presidential election of 1856, the Republican nominee, John C. Fremont, carried eleven northern states and received no southern support, showing well against the Democratic winner, James Buchanan. The Republican's motto had decried "Bleeding Sumner" as well as "Bleeding Kansas," for just before the election an outraged South Carolina congressman, Preston Brooks, beat Phillips' friend senseless with a heavy cane, avenging "insults" to his family's honor uttered by Sumner during a speech, "The Crime Against Kansas." The following year, the United States Supreme Court announced its famous *Dred Scott* decision, which seemed to guarantee slavery the right to move wherever it wished. Black people, the chief justice affirmed, had "no rights that white men were bound to respect."

Phillips denounced all these developments with a predictable mixture of distress, disdain, and self-vindication. His public appraisal of the new Republican party rehearsed all the old themes. After all, he emphasized, most Republicans were even more conservative about the Constitution and immediate emancipation than the Free-Soilers had been. He lamented their moral shortcomings, vilified their leaders, and occasionally gave credit to the most advanced of them when they defied their party's "half-measures." Phillips also continued zealously to preach disunion, for the Kansas conflicts and the *Dred Scott* decision, he said, only reconfirmed what he had first said in 1842, that every attempt to hedge in slavery with constitutional restrictions was doomed. In 1858 he found American politics as bankrupted as they had been in 1840. "I have nothing new to say," he admitted, as he rose to address the Massachusetts Anti-Slavery Society in 1857. "You will not be surprised that at these gatherings, repeated year after year, there is very little new to be offered. We only repeat the same exposition of principle, varying it by application to the latest facts."[2]

The continuity of Phillips' behavior was equally clear when he reacted to the violence in Kansas. He showed his usual ambivalence about bloodshed, expressing the hope that the fighting presaged peaceful disunion even as he pledged a hundred dollars to a rifle fund for the free-soil guerrillas. Preston Brooks's attack on Sumner aroused in him the

2. *Liberator*, July 10, 1857, and see Phillips' speeches reported on May 19, 1854, August 8, 1856, February 30, 1857, and May 21, 1858, for his specific views on major sectional events from 1854 through 1858.

same wrath as had the Burns and Sims affairs, and again he blasted the "corrupted" leaders of Massachusetts politics from the platform. When anti-Catholic nativism surfaced in Massachusetts as the Know-Nothing party, Phillips condemned it as yet another conspiracy of "cotton Aristocrats" against Irish Catholics, slaves in the South, and the health of republicanism in the free states. To all who remembered, of course, such words echoed his gestures to the Irish in 1842.[3]

All the while, Phillips continued as ever to sustain his fellow Garrisonians by emphasizing the overriding power of their movement and predicting its eventual triumph. He also acknowledged, however, that the Republicans now absorbed disunionist agitation far more completely than the Free-Soil party ever had. In moments of public candor, he could even be heard lamenting that after "twenty years of incessant strife . . . the treasury is empty, the hand is tired, the toil of many years had gained but little. . . . There is no Canaan in Reform. There is no rest ahead. All is wilderness."[4] In August, 1857, when Phillips made this beleaguered-sounding admission, northern disunion certainly remained as elusive and unpopular an ideal as it had been in 1842. Nevertheless, even as he confessed his deep discouragement, Wendell Phillips had also begun to make his name as a public speaker without peer, as the matchless orator of Yankee abolitionism.

As an undergraduate, one recalls, Phillips had once hailed the fast-multiplying number of books, newspapers, and pamphlets as the most important achievement of his own age, but he could never have foreseen the length to which Yankee culture would go to advance public enlightenment. As populations grew by millions, so did the literacy and sophistication of readers and audiences. By the 1850s, the North had become a hive of reading rooms, libraries, debating societies, and civic-minded voluntary associations, which were founded, staffed, and attended by the rapidly developing business and professional classes found in many cities and towns. Meanwhile, expanding networks of roads, railways, canals, and telegraph lines meant swifter, cheaper, and wider distribution of all kinds of information. Lecturers could now venture with unprecedented speed into places unreachable years before. In pub-

3. *Ibid.*, June 15, August 10, 1855, January 30, 1857; New England Emigrant Aid Society Papers, Amos Lawrence Papers, MHS; Phillips to Pease, November 9, 1856, Garrison Papers, BPL. For more details on Phillips' activities relative to these issues, see Bartlett, *Phillips*, 188–91, 199–207.
4. *Liberator*, August 14, 1857.

lishing, too, advances in the production of cheap reading materials meant that by 1847 an up-to-date press and new stenographic techniques could turn out twenty thousand impressions an hour and disseminate a speaker's remarks just as they had been delivered. Editors, moreover, gladly filled their newspapers with densely printed multiple columns, sometimes in several installments, that reproduced to the last word even the lengthiest of speeches. Newsmen assumed, quite accurately, that subscribers made few sharp distinctions between hearing a speech and reading it (a dichotomy far more significant for readers in an age of radio and television). Instead, both activities were seen as complementary parts of one's larger interest in remaining informed. As a result, a huge reading public now formed the popular orator's second audience, participating in lectures at one remove while scanning their newspapers.

Far and away the most popular of all these new educational organizations was the lyceum movement. Before the Civil War, every lyceum was self-supporting, controlled by a local board in each town that sponsored a lecture series. Nearly every ambitious northern community had such an organization by the 1850s, managed by its respectable bankers, attorneys, and commercial entrepreneurs, whose goal "was the mutual benefit of society." Those who joined thereby indicated their "wish to share their knowledge, and from the manner in which they associate, each may become by turns a learner and a teacher." It all amounted, most simply, to an effort to extend the goals of the public school into the larger community. Lyceum organizers promoted middle-class values among their town's citizenry, recruiting instructive speakers who would, they hoped, infuse their community with the moral direction that they feared individual families could no longer supply. Phillips, as a self-professed agitator, hailed this effort to promote self-improvement as "God's normal school for educating men, throwing upon them the grave responsibility of deciding great questions, and so lifting them to a higher level of intellectual and moral life."[5] In his assumption about social

5. Russel B. Nye, *Society and Culture in America, 1800–1860* (New York, 1974), 245–46; Phillips, "Scholar in a Republic," 342. On the relationships between speech, print, and information, see Alvin W. Gouldner, *The Dialectic of Ideology and Technology: The Origins, Grammar, and Future of Ideology* (New York, 1976), 91–137; Paul E. Cochran, *Political Language and Rhetoric* (Austin, 1979), 52–136. For the best treatment of the lyceum movement, consult Carl Bode, *The American Lyceum: Town Meetings of the Mind* (New York, 1956). See also John Mayfield, *The New Nation* (New York, 1982), 168–69.

aims, although not in abolitionist ideology, he therefore supported the Lyceum's ends completely. A well-run lyceum series might present in one season lectures on literature, science, philosophy, and current events, as well as humorous talks and travel accounts. A rich mixture of politicians, authors, and reformers—from Webster to Stowe—took to the circuit. National favorites included John B. Gough, the reformed alcoholic; Bayard Taylor, the brilliant travelogue lecturer; and increasingly, Wendell Phillips, who offered sectional inspiration as well as spiritually edifying entertainment.

Phillips developed a popular repertoire of noncontroversial, "elevating" topics. Audiences were eager to hear speeches titled "Chartism," "Water," "Geology," or "Street Life in Europe," but the universal favorite was "The Lost Arts," a speech Phillips repeated many hundreds of times and from which he made many thousands of dollars in fees. Read today, it seems an innocuous little talk. Phillips simply explains that most modern inventions of which people boasted so proudly had really been put to use ages before. In the realms of new discovery, in fact, there had actually been little progress for many centuries, said Phillips, reciting a string of fascinating examples. Ancient chemists and physicists, for instance, knew as much about glass, refraction of light, magnets, gunpowder, and metallurgy as any nineteenth-century scientist. Indeed, the engineers who had moved the Pelham Hotel in Boston (weight fifty thousand tons) only repeated procedures used in the sixteenth century by a handy Italian to set up a huge Egyptian obelisk in Rome. The theme justified itself easily as pure entertainment.

An audience of the time, however, would have recognized a powerful sectional message half hidden in the talk. Phillips always emphasized that these arts had been lost because privileged aristocrats had monopolized them in past times. In the nineteenth century, a democratic age, people had been forced to tear aristocracy apart in order to rediscover them and apply them for the benefit of all. He then began a paean to the same belief in free inquiry and the individualistic values of self-improvement that, not so coincidentally, inspired some of the North's deepest hatred of southern civilization. Remembering Phillips' reputation for extreme abolitionism, middle-class Yankee audiences knew, of course, exactly what he was actually driving at. "Today learning no longer hides in the convent or sleeps in the palace," he asserted. "No! She comes out into every day life and joins hands with the multitude." Astronomy dwells no more in the stars alone, but "serves navigation

The quick strokes of this pencil sketch suggest Wendell Phillips' animation as public speaker and agitator.

Chicago Historical Society, ICHi-18542

and helps us run boundaries." Alchemists no longer hoard the secrets of chemistry, which had now become the gift of the agronomist, "with his hands full for every farmer. . . . Our distinction lies in the liberty of the intellect and the diffusion of knowledge." Every individual, Phillips proclaimed, "has a right to know whatever may be serviceable to himself or to his fellows." For this reason, schoolhouses, town halls, lyceums, and churches—all dispensaries of democratic learning—were now the symbols of American culture, and "The care of Humanity" now constituted the nation's principal mission.[6]

Rome had once achieved all this and had yet relapsed into savagery, Phillips would warn in conclusion, asking "What is to prevent history from repeating itself? Why should our arts not be lost?" Citizens, he answered, must beware those who claimed an exclusive right to knowledge or who tried to keep art and science a secret from the people. Not once had Phillips mentioned either American slavery or the planter class, but not once had he departed from themes that made inherited inequality and hierarchy the mortal enemies of democratic knowledge and the programs of a free-labor civilization.[7]

Simply by inviting Phillips to lecture, local lyceums automatically created widening opportunities for him to speak of abolition. It was a plain fact, after all, that Phillips' claims to forensic authority were as a great abolitionist, not as a hydraulic engineer, though he spoke about water, or as a tale-spinner, though he also talked about lost arts. People obviously were drawn to lyceum meetings by Phillips' notoriety as "abolitionism's golden trumpet"; they wanted to measure their own beliefs about slavery against his. "The Lost Arts," though provocative entertainment, still furnished only a partial, unfulfilling exposure to the *real* Wendell Phillips, a Utica, New York, correspondent once complained. "Beautiful and golden as the speaker's oratory was, the audience, we think, was not satisfied," he wrote. Instead of "The Lost Arts," listeners wanted Phillips' "latest research and thoughts, lit up by the light of the latest events. . . . If a man (as Wendell Phillips) who has devoted his life to the negro question is to lecture, by all means let him lecture on the negro, or some subject akin to that."[8]

6. "The Lost Arts" is reprinted in Martyn, *Phillips*, 533–47.
7. *Ibid.*
8. The theoretical underpinning for much of my discussion of Phillips' rhetoric and the settings in which it took place derives partially from Erving Goffman, "The Lecture," in his *Forms of Talk* (Glencoe, Ill., 1981), 162–96, and from two fine essays

Lyceum directors, well aware of such complaints, sometimes found their meetings growing rancorous as they debated whether or not to permit Phillips to speak on slavery. As early as 1845, for example, the board of the Concord lyceum experienced great turmoil, including several resignations, before inviting him back to speak as an abolitionist. Phillips, in turn, manipulated these difficulties for his own ends by agreeing to lecture for no fee on slavery *if* the lyceum boards would also invite him to speak for pay on a noncontroversial topic. This gracious offer often relieved a divided board of the dilemma created by his notorious but popular reputation. Before proceeding directly into a lecture like "Chartism" or "The Lost Arts," Phillips would fashion an antislavery prelude, which he humorously called "The Portico."[9] He took such liberties because he knew full well that his audience came to hear him as an abolitionist, whatever his announced topic. After all, as he once shrewdly observed, people did not attend his lectures out of a sense of obligation but because they desired vicarious participation in the great events and controversies associated with Phillips' name. People did not say, "If I don't go, my neighbors won't do their duty. I'm sorry to waste the hour, but . . . I must set a good example for my children." Rather, he observed, the listener hastened to the lecture hall "because his heart is there a half hour before he is. He goes because he cannot stay away. . . . He goes to share in the great struggle, and glow in the electric conflict."[10]

As sectional tensions deepened and spread, Phillips made his abolitionist tactics even more direct, adding to his list of historical topics "Toussaint L'Ouverture" and "Crispus Attucks," his great heroes of black revolution. At times, he simply loaded his talks with keen antislavery humor. In "The Lost Arts," for example, he loved to describe an ancient Syrian's beautiful steel sword as so flexible "that it could be put into a scabbard like a corkscrew, and bent every way, without breaking— like an American politician." It pleased Phillips most of all when lyceum

---

by Donald M. Scott, "Print and the Public Lecture," in William L. Joyce *et al.* (eds.), *Printing and Society in Early America* (Worcester, 1983), 278–99, and "The Popular Lecture and the Creation of a Public in Mid–Nineteenth-Century America," *Journal of American History*, LXVI (March, 1980), 791–809. See also the Utica *Herald*, reprinted in *Liberator*, April 21, 1865.

9. Bartlett, *Phillips*, 124–25; *Liberator*, February 10, 1844, March 28, 1845, December 2, 1860; Aaron Powell, *Personal Reminiscences of the Anti-Slavery and Other Reforms and Reformers* (Plainfield, N.J., 1899), 86–87; Phillips to Pease, December 30, 1842, Garrison Papers, BPL.

10. Phillips, "The Pulpit," in his *Speeches, Second Series*, 264–65.

boards simply gave in and let him talk as he wished under their formal auspices. When they did so, of course, they became publicly associated with a sectional posture simply by attaching their organization's name to his speech. When Lee, Massachusetts, gave him his head, Phillips exulted to Ann that "the guns are spiked. . . . So the walls fall down and prejudice melts year by year—I see more and more the wide influence of the Lyceum movement in smoothing the path for other things."[11]

Phillips possessed the freedom to behave so independently because he had become a star. Following foreigners Fanny Kemble and Jenny Lind, he was among the first generation of Americans to achieve national visibility as popular figures whom people would pay to see. The public, already aware of his reputation, wanted to find out what Wendell Phillips looked like, how he behaved, and what he "really" said. News reporters, therefore, started publishing analytical pieces on all these topics, thereby assisting all the more in the promotion of Phillips as a public personality. Before he spoke in large cities, mass-circulation newspapers carried notices that drew audiences from great distances, and people hounded him for autographs, artifacts that testified to a personal encounter with the famous man. The casual researcher can stumble upon Phillips' "marks" in practically every northern historical society's autograph file, his signature commonly scrawled below his favorite slogan: "Peace, if possible—Justice at any rate!" As people entered the lecture hall, they did not simply expect to hear a man give a talk about slavery; instead, they were well prepared and eager to participate in a significant dramatic event, orchestrated by the powerful presence of Wendell Phillips. In no respect did Phillips disappoint them. His platform style was by all accounts arresting, his impact unforgettable.[12]

People often expressed great surprise at their first sight of Phillips, for his appearance greatly contradicted their expectations. He seemed not an energetic extremist but a humble, open, and friendly man. "Can this be the fiery reformer. . . ? Can this be the rank agitator. . . ? Could this easy, effortless man be Wendell Phillips?" Such exclamations echo through contemporary descriptions of Phillips' public demeanor. He projected great physical authority, to be sure, for he was full framed and athletic looking, with thinning sandy hair and a profile that grew more

11. Higginson, *Phillips*, viii; Phillips to Ann Phillips, February 25, 1855, Blagden Papers.
12. On audience expectation, see Goffman, *Forms of Talk*, 176–79.

rugged with age. There was an "absence of vindictiveness, or even sever-
ity, though not of firmness in his appearance." He seemed the complete
opposite of the flint-skinned fanatic. Instead, a "genteel man" stepped to
the platform, "neatly, not foppishly dressed," his face wearing a "pleasant smile." He carried no notes and stood directly before the audience.
Since he never used the podium, neither script nor props ever separated
him from his listeners. He suddenly but quietly seemed to leap "at a
single bound, into the middle of his subject." The "keynote to Phillips'
oratory," Higginson wrote perceptively, was its conversational quality,
raised "to the highest power." No other orator, in Higginson's opinion,
"ever began so entirely on the plain of his average hearer. It was as if he
simply repeated, in a slightly louder tone, what he had just been saying
to a familiar friend at his elbow." The moment Phillips began to lecture,
the psychological distance between himself and his audience collapsed
almost entirely. He "held them by his very quietness," according to Higginson, establishing a powerful atmosphere of intimacy with audiences
of many hundreds.[13]

As Phillips developed his subject, none could doubt that they were
hearing inflammatory language from an authentic extremist who aimed
his words at their deeper passions. Nevertheless, by every account his
delivery (so unlike Webster's) was absolutely calm. He looked, one listener recalled, "like a marble statue, cool and white, while a stream of
lava issued red hot from his lips." Another witness suggested similarly
that he "resembled a volcano, whose bosom nourishes inexhaustible
fire . . . while all without is unruffed and unindicative of the power
within." As he continued speaking, Phillips' voice would grow deeper,
and his sentences would begin following each other in "a long, sonorous
swell, still easy and graceful, but powerful as the soft stretching of a ti-
ger's paw." He used simple, democratic language, including slang con-
tractions, such as "ain't," often encased in short sentences. Yet, it
seemed that he never let a note of inelegance intrude as he maintained
familiarity with his audiences.[14] A certain E. A. S. Smith, no prominent

13. Higginson, *Phillips*, 265–67; Andover (Mass.) *Advertiser*, reprinted in *Liberator*, March 20, 1857; *New Englander Magazine*, reprinted in *Liberator*, November
15, 1850. See also Thomas W. Higginson to L. Higginson, July 9, 1845, Higginson
Papers.

14. Wyman, "Reminiscence of Wendell Phillips," 732; *Liberator*, August 6, 1852;
Martyn, *Phillips*, 493–94. For a discussion of elocution and speaking style in relation
to the impact of lecturing, see Goffman, *Forms of Talk*, 162–96.

abolitionist or culture critic, summed up his reaction on first hearing Phillips:

> I have never been so completely absorbed by a speaker. . . . He had all the ease and manner of one who is the perfect master of his subject and is confident of its truth and all the grace of a graceful man. The topics that he touched upon were all powerful, finely illustrated, and it appeared to me that they must convince every one there that they must be up and doing. His manner was so easy and every thing about his address so informal that I thought we might [call it] a talk rather than an address.[15]

In one way or another, all these responses suggest the crucial forensic point that goes far to explain why audiences found Phillips so captivating. He was a complete master of what sociologist Erving Goffman has called "fresh talk," the speaker's ability to appear immediately receptive to the feelings of his audience, even as he speaks with seeming authenticity of his own thoughts and emotions. The effect is one of complete spontaneity, unencumbered by physical props and rhetorical "noise" (exaggerated gestures, superficial hyperbole, or stumbling diction), which tend to heighten the audience's sense of distance from the speaker. Phillips, in other words, conveyed the impression that he was revealing his true self as he spoke, offering his listeners "a sort of common people honesty," as one reporter described it. He appeared to be a "plain, honest man that loves sincerity and the truth . . . and can tolerate no mock shows or false dignity." Another witness agreed, "He opens his heart to you as the spring buds do theirs. You never think of asking from whom he learned to do so." Thoreau had the same impression, observing that Phillips' rhetoric was unique because he was "at the same time an eloquent speaker and a righteous man." All these observations echo precisely what Phillips' college friends had said of him decades before, that he was transparent and wholly without guile.[16]

It was all arrestingly simple. Phillips seemed to stand before each individual in his audience and say honestly what was on his mind. He "forces upon his audience the belief that he is speaking exactly the convictions of his own understanding," one observer noted. Moreover,

---

15. E. A. S. Smith to Caroline Weston, n.d., Weston Papers.
16. *Liberator*, March 20, 1857, December 4, 1863, March 25, 1845.

Phillips projected this impression so placidly that his most denunciatory words actually made his listeners feel serenity. (Demagogues, Phillips had always believed, inflamed the passions of mobs. Orators, by contrast, elevated audiences' interests.)[17] His words seemed like "oil on the troubled billows of the chafed sea; he rebukes the winds of strife and the waves of faction. . . . The severe front of a turncoat or tyrant present begins to relax. . . . He is the mobber of mobs." The point is crucial. Phillips' speeches have always repelled or inspired modern readers (depending on their politics) for their unabashedly extremist language. The listeners of his day likewise reacted within this range of judgment, but unless intent on harassing him, audiences never felt that Phillips was trying to intimidate them or to lead them to abandon their emotional self-control. "How well he speaks," enthused another reporter, confirming this aspect of Phillips' appeal. "No waste of power. No 'bursts of eloquence.' Everything is subdued, strong, and telling. He steals upon the audience . . . and surprises them into enthusiasm." As all these qualities came together, listeners found themselves imaginatively lifted beyond the confines of the lecture hall, emotionally absorbed in Phillips' actual speech. "You heard him . . . an hour, two hours, three hours," a colleague recalled, "and were unconscious of the passage of time. . . . He had exactly the manner of an agitator. [But] it was entirely without agitation."[18] In rhetoric, as in so many parts of his life, from marriage to social ideology, self-control once again provided the basis of self-expression. This time, self-control allowed Phillips to achieve spontaneous interaction with his audiences, orchestrated in the same general way that he managed so much else, with a blending of "fire and ice." The experience, from the viewpoint of lyceum managers, was certainly worth Phillips' $250 fee.

There was much more to Phillips' rhetorical power than style, however. In successful forensics there is a point at which content and manner unite and begin to reinforce each other, endowing the orator's presentation with a compelling unity. What Phillips actually said, therefore, was just as important as his way of expressing himself, for the two elements seemed to combine in a single artistic creation. Audiences felt invited to respond to his speeches in toto, as one might to a provocative painting or piece of sculpture. One commentator, suggesting that

17. Phillips, "Attachment to Ancient Usages."
18. *Liberator*, December 15, 1850, February 19, 1855; Martyn, *Phillips*, 493.

Phillips' rhetorical artistry evoked pictures of "a beautiful damsel in *deshabille*" wrote: "His quotations, then, are ringlets rolled up in papers, and the main part of his lecture like a loose gown which now and then reveals a neck of pearl and a voluptuous bust of snowy whiteness and beautiful proportions."[19] Another observer, writing for the moderate Republican *Ohio State Journal*, also found Phillips' artistic synthesis remarkable, but chose a military rather than a sensual metaphor to describe it: "Those simple, brief sentences of which his speeches are made up, form a coat of mail so cunningly and closely wrought that no lance can pierce it." Phillips' friend and son-in-law George W. Smalley resorted to classical parallels: "There was much of the Greek in him; the sense of ordered beauty and art. . . . They were still the more evident when you heard him. . . . The symmetrical quality of mind and speech, which is almost the rarest in modern oratory and modern life."[20] A sensual maiden, chain mail, and Grecian symmetry—the diversity of imagery that Phillips' rhetoric inspired also suggests some of the deeper reasons why people flocked to hear him. By opening his rhetorical world to others, he allowed each listener to explore powerful imaginative visions of his or her own creation.

Yet the writer from the *Ohio State Journal* went on to register a warning about Phillips' speeches, which was actually a compliment of the highest order: "For the present generation, he is a most dangerous agitator. Wendell Phillips is the subtlest, stubbornest fact of the times." Continuing, this critic next touched on the most significant political element of Phillips' oratorical power. Phillips, he emphasized, had an unmatched ability to "take premises which we all grant to be true" and to "weave them into an enchantment of logic from which there is no escape." In other words, Phillips anchored the content of his rhetoric firmly in republican political axioms that few in his audience were inclined to question; no matter how extreme his doctrine, he always enunciated it in the dominant language of northern political culture. When, for example, he propounded disunion, this analyst continued, Phillips pictured it as the essence of patriotic freedom, which left "God's natural laws to work out their own solution" in destroying tyranny. "You are hurried along by reasoning like this," the reporter complained, "and

19. *New England Magazine*, reprinted in *Liberator*, October 15, 1850.
20. *Ohio State Journal*, reprinted in *Liberator*, April 5, 1861; Smalley, "Memoir of Phillips," 141–42.

cannot make a ready answer. The more you consider it, the more mer-
cilessly logical it appears. It strikes deep and pervades the ideas you have
cherished." Still another critic, equally impressed by Phillips' republican persuasiveness, emphasized that he always "appeal[ed] to men on
behalf of old and established principles. . . . His position accordingly
supposes in his audience a pre-existing community of faith, a pre-existing wealth of affection for certain ideas and institutions."[21]

In the face of statements such as these, historians of the sectional
conflict put their judgments in jeopardy when they dismiss the abolitionists' "hyperbole" and "rhetoric" in favor of election results plotted
from computer tapes. Perhaps Phillips made only a few heart-and-soul
converts to disunionism, but there surely can be no doubt, in light of all
these statements about the impact of his speaking, that he exercised a
pervasive influence upon a receptive middle-class northern popular culture, sectionalizing it in ways that had enormous political implications.
In this most important sense, every one of Phillips' claims for the political efficacy of the agitator, no matter how self-serving otherwise, was
grounded in firmest fact, describing surprisingly well his formidable national career as a rhetorician.

"He had many surprises in thought and diction," one contemporary
recalled, trying to explain the sources of Phillips' oratorical powers.[22]
The level of understatement achieved here is surely sufficient to depress
any modern scholar who has carefully read the mass of Phillips' printed
texts. Epigrams, analogies, parables, tall tales, teeth-grating sarcasm,
torrents of personal abuse, one-liners, vignettes, candid self-revelations,
historical meditations, and large thematic structures crowd the reader
from every direction. By themselves, Phillips' speeches are worthy of
their own book, and it would be patently untrue to suggest that any
analysis of representative technique could be accomplished here without subverting the larger intentions of this biography. Yet one loose
blending of elements did appear so repeatedly in Phillips' speeches that
it is worth examining for a moment.

It was an endlessly flexible formulation that Phillips developed by
fusing into a single evocative vision America's history, geography, economy, and moral foundations. In the many such passages that appear in

---

21. *Ohio State Journal*, reprinted in *Liberator*, April 5, 1861; *Christian Exam-
iner*, reprinted in *Liberator*, December 4, 1863.
22. Martyn, *Phillips*, 494.

his speeches, he elaborated what might be called the "moral terrain" of America's past, present, and future, while invoking every compelling value of a dynamic, free-labor republic that imagination could supply him. It is, one hopes, better to furnish one example of this trope than to attempt any analysis. The following is part of a stenographic report by James A. Yerrington of what Phillips said on July 4, 1859, to an audience in Framingham, Massachusetts. It is not typical, except as it suggests themes that Phillips endlessly reorchestrated with varying emphases and in differing contexts during his speaking career:

It is a glorious country that God has given us, fit in every respect but one to look upon, this holiday of the Union, and seem worthy of the sun and the sky that look down upon us; for it is the people taking possession, by right, by inheritance, by worth, of the wealth, the culture, the happiness, and the achievements of the age. Show me such another! In the rotten, shiftless, poor, decrepit, bankrupt South, can you find the material that can erect a barrier against the onward and outward pressure of such a people as ours? Yes,—when the dream of the girl dams up Niagara, when the bulrush says to the Mississippi, 'Stop!' then will Carolina or Mississippi say to the potency of New England, with her three million educated, earnest, governing hearts,—say to her, in the tone of this worn-out, effete, rotten whiggery of Harvard College, 'Stop here!' (Great enthusiasm.) Why, by the vigor of such a civilization as ours, we shall take the State of Mississippi by the nape of its neck, and shake every decrepit white man out of it and give it into the hands of the slave that now tills it, and make America to represent the ideal to which our fathers consecrated it. Be worthy of this day! Create a sympathy among these toiling millions for liberty. What is it that makes us powerless? It is that your Church teaches us to look down on the black man; it is that your State teaches us, with this letter of Winthrop, that we have no duty outside the narrow circle of Massachusetts law. Here, under the blue sky of New England, we teach the doctrine, that wherever you find a man down-trodden, he is your brother; wherever you find an unjust law, you are bound to be its enemy; that Massachusetts was planted as the furnace of perpetual insurrection against tyrants, (loud applause); that this is a bastard who has stolen the name of Winthrop, (tremendous cheering)—been foisted into the cradle while his mother was out (loud laughter and applause); that the true blood of the Bradfords, the Carvers, the Endicotts and the Winthrops crops out in some fanatical abolitionist, whom the Church disowns, whom the State tramples under foot, but who will yet model both, by the potency of that truth which the elder Winthrop gave into our hands, and which we hold to-day as an example for the nation. (Prolonged applause.) This is my speech for the Fourth of July.[23]

Historians have skillfully analyzed the free-labor ideology that suffuses so much of Phillips' speech, and of course, a similar cluster of values had, from the beginning, inspired Phillips to frame his abolitionist visions. But no scholar, no matter how adroit, can ever recapture the evocative power and egalitarian universality that Phillips' rhetoric supplied to this ideology. All one can finally do is reread the printed pages and imagine what it might have been like to have actually heard the words. One must also remember that Phillips' audiences of respectable Americans, comprising commercial and business leaders and many farmers and artisans as well, did indeed come to believe strongly (as he asserted above), that northern "wealth, culture and happiness" must triumph, even by warfare, over a "rotten, shiftless, poor, decrepit, bankrupt South." Phillips, in sum, invited his audiences to picture a glorious new era of republican freedom, supported by unvarying law, biracial egalitarianism, and a prosperous economic harmony that incorporated all classes. In so doing, he also addressed the least common denominator of northern political belief, from which came finally the Republican party, with its uncompromising demand for "free soil, free labor and free men."[24]

All politically literate southerners and northern conservatives appreciated full well the dangerously disruptive qualities of Phillips' rhetoric. From a slaveholder's perspective, Phillips might seem a potent, aggressive monstrosity, an "infernal machine set to music," as the Richmond *Enquirer* once called him. Yet Phillips could also appear as the most maddening kind of effeminate incendiary. He warred with language, after all, not pistols or heavy canes, and surrounded himself with

23. *Liberator*, July 18, 1859. The reader is simply encouraged to peruse either volume of Phillips' collected speeches to learn more about what I am arguing and describing here.
24. See Foner, *Free Soil, Free Labor, Free Men*; and Holt, *The Political Crisis of the 1850s*, for the most useful analyses of republican political ideology in the prewar era.

others whom white southerners believed were as unmanly as himself—temperance advocates, pacifists, male feminists, and (of course) women. In the judgment of slaveholders, proud guardians of their own masculine positions, Phillips attacked as only a feminized coward would. "Perhaps if civil war should come," jeered the editor of the Baltimore *Patriot*, "Mr. Phillips would be surrounded by a life-guard of elderly maidens [and] protected by a rampart of whale bone and cotton wadding." Whether he was seen as effeminate or as a terrible machine, Wendell Phillips spread deep anger and fear far and wide within the planter class.[25]

Boston's conservative unionists had no easier a time of it than slaveholders from their famous local agitator. They, after all, had been forced to endure nearly four decades of unceasing Phillips invective. Plainly, they hated him, and for the best of reasons. He slandered their characters, assailed the morality of their economic endeavors, assisted their political enemies, degraded their reputations, sneered at their social pretensions, accused them of racial barbarianism, and indicted them as traitors to their city and state. They, in turn, vilified him in their presses, raised mobs against him, and packed his speeches with disrupters. In 1860 and 1861, as we shall see, Phillips literally risked his life, thanks to such opponents, when he walked the streets of Boston.

This unceasing local war finally became grist for the revealing newspaper satire of one "Solomon Sizzle," who quotes an unhappy textile merchant: "Wendell Phillips—I shudder with horror at the theme—I am nauseated at the remembrance that his name brings up." Phillips, the merchant complains, had turned Boston "into a reproach in our eyes and in the eyes of the world. . . . He has bruised us, he has made us sore; and the sores will not heal because he does not let them alone." Once, he recalls, the aristocrats had "spoken with authority" and had been obeyed, but now, whenever they organize a political meeting, "the very people who hear us talk go straight from us to him, to hear what he says about it, and laugh at the fun he makes of us." Finally, the merchant decides "there is nothing left to be done but to shoot Phillips." Although he fears "the noise, and the risk of hitting the wrong man" or "worst, [being] hit in return," he concludes that assassination should be tried anyway, observing that "no man will be to blame. . . . We can afford to make an example of him for the sake of peace and Union."[26] The mer-

25. *Liberator*, June 2, 1854.
26. *Liberator*, May 22, 1861.

chant's confused solution was, of course, also Solomon Sizzle's brilliant confirmation that Phillips had developed a pervasive impact on day-to-day politics in Boston. In an entirely opposite way than his father's, Phillips had actually become a community leader as important for his own time as even the greatest of the earlier Phillipses for theirs.

How, one finally wonders, did Phillips generate such seemingly effortless rhetorical power? The answer is simply that he worked at it tirelessly. To maintain his spontaneous flow of ideas and images he disciplined himself constantly not by memorizing or outlining his remarks but by working systematically in his Commonplace Book, as he had since he first invented this system as a Harvard undergraduate. Then, Phillips had begun copying passages that he wished to retain in his memory for speeches, and by the end of his life Phillips had written over a thousand pages, certainly a testimony both to his persistence and to his accomplishments as a reader, for the range of authors he drew upon was extremely large. He had actually become something of the scholar as well as the activist that he had fantasized about in his youthful meditations on history. Dryden, Swift, Burke, Machiavelli, Sidney Smith, Arnold, Paine, Carlyle, Dumas, Fontenelle, Jefferson, Madison, George Tucker, Coleridge, Robert Browning, Tocqueville, Gibbon, Peel, Milton, Harrington, Cobden, Bright, McCauley, the *Edinburgh Review*, the *Tatler*, Emerson, John Jay, Sr., and Henry Cary make up a representative list of citations over a two-year span.[27]

As Phillips assembled this rhetorical raw material in the Commonplace Book, he also developed various forms of self-therapy and intellectual play. Many of the passages he transcribed were actually descriptions of, or sayings by, other great orators with whom he felt kinship. Robert Peel, for example, attracted Phillips' admiration because, as he copied from an article, Peel was "the father of political out-of-doors agitation." Tom Paine, by contrast, wrote libertarian doggerel that Phillips transcribed, first, because he agreed with it and, second, perhaps, because it rhymed almost as badly as did his own. Revealing another mood, Phillips once set down a grand historical chart that outlined the rise of freedom in Europe from A.D. 957, when the city-state of Cambrai adopted uniform taxation, through the late thirteenth century, when the king of Aragon promulgated a charter of liberties. On still other occasions, he set down passages that were clearly meant as cautionaries to himself: "It

27. See generally the Phillips Commonplace Books, BPL.

is a difficult matter to set a weak man right and it is seldom worth the trouble. But it is infinitely more difficult, when a man is intoxicated by applause, to persuade him that he is going astray."[28] No one, however, can explain how Phillips transformed these fragments, quotations, charts, and aphorisms into golden rhetoric, though clearly the process was automatic, and his persistence was richly rewarded.

Someone once asked Phillips to comment on his lecture preparations. The speaker, he replied, should always "think out" the subject with care. "Read all you can," he advised, "Fill your mind." Preparation, bluntly, meant disciplined study, but delivery required spontaneity. "Forget that you are to make a speech, or are making one," Phillips instructed, for the powerful orator must first become inspired "with the idea that you are going to strike a blow, carry out a purpose. . . . having forgotten yourself, you will be likely to do your best. Be simple; be earnest."[29] His candid advice was of little use to anyone wishing to emulate him. Since his youth, the counterpoint between self-discipline and passionate self-expression revealed in this advice had given Phillips a special design for living, as well as for speaking, which no one else could possibly set out to learn. Ralph Waldo Emerson once observed that Phillips gave "no indication of his perfect eloquence in casual intercourse. How easily he wears his power, quite free, disengaged, in no wise absorbed in any care or thought of the thunderbolt he carries within."[30] It was, of course, quite possible to emulate Phillips' style of speaking, as many would, but never could another speaker hope to duplicate the sources of his peculiar forensic power.

By 1857, however, political revolution, not rhetorical thunderbolts, held greatest attraction for some of Phillips' abolitionist friends. For some disunionists the later 1850s had become times of terrible frustration, but to others it seemed as if substantial progress against slavery was finally taking place. One's judgment depended on one's view of that massive new antislavery enterprise, the Republican party, which had swept into so many northern statehouses in 1856 and had shown such

28. *Ibid.*, 220–25. I have purposely quoted from a very few pages here, to indicate the range of Phillips' activity in the books over a few days' time. (He dated his entries sporadically at best.)

29. Joseph Cooke quoting Phillips in the New York *Independent*, February 14, 1884, reprinted in Martyn, *Phillips*, 362–63. See also Phillips to Aaron Powell, n.d., in Powell "Reminiscences of Wendell Phillips," 86.

30. Emerson is quoted in Oswald Garrison Villard, "Wendell Phillips After Fifty Years," *American Mercury* (January, 1935), 96.

strength behind John C. Fremont. It also depended very much on which part of Wendell Phillips' ambivalent view of politics one chose to emphasize. By general Garrisonian standards, of course, all Republicans had grave shortcomings when it came to the Constitution, abolishing slavery, and treating blacks as equals. Yet William Lloyd Garrison had also begun to suspect that his years of crying in the wilderness were finally starting to be vindicated. These politicians (as Wendell Phillips had always said) must after all be claimed as the legitimate offspring of the movement that now called Garrison himself the founder. Garrison, in fact, came as close to endorsing the Republicans as possible in the 1856 elections, declaring in the *Liberator* that "if there were no moral barriers to our voting, and had we a million ballots to bestow, we should cast them all for John C. Fremont."[31] On the other hand, Parker Pillsbury, the Fosters, and several others saw Republican party growth only as a measure of the disheartening spread of proslavery constitutional compromise within the electorate. Certainly (as Wendell Phillips had always said) oath-swearing politicians like these Republicans deserved from Garrisonians not support but only sternest censure. To this faction, Garrison's warm words only indicated that he was growing soft and more eager for personal congratulation than for the slaves' freedom. "Advancing age always tends to conservatism," Abby Kelley Foster acidly observed, and Stephen S. Foster wrote vehemently to Phillips that abolitionists had always refused to be charitable toward well-intentioned politicians. Why, he demanded, should Garrison reverse himself now? "Our business is to cry 'unclean, unclean—thief, robber, pirate, murderer'—to put the brand of Cain on every one of them." He also wondered pointedly why Phillips had made remarks supportive of Charles Sumner in a recent speech. Was Phillips, too, losing his backbone? In 1857, Foster openly attacked Garrison for displaying a pro-Republican bias, and a major schism threatened the Garrisonians' ranks.[32]

Quincy, May, Maria Weston Chapman, the Weston sisters, Oliver Johnson, and the rest of the Boston clique sided at once with Garrison. Both factions began complaining to Phillips about "the impossibility of associating further" as conflicts sputtered over the next two years. By

31. *Liberator*, quoted in the *National Anti-Slavery Standard*, October 25, 1856. See also William L. Garrison to Helen B. Garrison, February 18, 1857, Garrison Papers, BPL.

32. Abby Foster to Phillips, June 24, 1859, Foster Papers; Stephen S. Foster to Phillips, March 29, 1857, Blagden Papers.

early 1858, the American Anti-Slavery Society and its state auxiliaries briefly faced open war when the Fosters and Pillsbury defied Garrison by declaring that moral suasion had failed completely. "Our people believe in a government of force," Foster emphasized, not in boycotting elections. "They wish to vote." He proposed a new abolitionist political party that would actually offer a disunion ticket at the ballot box. Higginson, always ripe for conflict, supported the Fosters while the rest of the Boston clique rallied to crush the idea. Still the Fosters persisted, hoping, in Pillsbury's words, to "build a great national party whose avowed aim shall be the overthrow of the government." By 1859 Abby Kelley Foster and Garrison had temporarily ceased communication, and she had refused to reassume her position on the Executive Committee of the American Anti-Slavery Society.[33]

These battles almost exactly foreshadowed the ideological differences that finally did split the American Anti-Slavery Society in 1865.[34] After 1857 the Fosters, Pillsbury, and many less well known abolitionists clearly equated their movement with egalitarian revolution to be accomplished by stringent political means. They would, moreover, hold fast to these goals even after the Thirteenth Amendment had abolished chattel slavery, arguing then that true enslavement would not be crushed until the legalized power of the state abolished the masters' social authority as well. Only then would black people actually be guaranteed political freedom and equality of economic opportunity. Garrison, Quincy, and the rest, however, were already looking to a day of jubilation when slaves would be free and they themselves would be vindicated as true prophets who could stand aside in triumph.

Phillips certainly shared the Fosters' anger over the North's timorous political attitudes in the later 1850s. "We had hoped for some . . . *reaction* if Buchanan were elected and when he crushes Kansas, and steals Cuba . . . and sets up the slave trade such a reaction may come," he

33. *Liberator*, February 5, 1858; Pillsbury to Giddings, February 14, 1859, Giddings Papers. See also Pillsbury to Phillips, July 15, 20, August 8, September 9, 1859, May to Phillips, June 10, August 6, 1859, Abby K. Foster to Phillips, July 24, 1857, all in Blagden Papers; Pillsbury to Nichol, February 17, 1859, Garrison Papers, BPL; Maria W. Chapman to Ann W. Weston, April 19, 1857, Weston Papers; Johnson to May, March 20, 1859, May Papers.

34. Friedman, *Gregarious Saints*, 255–80, discusses this final schism of 1864–65 in detail but gives these earlier conflicts little attention. Friedman's idea that Garrisonians sought prophetic vindication is, however, of great use to my discussion of this disagreement.

wrote Elizabeth Pease. "But all seems now settling down into the same old indifference. If Sumner's outrage did not rouse them, what can we expect will have an effect?" No less than the Fosters, he hated and envied the Republican stranglehold on antislavery politics. Whenever he heard that party claim antislavery supremacy, Phillips confessed in anger, "I think of the wealth of sacrifice, of the lives that have been devoted to this cause—I think of the tombs round which I have stood of those called from the struggle, [and] I say, 'In God's name beware how you peril what so much toil and so much self-devotion have purchased for us. This is holy ground that you tread!'" In addition, he showed himself wary of becoming entangled with individual Republicans, and he provoked protests from Senator Henry Wilson and Abraham Lincoln's law partner, William Herndon, for attacking their party so savagely. When Herndon came to Boston for a visit, Phillips snubbed him. Yet despite his abiding distrust of this and all parties, he nevertheless continued to claim the Republicans as direct products of Garrisonian agitation, and he opposed the Fosters' disunionist party proposal.[35]

In this way, Phillips' double vision of politics allowed him to live in both camps of feuding Garrisonians, arbitrating between them and relying on cajolery, humor, and painstaking explanation to maintain communication between political visionaries and prophets of righteousness. Still, at times he felt forced to issue blunt warnings to the Fosters. "Your danger and Pillsbury's," he wrote Abby Foster, "is intolerance—you are leaning to sectarianism and bigotry. You incline to suspect the honesty of those you cannot at once convince to your views."[36] The breach never entirely closed, but thanks in large measure to Phillips' diplomacy, the American Anti-Slavery Society continued for several years more to maintain a semblance of unity between its saints and its radical politicians.

As they fought over the politics of disunionism, Garrisonians of all persuasions also continued as a group to reflect an increasingly accepting attitude toward sectional violence. Sims, Burns, Sumner, Kansas, and *Dred Scott*—all became symbols to them of the triumph of proslavery force since 1850 and helped justify the Fosters' contempt for

---

35. Phillips to Nichol, November 9, 1858, Garrison Papers, BPL.; *Liberator*, August 14, 1857; Henry Wilson to Phillips, September 28, 1856, William Herndon to Phillips, March 9, May 12, 1857, July 2, 1858, all in Blagden Papers, HL.

36. Phillips to Abby K. Foster, June 30 (quotation), 10, 19, July 20, 1859, all in Foster Papers.

moral suasion. Other names, however, became symbols of an aggressive counterthrust by antislavery forces. There was Christiana, where the slave catcher had died, and Sherman Booth, the Milwaukee abolitionist who succeeded where Higginson had failed, leading a mob that freed a captive fugitive slave. "Jerry" recalled the liberation-by-force that took place in Syracuse, and "Oberlin-Wellington" referred to a similar action in Ohio. Phillips, along with the others, made his flirtation with violence increasingly obvious. In February, 1859, for example, he demanded that there be "no slave-hunting in the Old Bay State," assuring the state legislative committee before which he testified that whites were about to nullify the Fugitive Slave Law by force of arms. He also began delivering his "Crispus Attucks" and "Toussaint" speeches more and more frequently, accompanying them with predictions of insurrection and taunts at his white audiences for their "thin blooded" failure to match the courage of these black heroes. "It is a very easy thing to . . . imagine what we would have done" in Attucks's place, he declared, but "it is a very hard thing to spring out of the ranks . . . and lift the first musket." In all these ways, Phillips both shared and spread the conviction that every plantation had its own Toussaint, who was arming and would soon rise up.[37]

Phillips first extolled the heroic Crispus Attucks in Faneuil Hall on March 5, 1858, when abolitionists of both races gathered for a highly symbolic ceremony. It was organized by prominent black leaders William Nell and John Rock to commemorate Attucks' death in the Boston Massacre of 1774. Space in front of the speaker's platform was decorated with some of Attucks' personal belongings, along with a wealth of other relics that attested to black heroism during the revolution, including "a banner presented by John Hancock to a colored company called 'The Bucks of America.'" Rock and Nell invited Phillips to join them on the rostrum and participate in rituals to honor forcible resistance.[38] The setting and Phillips' words in celebration of Attucks that day accurately forecast some of the flesh-and-blood violence soon to come.

Not long thereafter, Phillips received a letter from Lysander Spooner,

37. Phillips, *No Slave-Hunting in the Old Bay State* (Boston, 1859); Phillips, "Crispus Attucks," 69–95. Friedman, *Gregarious Saints*, 196–222, is an excellent analysis of abolitionists' flirtation with violence.
38. *Liberator*, March 12, 1858.

his old foe in debates over slavery and the Constitution during the 1840s. This time, however, insurrection, not law, was on Spooner's mind. The letter asked Phillips' endorsement for a plan to infiltrate the South with armed cadres that would join with black escapees and poor whites to set up insurgent groups in the wilderness. "I think that in five years, 500,000 men in the North would join," Spooner explained with stunning innocence, "and that nearly all the non-slave holders of the South would be with us." Finding themselves surrounded and outgunned, the planter class would then capitulate in terror, free their slaves, "and the work would be done without shedding a drop of blood," he concluded lamely.[39] Hearing the idea, most Garrisonians, even those with the most tattered nonresistance banners, recoiled, but some militant souls, Parker, Higginson, and Stephen Foster included, bid Spooner Godspeed in his plan. Even if few volunteered, these supporters hoped that knowledge of the plan would "excite terror among the slave holders." Spooner showed Phillips his plan four months before he mustered sufficient courage to circulate it more widely, and Phillips' objections to it were practical ones only. The state would certainly crush such a movement as an act of treason, he wrote Spooner, for no voluntary effort like his could ever "compete with an organized despotism like ours." But Richard J. Hinton, a visiting British journalist who was particularly fascinated by the idea of slave revolts, amplified on Phillips' reaction to Spooner's fevered inspiration. Phillips, Hinton assured Spooner, had agreed to put up cash for printing five hundred copies of a handbill explaining the plan, which were to be distributed in order to "help to spread the panic." Indeed, by December, 1858, Spooner was busily mailing fresh copies. Short of actually picking up a gun, Phillips clearly was trafficking with insurrectionary violence as heavily as he could. He had experienced no bright illumination or flash of anger to bring him to this point, but by the end of this violence-filled, frustrating decade, he had, without thinking much about it, simply allowed his long-standing belief in the justice of armed resistance to assume dominance over his deep commitment to moral suasion.[40]

39. "A Plan for the Abolition of Slavery, Addressed to Non-Slaveholders," Lysander Spooner Papers, New York Historical Society; Spooner to Phillips, July 6, 1858, Blagden Papers.

40. Francis Jackson to Spooner, December 3, 1858; Stephen S. Foster to Spooner, January 1, 1859; Thomas W. Higginson to Spooner, November 30, 1858; Parker to

Phillips also knew, however, that some of his close friends were consciously sponsoring violent enterprises. Since 1857, some of his vigilance committee partners—specifically Samuel Gridley Howe, Parker,
and Higginson, as well as George L. Stearns and Franklin Sanborn—had
all been holding confidential discussions with a certain John Brown.
Brown was fresh from the Kansas border wars with the taint of premedi-
tated murder on his hands, having ordered through his sons the deaths
of six unarmed settlers there. Phillips had first met Brown in the home
of Theodore Parker, where he had listened as this magnetic holy warrior
had debated nonresistance with William Lloyd Garrison. Whenever
Garrison had appealed to the pacifism of the Savior, Brown had countered with bloody prophecies from Jeremiah. Soon Brown had become
most familiar in abolitionist circles, drumming up funds for his Kansas
campaigns from Free-Soil politicians as well as Christian perfectionists. Brown was now talking warmly with Higginson, Parker, Stearns,
Sanborn and Howe, as well as with New York philanthropist Gerrit
Smith, about fomenting black insurrection in the South. They gave him
cash and encouragement, and they asked few specific questions. Finally, on October 16, 1859, Brown and a band of eighteen descended on
Harper's Ferry, seized the federal arsenal, took hostages, and waited
for the slaves to rise. Two days later, Brown lay in prison seriously
wounded, his brigade having been routed by troops under the command
of Colonel Robert E. Lee. Waves of vengeful anger swept through the
plantation South.

Brown was indeed a personality of unfathomable personal power. Yet
his raid was no more a supreme act of his personal will than it was the
predictable result of the abolitionists' half articulated desire for a righteous triumph by blood sacrifice, which Phillips and many others had
indisputably helped to foster. Certainly it had been Phillips, far more
than anyone else, who had given compelling rhetorical witness to the
widely accepted prophecy that slaves would soon strike for freedom by
themselves. The Boston *Post*, a moderate Republican newspaper, put
this truth succinctly: "John Brown may be a lunatic, [but if he is,] then

---

Spooner, November 30, 1858; Phillips to Spooner, July 16, 1858; Richard J. Hinton
to Spooner, n.d. [1858], all in Spooner Papers, BPL. Friedman, *Gregarious Saints*,
196–222, is an effective treatment of the counterpoint between violence and moral
suasion in abolitionist attitudes. So is Wyatt-Brown, "Garrison and Antislavery
Unity," and especially Rossbach, *John Brown*.

one-fourth of the people of Massachusetts are madmen."[41] There was never a doubt that the orator had prepared the way for the insurrectionist. Within two weeks of his capture, Brown was arraigned, tried, and hanged for treason, as abolitionists and Yankee intellectuals sang paeans to his courage and inspiration.

Phillips was surprised not at all by the first news of Brown's attack. Back in 1857 he had given Brown a contribution, and years after the raid he told a friend that he was aware Brown "was working in such ways." Phillips had remained studiously uninformed of Brown's specific plans, however, even as close friends like Higginson, Parker, and Stearns became directly involved. He wrote to Brown to refuse an invitation, for example, in the fall of 1859, a date confirmed by his reference in the letter to a relapse in his own health that he claimed had occurred in August of that year. Actually, it was Ann who was ill, but clearly Phillips did not wish to make her condition his stated reason for declining to attend a meeting with Brown and some of his Harper's Ferry supporters. Nevertheless, the moment the news broke that Brown had been captured, conspirator Franklin Sanborn, obviously assuming Phillips' foreknowledge of the raid, beseeched the orator for legal opinions and news. Phillips then plunged actively into discussions of guerrilla conspiracies, concocting a wild plan to free Brown by kidnapping the governor of Virginia and then working out an exchange of prisoners.[42]

Obviously Phillips had been caught up in John Brown's general course of action well before Harper's Ferry and, like so many others, had become greatly enamored of him as an individual. For years Phillips had paid homage only to violent men and deeds, while counseling law and order. When he had been pressed toward resistance by the most excruciating circumstances, as in the Sims and Burns cases, he had not been able to bring himself to call for mobs or guns. Now, however, after several ensuing years of slave power victory, John Brown had acted for him, just as Elijah Lovejoy had once acted for him many years before. As in 1837 Phillips felt a deep sense of release from tensions and frustrations that he had been forced to control for so long. At once, after the

41. Boston *Post*, quoted in C. Vann Woodward, "John Brown's Private War," in his *The Burden of Southern History* (Baton Rouge, 1960), 48.

42. Bartlett, *Phillips*, 419, n. 6; Wyman, "Reminiscence of Phillips," 728; Phillips to John Brown, [1859] (photocopy), Frank Stanley [Franklin Sanborn] to Phillips, October [?], November 7, October 22, 1859, all in Blagden Papers.

fact, Phillips began to participate vicariously in the Harper's Ferry raid, offering lyrical praise and acts of devotion to his new hero-saint, John Brown.

Phillips now developed an intense concern for the welfare of Brown's family, who lived a hardscrabble rural existence in remote North Elba, New York. To help them, Phillips arranged fund-raising meetings, and as he did so, he also gathered up memorabilia that had belonged to the "great old man." A Virginia slaveholder unwittingly did Phillips a great favor in this respect, sending him a lock of Brown's hair, which the orator rejoiced over as a great treasure. He was greatly disappointed to learn that a friend, J. Miller McKim, "had not *given*, only *lent*, the envelope on which Brown marked his route" to Harper's Ferry. McKim did give him a pike used by Brown's son Oliver, and Phillips made it into an object of veneration, as he did a daguerreotype of Brown's wife "taken from Oliver Brown's breast after he was shot." With Ann's enthusiastic approval, Phillips made an even more personal gesture of honor to Brown, for he embarked on a pilgrimage to North Elba to witness the funeral of his insurrectionist hero. Traveling to Philadelphia he met Mrs. Brown and her husband's casket. With McKim he then accompanied her on the long trip back to the bleak hills of eastern upstate New York.[43]

His time with Brown's family moved Phillips deeply. "If you could have seen those young widows and children, in that rude roof on the hills, so serenely meeting and accepting their part in the martyrdom, as good and grand in their places as the old man in his," Phillips exclaimed to Ralph Waldo Emerson a short time afterwards. The spiritual wholeness Phillips attributed to Brown's family seemed to confirm their patriarch's stunning moral completeness, "showing what a grand whole his life was to have bred such." When others suggested that Brown's body should be put on tour as a means for fanning popular indignation, Phillips initially approved but quickly changed his mind when Brown's widow protested. Instead, he presided over a small family service in Brown's little house. The casket rested on the kitchen table, and Phillips

43. *Liberator*, December 9, 1859; "A Slaveholder" to Phillips, November 22, December 19, 1859, Phillips to Ann Phillips, n.d. [1859], December 5, 1859, all in Blagden Papers; Phillips to Ralph Waldo Emerson, December [?], 1859, in Ralph Waldo Emerson Papers, HL; Phillips to McKim, April 7, 1860; May-McKim Papers; New York *Tribune* reprinted in *Liberator*, December 16, 1859.

stood next to it, surrounded by a few friends and four grieving widows—
Mrs. John Brown, the widows of Oliver and Watson Brown, and the
widow of another fallen warrior, William Thompson. Phillips, in his eulogy, insisted that John Brown had not failed at Harper's Ferry, that he
had actually dealt slavery its fatal blow. "John Brown has loosened the
roots of the slave system;—it only breathes, it does not live—hereafter." Americans would surely consecrate themselves afresh to the
great cause precisely because Brown had given all, Phillips assured the
company. "Only lips fresh from such a vow have the right to mingle
their words with your tears." As the casket was lowered into the grave, a
black family from a farm nearby sang several of John Brown's favorite
hymns.[44]

"I am so sad about poor Brown," Ann Phillips wrote Wendell in November, 1859. "My heart aches for him. . . . I hope you talk about Brown
whenever you get the chance." He needed no such encouragement. Even
as the news of Harper's Ferry began to spread, Phillips burst forth with
waves of rhetorical inspiration on the subject of his newfound hero. He
set off immediately on tour, speaking in New York City and as far west
as Cleveland before returning to Philadelphia. When he was not spreading the mythology of John Brown himself, he was arranging for others to
do so, besieging Emerson, for example, with pleas to speak at John
Brown memorial meetings. "You know what a vein and stratum of the
public you can tap," he wrote, "far out of the range of our bore."[45]

Most important was the personal tribute Phillips paid his hero in a
series of extraordinary speeches. Only once before, when Lovejoy's death
had first driven him to action, had Phillips felt himself so deeply involved in someone else's heroic gesture. Lovejoy's act had opened a new
era in Phillips' life, lifting him beyond vocational crisis into the great
crusades against slavery. Now, in Brown, Phillips sensed the same moment of liberation for the entire nation and for himself as well, for
Brown, as Phillips saw him, possessed superhuman qualities. In his apo-
theosis of Brown, Phillips once again recapitulated the same all-pervasive
interplay of order and passion that had long ago shaped the inmost

44. Phillips to Emerson, December [?], 1859, Emerson Papers; Phillips to Ann
Phillips, December 5, 1859, Blagden Papers; New York *Tribune*, reprinted in *Liberator*, December 16, 1859; Phillips, "The Funeral of John Brown," in his *Speeches*,
289–94.

45. Ann Phillips to Phillips, December 1, 1859, Blagden Papers; Phillips to Emerson, January [?], 1860 (quotation), December 12, and [?], 1859, Emerson Papers, HL.

parts of his own life and thought. Brown had become for him a figure who had transfigured the national experience by the exercise of inner power. Harper's Ferry, Phillips therefore announced, had closed a corrupted era in American history, for Brown had released enormous forces, which were creating a pure new republican order that fullfilled the nation's oldest promises of liberty and fostered the spread of freedom as never before. "Why this is a decent country to live in now," Phillips rhapsodized.[46]

Whenever he spoke on Brown, Phillips made one crucial point. Although the "lesson of the hour," he always declared, was insurrection, Brown himself most certainly had been no bringer of social chaos. Obeying his abiding devotion to order, Phillips embraced Brown's violent actions by sincerely denying all possibility that the "Old Puritan" had played a subversive role. To charge him thus, Phillips insisted, was a "great mistake," for the forces he had unleashed at Harper's Ferry were anything but disruptive. Instead, Phillips insisted, they had put an end to a most turbulently immoral society. This, according to Phillips, was the essence of Brown's genius, for he had struck out boldly to suppress forever the chaotic tyranny of slavery. Anarchic Virginia, long in a state of "chronic insurrection," contained "no basis of a government," Phillips held, for she was peopled by a "barbarous horde who gag each other, imprison women for teaching children to read, abolish marriage, condemn half their women to prostitution and devote themselves to the breeding of human beings for sale." Into this pit of licentiousness had marched Brown, the bringer of civilization, armed with God's warrant to enforce iron-handed control. "He stood as a representative of law, of government, of right, of justice of religion," Phillips declared, and therefore only the opposite could be said of Brown's captors, depraved slaveholders characterized by Phillips as "a mob of murderers who gathered about him, and sought to wreak vengeance by taking his life." What Phillips had long ago praised in Lovejoy and before that in Burke, he now attributed to Brown with even greater force. Here was a man so wholly self-disciplined that he could act completely from self-will, forcibly bringing order where chaos had once reigned. "John Brown," Phillips exclaimed in triumph, "is the impersonator of God's law, moulding a better future, and setting it for an example."[47]

46. Phillips, "Harper's Ferry," in his *Speeches*, 274.
47. *Ibid.*, 271–72; Phillips, "The Puritan Principle and John Brown," in his *Speeches, Second Series.*, 308 and *passim*.

It is important to notice that Brown's rhetorical image, as Phillips constructed it, sharply contrasted with the version of Webster he had created in the early 1850s. Brown, according to Phillips, derived his vital inspiration from the traditions that the impotent Webster had forfeited to pursue selfish gain. Brown, in contrast to Webster, had marched into battle as the primal exemplification of oldest Anglo-Saxon freedoms, reclaiming traditions of liberty that stretched back to the England of "two hundred years ago," when the bold Cromwell had beheaded a king and had mustered a New Model Army in defense of freedom. An "impulsive, enthusiastic aspiration . . . which obeys ideas . . . with *action*" was the Puritan principle that Phillips believed had given Brown his animating strength; Brown was a "regular Cromwellian, dug up from two centuries" ago. Like the old opponents of Stuart tyranny, he had defied the state to defend liberty. Centuries ago "Puritanism went up and down England" and "tore off the semblance of law to reveal despotism," Phillips declared, as his emotional distance from the past collapsed almost entirely. "John Brown has done the same for us today," not "hesitating to ask what the majority thought" but striking boldy, inspired by the "great idea of crushing tyrannical power."[48]

As Phillips repeated these themes from platforms across New England and the Midwest, he fused his autobiography and rich historical imagination with his rendering of his subject. In Webster, he had discovered a hateful personal symbol whom he had rhetorically reduced to impotency. Brown, by contrast, seemed to him a towering embodiment of all the elements that the orator himself believed were giving emotional richness, spiritual harmony, personal vitality, and ideological coherence to his own life. Self-control and spontaneous expression, together with a powerful supportive vision of the past, had always supplied Phillips with inspired designs for living. Now, in his view of Brown he discovered a transcendent figure who united these elements, achieving a complete reconciliation of submission with liberation, restraint with passion, and tradition with revolt. "Prudence, skill, courage, thrift, knowledge of his time, knowledge of his opponents [and] undaunted daring"—these were the traits that Phillips saw fused in Brown's character. In addition, the Brown family was whole-mindedly devoted to their patriarch's cause; he was "girded about by his household." This family solidarity confirmed

48. Phillips, "The Puritan Principle," 295–300.

all elements of the vital symmetry. Brown's was no "spasmodic" act of simple passion, Phillips insisted, but the "flowering of sixty years," the supreme expression that endowed his life with perfect wholeness. "Everything about him grouped itself harmoniously," Phillips exclaimed, "like the planets and the sun."[49]

Phillips certainly appreciated that he and Brown were hardly identical people. Yet in this realization he identified with the "Old Man" all the more, for Brown, after all, had mastered manly action as well as talk, and Phillips knew full well that he would never be able to duplicate that mastery. Brown, as Phillips saw him, had achieved unmatchable levels of spiritual liberation and primal masculine energy. "The very easy thing [is] to say; the difficult is to do," Phillips admitted. For decades he had called from the speaker's platform for people to trample on the law; Brown had simply marched southward, gun in hand, achieving an eloquence in his deeds that no mere speaker could ever match. Brown, therefore, had shown the American people a "true manhood" that Phillips could only admire; he had stilled the chaos of slavery and faced death "with two hundred thousand broken fetters in his hands."[50]

As enraged planters escalated threats of secession, Wendell Phillips continued to talk. His principal themes, following his characterization of Brown, urged his listeners toward a final accounting with slavery. Disunion was now inevitable, he declared; it would bring either race war or the planters' terrified capitulation. Blanching at such doctrines, the Republican party's leaders counseled moderation and rallied voters to the standard of Abraham Lincoln. Yet to slaveholders' well-educated ears, the Republicans' message in the 1860 election and Phillips' urgings to violence sounded awfully much alike. Both Phillips and Lincoln, after all, demanded an America where slavery could expand no further. Both, moreover, envisioned a nation of "free people," economically self-sufficient and spiritually self-disciplined, whose creative energy would expand republican liberty from ocean to ocean. Both, in the final analysis, accused a morally barbaric, economically benighted slave power of stifling and corrupting the creative energy of American free labor. By 1860 much of the same broad counterpoint of order with liberation that

49. *Ibid.*, 303; Phillips, "Harper's Ferry," 274.
50. Phillips, "Burial of John Brown," 291–93; Phillips, "The Puritan Principle," 296, 302.

had enriched Wendell Phillips' portrayals of John Brown, had begun to inspire the fighting of the Civil War.[51]

51. Foner, *Free Soil, Free Labor, Free Men*, 1–72; Major L. Wilson, *Space, Time, and Freedom: The Quest for Nationality and the Irrepressible Conflict, 1815–1860*, (Westport, Conn., 1974), 120–47, 178–200; Richard H. Sewell, *Ballots for Freedom: Antislavery Politics, 1837–1861* (New York, 1976), which is the best narrative analysis of its subject, and a sensitive explanation of the relationships between racism, egalitarianism, and sectionalism in Yankee political culture. Slotkin, *The Fatal Environment*, 227–78 and *passim*, explores the relationships between sexual metaphors (like those Phillips used in reference to John Brown), racism, and class antagonisms as these bore on the larger political conflict over slavery.

TEN

Citizen Wendell Phillips

Sounds of competing voices rose from northern lecture halls as the 1860 elections neared, for in Boston and throughout the North, three great organizations contested for the future of the Union. The Democratic party had finally succumbed to sectional rupture. Northern Democrats backed Stephen A. Douglas and popular sovereignty, while John Bell of Kentucky and Boston's Edward Everett spoke for the Constitutional Unionists, offering sectional reconciliation and addressing the fears of Massachusetts' cotton industrialists. Republican candidate Lincoln was pledged to arrest the westward march of slavery. As usual, Wendell Phillips did not participate in the canvass. Instead, he and Ann vacationed from June to November in Milton, Massachusetts, with their friends George and Mary Stearns. "I am as idle as the trees and grow fat with them," Phillips wrote Samuel J. May complacently. He mourned the sudden death of Theodore Parker, discussed religion and abolitionism with his youngest brother Thomas, and labored over the tangled finances of his brother-in-law George Greene. Greene was ill, abused drugs, and believed that Christ was returning soon. He had trouble keeping track of his affairs, and Phillips worked hard to lead him back to economic self-sufficiency.[1]

1. Phillips to May, July 18, 1860, May-McKim Papers; Thomas Phillips to Phillips, June 16, 1860, Grew to Phillips, October 16, 1860, both in Blagden Papers. See the Mary Grew correspondence file and the Jennie Greene correspondence file, Blagden

Although he did not campaign, Phillips certainly became involved in the election simply by tagging Lincoln with the sobriquet "The Slavehound of Illinois." It was a typical Phillips turn of phrase, which referred to Lincoln's support as a Congressman in 1849 for a bill that had sanctioned the old 1793 Fugitive Slave Law. Phillips' larger purpose was, as usual, to expose the Republican party's antislavery pretensions, and the New York *Tribune*, as well as prominent Republicans like Joshua R. Giddings, issued strong rebuttals.[2] Phillips continued to sneer at Lincoln ("This huckster in politics . . . this country court advocate") and to accuse the Republicans of corruption, but he simultaneously displayed the other part of his political ambivalence by becoming increasingly optimistic. "The sky grows bright," he assured his fellow Garrisonians; their agitation was finally leaving parties and churches "broken in pieces." Showing his similarly divided feelings about the Republicans, Phillips characterized William Seward as a politician whose every gesture showed "his two hands filled with lies," but he also praised the very same Seward, then a candidate for the Republican nomination, as a leader who would "enter the Presidential chair, mean[ing] that his portrait . . . shall be painted with one hand upon the American Eagle, and the other on the jugular of the slave system."[3]

As the campaign progressed, the Garrisonian movement proved unable to sustain this ambivalence and divided along the lines set out by Phillips' double-mindedness. Garrison, Quincy, the Mays, Maria Weston Chapman, and others of the clique showed an ever-increasing disposition to support the Republicans. Conversely, the Foster-Pillsbury circle attacked the party and its abolitionist apologists with greater zeal than ever. Phillips as usual negotiated, cajoled, and tried to inspire everyone by lauding the beauties of disunionism.[4] By November, Lincoln had won, taking not a single southern electoral vote, and South Carolina girded for secession. As a war to save the Union drew ever closer, Phillips clung even more doggedly to disunion, the political foundation of his

Papers, for numerous letters regarding the problems of George Greene. Phillips, "Theodore Parker," in his *Speeches, Second Series*, 421–37.

2. *Liberator*, June 22, July 13, August 24, 1860; Herndon to Phillips, November 26, 1860, Blagden Papers.

3. *Liberator*, May 18, June 8, 1860.

4. Grew to Phillips, October 15, 1860, Blagden Papers; *Liberator*, May 18, 1860; and *National Anti-Slavery Standard*, October 13, 20, 1860.

abolitionist creed and the sole remaining support for unity among feuding Garrisonians.

Phillips had returned from Milton with Ann to Essex Street just before the telegraph confirmed Lincoln's election. Soon thereafter, on the evening of November 7, he stood before a crowded audience in the Tremont Temple, proclaiming the results a watershed victory for the American Anti-Slavery Society. For the first time in American history "the *slave* has chosen a President of the United States," he announced. "We have passed the Rubicon." Although Lincoln, as Phillips stressed, was "not an abolitionist, hardly an antislavery man," he nevertheless "consents to represent the antislavery idea," for behind the "pulling of wires and creaking of wheels" that manufactured his election stood the true orchestrators of sectional politics—the abolitionists. Lincoln, Phillips assured his listeners, was only *"in place."* Garrison was *"in power!"* The Constitution, of course, remained firm under Lincoln's control, and the Republicans would never be able to crush slavery until the sectional conflict grew so severe that it would "force them into our position" of disunion. Meantime, Phillips counseled, Garrisonians must agitate steadfastly and await the inevitable triumph. "Wait! Be Patient! In 1760, what Boston rebel boys felt, James Otis spoke, George Washington achieved and [Edward] Everett praises today. The same routine will go on."[5]

As abolitionists discharged these high duties, the spread of free-labor values that their movement had always championed would propel the North forward, Phillips continued. "Sewing machines lift women out of torture, steam marries the continents, and the telegraph flashes news like sunlight across the globe. Every step makes hands worth less and brains more," he rhapsodized. In the end, people would realize what disunionists had always known, that it was "impossible to make a nation with one half steamboats, sewing machines, and Bibles and the other half slaves." Not Lincoln's leadership but machines and morality, he said, would finally overwhelm slavery, for abolitionists would fuse them into a single potent force for freedom. Their agitation would endow "this mere industrial value" of America with "the nobler elements of national purpose and life, a love of right . . . a higher plane of Christian manhood." In this way, slavery would finally fall, Phillips declared, and the

5. Phillips, "Lincoln's Election," in his *Speeches*, 294–314.

abolitionists would stand vindicated as "the children of a purer civilization, the pioneers of a Christian future." Supported and inspired by this
moral economy, Americans of all races and classes would then unite to
fashion a "government whose cornerstone is Justice and whose top
stone is Liberty. Crowding into the shelter of its stately arches, I see old
and young, learned and ignorant, rich and poor, native and foreign,
Pagan, Christian, Jew, black and white in one grand, harmonious procession."[6] Wendell Phillips spoke many times of his vision of America's
grand future as an egalitarian, socially harmonious free-labor republic.
Seldom, however, did he frame all of its elements in with greater dramatic symmetry.

In so titanic a drama of forces and principles, Lincoln was simply a
pawn in God's most obvious design, which destined the abolitionists to
"sweep the board." Therefore, Phillips concluded, if the South truly
wished to leave the Union, the North should hasten its peaceful departure, thereby securing a victory no less majestic than that of 1776. Once
separated from the free states, the slaveholding oligarchs would find
themselves subjected to the ceaseless onslaught of northern antislavery
opinion and economic power. Slave insurrection might follow, or perhaps the planters would simply capitulate without a struggle to their
cultural superiors. In any event, Phillips maintained, Lincoln's election
only multiplied the reasons for continuing to demand dissolution of the
Union. In the wake of disunion, he foresaw "Northern pulpits can-
nonading Southern consciences; Northern competition emptying its
pockets, educated slaves awakening its fears. . . . Disunion leaves God's
natural laws to work out their own solution," he exclaimed. "Let us
stand out of God's way."[7]

By December, 1860, nearly everyone involved with Massachusetts'
industry was cursing Phillips for saying such things. Southern threats of
secession had begun to destroy the state's North-South trade as nervous
bankers clamped down on credit, mill owners laid off workers, and businesses failed. Seeking to placate the South, Amos Lawrence, Nathaniel
Appleton, Edward Everett, and other former Cotton Whigs pressed the
state legislature to repeal Massachusetts' Personal Liberty Law of 1842.
(Phillips responded by testifying for the need for a much more stringent

6. *Ibid.*
7. Phillips, "Disunion," in his *Speeches*, 369 and *passim*; *Liberator*, April 5, 1861.
See other of Phillips' statements on disunion in *Liberator*, December 2, 1860, January
20, 1861, and also Phillips, "Mobs and Education," in his *Speeches*, 319–42.

bill.) They organized Union meetings, circulated petitions favoring compromise, and hurried to Washington in a frantic effort to avoid Civil War.[8] Finally, they moved to overcome the abolitionists of Boston, and silencing the abolitionists came to mean, above all, silencing Wendell Phillips.

Hardly a citadel of antislavery, Boston contained many who sympathized heartily with all such plans. Lincoln had carried just a bit less than half the city's vote, and a Unionist Democrat, Joseph Wightman, had been elected mayor by a large majority. Mill hands and day laborers from outstate factories, seeking work, crowded Boston's rooming houses and nursed resentments against upper-crust extremists like Phillips who further dimmed their economic prospects by sermonizing on disunion. From early December, 1860, until late January, 1861, Phillips made four public appearances in Boston. On each occasion, predominantly working-class audiences greeted him with seething resentment or threatened him afterward in surly mobs. Following the last such confrontation, a riot-torn meeting of the Massachusetts Anti-Slavery Society held in the Tremont Temple, Phillips even appealed personally to the Republican governor, John A. Andrew, to call out the militia, but Andrew refused. Instead, the police chief, at Mayor Wightman's urging, closed Tremont Temple to the abolitionists before they could start their afternoon session.[9]

Phillips, of course, did everything possible to inflame the already angry atmosphere, speaking on announced topics such as "Mobs and Education" or "Disunion, the Lesson of the Hour." Neither did he design his specific remarks to soothe the feelings of his greatest enemies, union-loving "cotton aristocrats," whom he assailed as "narrow men, ambitious of office, fancying that an inheritance of millions entitles them to political advancement." He called them "bloated distillers, "some without the wit to keep the money they stole. Old families run to respectable dullness. . . . Snobbish sons of fathers lately rich, anxious to show themselves rotten before they are ripe."[10]

For years, Phillips had hated this so-called association of gentlemen

8. Thomas O'Connor, *Lords of the Loom: The Cotton Whigs and the Coming of the Civil War* (New York, 1968), 132–53; *Liberator*, February 8, 1861; William L. Garrison to Phillips, January 30, 1861, Blagden Papers.

9. For a more detailed narrative of these speeches and notes, see Bartlett, *Phillips*, 225–35. See also Lane, *Policing the City*, 121–25, for Mayor Wightman and his role with the Boston police.

10. Phillips, "Mobs and Education," 325.

from which he had long ago broken away. Seeing them as infected by the corrupting spirit of Daniel Webster, he had arraigned them ceaselessly for polluting the commonwealth's "moral economy" with "southern gold" and turning its politics into a playground for slaveholders. They, of course, had long reciprocated his enmity, and now, with renewed zeal, they rose as never before against him. Phillips welcomed the combat, clinging to his disunionism all the more fiercely and flaunting it provocatively in the faces of his elite opponents. After the first mobbing, a violent affair that occurred in a black church on Joy Street, Phillips eagerly challenged the powerful Amos Lawrence: "I hold you responsible . . . for this infamous proceeding, which has resulted in serious, if not fatal injury to ten of our colored citizens." Lawrence, Phillips charged, was the silent sponsor of "brutal associates" who had committed a "brutal outrage."[11] Meanwhile, Phillips wisely took measures to protect himself, collecting a bodyguard of young admirers like Oliver Wendell Holmes, Jr. (a distant relative), George W. Smalley, and Higginson, who were joined by various militant blacks. A neighborhood club of German turners volunteered as full-time guards for 26 Essex Street, and Phillips let everyone know that he now carried a gun. Twice, as they escorted him back to his home after speaking, his guards hurriedly formed a cordon around him to turn back cursing, spitting protestors. They left Phillips at home, grimly standing sentinel, holding the pike from Owen Brown that J. Miller McKim had given him.[12]

All the guards and precautions are an indication of the genuine fear among abolitionists that armed assassins had been hired to kill Phillips. None could deny that he had been marked as an object of "special violence," and Phillips did receive at least one private threat, as well as a carefully wrapped box that Ann feared might contain a bomb. She opened it to find instead only a dead cat.[13] Phillips also noticed several

11. Phillips to Amos Lawrence, December 5, 1860, Lawrence Papers.

12. *Liberator*, December 21, 28, 1865, January 25, 1861; Bartlett, *Phillips*, 303–305; "Reminiscences of Charles Slack" and "Letters of Lydia Maria Child," both reprinted in Martyn, *Phillips*, 303–305, 307–309; Smalley "Reminiscences of Phillips," 133–41; Phillips to Grew, December [?], 1860, reprinted in Martyn, *Phillips*, 305–306; Grew to Phillips, December 18, 1860, Maria W. Chapman to Ann Phillips, n.d., both in Blagden Papers; Phillips to Sidney H. Gay, October 18, 1861, Gay Papers; Howe to Sumner, January 20, 1861, Sumner Papers.

13. Johnson to William L. Garrison, January 19, 1861, E. W. Wedgewood to May, December 19, 1860, both in Garrison Papers, BPL; "All Up" to Phillips, December 8, 1860, S. A. Mapes to Phillips, November 30, 1868, both in Blagden Papers; Bartlett, *Phillips*, 230.

men brandishing arms in the crowds that attempted to waylay him. "I am glad he has a strong, brave wife," wrote Mary Grew to Garrison. She had feared that all this danger would devastate Ann's health, but Ann held up well this time, notwithstanding the cat.[14]

Phillips himself was greatly elated by his dangerous situation. Armed with his revolver and clutching his pike, he regarded himself as a defiant example of law and order in a city exploited by mobs and conspiring cotton brokers. He delighted in surrounding himself with his German bodyguards, chuckling to Mary Grew, "That's worth being mobbed for. There is some good in the world, despite original sin." Higginson confirmed Phillips' highly excited mood. As one of the protective entourage, he noticed "something peculiarly striking and characteristic" about Phillips' demeanor. Phillips hardly seemed angry, certainly not intimidated, Higginson thought. Instead, he projected "a careless, buoyant, almost patrician air," as if wishing to tell his Brahmin adversaries that "all threats of opponents were simply beneath contempt."[15] For Phillips, this was now a far different Boston from the city it had been back in the early 1850s, when overwhelming armed might, backed by the president of the United States, had crushed his efforts to save Burns and Sims and to dethrone Daniel Webster. Now, no Marine bayonets protected the forces of slaveocracy; there were only these "lords of the loom," whom he met face-to-face on the city's streets and humiliated, flaunting his version of aristocratic disdain. It was as close as Phillips would ever dare to come to matching the heroic actions of his beloved John Brown.

In February, 1861, however, when the crowds finally dispersed for good, Phillips showed that his outwardly defiant behavior had not left him in a triumphal mood. In fact, the mobs had actually unsettled him deeply, as became clear when he began expressing some altogether new concerns about law and liberty in Boston. In March he revealed some of these anxieties when he appeared before the state legislature to argue in favor of a proposal to remove the Boston Police Department from the control of the city's citizens. The bill provided that the governor appoint a board of commissioners, independent of the city's elected officials, to run the police force. In supporting this idea, Phillips argued that the recent riots had proven Boston's voters incapable of behaving in a republi-

14. Grew to William L. Garrison, January 13, 1860, Garrison Papers, BPL.
15. Phillips to Grew, December [?], 1860, reprinted in Martyn, *Phillips*, 305–306; Higginson, *Phillips*, ix–x.

can manner; they should therefore be stripped of electoral power over the police. Certainly it was a strange position for an agitator who had always demanded that voters keep their representatives under the closest possible scrutiny. Yet Phillips' stance was actually a clear extension of his reliance on positive laws to supersede the judgments of corrupted individuals and interests and so guarantee the expansion of freedom's boundaries. He had demonstrated this belief years before in his struggles to desegregate schools and transportation, and his position on the police represented a portentous foreshadowing of his approach to Reconstruction after the Civil War. Then, he was to demand that federal statutes and officials obliterate all hint of white people's localistic rights to regulate race relations and civic liberties at the expense of emancipated slaves.

In the case of Boston police, however, alcohol, not race, was the source of society's transgressions in Phillips' view. He maintained that since the city contained two thousand places that illegally sold liquor, friends and relatives of the owners and patrons of these establishments naturally elected public officials who flouted the law to protect these illegal traders. No wonder that the police force had stood idle as mobs attacked the abolitionists; they had been encouraged to do so by a complicitous mayor who was beholden to law-breaking tavern keepers. The "mob that broke up that Tremont Temple meeting reeled into it from the grog shops," but the mayor had not ordered the police to shut the bars. Instead, he had closed the temple to the mob's victims, the abolitionists. Therefore, freedom of speech and the right of peaceful assembly in Boston could be protected from a liquor-corrupted electorate and city government only if the state legislature intervened by agreeing "to take the police force of Boston out of *the control of its voters.*" Independently appointed commissioners were absolutely essential to guarantee equal police protection under the law to all classes and groups. "We want only the law. The law we shall never have if you leave us with the voters of the city of Boston."[16] The proposed bill did not pass, but Phillips pressed for it again when it reappeared before the legislature in 1863.

As Phillips' remarks suggested, Boston itself had changed greatly since the days he remembered when Beacon Hill residents had pastured their cattle on the Common. Between 1820 and 1860, the city's population had expanded from 43,000, to 178,000. By 1870, it would reach

16. Phillips, "Letter to Shaw and Walker," in his *Speeches*, 237–41; *Liberator*, March 29, 1861.

251,000. When Phillips' father had been mayor, the town had been populated almost exclusively by Anglo-American Protestants, and its budget
had been $171,000. By 1865, however, 45 percent of the residents were
immigrants, mostly Irish Catholic, and the city spent $6.5 million on
its annual operations. Just five years later that figure would rise to $12.4
million. Originally, a small, personalized social and economic setting
had nurtured ideals of republican liberty that Phillips had learned in his
youth. But now, as factory production, urban growth, and administrative
bureaucratization spread across New England, this rapidly vanishing
milieu was being replaced by deepening class estrangements. In the
northern interior, Erie, Pittsburgh, Cleveland, Cincinnati, Chicago, and
Detroit reflected the same trends so visible not only in Boston but also
in the factory town of Lynn, close to Ann and Wendell Phillips' summer
residence. There, shoemakers had just recently laid down their tools,
striking in 1860 for higher wages, union recognition, and "the rights
of labor" in general, protesting in this way their declining economic
power and personal autonomy in the new factory system. It was the
largest, most protracted working-class protest action the nation had yet
witnessed.[17]

When Phillips had first joined the abolitionists, he had taken it on
deepest faith that harmony between classes, races, and ethnic groups
could only be assured through the ennobling exercise of individual initiative, and it was the primacy of law that would secure individual freedom. As the Civil War drew ever closer, however, urban growth and industrial expansion had already begun to cast serious doubts on these
axioms by generating class enmity, intensifying ethnic and racial divisions, and spawning violence. As his support for the Municipal Police
Bill revealed, Phillips already regarded these transformations as indisputably clear threats to his republican creed. The working-class mobs of
1860–1861, moreover, had led him to believe that the cause of urban
lawlessness was alcohol.

By midcentury, most upper- and middle-class Yankees had concluded

17. Lane, *Policing the City*, table, 238; Oscar Handlin, *Boston's Immigrants* (Boston, 1959), table, 246; Faler, *Mechanics and Manufacturers*, 222–33; Dawley, *Class
and Community*, 78–79, 102–103. For a view of abolitionists' general reactions
to the rise of working-class consciousness, see Foner, "Abolitionists and the Labor
Movement," 254–71. An excellent treatment of popular response to the Lynn strike
of 1860 is offered by James L. Huston, "Facing Angry Labor: The American Public
Interprets the Shoemakers' Strike of 1860," *Civil War History*, XXVII (September,
1982), 198–212.

that sobriety was essential to maintain a work force that was self-controlled and therefore efficient and manageable. For this reason, many temperance advocates also tended to reveal strong desires to undercut both lower-class work habits, carried over from earlier prefactory experiences, and the social networks of working people's neighborhoods. These privileged reformers also supported the creation of such new public bureaucracies as independent police commissions as a means to place city administration beyond the control of their own employees and to shape the urban environment to fit their own needs. Phillips, who put the highest premium on self-disciplined personal initiative, certainly hated intemperance as subverting this trait, for a person could become, in his view, no less enslaved to alcohol than to the dictates of the South's masters. Nevertheless, his advocacy of the municipal police proposal reflected none of these elitist motives. Instead he supported it as a means of separating alcohol from politics in the hope that such separation would restore civil liberties that belonged to all classes. Certainly he did not seek to wrest power from Boston's lower class in order to give it to the same merchants, bankers, and Harvard clubmen whom he despised so deeply and whom he blamed for the riots in the first place. There was, moreover, no hint of anti-Catholicism or anti-working-class bias in Phillips' arguments, for he made clear that he simply wanted to see Boston secure for all its citizens to assemble in peace. One might argue that despite his own egalitarian goals, his advocacy of police reform and hatred of alcohol reinforced, albeit inadvertently, upper-class programs for dominion in the city.[18] It is clear, nevertheless, that Phillips' republican values had begun to heighten his awareness of the costs of industrialization. Soon he would begin to insist that labor and temperance reform were no less vital to America's social reconstruction than was the achievement of racial equality.

In the spring of 1861, however, it was the Union, not alcohol, that preoccupied everyone in Boston. On April 12, South Carolina militia units opened fire on the federal installation of Fort Sumter in Charles-

18. For many of these developments of urban, upper-class social control, see Paul Boyer, *The Urban Masses and Moral Order in America* (Cambridge, Mass., 1978), 3–191. The best discussion of alcohol, temperance, and the changing economy of the Northeast is found in Paul Johnson, *Shopkeepers' Millennium: Society and Revivals in Rochester, New York* (New York, 1978). For an excellent examination of the egalitarianism and elitism to be found in Victorian moral reform ideology, see Thomas L. Haskell, "Capitalism and the Origins of Humanitarian Sensibility: Part 1," *American Historical Review*, XC (April, 1985), 339–61.

ton Harbor, and Abraham Lincoln called for seventy-five thousand volunteers. The war to preserve the Union had begun, and Governor John Andrew declared a mobilization of Massachusetts troops. Cotton aristocrats led the vanguard of war, hoping to force a rapid conclusion. Daniel Webster's son Fletcher stood patriotically on the the statehouse steps and announced that he would lead a regiment into battle, while Amos A. Lawrence spent spare hours instructing Harvard undergraduates in weaponry. Boston bankers even lent $3.6 million to the state government to underwrite the purchase of war materiel, and militia units drilled up and down State Street.[19] The last anyone had heard from Wendell Phillips had been his cry that peaceful disunion accorded with "God's natural laws." As waves of militant patriotism swept through Boston, its greatest radical censor, so hated and venerated just a few months before, remained silent. Nine days elapsed after Lincoln's call for war before he finally spoke, and little is known about Phillips' activities during this interval, except that he looked haggard, acted distracted, and complained that everyone he talked to was pressing him to support the war. If he complied, he lamented, he would also be forced to "renounce my past . . . belie my pledges, disavow every profession of faith, bless those that I have cursed, start afresh with a new set of political principles, and admit that my life has been a mistake."[20]

No doubt Phillips cringed at the thought of recanting. Just three months before, he had gloried in defending against mobs and hated cotton aristocrats the doctrine of disunion, which had given him ideological and personal inspiration for two decades. Yet it is also clear, even before Sumter was attacked, that Phillips had welcomed the general prospect of war, the bigger and bloodier the better. "I trust *events*," he had confided to Gerrit Smith before Lincoln gave his call for arms. "The *Adm*[inistration] means war. . . . There must be *bloodshed*." Whether the North met defeat or was victorious with "great loss" mattered little, Phillips thought, for the first result would be "disunion (which is freedom)," and the second "emancipation by the war power of the President." No matter what the outcome, Phillips rejoiced in the crisis of 1861. It presaged abolitionist triumph, Phillips assured Smith, and all reformers should therefore give thanks to God. "Did you ever expect to see such a day—we truly are blessed to see the fruits of our toil." The

19. Bartlett, *Phillips*, 236; O'Connor, *Lords of the Loom*, 165–77.
20. George W. Smalley, *Anglo-American Memories* (London, 1911), 96.

thought that he and Garrison, not Lincoln and Confederate President Jefferson Davis, stood central in the secession crisis clearly had begun helping Phillips to accept the obvious. Unless he wished the culminating crisis of the sectional conflict to pass him by, he had no choice but to join the war to save that same polluted Union that he had denounced for so many years. Phillips suddenly announced without elaborating further that he wished to air his views on the war, and a date and a place were set, April 21 in the cavernous Boston Music Hall. Once again, Phillips had met a personal dilemma by making a bold choice that led him, as usual, to a speaker's platform.[21]

Phillips was about to eat his words, the "cotton press" reported gleefully. In all likelihood, Phillips had leaked just such information, hoping to control the setting in which he was to speak and the expectations of his audience. Charles Follen, a prominent abolitionist who was in charge of decorating the Music Hall, also helped Phillips reach these ends. When Follen asked Phillips if he could hang a flag behind the speaker's platform, the orator replied, "Hang as many flags as you like. I am going to speak for the flag." Follen festooned the hall in red, white, and blue, fashioning over the rostrum an arch wrapped in bunting accented with sprigs of laurel and evergreen and hanging banners from ceilings and walls. "The atmosphere was charged with patriotism," a witness recalled. Since Phillips had now decided to march "under the flag," the decorations created a setting that dared any heckler to cry out "I told you so," and he was certain now to face "an audience wholly in sympathy with his expected speech."[22]

Phillips rose to face the crowd that filled the Music Hall and in an instant convinced everyone, including himself perhaps, that he was not really recanting the essence of his disunionism at all. All winter he had counseled "peaceful separation," he acknowledged, as he began his address. Now it had been said that "I am here this morning to retract these opinions." He paused and then cried out, "No, not a one of them." The audience applauded loudly, but Phillips continued quickly: "I need them all—every word I have spoken this winter, every act of the past twenty-five years, to make the welcome I give this war heavy and hot. . . . I speak under the stars and stripes, and welcome the tread of Massachusetts men marshaled for war." At this the crowd sprang to its feet and

21. Phillips to Gerrit Smith, [March–April?], 1861, Smith-Miller Papers.
22. "Reminiscences of Charles Slack," in Martyn, *Phillips*, 316–17; Smalley, "Reminiscences of Phillips," 141.

In this engraving by Augustus Robin of New York, Phillips, about fifty years old, is idealized as an exemplar of Victorian manhood and as the heroic defender of liberty.

burst into prolonged cheers. With a smooth rhetorical transition (and some clever advance preparation) Phillips had maintained the public reputation for moral consistency he so cherished, even as he dramatically reversed his entire political position. Never again could he persuasively act as an independent censor of politicians. Although he would often make claims to the contrary and would attack with customary ferocity the acts of congressmen and presidents, there was no denying that Wendell Phillips now accepted the legal premises on which the federal government based its rule. His many years of political ambivalence had certainly not ended, but it was clear, as he himself confirmed later in this speech, that his orientation had changed forever. He had always upheld a full American allegiance; now he had also reentered the electoral population. "Yes," he declared, "today the abolitionist is merged in the citizen, in America."[23]

As a disunionist, Phillips had for decades defended Massachusetts' right of secession. Now, as a citizen, he denied that very same right for the South, which, he now contended, would possess the North's permit to rebel only to seek freedom for all her citizens. Since the South had seceded to protect white tyranny, however, she could claim no legitimate right to revolt. In a truly republican nation, he asserted, no oligarchical faction "can claim, by any law, the right of revolution . . . to preserve a system which the common conscience of mankind stamps as wicked and infamous." Nevertheless, Phillips declared, southern secession, though illegal, had finally put into military terms the cosmic struggle that had already been going on for decades between two fundamentally opposite civilizations. "Our struggle is between barbarism and civilization, between a North that *thinks* and is the nineteenth century," and a South that "*dreams*" and "is the thirteenth or fourteenth century— baron and serf—noble and slave." The nation, he rejoiced, had finally broken through thirty years of artificial "conciliation and compromise" to confront the terrible battle that had always raged within it between two antithetical definitions of American nationality. Only slave emancipation would truly assure that the nineteenth century finally triumphed, for as the historical precedent of Haiti proved, black freedom was, "in every instance, the child of convulsions."[24]

23. Phillips, "Under The Flag," in his *Speeches*, 396–415.
24. *Ibid.*, 396–404.

The struggle to attain a common nationality, therefore, gave the war its transcendent meaning, Phillips told his listeners. Clearly, the fourteenth-century South must be obliterated from every corner of the American map. Warfare alone could finally release the full dynamic power of the North's mighty free-labor system. Three months before, of course, he had asserted to many of these same people that peaceful disunion would slowly allow the Yankee civilization to overwhelm a despotic South, but now he insisted that armies, not economics alone, would be needed. "I know what the sewing-machine and reaping machine and ideas and types and school houses cannot do, the muskets of Illinois and Massachusetts can finish up." All now "turned on . . . liberty and the slave," he emphasized, and northern victory was surely inevitable. "I know that free speech, free soil, school houses and ballot boxes are a pyramid on its broadest base," the material for building a new nation. Every New England man, Phillips assured his listeners, already possessed the social and economic power "to wipe away the stain which hangs about the toleration of human bondage." Although the "just converted hucksterism" of Amos Lawrence and the "mere enthusiasm" of shallow patriots would certainly wane, the war would nevertheless fuse together all the North's great productive classes against the tyrants of the South. The very same class alienation that Phillips feared was being created by the industrial revolution and the spread of urban culture would be erased by the Civil War. "The cordwainers of Lynn, the farmers of Worcester, the delvers of the prairie—Iowa, Wisconsin, Ohio and Maine" would be united into one vast community of soldiers, for these hard-working, practical people, "who have no leisure for technicalities," had "waited long enough. . . . they have quieted their consciences long enough . . . split logic with their abolitionist neighbors long enough." Now, Phillips declared, "the great body of the people itself . . . have got their hand on the neck of a rebellious aristocracy," and in throttling it, the North's productive classes would finally endow America with true nationhood. The chaos of war would finally surmount the discord of both slavery and urbanization, inaugurating a new era of unmatched social harmony, political freedom, and technological progress. In this manner, Phillips believed, all classes and races would find reconciliation in their common struggle for nineteenth-century civilization.[25]

25. *Ibid.*

Phillips had now embraced a vision of a union socially and morally transformed, instead of militarily restored, a union made tangible by an egalitarian national culture of republican freedom rather than by parties, race hierarchies, frozen class structures, and discriminatory laws. "Years hence," he assured his audience, "when all the smoke of this conflict clears away, this world will see under our banner all tongues, all creeds, all races—one brotherhood—and on the banks of the Potomac the genius of liberty robed in light, thirty-four states in her diadem, broken chains under her feet, and an olive branch in her right hand." For twenty-five years he had despised the Constitution of 1787, but now, as troops marched and cannons rolled, Phillips had realized that the "possibility of justice" could be entertained "in the certainty of the union" and nowhere else. The rebellious South must be wholly remade before assuming its place in a union where racial freedom and unlimited possibilities for individual advancement held sway from ocean to ocean.[26]

Wendell Phillips had now transformed himself from a New England disunionist into a radical prophet of democratic nationalism. In becoming "citizen Wendell Phillips," he, and most other abolitionists, had taken irrevocable steps across barriers that had for so long kept them outside of any larger political consensus. Stephen S. Foster sensed this change in Phillips' position, and in his own as well, when he wrote, after the Music Hall speech, that "the orator is the natural aristocrat . . . when the nation is to be aroused to the performance of some great deed of honor, heroism or justice." He advised Phillips, "You must now place yourself before the country in a true, national position so to gather around you the popular heart that the White House itself shall reverently ask its order at your lips." Foster's undoubted overstatement of Phillips' new position nevertheless perfectly captured the hopes Phillips harbored for himself as he launched a campaign to remake the Union into an instrument of national liberation. Meanwhile, abolitionists everywhere joined ranks with Phillips. Referring to his Music Hall address, Susan B. Anthony reported that she and all of her friends were "delighted with your speech. What a glorious revolution we are in—

26. *Ibid.* See Peter Walker, *Moral Choices: Memory and Desire in Nineteenth-Century American Abolition* (Baton Rouge, 1978), 8–11, for an interpretation of Phillips' views on disunion and the secession crisis that varies from the one presented here. In my opinion Walker errs in questioning the authenticity of Phillips' profession of peaceable disunion.

emancipation must come out of it," though, as she added especially appropriately, "It is strange to go in for the union."[27]

It quickly became apparent that his new unionism presented Phillips with vexing problems, so different was it from Abraham Lincoln's. In his first proclamation calling for volunteers, the president had made plain his intention not to disrupt slavery but to restore the union as it had been prior to 1861. Ambassadors then carried Lincoln's message to foreign capitals, and commanders reinforced it by returning escaped slaves to their masters across the battle lines. By July, 1861, Phillips was writing in hot fury to Sumner, having learned that two Massachusetts commanders had sent back fugitives. "Are colonels to resolve themselves into *judges* as Slave Bill Commissioners?" he demanded. Sumner must denounce them from the floor of the Senate and force their removal, for in Phillips' view, "this much is due to the hope that the *Govt.* means *freedom* by this war." He did not feel his outlook improve at all the following month when the Union army was routed at the first battle of Bull Run. As Federal forces straggled back to Washington, Congress resolved that the sole purpose of the war was "to preserve the union, with all the dignity, equality and rights of the several states unimpaired." Plainly, Republicans were not anxious to plunge into an antislavery war. It also must have especially galled Phillips to reread a letter he had received from M. J. Flanders, just after the Music Hall speech. She had asked Phillips, "What means are now being taken to arm the race so long oppressed—?" She herself volunteered to solicit funds for equipping black soldiers, even if no one else joined her. "If men are not working for that object, women should," she added pointedly.[28]

There were, from Republican party perspectives, good reasons for keeping the emancipation issue out of the Civil War. Politicians greatly feared alienating the strategically crucial border states, unionist parts of the South where slavery remained in full force. Republican leaders also knew that they must not upset the delicate coalition that kept radical Charles Sumner and his great Cotton Whig antagonist Amos A. Lawrence together in the same party. Among seasoned Garrisonians, how-

27. Stephen S. Foster to Phillips, November 8, 1861, Susan B. Anthony to Phillips, April 28, 1861, both in Blagden Papers.
28. Sumner to Phillips, July 15, 1861, M. J. Flanders to Phillips, April 22, 1861, both *ibid.* See Stewart, *Holy Warriors*, 179–80, for a summary of Lincoln's and the Republicans' early approach to the war.

ever, such caution carried the familiar ring of proslavery expediency that they had always expected from union-loving politicos. In wartime, reformers like Phillips discovered, northern party leaders placed an even higher premium than usual on maintaining compromise and consensus. As a result, Phillips soon found himself answering an intense letter from Stephen S. Foster, denouncing the Republicans wholesale as cat's-paws of slavery. The old tension among Garrisonians between political revolutionaries and half-vindicated prophets began to surface once more, for Foster was again proposing a new political party, this one pledged to emancipation, complete civil equality for blacks, and the scourging of the Republican party.

The Fosters and Pillsbury, in deadly earnest about their proposal, twice interrupted antislavery society meetings in 1861 with resolutions that called on abolitionists to withdraw all support from the proslavery government. It was, of course, Phillips' old disunionism, now applied to wartime conditions, but he had absolutely no time for it. Instead, Phillips counseled patience with Lincoln, observing that "no man can mould the world in exactly his method." Abolitionists must bring public pressure for emancipation to bear on the Republicans, not risk being seen as traitors by opposing the wartime government. Clearly, Phillips was now advising his colleagues to submit to Lincoln's leadership on practical grounds; it was advice wholly at odds with his abiding desire to continue believing in the absolute political independence of the American Anti-Slavery Society. Caught in an excruciating conflict between this powerful abolitionist tradition and the exigencies of Civil War politics, Phillips attempted to reconcile these opposites, just as he had always resolved his ambivalence before. This time, however, he failed miserably. Just "as of old," he insisted lamely, abolitionists must conduct themselves as nonpartisan agitators, who would yet see their work bear fruit in government policy. "To-day belongs to the Negro," he emphasized. "Whatever question we discuss to-day, we should discuss as the slave looks at it—from no other standpoint."[29] Yet he had also just told his colleagues that Lincoln's judgment, not the slaves', should define abolitionist behavior. Even as the Fosters' resolution went down to handy defeat, it was obvious that Phillips, in all innocence, had misspoken badly when he claimed that the American Anti-Slavery Society could

29. Stephen S. Foster to Phillips, November 8, 1861, Blagden Papers; *Liberator*, July 12, August 9, 1861.

still operate "as of old." As much as he wished to believe otherwise, Garrisonians had now become a loyal opposition to the regime in power. Whatever had been its original value, they had abandoned disunionist politics forever, and Phillips, like the rest of them, now found himself committed to the not inconsiderable task of rousing the nation to goad Abraham Lincoln into emancipation.

In the winter of 1861–1862, Phillips toured New England, speaking on the war to larger audiences than ever before. New York *Tribune* editor Horace Greeley, who had the credentials to make such an estimate, calculated that at least fifty thousand people heard Phillips that year and five million more read his speeches in Republican party newspapers. Phillips' speech titles suggest some of the reasons, apart from his magnificent platform skills, why he achieved such enormous wartime appeal and growing influence. He gave his talks catchall titles, such as "The Times," "The War for the Union," "The Present and Future of the Country," or simply "The War." By using such up-to-the-moment rubrics, vaguely suggestive of newspaper headlines, Phillips was able to revise his remarks continuously so that he always addressed the latest developments in the war or in Washington politics, condemning generals and politicians for their most recent acts of treason, and extolling those who had, in his opinion, struck blows for emancipation.[30]

"Someone has said that he always read Wendell Phillips' speeches to get the latest news," observed one shrewd reporter toward the end of the war. Phillips, in other words, had begun delivering an endless stream of "fresh facts" in his compelling "fresh talk" style to an audience of unprecedented size. People no longer regarded him as only an extremist or an agitator; they now saw him as a critically astute and knowledgeable observer. Phillips, indeed, had become an editorialist-at-large, a pundit, whose views on rapidly changing current affairs were somehow worth knowing simply because he uttered them. When he profitably published his collected speeches in one large volume late in 1863, his influential new status was confirmed. It was even reported that the only book in English catalogued in the only library in Alaska was a copy of Phillips' speeches, so widely circulated had they become. "It is a peculiarity of Phillips' speeches that they read admirably," said one reviewer.[31] News-

30. Phillips, "The War for the Union," in his *Speeches*, 438–39.
31. *National Anti-Slavery Standard*, July 29, 1865, February 8, 1868; *New York Home Evangelist*, quoted in *Liberator*, December 7, 1864.

paper editors Edward L. Godkin, James Gordon Bennett, and Horace Greeley had begun developing the pundit style too, but they were hard pressed to match Phillips in this kind of newsmaking, for he could be heard in dynamic personal appearances as well as read in print. When Phillips spoke in New York City's Cooper Institute in late 1861, for example, people lined up hours before the doors were opened, and over a thousand were turned away while New York's police (supervised by an independent commission) kept the crowds well in hand.[32]

Still another factor in Phillips' burgeoning popularity, and that of other abolitionists as well, was the fact that two of his friends, Sidney Gay and Oliver Johnson, had now risen far in the world of journalism. Gay had developed considerable influence at the New York *Tribune*, and Johnson at the *Independent*. Both papers were supported by large Republican readerships, and when Phillips' co-workers arranged for him to have access to their columns, the results amazed veteran abolitionists. Mary Grew, Ann Phillips' aunt, read the papers and shook her head in happy bewilderment at the public's evident acceptance of the abolitionists. "It is hard to realize the wondrous change that has befallen us," she wrote to Wendell Phillips Garrison in early 1862. "After thirty years of persecution . . . abolitionists read with wonder, in prominent journals . . . respectful tributes to men whose names had been hitherto used as cries where with to rally a mob; and see with joy their own arguments and phraseology adopted by these journals."[33] With assistance such as this, Phillips was hardly the only abolitionist to rise so rapidly in the public's esteem during the war; many others prominently associated with the cause also became celebrities. Douglas, Garrison, the Mays, the Fosters—all returned in triumph to speak in places where they had earlier been mobbed.

If his growing power and popularity pleased Phillips or made him feel uncomfortable, he never said so. All the appreciative press notices clearly meant little, judged against his evident lack of actual influence on the conduct of the military conflict. The Bull Run disaster, which Phillips had first hoped would stun the North into action, had instead delivered the army to General George B. McClellan, a Democrat and a conservative unionist who never seemed eager to fight aggressively. Lincoln, moreoover, had snuffed out Phillips' only glimmer of military

32. Johnson to William L. Garrison, December 20, 1861, Garrison Papers, BPL.
33. Grew to Wendell P. Garrison, January 9, 1862, *ibid.*

hope in 1861 when, to the abolitionists' universal dismay, he overruled the order of John C. Fremont, commanding general in the West, declaring martial law in Missouri and freeing all slaves of rebels in the state. Garrison fumed that Lincoln, though "six feet four inches high . . . is only a dwarf in mind." Meanwhile, Phillips, Garrison, Quincy, John Andrew, Franklin Sanborn, George L. Stearns, and others discussed ways to push public opinion and the president toward emancipation, but by December, their Emancipation League, for all its size and noise, seemed to have done little good. Lincoln, in a message to Congress early that month, again made plain his determination to soft-pedal the slavery question.[34] He endorsed colonization for voluntarily emancipated slaves (anathema to every abolitionist) and repeated that he would not touch slavery in the South. In January, 1862, in Tremont Temple, Phillips finally announced that Lincoln had taxed his patience too far, and he gave voice to the major themes about the war that he was to repeat in his speeches for the next two years.

"I have addressed many audiences in the different cities in the past ten months," he began, always counseling "matchless patience" with Abraham Lincoln, but "I must say that the past ten months have exhausted my patience." The nation now found itself burdened by a "President who could not open his eyes any wider than to take in Kentucky." If he persisted in his policies and disaster befell the country, "posterity will henceforward divide the curses that have usually been monopolized by Aaron Burr and Benedict Arnold. We have poured out two million a day," Phillips charged, "and we have purchased nothing but disgrace." Lincoln had allowed danger to crowd the republic from every side, for McClellan's noxious influence dominated Lincoln's cabinet, and England and France awaited the first ripe moment to recognize the Confederacy and split the Union. Most of all, Phillips insisted, the South was fighting with admirable valor and, because of the president's manifest failures, should by all rights win the war. Only God's hatred of slavery, nothing that Lincoln had done, had prevented the Confederacy's overwhelming triumph, for the South, Phillips declared, was fighting sincerely in defense of its ideal of nationality. "She is true to her idea, slavery," said Phillips. "She makes everything bend to it and deserves to succeed." The North, by contrast, "dare[s] not whisper the idea on which it rests,"

34. William L. Garrison to Johnson, October 7, 1861, *ibid.*; Frank P. Stearns, *The Life and Public Services of George Luther Stearns* (Philadelphia, 1907), 265–66.

he charged, for she sent "her armies into the field and the only thing they have done for ten months is to catch negroes and find owners for them. We have not yet vindicated our title to govern by the exhibition of a civilization and an earnestness of idea superior to the South." Phillips had envisioned a great war for American nationality, but the North seemed to be succumbing to defeat from a lack of spiritual conviction caused, surely, by Lincoln's failure to act boldly, as a Burke or a John Brown certainly would have.[35]

Union defeat was rising on the horizon, Phillips warned his audiences, threatening economic and moral anarchy, the nightmarish collapse of the same free-labor republic he had so often extolled. "Two unions mean no tariff . . . mean bankruptcy at Lowell, bankruptcy at Lawrence . . . a very radical change in the manufacturing and the mechanical interests of these states . . . a John Brown in every northern village and fear in every Southern Harper's Ferry that he attacks . . . constant, bloody bitter strife, until in thirty or fifty years, perhaps, natural law kills slavery." He was now warning the North as no "mere abolitionist," Phillips insisted, for although he demanded that the country repay "what it owes the victim race," he also spoke "from the broadest motives of an American" who now marched "under the flag." As such, he declared himself to be "charged with the welfare of all races, white, black, foreign and native," and every other citizen must be made to learn to feel likewise, to speak out, and to defend the republic by demanding an end to slavery. "Let the year 1862, by its success, blot out the disaster and disgrace of 1861."[36]

Even as he denounced Lincoln and demanded new vigor from the North's politicians, Phillips noted signs of such leadership emerging in Congress. Early in 1862, the House of Representatives dissented from Lincoln's mild annual message by rescinding its earlier resolution that the war aimed only at restoring the Union. To monitor Lincoln's leadership, Congress created the Joint Committee on the Conduct of the War, and as the new year opened, a group of antislavery dissenters started emerging in Washington. Ohio's Benjamin Wade and Michigan's Zachariah Chandler spoke especially strongly against Lincoln in the Senate, as did Henry Wilson and Charles Sumner. In the House, George W. Julian assumed the mantle of his father-in-law Joshua R. Giddings and was

35. *Liberator*, January 31, 1862.
36. *Ibid.*

joined by a cluster of others, led by Henry Winter Davis of Maryland, Thaddeus Stevens of Pennsylvania, George Boutwell of Massachusetts, and Elijah Lovejoy's brother Owen, congressman from Illinois. Although hardly united in policy, these Congressmen did share a persuasion people were increasingly referring to as radical Republicanism. All insisted that defeating the South demanded direct warfare against slavery and that Congress should legislate against the peculiar institution and shape military policy to secure a final victory.[37]

Phillips immediately felt drawn to this developing circle of insurgents and lamented his lack of strong contacts in Washington. He could count as reliable only Sumner, who began receiving the first of dozens of letters from Phillips, urging him to "go forward with your bill for total emancipation. . . . don't let others steal all your laurels, when you have stirred the game, by bagging it themselves."[38] In the spring of 1862, Phillips took a far more significant step, one he hoped would secure the political power he had always so wanted to wield. He arranged a very special speaking tour to the Midwest with a first stop scheduled in Washington, D.C. For decades he had sought to shape the nation's destiny even as he declared himself far above the "taint" of office holding and electioneering. Now, however, he was deciding that close ties with the Republicans' foremost congressional radicals were compatible with his self-ascribed role as impartial public censor. Actually, however, his independent position was eroding rapidly, for he now sought what only the most powerful journalists and lobbyists possessed—inside contacts created through close associations and understandings with powerful elected officials.

Ann Phillips disapproved, adamantly and completely, of what Wendell now proposed to do. She deeply feared that he was about to forfeit his status as an uncompromised moral spokesman, the high-minded vocation that had seemed, thus far, so worth her great sacrifices. When Wendell departed for Washington in March of 1862, Ann repeated warnings she had voiced before his departure. "I fear you are nearly popular *because* you have gone over to worldly men," she began, before subjecting him to a fast review of basic Garrisonian axioms. Influential men " have not come to you," she insisted, but instead, "their own selfish interests

37. The best study of this group is Hans L. Trefousse, *The Radical Republicans: Lincoln's Vanguard for Racial Justice* (New York, 1974).
38. Phillips to Sumner, December 16, 1861, Sumner Papers.

carry them to emancipation. I see no change in them, and feel no encouragement *whatever* in it." Abby or Stephen Foster certainly could not have put such views more forcefully. Since Ann Phillips clearly shared the Fosters' opposition to the Republicans, she feared all the more deeply for her highly prized moralistic vision of her husband. Republicans, not Democrats, "have brought us where we are," she reminded him urgently. "Let them see that you are not one of them, and be bold and thorough in urging what you want. I think you mire yourself too much with them. . . . I hate having you mixed up with them." Afraid that his gregariousness might make him easy prey for the unscrupulous power brokers of Washington high society and that he himself might well become carried away with the experience, she wrote, "They think of you as a 'brother well met' and go right on with their villainous time serving." She reminded him that "in making speeches now, men wish to be serious, for the time, makes them [so]." She implored Phillips to take Garrison along, so that at least they could protect one another from unscrupulous politicians, and then she pled the same case directly to Garrison: "Wendell needs *you*, otherwise you leave him alone with *politicians* and his influence *without* you *must* be comparatively null." As it turned out, Garrison declined, and despite all of Ann's entreaties, Phillips clambered down from his lofty perch as an independent agitator to seek power on the broad plain of Republican party politics.[39]

For decades, Ann Phillips had lived out her abolitionist faith vicariously, and at heavy personal cost, through Wendell's uncompromised career. Now, though she feared that he was risking all that they stood for together, nothing she could say had been able to dissuade him. They had not achieved a meeting of minds, she wrote bitterly. Instead, he had simply defied her and gone his way, defining his quests for power and black emancipation apart from their relationship. "I am sick at heart, as it was your judgment to go," she wrote, for he had given her no choice but submission. "I know that I must let you do what you conscientiously think is right after weighing what I say," she continued bitterly, "but I do not feel that you did *weigh*. That's the trouble." All she could do now, she concluded, was to trust him and to assume that time and

39. Ann Phillips to Phillips [March], 1862, Blagden Papers; Ann Phillips to William L. Garrison, March 4, 1862, William L. Garrison to Johnson, March 30, 1862, both in Garrison Papers, BPL.

more discussion would put things right. "I wish I had something more to tell you," she assured him in closing, "but can only repeat the old story that you are my life." In her next letters, she changed her tone from anger and resigned admonition to supportive advice: "I am thankful you are doing much good, and only wish I could spare you more." She even began instructing him as to whom to see and what to say in his explorations of the corridors of power. "Do be *terribly* in *earnest* and grave to all members of Congress," she advised, and "if you can do anything by seeing Stanton and Co., I should do [so]." Once again, she and her husband had confirmed the inseparable bonds between the direction of his career and the texture of their private lives, and again this achievement had been gained only by Ann's sacrifice. As in the depressing aftermath of the Anthony Burns affair, when he had first gone on an extended speaking tour, Wendell Phillips had placed himself in her debt. In 1863, when his collected speeches were first published, Wendell, in recognition, presented Ann with a copy, the title page of which was inscribed, "Speeches and Lectures, by Ann Phillips."[40]

In the spring of 1862, Washington, D.C., suggested some of the ambiguities and frustrations of the war that was being fought around it. Slavery still flourished there because the Republican majority in Congress feared the divisive political implications of trying to abolish it. At the same time, however, once-notorious abolitionists now mixed easily as guests of honor at Washington soirées, and antislavery ministers held forth confidently before audiences of attentive Congressmen. But despite Union victories in the West, the troops surrounding the city occupied battle lines that had changed very little since the first Bull Run. The South, from a Washington perspective, could seem as entrenched and intransigent as ever. Phillips' train pulled in on March 15, and as he peered out the window of his car at the skyline, he enquired "what that engine round house" was used for. "Speak respectfully," replied a companion. "That is the *Capitol* Dome."[41] Phillips indeed had much to discover about the workings of Washington, D.C.

40. Ann Phillips to Phillips [March], April 3, 1862, and for Phillips' reply to Ann's concern, see Phillips to Ann Phillips, March 28, 1862, all in Blagden Papers; Martyn, *Phillips*, 325.
41. Phillips to Ann Phillips, March 31, 1862, Blagden Papers. This is an extremely long and valuable letter, in which Phillips recapitulated for Ann many aspects and events of his western tour. It provides much of the detail and documentation for the next several paragraphs.

The next morning, Charles Sumner escorted Phillips to the floor of the United States Senate and plunged his friend directly into Washington politics. Henry Wilson, John P. Hale of New Hampshire, and the powerful Lyman Trumbull of Illinois came over at once to renew acquaintances, and the effusive reception surprised Phillips as much as it gladdened him. Many other senators also made a special point of introducing themselves before everyone repaired to private chambers, where "they crowded around me still more and numerous," as Wendell wrote in high excitement to Ann. That evening, Phillips delivered his fullest dress abolitionist lecture in the Capitol, from which hundreds were turned away. The senators and representatives present helped make up a "warmly applauding audience," the *Liberator's* correspondent reported, as Phillips demanded immediate freedom for every slave. Behind him on the speaker's platform, apparently listening intently, sat Hannibal Hamlin, the vice-president. Abraham Lincoln through his private secretary had sent his regrets.[42] The congressmen and cabinet members who crowded around to shake his hand after the speech were clearly acknowledging that Phillips' political standing was considerable indeed. "Phillips manufactures a vast amount of popular opinion," the ambitious Massachusetts politician General Benjamin F. Butler was told by one of his advisers. "No man will speak oftener or to larger audiences in America. . . . the masses in New England or New York and Ohio are reached by Phillips, who has the public ear in the Lyceum Halls." As a radical orator, a pundit, and a fixture of popular culture, Phillips had actually begun to attain much of what Stephen S. Foster had prophesied, "that the White House itself shall reverently ask its orders at your lips."[43] Though motivated by political practicality, not reverence, Abraham Lincoln would, in fact, soon invite Phillips to a private interview.

Phillips joined a gathering of the influential for dinner at House Speaker Galusha Grow's residence. There, for the first time, he met John C. Fremont and began to suspect that he was encountering a new antislavery hero, the Cromwell he was calling for who could put slavery into its grave. Some of Ann's concerns about her husband's political innocence and sociability were starting to prove well founded. Fremont, of

42. *Ibid.; Liberator*, March 21, 1862.
43. Stephen S. Foster to Phillips, November 8, 1861, Blagden Papers; J. O. A. Griffin to Benjamin F. Butler, January 18, 1863, in Jessie A. Marshall (ed.), *The Private and Official Correspondence of General Benjamin F. Butler During the Period of the Civil War* (5 vols.; Norwood, Mass., 1917), II, 580.

course, had made himself a favorite of abolitionists by his Missouri emancipation order, and Phillips was quite taken by this dashing, romantic figure and his vivacious wife, Jessie. "Fremont was all that I fancied him, modest, able," he reported to Ann. What particularly impressed him was Fremont's story of listening incognito to Phillips when he spoke in New York City. When the orator had referred to General Fremont, the crowd had erupted in grand uproar, convincing the disguised commander that "the *masses* really loved him." Perhaps, Phillips had already begun wondering whether Fremont would make a popular replacement for Lincoln in the next election. Meantime, Jessie Fremont certainly enhanced her husband's standing in Phillips' eyes, for at dinner she spurned Sumner's company for his and "told me many good things," he reported enthusiastically to Ann. Two months after this first meeting, Phillips was to inform an audience in New York City that "Abraham Lincoln simply rules; John C. Fremont governs," and although Fremont had lost the presidential campaign in 1856, "the people buried him in their hearts, and reproduced him . . . and elected him the President of the crisis."[44] Already he had begun to involve himself in the bareknuckle politics of the Republican party, and within two years Phillips was to find himself working openly to replace Lincoln with Fremont as president.

Lincoln, however, was the past master of those politics. Phillips prepared for his interview with the president by touring the countryside around the capital and visiting some Massachusetts troops. On the soil of Virginia he spoke to them of black emancipation as the only justification for fighting, and they responded with choruses of "John Brown's Body." Thus fortified, he went to the White House for a conversation that would last over an hour. As he prepared to meet the president, Phillips actually felt more positively disposed toward Lincoln than he had for several months. A few weeks earlier, Lincoln had approved of giving federal compensation to any state that enacted a plan of gradual emancipation, and Phillips, to Ann's dismay, had endorsed Lincoln's idea as "one more sign of promise. . . . If the President has not entered Canaan, at least he has turned his face Zionward." ("It is not right to bribe people to do right," Ann had protested.)[45] Phillips could take hope from

44. Phillips to Ann Phillips, March 31, 1862, Blagden Papers; *Liberator*, May 16, 1862.
45. Phillips to Ann Phillips, March 31, 1862, Blagden Papers; *Liberator*, May 16, March 14, 1862; Ann Phillips to Phillips, March 20, 1862, Blagden Papers.

his agreement with Lincoln about at least one matter of substance prior to their conversation.

Lincoln offered a mild joke as he entered the room, and Phillips replied in kind, each trying to put the other at ease. "The beard and his hair make [him] look better, less quaint, than his pictures show him," Phillips decided. The president seemed "perfectly honest—trying to do what he thought was his duty, but a man of very *slow mind*." Phillips first told Lincoln that his latest message to Congress was too timid, that he must attack the South as an emancipationist. In reply, Lincoln reminded Phillips of the problem he faced. The border states (as Phillips quoted the president) "loved slavery—meant it should last—he [Lincoln] hated it and *meant it should die*." Phillips responded by insisting that Lincoln must dismiss his conservative secretary of state, William Seward, and by so doing rally the people behind a proclamation of emancipation. Lincoln then offered a humorous story, illustrating his claim that he was much more devoted to abolition than his critics appreciated, but talking so rapidly that Phillips found it "hard to get a word in edgewise." When the interview concluded, Phillips felt "rather *encouraged*," for Lincoln had, after all, made it clear that all his instincts inclined him to emancipation. From this moment forward, Phillips would react as did all the other radical Republicans; that is, he would follow Lincoln's direction. When the president took an antislavery step, he could rely on the support of the North's most powerful rhetorician, and when he refused to act boldly, it was because the risks of doing otherwise clearly outweighed the inevitable protests of Wendell Phillips. In such a relationship, Phillips always used his great public influence to make it as costly as possible for Lincoln to hesitate. Yet, as an agitator who had always sought his own centrality in sectional politics, Phillips found it extremely frustrating that White House policies increasingly dictated much of his own behavior, even as he tried to gather power for himself. He could denounce or praise Lincoln's actions as the occasion warranted, and his impact on the public surely added pressure on Lincoln to act against slavery, but never again could he truly question the fundamental premise of the government. Beyond this, all he could do was work hard for the election of a president more congenial to his views, just as any other voter might.

The day after conversing with Lincoln, Phillips spoke on Toussaint at the Smithsonian Institution, and "gave the *negro* in full style." Then he boarded the train for appearances in Cincinnati, Chicago, Milwaukee,

Madison, Detroit, and Cleveland before returning home. Having developed new power centers and contacts in Washington, he now judged it essential to enhance his stature with audiences in the politically crucial Midwest. He had visited these cities before, so past associations guaranteed that people would be eager to listen to him again, especially in his wartime capacity as patriotic opinion-maker.[46]

The vicious mob that attacked him in Cincinnati, his first stop, was therefore the most fortunate thing that could have happened, in his opinion. Eggs flew as he spoke in this city so close to the borders of slavery; a mob charged from the gallery, and afterward officials found a bottle of explosives in the lobby of the lecture hall. Phillips saw no disturbing implications in this display of urban violence, unlike the mobbing in Boston the previous year. This time he considered it far more important that news of the outrage made headlines in every other city on his trip. While Ann felt terrified for her husband's safety, Wendell expressed his delight at the political gains he was making. Most of all, he rejoiced that the news of the mob had furnished him with free mass advertising and had greatly enhanced his appeal as a touring celebrity. Reporting happily from Chicago, he assured Ann, "I had a tremendous house—the whole city and the best men. The Cincinnati mob has caused the whole midwest to hear me." As in Washington, every reception was overwhelming, every committee large and effusive, every speech an unquestioned success. More than ever, he felt himself to be the bridge between electorate and politicians, the Garrisonian whose role was crucial in maintaining republican politics. The mayor of Cincinnati even begged him to come back, so his city might erase the stigma placed on it by the mob. Ann insisted that he refuse, and he complied, for he knew well that he had already treated her wishes far more cavalierly than their relationship could normally permit. Besides, as he reassured her, he felt he had plenty to do without returning there: "I have never regretted more my inability to work at a distance from home," he told Ann, in thanking her "for letting me spend this month here. It has done more good than ten times as much New England lecturing."[47]

His audiences, as always, thrilled to his speeches, and whenever he spoke, the lecture halls were jammed. Every day, moreover, Phillips pri-

46. Phillips to Ann Phillips, March 31, 1862, Blagden Papers; Martyn, *Phillips*, 325.

47. Phillips to Ann Phillips, March 26, 27–28, 29, April 9, 1862, Ann Phillips to Phillips, March 26, April 2, 1862, all in Blagden Papers.

vately received "at least *two* delegations" from other cities, as well as telegrams and letters, requesting that he visit. "I could stay here two months," he assured Ann; "public opinion is ripening out here fast." As always, local papers reprinted his speeches as editorial commentary and as news, but far more important, politically, were the periods of "pre-play" and "post-play" (to use the terms of sociolinguist Kenneth Pike) with which Phillips bracketed his days of lecturing. Simply put, he always tried to make himself accessible to people who wished to claim face-to-face contact with the famous individual behind the headlines. Invariably available for private conversation before he gave a lecture, Phillips could always be sought out afterward for dinner or for a chat in the hotel lobby. In such situations, Phillips' friendly, candid style must have been particularly effective, even with strangers, and most significantly its recipients were usually the elite of the local community. "Judges, lawyers and old Congressmen in heaps" took up his time for hours. "I did not have my room empty one moment yesterday, from 8 A.M. to 8 P.M. and as often as once an hour came a fresh visitation," he reported from Chicago. "All day my room is full of *first citizens*."[48]

In these endless private conversations, as well as on speaking platforms and in print, Phillips deepened his dialogue with middle-class Yankee political culture. Professional men, editors, judges, and local politicians constituted the organizational backbone of the Republican party, the people who translated its free-labor credos into party organization, nominating conventions, editorials, and get-out-the-vote campaigns. Moreover, these individuals also made up an influential sector of the public, possessing fixed reading habits that Phillips, as newsmaker and political pundit, depended upon most of all. Especially after meeting with him personally, their eyes would light upon his name whenever they scanned the daily paper. Thus, as Phillips returned to Essex Street in mid-April, he left behind an enormous mass of people, some extremely influential, who felt as if they knew him and who were tied to him by a network of newsprint. When next he spoke in Faneuil Hall, they would notice his message reprinted or summarized in their own local newspaper. This, roughly, was the process to which Benjamin Butler's adviser had referred when he observed that Phillips "manufactures a vast amount of popular opinion." After 1862, no Radical Republi-

48. Phillips to Ann Phillips, March 28, 29, 1862, both *ibid.*; Kenneth Pike cited by Erving Goffman, "The Lecture," in his *Forms of Talk* (Glencoe, Ill., 1981), 167.

can, in Congress or out, brought a more pervasive political influence to the cause of emancipation than did Phillips.

Yet in the six months following Phillips' encouraging foray into "Washington and the West," as he called it, little good seemed to follow. In May, 1862, Radical Republicans in Congress failed to repeal the Fugitive Slave Law. In Union-occupied South Carolina, General David Hunter declared that captured slaves were to be freed as "contraband of war," but Lincoln overruled him. Meanwhile, Phillips' new favorite, Fremont, resigned, disgusted at the president's approaches to strategy. Even Samuel J. May, one of the most soft-spoken and pro-Lincoln of the Garrisonians wrote privately in July, "We find ourselves outwitted, beaten and defeated at every point. Lincoln is the criminal."[49] Phillips found his own impatience with the president turning first to frustration, then to rage. Although his political stature was growing, he needed to feel that his attempts to gather power were having an immediate, dramatic impact on Lincoln's policies. He had, after all, jeopardized his highly prized political "independence" by going to Washington and, in so doing, had even challenged the basis of his relationship with Ann. She, of course, had warned that his dalliance with national politicians would only serve him ill. In his own eyes, therefore, Phillips could justify his recent behavior only by the certainty that Lincoln, Congress, and the United States army had now begun to do his bidding. The patience that Phillips had once counseled for his fellow disunionists now proved impossible for him to practice himself. Instead, he struck out in great anger at the immediate object of his frustration, the president who refused to give him immediate heed.

Reflecting this dark frame of mind, Phillips filled pages with acrimony and sent them to Sumner. All of Lincoln's generals had proven incompetent or worse, he lamented. "I wish I could nominate *one*. . . . God grant soon the *Cromwell* that will clear such Essexes and Manchesters out." Sumner must organize the Radical Republicans in Congress to defy the president at every point. "We are paying thousands of lives and millions of dollars for having a *timid* and *ignorant* President, all the more injurious because he is *honest*. . . . there is not one chance of saving the Union under this administration," he wrote. "Put your feet down and make the cabinet *fear* your opposition, you Republicans." To

49. May to Charles C. Burleigh, July 17, 1862, May Papers.

Gay, at the *Tribune*, Phillips now declared that he had tried flattery and persuasion on Lincoln for two years, but to no avail. "If the proclamation of emancipation is possible at any time for Lincoln (which I doubt) it will be wrung from him only by fear. He is a spaniel by nature." As if to prove this claim, Phillips next composed an editorial, "Leaders as Well as a Party," which blasted Lincoln's presidency. From his first day in office, "we have had our sham fights and rose-water, imbeciles and traitors till the land is satisfied." Oliver Johnson arranged to have it published in the *Independent*, and it raised a storm of controversy, for the North's most fearfully regarded manufacturer of public opinion had again opened a sustained assault on the president.[50]

Republican moderates led by Horace Greeley leapt to defend Lincoln, feeling it politically essential to counteract Phillips' virulence. Just the month before his editorial appeared, Phillips had attacked Lincoln with unprecedented fury at a meeting of the Massachusetts Anti-Slavery Society. "I do not believe in this government," he had said. "It drifts with events." He had derided Lincoln as a "first rate *second rate* man"; he might be honest, but "who cares whether a tortoise is honest or not?" McClellan could not have served the South better if "he had been a traitor from the crown of his head to the sole of his foot. Almost the same may be said for Mr. Lincoln." Northern presses had reprinted these sulphuric remarks widely under such headlines as "Wendell Phillips Spouting Foul Treason." Phillips, of course, had counterattacked with a long rebuttal, defending his original assertion.[51]

Thus, when Phillips issued his editorial blast against Lincoln, and Greeley replied so heatedly, the orator had already provoked a widespread controversy over administration policies. Sidney Gay, in turn, cited this volley of argument when he appealed directly to Lincoln, writing him that public opinion had far outdistanced the president on the question of emancipation. Then, as if to prove Gay's point, Greeley, one of Lincoln's most vocal defenders, published a dramatic "Prayer of Twenty Million," demanding an end to slavery. Lincoln, to everyone's surprise, replied publicly; but maddeningly, for Phillips, he still put sav-

50. Phillips to Sumner, March 29, June 29, 1862, Sumner Papers; Phillips to Sidney H. Gay, September 2, 1862, Gay Papers; *Independent*, reprinted in *Liberator*, September 19, 1862.

51. *National Anti-Slavery Standard*, August 16, 1862; Phillips, "The Cabinet," in his *Speeches*, 448–63; Phillips to Sidney H. Gay, September 2, 1862, Gay Papers; *Liberator*, August 15, 22, 1862.

ing the Union—even with slavery—above emancipation. Lincoln's reply was the most disgraceful statement "that ever came from the head of a free people," Phillips fumed to Gay.[52]

Yet Lincoln's reply showed that he now felt sufficiently in control of conflicting diplomatic and political pressures to recognize the rising sense of public opinion favorable to emancipation. That was in August. Finally, on September 22, he concluded further that abolitionist pressure was compatible with Republican political aims and issued a preliminary Emancipation Proclamation, which ordered that on January 1, 1863, all slaves in rebel states would be declared free, but that those living in states that returned to the Union before that date would remain unaffected by the order. Once in force, the proclamation made Union troops into true armies of emancipation as they advanced into hostile territory, and for this reason above all others, most abolitionists rejoiced at Lincoln's new policy, drowning out Pillsbury, Foster, and others who protested that it failed to touch slavery in parts of the South presently occupied by Union forces.

Initially, Phillips added a restrained voice to the celebration. "I am not going to criticize the President," he told a Boston audience in early November. "I believe that today he has turned the corner and recognizes the fact not simply that the slaves of rebels, but that the *slaves* must be freed."[53] But this self-declared truce lasted barely six weeks. On January 1, 1863, the day the proclamation took effect, Phillips again stood beneath the American flag before a huge celebration in Tremont Temple. At last, he declared, "the nation unleashes the sword and announces its determined purpose to be a nation. . . . It grasps the hilt of the handle firmly and unleashes the glittering blade." But Lincoln received not an ounce of his praise for this momentous turn to emancipation. Instead, Phillips declared that the people had wrung the proclamation from this reluctant president, who had now taken only the "first step in the direction of a union that every man may love and die for." The proclamation itself did not secure an American nationality, Phillips insisted, for it offered no guarantee for a "Union of the future . . . as indestructible as the granite that underlies this continent." That Union, he emphasized, would never be created simply because three million slaves had been forcibly

52. Phillips to Sidney H. Gay, September 2, 1862, Gay Papers; James M. McPherson, *The Struggle for Equality: The Abolitionists and the Negro During the Civil War and Reconstruction* (Princeton, 1964), 112–17.
53. *Liberator,* November 28, 1862.

unshackled. The entire structure of southern society would have to be recast in a new, republican mold. "The nation knows no limits," he insisted to his listeners; "*salus populi, suprema lex*: The safety of the people is the highest law." If this maxim, which for Phillips embodied nationality, did not hold true at the end of the war, then America was "merely a Confederacy, [and] secession is right."[54]

Phillips, in other words, was now demanding national laws to enforce a completely national definition of freedom, not just executive orders that took slaves away from their masters. Just as he had argued in the Boston school desegregation battles of twenty years earlier, he now insisted again that no truly free society could maintain itself unless government power secured liberty for everyone. So as to the South, Phillips demanded that the government create a bureau of freedmen to "guard and aid the advent of these three million" into the status of citizens and allow the slaves to confirm that citizenship by arming them to fight. "Nationality! It is built on races," Phillips told his audience in conclusion. "The despised negro . . . comes in with the sound of trumpets, an army with banners, in the terror of the conflict, to insure us success."[55] Lincoln, to be sure, had proclaimed an end to chattel slavery. Wendell Phillips, however, had now begun to detail his sweeping programs for a reconstructed America, where federal law would prevent racial exploitation from ever again restricting individual freedom and where aristocracy could no longer pervert the values of republicanism.

54. *National Anti-Slavery Standard*, January 12, 1863.
55. *Liberator*, January 9, 1863.

ELEVEN

Reconstruction, Capitalism, and the Franchise

On December 4, 1863, members of the American Anti-Slavery Society convened in Philadelphia to mark three decades of activity. It was a time to reflect and celebrate. Garrison presided, and Samuel J. May, J. Miller McKim, and other veterans made speeches in which they cast their thoughts back to the 1830s, when they had been young and their movement small and despised. Now, vindication sat on the platform in the person of Senator Henry Wilson of Massachusetts, who told the abolitionists how great an inspiration the cause had been to him as he promised to work to "break the last fetter of the last slave." Then as Garrison read their names, charter members of the society arose to great applause. Wendell Phillips did not add to the cheering, however, for he was in New York City's Cooper Institute, assailing Lincoln's Reconstruction plans before a distinguished audience of Republicans. As Garrison well knew, Phillips had boycotted the festival to protest disagreements with its sponsors.[1]

From the first, Civil War had brought confusion to the American Anti-Slavery Society, for dozens of prominent people joined the organization they had denounced for so long. Some, including Elizur Wright, Jr., Lewis Tappan, Gerrit Smith, and Frederick Douglass, had returned from the Liberty party and its successors, and others, such as George B.

1. *Liberator*, December 25, 1863; *National Anti-Slavery Standard*, January 9, 1864; William L. Garrison to Ellen Wright, December 11, 1863, Garrison Papers, SCL.

Cheever and Henry Ward Beecher, were great evangelical preachers. Still others, seasoned politicians like Senator Wilson, George W. Julian, and John A. Andrew, had furnished the best proof of all that the old dis-unionist community of saints was rapidly vanishing, but in a way that could only make many longtime Garrisonians rejoice. Since the war was leading the North to abolition, it was now time, some of these veterans had concluded, to lay the cause aside. As early as 1862, Maria Weston Chapman, the Weston sisters, and J. Miller McKim had resigned from the American Anti-Slavery Society and had called instead for mission-ary efforts to former slaves.[2]

Then Lincoln issued his Emancipation Proclamation, and Garrison declared his eagerness to dissolve the society, despite Phillips' immedi-ate objection that the nation needed the abolitionists now more than ever. In January, 1863, for example, Garrison hinted at an antislavery gathering that final victory lay just ahead. Phillips praised Garrison's "encouraging faith" in "the progress of the antislavery idea," but he went on to lament the weaknesses of the Emancipation Proclamation and the need to stand by Lincoln for two more years. Phillips heaped praise on John C. Fremont and Benjamin F. Butler, the military governor of Union-occupied New Orleans, whose stringent policies were protect-ing blacks and repressing white obstructionists. These were men Lin-coln ought to emulate. The Fosters and Charles L. Remond, displaying less diplomacy than Phillips, then pointedly reminded Garrison of the original Declaration of Sentiments of the American Anti-Slavery So-ciety, specifically the clauses that bound abolitionists to eradicate not just chattel slavery but white racism itself across the land. This part of the abolitionists' work was far from complete. Thus, when Garrison again spoke in favor of dissolution, during the anniversary celebration in Philadelphia, Foster and Frederick Douglass were already well prepared. Denouncing Lincoln's proclamation as the product of expediency, they warned Garrison that white supremacy reigned as widely as ever in American political culture. As Douglass put it, abolitionists must never disband until "the black man of the South, and the black man of the North, shall have been admitted fully and completely into the body poli-tic of America."[3] He was clearly reflecting the sentiments of the con-spicuously absent Wendell Phillips as well.

2. Friedman, *Gregarious Saints*, 256–61.
3. *Liberator*, January 7, 1863; *Proceedings of the American Anti-Slavery Society at Its Third Decade Meeting. . . .* (New York, 1864), 1–175.

Just prior to this Philadelphia meeting, Lincoln had outlined some of his Reconstruction plans, which seemed to Phillips to reconfirm the folly of Garrison's call for dissolution. The president offered pardons to all who would swear loyalty to a Union without slavery, excluding only the most prominent Confederates; and he suggested that any rebel state should be readmitted when one-tenth of its 1860 population had taken this oath and had established an acceptable new state government. As to race relations, Lincoln insisted only that there be no more slavery; other "temporary arrangements" would be acceptable. Southern whites, understanding Lincoln's willingness to let them manage the freedmen alone, perhaps through peonage or apprentice systems, of course felt no compulsion to grant civil and political rights. Lincoln, moreover, had seemingly excluded Congress from the Reconstruction process. Charles Sumner, Ben Wade, and the rest were, presumably, to have no voice in determining readmission policy.[4]

Some took Lincoln's statements as pragmatic efforts to weaken the rebellion and placate the border states, not as fixed policy. To Phillips, however, they seemed to fit a distressing pattern in which his own impact was hard to document. In 1863, for example, Lincoln had undercut Benjamin Butler's iron rule over "disloyal" whites in New Orleans by appointing Nathaniel P. Banks, an old Cotton Whig, as military governor of Louisiana. Banks had then conducted elections under the state's antebellum constitution that returned power to the old planter classes and had instituted a labor system that forced former slaves to work under restrictive labor contracts. Some abolitionists, Garrison among them, had justified Banks's regime as necessary to bring social order to chaotic Louisiana. Phillips, however, and the black abolitionists who had flooded Washington with protest petitions saw it as slavery in disguise. "What you call the freedom of Louisiana is 'Banks' freedom,' and it is no freedom to me," Phillips had declared, insisting on the contrary that no class or race was safe, "no freedom real . . . which does not place in the hands of the man himself the power to protect his own rights." As the Christian paternalist Garrison supported Lincoln and Banks, the Radical Republican Phillips began demanding that black men be granted in-

4. The political background of Reconstruction developed here and in succeeding paragraphs of this chapter and the next is heavily influenced by Michael Les Benedict, *A Compromise of Principle: Congressional Republicans and Reconstruction, 1863–1869* (New York, 1973); John H. Cox and LaWanda Cox, *Politics, Principles, and Prejudice, 1865–1866: The Dilemma of Reconstruction America* (New York, 1963).

dependent citizenship, "in accord with our philosophy of government since the 4th day of July 1776."[5] He now feared that Lincoln meant to extend his Louisiana policies throughout the rebel states.

After meeting with the president again early in 1863, Phillips came away certain that Lincoln had personally confirmed all such misgivings. In deciding to revisit the White House, Phillips had hoped to persuade Lincoln to appoint an antislavery leader like Fremont to administer subjugated areas of North Carolina. Instead, Lincoln had installed a unionist from that state, Edward N. Stanly, a former slaveholder who had once threatened Joshua Giddings with physical assault on the floor of the House of Representatives.[6] Little wonder, then, that Phillips much preferred denouncing Lincoln at Republican gatherings to contemplating "victory" and retirement with Garrison. As his debates with abolitionist colleagues grew sharper, Phillips' attacks on Lincoln and his demands for reconstructing the South also became more wide-ranging.

In his speech before the New York City Republicans at the Cooper Institute Phillips rehearsed all his disagreements with the president. If he began rather mildly, it was only because he wished to develop many more fundamental criticisms. He could grant, he said, that the president was a "growing man, with his face zionward," but Lincoln's greatest merit, in Phillips' view, was that his obstinacy was weaker than "the force of events and the public pressure which crush it." In short, Lincoln could be pushed by abolitionist agitation, but even such pressure would not prevent the catastrophe Phillips foresaw should the president proceed as he wished with Reconstruction. Great secessionist planters would regain control over the South's economy, its politics, and its black labor force, reinstituting slavery under one guise or another and leaving the freedmen as helpless as they had been in 1860. Lincoln, according to Phillips, proposed that "we should stand and see the freedmen, whose arms helped us to victory, robbed of their liberty at the sight of its reality. Mr. Lincoln is a very prudent man, people say. Well, prudence is a worthy virtue, except when exercized at other people's expense."[7]

As Phillips next detailed what he believed could be a truly effective

5. *Liberator*, December 11, 1864, February 10, 1865; Phillips, *"The Immediate Issue": A Speech Delivered at the Annual Meeting of the Massachusetts Anti-Slavery Society* (Boston, 1865).
6. Moncure Conway, *Autobiography* (2 vols.; London, 1914), I, 377–84; Stewart, *Giddings*, 220 n.
7. *National Anti-Slavery Standard*, January 9, 1864.

Reconstruction policy, some of his reasons for boycotting Garrison's victory celebration suddenly became clear. Slavery would never truly be destroyed, he insisted, until the federal government "crumbled up the nobles' estates into small farms" and put them "into the hands of the negroes and white men who fought for [them]." Only by redistributing rebel lands and by subjecting the South to military occupation could a truly victorious North expect to "plant a union as sure to grow as an acorn to become an oak," said Phillips. "Plant two hundred thousand negro farmers, and by their side two hundred thousand white soldiers, and I will risk the South, Davis and all."[8]

But confiscation would be only the first step. White Americans must never forget that they had "robbed four million men and their ancestors for seventy years" by practicing slavery. Every black had more than earned from them the "substantial protection in all his rights." And so Phillips returned to his lifelong reliance on the power of the state to institute a sweeping agenda of nationally legislated black equality. He called for the enactment of two constitutional amendments, one prohibiting slavery and the other providing that "no state shall make any distinction among its citizens on account of race or color." Then he demanded even more, proposing federal laws that guaranteed land and public education for every former slave. "The nation owes the negro not merely freedom," Phillips insisted. "It owes him land; it owes him education also. It is a debt that will disgrace us before the people if we do not pay it." Anything less, he warned, would lead to another fatal compromise similar to those of 1787 or 1850, exactly the direction in which Lincoln's plans inevitably led. "The President's plan is not feasible," Phillips warned, "and ends in shame or defeat. . . . A union so reconstructed would be sure not to work. Such a peace would be war in disguise." The great struggle between antagonistic nations that Phillips had spoken of so often would certainly continue, he believed, until the North realized that the slaves, to be truly free, must be protected with preferential legislation. And to achieve these goals, Phillips vowed finally, he would never rest until the nation had a president better than Lincoln, "someone whose character this war has brought to the surface. . . . In other words, until either Butler or Fremont mans the guns."[9]

If Phillips had not quite made a presidential endorsement, he had cer-

8. *Ibid.*
9. *Ibid.*

tainly highlighted his disagreement with Garrison. He had also unveiled
the rudiments of southern Reconstruction policies that he would ceaselessly reiterate during the next six years. Fremont (Phillips' new hope for
achieving his sweeping objectives) and Lincoln (Garrison's agent of vindication) now represented opposite political poles for feuding abolitionists, and as they began to gravitate toward one leader or the other,
division within the movement quickly grew. The wide differences now
separating Phillips from Garrison also became dramatically public when
the Massachusetts Anti-Slavery Society met in January, 1864.

In this first face-to-face debate with Garrison, Phillips delivered
blunt warnings about the white South's intransigence, the importance
of the upcoming presidential elections, and the dangers he saw in supporting Lincoln. Lincoln, a bigot, "does not recognize the negro as a
man; he does not blot out races," Phillips charged, calling once more for
laws that would revolutionize southern society—land redistribution,
black suffrage, compulsory education, and an amendment banning racial discrimination. "As the educational apparatus of New England follows close behind the garrison," Phillips rhapsodized, technology and
moral enlightenment would reshape the slaveocracy in the image of
Massachusetts. "The moment we get an acre, we set a school house on
it. God speed New England! and next door to it we set up a spinning
machine; and next to that we plant in the sweat of each man's brow the
harvest he is to gather and eat. Civilization taking possession of the recovered states!"[10]

Lincoln wanted to stifle the liberating spread of free-labor civilization
before it even began, Phillips asserted in conclusion, and he put forward
a resolution condemning the president's haste to fabricate a "sham
peace" that would return embittered whites to power and "leave the
negro in a condition little better than slavery." Garrison then leapt to his
feet and offered his own motion, which endorsed Lincoln's reelection
and disagreed vehemently with Phillips' assessment. "Now Sir," said
Garrison, "I do not believe a word of it, and cannot vote for it. . . . In my
judgment, the re-election of Lincoln would be the safest and wisest
course." When the vote was finally taken, Phillips' resolution prevailed
by a three-to-two margin. The Massachusetts Anti-Slavery Society was
now on record in opposition to Lincoln's second term, in favor of social

10. *Liberator*, February 5, 1864.

revolution in the South, and controlled by a majority loyal to Wendell Phillips.[11]

The victory itself actually meant far less than the dynamics that lay behind it. Garrison, in defending Lincoln, had rejected all that Phillips was seeking in his quest to create a republican South and to fulfill his vision of a nation whose laws secured harmony and freedom for all its races and classes. Phillips' own personal liberator seemed instead to favor replacing the crusade for equality with an "old clothes movement" that would "dish out thin soup" to the freedmen and hand their liberties to vengeful planters. Abolitionists would argue interminably over the next year as Garrison and his supporters prepared to leave the movement. Nothing anyone said, however, modified the fundamental clash of assumptions that Garrison and Phillips explored in this first exchange. A young abolitionist who listened to them argue sensed quite correctly that "something terrible" lay behind the more obvious points in Phillips' and Garrison's exchanges.[12]

Garrison, to be sure, felt he had persuasive grounds for resenting Phillips' charge of abandoning the freedman. Like Quincy, the Westons, the Mays, Maria Chapman, and Oliver Johnson, Garrison believed that he was remaining truly faithful to one of abolitionism's oldest tenets. As a founder of the American Anti-Slavery Society, he had long ago declared it his obligation to prepare blacks for freedom by furnishing Christian assistance. Paternalism it certainly was, but Garrison believed it his duty to aid those whom society had so grievously wronged. From his perspective, Phillips' exclusive emphasis on legislation seemed dangerous. After all the statutes had been enacted, he feared, freedmen would still be left with no cultural or religious supports for their freedom. Phillips, in turn, regarded Garrison's quest for vindication as a serious threat not only to black emancipation but also to his self-conceived political role, which was continuing to expand as rapidly as debate over Reconstruction itself.[13]

Having fashioned himself for decades to be a latter-day Edmund Burke, Phillips finally had begun to achieve the national stature he had

11. *Ibid.*
12. *Ibid.*, May 6, 1865; Lillie Buffum Chace Wyman and Arthur Wyman, *Elizabeth Buffum Chace* (2 vols.; Boston, 1914), I, 258–59.
13. See *Liberator*, February 10, 17, 1865; and *National Anti-Slavery Standard*, May 1, 1864, for a sample of these views.

dreamed about as a college student and even before. He had demonstrated that he was a newsmaker of indisputable authority, a radical spokesman for powerful constituencies, and he had taken pains to develop connections with influential politicians. Yet Lincoln seemed impervious to his influence. Now Garrison was joining the president to stand directly against all that Phillips wished to achieve. Content with the person in office, Garrison felt placidly removed from political struggle. Phillips, by contrast, was becoming ever more deeply enmeshed in partisan activities, seeking to translate his indisputably great influence into explicit political control. To those ends, he sought out Benjamin Butler as confidant and assured Sumner and George W. Julian that he intended "to work with your gang" to ripen "public opinion sufficient to control legislative action in . . . reconstruction." Little wonder, then, that Phillips felt his anger grow as Garrison challenged his loftiest social visions and most private political ambitions.[14]

Major newspapers soon began speculating about an open break, while abolitionists tried to minimize the conflict. Garrison and Oliver Johnson wrote conciliatory editorials, asserting that "no schism exists in, or impends over, the Anti-Slavery body."[15] Yet in the weeks before issuing these denials, Johnson had editorialized that the antislavery societies must disband as soon as the states ratified the Thirteenth Amendment. He, McKim, Quincy, and Samuel J. May also assured Garrison that Phillips was behaving irresponsibly, and Ann Warren Weston bluntly conveyed the same opinion to Ann Phillips. Phillips, meanwhile, received assurances of support from the predictable sources—the Fosters, Pillsbury, Henry Wright, and most of the female and black abolitionists. Personal relations were souring quickly.[16] Phillips, for instance, hedged when invited to a recognition celebration for Garrison. "Give me a few days to consider when I return from a talking tour," he requested. Although he protested privately that he still loved Garrison like a "dear brother," when he had ended his trip, he did not attend Garrison's party. Moreover, on that talking tour Phillips announced that John C. Fremont, not Lincoln, should bear the Republican party standard in 1864. Shortly

14. Bartlett, *Phillips*, 261–68; Phillips to George W. Julian, March 27, 1864, Joshua R. Giddings–George W. Julian Papers, Library of Congress (hereafter LC).
15. *National Anti-Slavery Standard*, March 12 (quotation), February 13, 1864; *Liberator*, February 26, 1864.
16. Friedman, *Gregarious Saints*, 256–70; *National Anti-Slavery Standard*, February 6, 1864; Johnson to William L. Garrison, February 18, 1864, Garrison Papers, BPL; Ann W. Weston to Ann Phillips, February 15, 1864, Blagden Papers.

thereafter, when the American Anti-Slavery Society gathered in New York City, Phillips was ready with still more anti-Lincoln resolutions. Garrison, of course, issued his familiar protest, but the society, by a small margin, voted against Lincoln's renomination.[17] Twice now Phillips had demonstrated that he, not Garrison, controlled the anti-slavery societies.

John C. Fremont looked upon these developments with hope, for he wanted the nomination and had support in Congress. In late 1863, Fremont visited Boston, bought a summer home near the Phillips' place in Nahant, and delivered a stirring speech at the Music Hall. Phillips sat behind him on the platform, and enjoyed another friendly talk with Jessie Fremont. In May, 1864, when insurgent Republicans called for an independent nominating convention and demanded a platform of black suffrage and southern land redistribution, Phillips' interest in the candidacy of the "Pathfinder" had grown considerably. The convention was scheduled to meet in Cleveland before either of the two major parties selected its candidates.[18]

Hoping to create upheaval in the politics that so baffled him and eager to secure his influence with Lincoln's possible replacement, Phillips endorsed the convention and put Fremont forward as his own nominee. "If Mr. Lincoln is re-elected, I do not expect to see the union reconstructed in my day," he declared. "If I turn to General Fremont, I see a man whose first act was to use the freedom of the negro as his weapon." Phillips next traveled to Vermont to drum up anti-Lincoln delegates for the Republican nominating convention in Baltimore. Finally, as if to show everyone how completely he had abandoned his long-cherished independence, Phillips even appeared at his neighborhood Republican caucus, where he offered anti-Lincoln resolutions that party regulars roundly rejected. Then, in late May, the insurgent Cleveland convention met, adopted a platform of legal equality and land confiscation, and nominated Fremont. Meanwhile, at the Republican convention in Baltimore, Garrison was ushered to the speaker's platform as the delegates wildly cheered. Enjoying yet another moment of vindication, he wrote, "Even

17. Phillips to Charles Eliot Norton, February 14, 1864, Charles Eliot Norton Papers, HL; Phillips to Moncure Conway, February 16, 1864, Moncure Conway Papers, CL; *Liberator*, May 20, 27, 1864.
18. *Liberator*, September 5, 12, 1864; Phillips to Sumner, November 27, 1863, Sumner Papers; Maria W. Chapman to "Lizzie and Annie," May 15, 1863, Weston Papers.

my friend Phillips would have been highly gratified with the tone and spirit of the convention."[19] Now that he and Phillips were looking in such opposite political directions, Garrison could not have misspoken more completely.

Though Phillips plunged into electioneering with a will, he failed to transform himself into an effective political strategist. Actually believing that Fremont could win in a three-way election, he thought, at the least, that the Cleveland convention would frighten the Republicans so badly that they would abandon Lincoln for someone more radical. He even dreamed for a time that Fremont would become a "nucleus to which breaking parties may gravitate" as the entire structure of partisan politics collapsed.[20] Soon, however, Phillips saw his naïve hopes deflated. Instead of expanding his role in politics and reshaping the Republican party, he was charged with abetting prosouthern "copperheads." Fremont, as Lincoln's supporters pointed out, would draw votes away from the wartime president even as his commander, Ulysses S. Grant, prepared to move south. Both the *Liberator* and the *Standard* therefore editorialized persuasively that Fremont's radical supporters were actually crippling the war to end slavery, and even close advisers like Aaron Powell urged Phillips to give Fremont up as "the smallest specimen of manhood he had ever attempted to associate with." Pillsbury wrote him even more bluntly: "To speak for [the] Cleveland [convention] up here, or indeed anywhere," he reported from New Hampshire, "is to class yourself with the copperheads." Phillips soon found himself forced to rebut charges that he had become the unwitting cat's-paw of the slave power, and Garrison, of course, delighted in his opponent's discomfiture.[21]

As the summer wore on, Phillips grew increasingly irritated and confused. On the one hand, he insisted to detractors like Samuel May, Jr., that supporting Fremont had not really undermined his political independence. "Soon I shall find occasion to say why I shall remain a reformer—not a politician—still (as in 1843) prefer[ing] *justice* to the *union*." But to supporters like Elizabeth Cady Stanton he voiced a re-

19. *Liberator*, April 8, May 13, June 3, 1864; Bartlett, *Phillips*, 269; William L. Garrison to Helen B. Garrison, February 24, 1864, Garrison Papers, BPL.

20. Phillips to Conway, March 16, 1864, Conway Papers; Phillips to Wendell P. Garrison, July 12, 1864, Garrison Papers, BPL; Phillips to Elizabeth Cady Stanton, July 20, 1864, Wendell Phillips Miscellaneous Letters, Henry E. Huntington Library.

21. *National Anti-Slavery Standard*, June 18, July 9, 16, 1864; *Liberator*, July 29,

vealingly contradictory lament: "I wish I had more influence with F[re-mont] and some men less. But I believe in *him*." Wendell Phillips Garrison, Phillips' namesake, resolved his own divided family loyalties by lashing out at his second parent. "You surrendered your dignity and your independent position for a paltry equivalent," he wrote. By endorsing Fremont, the young Garrison lectured, "you left Olympus for a caucus." These words, of course, as Phillips surely appreciated, echoed his own assessment of Daniel Webster's political bankruptcy in 1850. He replied in patient tones but implausibly, for he insisted that he was now no less his own political man than he had been in the 1840s.[22] William Lloyd Garrison and his confederates wrote to each other in the meantime, lamenting poor Wendell's behavior. By June, Garrison knew "that our society must be rent asunder. . . . I fear that P[hillips] has made up his mind to leave us. He is evidently in a heated state."[23]

Garrison's was a noteworthy understatement. As Phillips' abolitionist friendships crumbled, so did his political aspirations, and he lashed out furiously at Garrison, now a "lost leader," and his followers. *Standard* editor Oliver Johnson became his target for special vehemence. Phillips claimed that Johnson's editorials criticizing Fremont had transformed the official voice of the American Anti-Slavery Society into a Lincoln campaign sheet. Johnson stuck to his position, however, and was supported by the society's Executive Committee. When negotiations failed, the Phillips camp withdrew financial support for the paper. Phillips, Pillsbury, and others also prevented income from the Hovey Fund, an abolitionist bequest for freedman aid, from falling into Garrison's hands, and by now everyone had become so upset that the Executive Committee canceled the American Anti-Slavery Society's usual round of summer meetings. The Fremont campaign meanwhile became mired in confusion as Sherman's army moved decisively upon Atlanta and military

---

1864; Pillsbury to Phillips, August 4, 1864, Powell to Phillips, June 28, 1864, Theodore Tilden to Phillips, June 30, 1864, all in Blagden Papers; Thomas, *Garrison*, 425.

22. Phillips to Samuel May, Jr., September 19, 1864, May Papers; Phillips to Stanton, August 22, 1864, Elizabeth Cady Stanton Papers, LC; Wendell P. Garrison to Phillips, June 30, 1864, Blagden Papers; Phillips to Wendell P. Garrison, July 12, 1864, Garrison Papers, BPL.

23. William L. Garrison to May, June 17, 1864 (quotation), May Papers; Johnson to William L. Garrison, June 20, 1864, May, Jr., to Webb, July 12, 1864; both in Garrison Papers, BPL; McKim to Caroline Weston, June 24, 1864, Weston Papers.

triumph made Lincoln politically invincible. Fremont hurriedly withdrew his name from contention, spurning Phillips' last-minute pleas that he remain in the race.[24]

Lincoln easily won the general election. The vast body of abolitionists, many of Phillips' usual supporters among them, rejoiced at the outcome even as the politically frustrated orator delivered a bitter post-election denunciation of the president at the Tremont Temple. His own association with Fremont had only hastened the collapse of abolitionist unity and cast doubt on his own political position. Indeed, from every perspective, Phillips' engagement in presidential politics could only be judged a debacle. In the aftermath nothing remained for him but to write Benjamin Butler sourly of his fears about the "too-hasty-peace-maker-on-any-terms" that the people had returned to the White House. Meanwhile, he tried to bolster his morale by believing that abolitionists could actually put aside their differences and "rally together to claim of the Republican party their performance of their pledge" of passing an emancipation amendment.[25] This vain hope represented Phillips' sincere gesture to the memory of a fellowship, now shattered, that had sustained his spirit and confirmed his social visions for nearly thirty years. Never did he reveal his deeper feelings about his many broken friendships; it was too painful a subject for him to address openly.

Had even the slightest grounds remained for reconciliation, Garrison dashed them in January, 1865, when he announced to a meeting of the Massachusetts Anti-Slavery Society that the enfranchisement of the freedmen, though proper, must not be imposed on the South. Phillips, as usual, had readied a counterresolution that "no emancipation can be effectual, no freedom real" until universal male suffrage was enshrined as constitutional writ. Moreover, Phillips maintained, defeated states must be forced by Congress to enact black enfranchisement before being readmitted to the Union, lest white obstructionism prevent subsequent ratification of a suffrage amendment. After savage exchanges among Stephen Foster, Quincy, and Garrison, the competing resolutions were put to the vote, and Phillips won overwhelmingly. Even before the balloting, however, Garrison stalked out, leaving Phillips to remark

24. Pillsbury to Phillips, August 27, 1864, Blagden Papers; *Liberator*, June 24, July 22, 1864; Bartlett, *Phillips*, 273.

25. *National Anti-Slavery Standard*, November 5, 1864; Phillips to Butler, December 5, 1864, in Marshall (ed.), *Correspondence of Butler*, V, 400; Phillips to Stanton, November 20, 1864, Stanton Papers.

magnanimously: "Whatever, therefore, may be the conclusion of the debate, I recognize the same leading mind at the head of the anti-slavery struggle. . . . In time to come we shall need, find and welcome the same leader."[26] There could be no denying that Garrison had lost badly. Twice now, the Massachusetts Anti-Slavery Society had rejected his views, concurring with Phillips instead that the franchise was crucial to all aspects of postwar reform.

Once war had broken out, Phillips, as we have seen, had greatly expanded his demands for legislated equality, insisting that a powerful central government must develop laws to reshape the South as a showplace of republican culture. In such a program, Garrison's states' rights notions obviously had no place. But despite his acquisition of power and his ever-growing reliance on state authority, Phillips harbored no fewer inherent suspicions of governments and political parties in 1864 than he had in 1844. He still believed that original sin held sway over human nature, officeholders still betrayed their constituents, governments still inherently tended toward despotism, and laws by themselves offered no automatic guarantees of liberty. Voters, however, most certainly did. At this point, Garrison's opposition to the national franchise constituted a declaration of total war against all that Phillips envisioned for America's reconstruction.

Just as in his disunionist days, Phillips held that public opinion, directed by agitators and expressed through the ballot, shaped the behavior of politicians. Officeholders reflected the popular will when they framed and enforced legislation, for when it came to political parties, the tails of the snakes continued to direct the heads, but the situation had also changed greatly since 1861. Before the war, in Phillips' view, Garrisonian agitators had been inspired to forgo the ballot, attempting instead to "persuade a mountain of prejudice," that is, a government directed by a racist majority, to move its moral center in behalf of powerless slaves. Now, however, as southern blacks took off their shackles, they must be enabled to "vote for themselves" to protect their economic standing and personal liberties, just as did all other classes and groups in America. Somewhat as James Madison had argued so many years before, Phillips approached Reconstruction assuming that the active pursuit of self-interest by every citizen would preserve the liberties of all. Unlike Madison, who had analyzed republican political culture as an aggregate

26. *Liberator,* January 1, February 3, 10, 17, 1865.

of contending factions, however, Phillips envisioned millions of voters, free laborers of every race, class, and occupation, expanding the boundaries of their individual freedom and promoting social harmony every time they cast their ballots. For this reason above all others, he dismissed Garrison's benevolent approaches to uplifting the freedmen as a dangerous sham. "I do not believe education for the masses has ever been wrung out of the upper classes by any such motive as philanthropy," he typically declared.[27] It was the ballot, Phillips stressed, that put power in the hands of poor people, forcing the wealthy to grant them their civil rights, promote their social interests, and expand their opportunities for self-improvement. The national franchise, in short, had become Phillips' most crucial mechanism of all for overcoming class divisions as well as racial barriers.

To illustrate this most important axiom, Phillips invariably related the history of Boston's Irish to the status of freedmen of the South, recalling his attempt to make common cause with these immigrants in 1842. Once, Boston's Irish had been few and unorganized, he asserted, and no one had respected their rights. Soon, however, they had grown in number and in political sophistication, and no politician "would dare to make a speech today without a compliment to Green Erin." This conviction above all led Phillips to contend that "the moment a man becomes valuable or terrible to the politician, his rights will be respected." As it had become for the Irish, he argued, so it must now be for the freedmen. Armed with the ballot and alive to protecting their rights and interests, blacks would find themselves courted by every politician "from Abraham Lincoln down to the laziest loafer in the lowest ward." Every male, no matter what his condition, should qualify to vote. "I don't care for his race," Phillips declared, "I don't care for his brains." Anyone with brains enough to get arrested "has brains enough to go to the ballot box." Phillips believed that people derived from the ballot all power necessary for creating a society dedicated to their individual economic improvement, to racial reconciliation, to harmony between classes, and to social progress. "From the possession of political rights," Phillips emphasized, "a man gets means to clutch equal opportunities of education and a fair space of work. Give a man his vote, and you give him tools to work and arms to protect himself."[28] In other words, the

27. *National Anti-Slavery Standard*, January 9, 1864.
28. *Liberator*, May 29, 1863.

very same franchise that Garrison refused to force upon the South would become, in Phillips' view, the wellspring of a comprehensive nationality, a national culture encompassing the North as well as the South, which he once described forcefully as follows:

> Wealth sees the ballot in the hands of poverty, and knows that its gold and its roof depend upon the use made of that ballot, and wealth hurries to put intelligence on the one side and religion on the other of the baby footsteps that will one day find their way to the ballot. That is the essence of democratic institutions. It mortgages wealth and learning and strength to lift up the poor man's cradle. I want that help for the black man. How shall I get it? I will explain. Go down to Broad Street and trespass on the rights of the raggedest Irish boy that sells newspapers in the streets, and in a week I will show you the *Advertiser* and the *Transcript*, the *Journal* and the *Herald*, the *Traveller* and the *Post* covering that boy with their advocacy, and Henry Wilson leading the van. (Laughter and applause.) And why do they do it? Because that boy is one of 80,000 living on this peninsula, who wield about ten thousand votes, and covered with the panoply of that defense, journal and political aspirants hasten to gain merit by conciliating the just regard and gratitude of that boy. I want the same thing for the black man, and I shall have it. The moment I give to the 40,000 black men in Louisiana ballots, Gen. Banks may then relieve himself from the labor of establishing schools; the white men of Louisiana will see to it that those black men, who have their hands on the helm of the State—whose purpose makes life and gold safe or otherwise, are educated. I plant myself always on democratic principles. I am a democrat, engrained, from top to toe; and I mean to welcome the negro to the same shield that has made me and the Irishmen of this peninsula equal and equally safe. I shall give myself no rest till the negro stands there.[29]

At this crucial point, Phillips' equation between southern blacks and Boston's Irish caused him to wrench his perspective northward. In doing so, however, he was also forced to expand the boundaries of Reconstruction far beyond all conventional understanding, for he suddenly found

29. *Ibid.*, February 17, 1865.

himself face to face with the obvious and enormous changes occurring in his very own state. He was demanding that industrializing New England's political culture be exported wholesale by force of arms into the South, but in his own Massachusetts, he had the indisputable impression that free labor had created drab factories, depressing neighborhoods, and angry class relations that fundamentally challenged his vision of nationality. Phillips, one must recall, had extolled abolitionism—and later the onset of civil war—for its ennobling influence on northern economic values and the solidarity it would bring to class relations. In 1860, however, even before the war had started, his municipal police and temperance proposals had conveyed his deep uneasiness over the spread of urban industrial society. That same year, moreover, the Lynn shoemakers' strike had given him strong indication that a worker's sense of injustice usually grew rather than waned with increased factory mechanization. Now, just as the war was drawing to a close, working-class leaders began again to protest against wage slavery, insisting that propertyless factory operatives had no chance to rise in a laissez-faire economy and must develop associations of their own to advance the interests of the producing classes. Technological development and an expanding marketplace did not offer them freedom, they insisted, only longer hours, harsher working conditions, and lower wages from the monied interests.[30]

Phillips had begun to suspect as early as 1864 that the war was bringing these grave developments into public view and had acknowledged his feeling that they profoundly contradicted his republican values. "The youngest of us are never again to see the republic in which we were born," he had announced at the American Anti-Slavery Society Annual Meeting of that year, for the war economy had already created a crushing national debt, debased the nation's currency, destroyed credit, and demoralized a generation of working people. In all these ways, Phillips had said, the war had "mortgaged . . . the labor of the next half century," exacerbating class oppression by depriving workers of the "surplusage of means" that had always insured their personal independence. The American artisan, he had insisted, had once used such extra funds "for books, for lectures, for amusements, for newspapers, for travel, for the education of his children." Now workers were being stripped of the

30. For an invaluable detailed analysis of the labor question during the 1860s and 1870s, see David Montgomery, *Beyond Equality: Labor and the Radical Republicans, 1862–1872,* (New York, 1967).

surplus dollar that had once "lifted labor [in America] to a higher level than the rest of the world knew." The working-class found itself being "robbed of that . . . which constitutes its nucleus of intelligence and moral progress." The grossly exploitative society that Phillips had found so revolting in Europe a quarter century earlier now seemed to be appearing in New England. In the hands of industrial entrepreneurs, he feared, his free-labor values were being perverted into a system in which workers' personal independence and horizons of individual opportunity were shutting down. Powerless and propertyless, they set off for the factory "each Monday morning almost as hopeless as the previous."[31]

Phillips, who had always so hated disorder and aristocracy, had now begun to see the challenges to his republican creed in New England mill towns and in Boston, as well as in the South. Contrary to his original expectation, the impact of Civil War had driven classes apart in the North instead of reconciling them. If, as it now appeared, the North was creating a permanently frozen class of hired laborers, Phillips wondered, could the proslavery apologists have been right in accusing Yankee capitalism of spawning wage slavery? In 1847 he had scoffed at such charges, but now he was not so certain. If wage slavery in the North was in fact supplanting southern chattel servitude, where then was the national victory Phillips had so long prophesied for free labor? Little wonder then, that in 1865, the same year that he split with Garrison and opened his campaign for universal male suffrage, Phillips also spelled out his support for temperance and for workingmen's rights. Contrary to oft-repeated assertions, Phillips did not move on to these other causes in 1870, after the ratification of the Fifteenth Amendment. Instead, from 1865 onward, he regarded labor and temperance questions as essential elements of the larger and long-continuing tasks of Reconstruction, the most pressing of which for the moment was black suffrage.

In February, 1865, therefore, Phillips declared his support for state-wide temperance laws, testifying before a legislative committee in Massachusetts against Boston's open defiance of codes forbidding liquor sales. As he took pains to emphasize at the start of his remarks, he feared for the deteriorating condition of all of Boston's voters, not just the drinking habits of the Irish-Catholics or the working class. After all, he contended, English-Americans had long been especially afflicted by a "peculiar temptation" for liquor that dated to the "drunken revels [and]

31. *Liberator*, May 20, 1864.

overflowing mead" of Anglo-Saxon days. The great peril, according to Phillips, was that drunkenness knew no class or ethnic boundaries in a society "where the heavy work of republican institutions rests on the people themselves," and the affliction had spread its influence so pervasively that state intervention alone offered respite from local anarchy and despotism. "A drunken people were never the safe depositories of the power of self-government," he insisted, for they invariably became "the mere victims of demagogues," with "uncontrollable passion and temptation their guide." Intemperance destroyed all moral progress and individual initiative, Phillips argued, utterly negating the social benefits of free labor and even the constructive expenditures that far-seeing governments devoted to public education. While school met, the bars were open and families perished, prostitution flourished, and the suicide rate mounted. Meantime, the liquor interest, "two thousand men with ten million dollars behind them, commanding three to seven thousand votes," manipulated elections, controlled the police, and profited from the illegal commerce.[32]

The commonwealth of Massachusetts must literally reconstruct Boston, Phillips declared. Clearly, he regarded the liquor interest as Boston's equivalent of the South's planter class; it too, was an aristocracy that, unless restrained by law and the state, would overawe the people, destroy their economic productivity, undermine their moral values, and subvert their power at the ballot box. In this instance, the Massachusetts legislature must enforce its own temperance laws ruthlessly in order to restore morality to Boston's economy and republican character to its politics. Moreover, Phillips argued tellingly, Boston's rapid growth had long ago transformed the city from the historical setting in which republican values had originally flourished. In "well educated, sparsely populated" Berkshire mountain towns, the moral consensus of public virtue might still "supply the place of force and compulsion," but in sprawling, ethnically divided Boston, only the intervention of a superior legal force could insure the restoration of civility and an end to exploitation of the poor by the liquor interest. Only if the state finally acted, Phillips believed, could the conspiracy of distillers and politicos be crushed and the city returned to a condition where "the mother can

32. Phillips, "The Laws of the Commonwealth: Shall They Be Enforced?" A Speech Before the Massachusetts Legislative Committee (Boston, 1865).

trust her boy, the wife her husband, the brother his brother, in the streets of the capital, for education, for trade, and for pleasure."[33] Although Phillips had seldom preached temperance at abolitionist meetings, he now integrated this crusade fully into his larger vision of an American nationality. Voters in New England, certainly no less than in the South, needed to be sober, self-directed, and alive to their interests at the ballot box if classes and races in America were to flourish in republican harmony.

Phillips called forthrightly for just such sober vigilance in late 1865, speaking to a gathering of workingmen at Faneuil Hall. This, however, was not his first appearance before the labor reformers. At least once that year, in Portland, Maine, he had addressed a similar gathering. On both occasions he voiced hearty support for legislation demanded by labor groups to shorten the workday to eight hours. Sometimes employees were forced to work twice that long, but twelve-hour days were the norm, and simple humanitarianism in the face of such excessiveness led some reformers to endorse the eight-hour day. Other proponents believed that a shorter workday would make prices and wages rise, for increased leisure would stimulate the working public's desire for nondurable goods. Yet the demand for a compulsory eight-hour day had far more enemies than friends, for it denied the conventional wisdom that laissez-faire labor and retail markets provided the highest form of economic freedom for all. It also suggested that workers would regain control of a far greater proportion of their own time, which they might spend not only with their families or on self-improvement activities, but also on organizing to protect their economic interest. Nearly all factory owners and most Republican politicians consequently opposed the idea.[34]

Phillips, however, hailed the proposed eight-hour law because it promised to restore the workers to social and economic independence, making each of them capable once again of exercising individual republican responsibility. Ceaseless factory drudgery, he announced in Faneuil Hall, had for too long been transforming free citizens into economic slaves. "Shut a man up to work ten, eleven, or sixteen hours a day, and he comes out the fag end of a man, with neither the brains nor the heart to

33. *Ibid.*
34. See Montgomery, *Beyond Equality*, 3–167.

discharge the duties of citizenship." Overwork, Phillips believed, no less than intemperance or caste exploitation, had become a great foe of a self-governing electorate. Eight hours of labor was certainly a sufficient workday, "a fair division of a man's day, with eight hours for sleep, eight hours for work, and eight hours for the soul." Employers' fears that workers would squander their leisure were groundless, Phillips maintained. The incentives of the marketplace itself would surely induce them to use their leisure constructively. To prove his assertion, he referred to the southern freedmen, again connecting black emancipation to the northern labor movement. In Port Royal, South Carolina, Phillips emphasized, former slaves who controlled their own work time had already transformed abandoned cotton plantations into models of free-labor civilization. This experiment, he declared, confirmed that increased leisure stimulated free workers to produce more, not less. "Mr. Cash is a more efficient master than Mr. Lash. I defy a million men, having got comfort and leisure, not to improve."[35] Phillips could hardly have stated his national vision of Reconstruction or his sweeping reliance on the socially mobile free laborer more directly.

In the labor movement, as in temperance and Reconstruction, Phillips therefore believed that the franchise counted for all. The key for the working class to leisure and comfort, Phillips announced, lay in a political crusade for the eight-hour day, not in strikes, which he denounced as unwisely disruptive and economically unnatural. Phillips strongly advised the workingman to avoid such actions because, as he explained, they violated the precepts of a republican economy. "Capital and labor are not enemies," he declared, "but friends [and] they cannot lead a separate life." As always, Phillips remained certain that class differences in America, no matter how stark, could be surmounted by political agitation, moral enlightenment, and technological progress—all supported by the work of free laborers. Capital, therefore, was but "crystalized labor," in Phillips' view, and labor "but capital dissolved and become active." Neither could prosper without the other, as his understanding of New England's history abundantly proved to him. "Six generations of Massachusetts workingmen," Phillips claimed, had made the state a "treasure house of capital. They have covered it with roads, dotted it

35. Phillips, *Address to the Mass Meeting of Workingmen in Faneuil Hall, November 2, 1865* (Boston, 1865); *Liberator*, March 17, 1865.

with cities; they have filled it with schoolhouses; they have joined it to the markets of the world." During the same era, "six generations of capitalists" had discovered vast markets for the goods that labor produced, had multiplied opportunities for workers to contract for employment, and had "made wages rise by competition." Therefore, working people should launch a great effort for the eight-hour day at the ballot box and so reclaim economic parity with their employers, instead of striking uselessly against them. Only by political methods, said Phillips, would all persons, owners and workers alike, be restored to a proper relationship in which there would be "no separate laborer or capitalist as such," since each person would "combine both in his own person."[36]

Strikes were "cumbersome and unnecessary," Phillips advised. Instead, "use your political power," he urged workers, "for the *ballot compels attention*." (These, of course, were precisely the same claims that Phillips was making for enfranchisement as the cornerstone of racial equality.) The question of the eight-hour day would be successfully legislated within five years, he predicted, if workingmen's associations would only "go into the political field," emulating the abolitionists' success in forcing the Republican party to take up their antislavery cause. "I want this platform occupied by Charles Sumner with his views on the [eight-hour] question," Phillips declared. "I want Henry Wilson with his tireless activity to do for the laboring man what he has helped to do for the negro."[37] Through the elective franchise, the advancement of liberty for working people of all races and in both sections had thus become wholly conjoined in Phillips' hopes for Reconstruction.

Phillips' memories and day-to-day experiences, no less than his abolitionist ideology, had brought him to this grand synthesis of individual freedom with the right to vote. Looking back over the decades, he felt certain that the vote had actually constituted his most important tool for securing all his self-declared antislavery triumphs. He believed that before the Civil War it had been nonvoting agitators like himself who had inspired the electorate to create the Republican party, thereby assuring the destruction of slavery. In addition, Phillips' great success as a public speaker could hardly have led him to question the claims of "Mr. Cash" as the liberator of peoples and societies. He, after all, had become

---

36. Phillips, *Address to the Mass Meeting*; *Liberator*, March 17, 1865.
37. Phillips, *Address to the Mass Meeting*; *Liberator*, March 17, 1865.

an outstanding personal beneficiary of both technology and the free market, for without railways, telegraphs, and steam-driven presses, Phillips could certainly never have become the great rhetorician-statesman. Moreover, unless he had been aggressively promoted by lyceum managers in the free marketplace of ideas, his doctrines, speaking style, and reputation would never have become so well known in northern popular culture. "Mr. Cash," in truth, had helped to secure Phillips' lifelong aspirations to act out republican heroism. And of course Phillips' great wealth hardly provided a critical perspective on industrialization's impact on people in the labor force. Pleading the slaves' cause had given him rich experience at imagining the plight of others, to be sure, and his lifetime of philanthropy had put him in close contact with poor individuals. He had developed considerable empathy with spindle keepers, miners, and factory hands. Still, privileged circumstance certainly encouraged his naïve conviction that unions and strikes were unnecessary, that class conflict and industrial exploitation could be legislated away once the election results had been tallied. Still, the ballot and the free-labor ethic greatly enriched Phillips' memories and inspired his ongoing commitments. William Lloyd Garrison, of course, had undercut these crucial supports the moment he denied Phillips' demand for a national franchise. Little wonder, then, that Phillips turned so furiously upon this dearest friend or that Garrison felt so eager to end the crusade.

As it turned out, Phillips saw both of his great opponents of the franchise removed in 1865. Only three weeks separated the assassination of Abraham Lincoln from Garrison's last appearance as a member of the American Anti-Slavery Society. Phillips received the news of the president's murder with badly divided emotions. Certainly he felt genuine grief. "I was very sad for Lincoln," he wrote privately, "very sad to picture that patient head bowed in death before that drunken and mad bullet." But he also betrayed considerable relief. "Providence," he declared, had wisely removed the most formidable opponent of black enfranchisement. "One bright spot in the cloud is Lincoln has won such living trust from the people that it is impossible to say anything against him," Phillips observed. "The removal of a man too great and too trusted is often a natural gain in times like these. It lifts off a weight and lets the people . . . think for themselves." In his eulogy on the martyred president Phillips praised Lincoln's patience and compassion but again conveyed an undercurrent of guilty satisfaction. "God has graciously withheld him from any fatal misstep," Phillips declared, "and has withdrawn him at the moment when . . . the nation needed a sterner hand for the work God has given to do."[38]

Shortly thereafter, Phillips reported to Ann from New York City that he had finally rid himself of Garrison at a meeting of the American Anti-Slavery Society held in the Cooper Institute. The gathering took two days, attracted huge crowds, and featured powerful speakers who debated all the issues. Phillips knew that he once again had the votes to defeat Garrison's dissolution resolutions; and he stood ready with his own resolutions, which pledged abolitionists to seek "absolute equality before the law—absolute civil equality for the freedman." Garrison's motion to dissolve the society was crushed by a vote of 118–48, and he spurned Phillips' invitation to assume the presidency despite the defeat. Every leading member of the Boston clique who had not done so already thereupon followed Garrison into retirement, as did English friends like Elizabeth Pease and Richard Webb. Oliver Johnson stepped aside as editor of the *Standard* while Garrison folded up the *Liberator*. As many of his oldest friends thus made their hostile departures, Phillips attempted to remain cheerful. "Our officers are nominated and we are having a good meeting," he reported to Ann.[39]

Although poorer in friends, Phillips still counted a goodly number of supporters as he assumed the presidency of the American Anti-Slavery Society, people who came from every stratum of the crusade against slavery. Gerrit Smith, George B. Cheever, and John Greenleaf Whittier, evangelicals with Liberty or Free-Soil party backgrounds, now served as vice-presidents. Anticlericals and political extremists like the Fosters, Pillsbury, Henry C. Wright, and Charles Burleigh also stayed with Phillips, as did Douglass, Remond, Purvis, George Downing, and nearly every other black abolitionist. So did Elizabeth Cady Stanton, Lucretia Mott, Susan B. Anthony, and others who increasingly equated black suffrage with feminist causes. Phillips could use the support of these people to help him deny the strong feelings of personal loss that must have come over him as many of his dearest friendships unraveled. Things could not have turned out any differently, he tried to assure himself, for "we have reached an age when the nature of our lives is *fixed*—I

38. Phillips to Stanton, April 23, 1865, Phillips Miscellaneous Letters, Huntington Library; Phillips, "Lincoln's Assassination," in his *Speeches, Second Series,* 446–54.

39. *Liberator,* May 26, June 2, 1865; Phillips to Ann Phillips, May 9–10, 1865, Blagden Papers.

do not look back with any regret on the path which events, rather than my own will selected for me. . . . I have at least done with some degree of efficiency work that few others were willing to undertake."[40] Such appeals to inevitability certainly furnished Phillips with solace and also allowed him to stifle his impulse to strike back at Garrison and the others. Though he soon became involved in fierce litigation with Garrison over a bequest in an abolitionist's estate, he never attacked his estranged colleague directly or slandered him privately to others.

Absorbing himself in Reconstruction politics was Phillips' best safeguard against anger or brooding, and Lincoln's death opened a multitude of possibilities. Congress had by now recessed for the summer and the new president, Andrew Johnson, issued vengeful statements about punishing traitors and fastening retributive justice upon the South. Phillips exulted in Johnson's powerful rhetoric, certain that his influence with a president was rapidly growing at last. "It is a great relief to be *assured* in regard to our President," he wrote Sumner in May. "Tell the President to give us time" to rally public opinion, he directed, and soon he began praising Johnson warmly as a supporter of black enfranchisement. "I believe him," Phillips declared. "I believe he means suffrage."[41]

By July, however, Phillips felt many familiar misgivings. He estimated that "*two thirds* of the North are willing that he [the black man] should vote," but he also knew that "the opposition is *very strong*" among "men in high places." By August, he had seriously begun to doubt Johnson's good intentions, and by December he had declared open war on the chief executive. "As for the cause," Phillips wrote to Mary Grew, "everything I hear, public and private, from Washington, increases my anxiety about the suffrage question. We shall get all we can bully out of this administration, and no more." All summer, Phillips' speeches became ever more stridently anti-Johnson and more emphatic about Negro suffrage. Without it, he predicted, the nation would relapse into a "horde of merchants lashing cotton out of unwilling blacks," which, he charged, was exactly what Johnson had in mind. The president, Phillips now declared, was an out-and-out "southerner, who cannot see the Negro impartially, who has the prejudice of the white race against him. . . . We must make up our minds that we must deal henceforth with a President

40. Phillips to Chase, July 23, 1865, Chase Papers.
41. *National Anti-Slavery Standard*, June 3, 1865; Phillips to Sumner, May 5, 1865, Sumner Papers.

implacably hostile to the only method of reorganizing that is safe, peaceful and permanent."[42]

Phillips this time had made a perfectly accurate political assessment. As a Tennessee unionist and prewar Jacksonian Democrat, Andrew Johnson had no intention of obliterating states' rights or equalizing the races. Throughout the summer, while Congress remained adjourned, Johnson began to direct the reorganization of the rebel states preparatory to their readmission. He did require each state government to abolish slavery, nullify its secession ordinances, and repudiate its Confederate debt, but he gave no direction about the status of former slaves. The whites, restored to power, were presumably free to arrange race relations as it suited them. Most Republicans, nevertheless, preferred to regard Johnson's actions as an experiment Congress could modify when it assembled again in January, 1866. In the meantime, however, Johnson pardoned many leading Confederates, restoring their titles to confiscated plantations that Phillips had earmarked for ownership by the freedmen. Responding to such leniency, southern whites began adding highly prejudiced black codes to their states' statute books, while in the North, white voters in Wisconsin, Minnesota, and Connecticut rejected black suffrage referenda. Most Republican leaders in these states had supported such reforms, but Democrats, most ominously, had opposed them in the name of their new patriot savior, Andrew Johnson, and had won.

Meantime, Phillips had begun receiving from observers in the South disheartening private dispatches that reconfirmed his worst fears. Albert G. Browne, a diligent treasury agent in South Carolina, filled dozens of pages in several letters on conditions in the South:

> I have been wandering to and fro and up and down the breadth of South Carolina, Georgia, and Florida, and have probably seen more of the working of the new system of labor, if system it may be called, when there is endless confusion, and absurd contradiction, and when in most cases the poor freedman is worse off, so far as food and clothing goes, than in a state of bondage when, in fact, he

42. Phillips to [?], July 16, 1865, Blagden Papers; Phillips to Boutwell, August 21, 1865, Washburn Family Correspondence, MHS; Phillips to Grew, December [?], 1865, in Martyn, *Phillips*, 351; *National Anti-Slavery Standard*, May 12, June 24, July 1, 17, 1865.

is made to do more work for less pay—and is subject to the most cruel treatment. "He's nobodys dog now." and everybody has a right to kick him. Tell about loyalty, there is no loyal sentiment in the South, not a bit of it.[43]

By October, Browne's letters, Johnson's policies, the white South's intransigence, and the Republicans' seeming timorousness had all finally inspired Phillips to open a full-scale attack. Selecting "The South Victorious" as the title of his newest speech on Reconstruction, he delivered it first in Boston, on October 17, 1865, and afterward repeated it in towns all over New England.

People jammed Faneuil Hall to overflowing, eager to find out why Phillips was declaring that the South had won the war. Six months before, had Lee not offered his sword to Grant, sending the North into days of celebration? Yes, agreed Phillips, but the surrender at Appomattox actually meant nothing now. "I think thus far and today, the South is victorious," he stated. The crowd's response was "deep silence." To prove his contention Phillips surveyed American history, invoking memories of the great struggle against "caste, aristocracy, mailed in states' rights . . . with the threefold whip of the slave, the poor white, and the northern slave," which had ruled the Union since 1787. Against this enemy Phillips pictured the North, arrayed in the Declaration of Independence, with its belief "that every child has not only a fair chance, but an equal chance with every other to develop his own nature and enjoy the blessings of God." In this great battle between "two antagonistic principles," Phillips asked, "where stands the South today? . . . How much has the South sacrificed? What one principle has she disowned?" His answer, of course, was "not a one. . . . they came into the Union as they went out of the Union, an aristocracy" wedded to "states rights, the subordination of labor and the impracticality of the two races living together."[44]

Part of the blame, Phillips declared, fell on Johnson, who was little better than Jefferson Davis. "He makes himself three fourths rebel in order that they [the old slave states] may be one fourth Union." The rest belonged to Republicans who excused Johnson's policies as an experiment, for by so doing they proved themselves either stupid or spineless. "No, gentlemen," Phillips assured his listeners, "the President's plan has

43. Albert Gallatin Browne to Phillips, June 16, September 17 (quotation), 1865, April 20, 1866, all in Blagden Papers.
44. *National Anti-Slavery Standard*, October 28, 1865.

none of the marks of an experiment. It is a fortification. . . . the President has put a bayonet in front of every Southern claim, has spiked every Northern cannon." Republicans who thought otherwise had forfeited all right to lead. "The Republican party has spoken, he declared, and "has dared not to utter the word suffrage; it has not dared to deny the President's plan." In truth, Phillips charged, the party itself no longer existed but appeared "only a spectre walking through the country in its shroud." The South had triumphed indeed, Phillips concluded. "We can trust neither Congress, nor Andrew Johnson, nor the Republican party. The only hope remaining is the people."[45]

Actually, there *was* someone else to rely upon, specifically Edward McPherson, Republican clerk of the House of Representatives. At the close of his speech, Phillips repeated a suggestion he had been making since midsummer. If representatives from the southern governments were actually permitted to take their seats in Congress, they would ally at once with the Democrats, form a majority, and direct Reconstruction as they pleased, but if the clerk of the House refused to call the southerners' names as part of the roll, then Republicans could organize the Congress on their own to combat Andrew Johnson.[46] McPherson, in fact, had already assured Phillips and many others that he would refuse to read their names when the southern delegations presented themselves in January, 1866. They would be forced to return home and await the judgment of the North following the Republicans' upcoming battles with their great new foe, Andrew Johnson. For Phillips, the war to create nationality, an America uniformly free of caste and class oppression, was only beginning.

45. *Ibid.*
46. *Ibid.*

TWELVE

Nationality

During the crucial congressional elections of 1866, Wendell Phillips noted two unusual developments. First, the president of the United States publicly denounced him as a traitor, and then, even as Andrew Johnson cried from the platform, "why not hang Thaddeus Stevens and Wendell Phillips?" the Workingman's party in Boston unanimously nominated him for Congress. The two events and Phillips' reactions to them nicely frame his central position in the great political drama of Radical Reconstruction. When Johnson assailed the orator, he spoke for a white South that sought "reunion without compromise." Stripped of their slaves, former masters were nevertheless struggling to retain racial supremacy and control of black labor as their states reentered the Union. Their presidential ally was therefore correct to consider Phillips a foe. Boston's workingmen, on the other hand, were also right to regard Phillips as a champion who served their special interests as well as those of the former slaves. Were he to be elected, they believed, his "advocacy of the interests of the working man" as well as his devotion to "impartial suffrage" would lead the Republicans to support "something even better" than black enfranchisement, specifically, the eight-hour movement and "an impeachment of the principal traitor," President Andrew Johnson.[1]

1. *National Anti-Slavery Standard*, September 15, 29, October 6, 13 (quotation), 1866.

Phillips found Johnson's charge amusing and the nomination a genuine compliment. He brushed off the one and graciously declined the
other, observing that were he to go to Congress, "I should, paradoxically
as it might sound, incur responsibility to a far greater extent than I
should gain power." It was perhaps the most intelligent tactical decision
about the acquisition of political power that Phillips ever made, for as
his close friend Aaron Powell observed, "The nation needs you more as a
delegate at large."[2] In the battles that lay ahead, Phillips would exercise
from the speakers' platform a voice in national politics that he could
never have equaled from a seat in Congress. "Impartial suffrage," workingmen's rights, and most of all the protection of black freedom now
constituted his most important national goals, and to achieve them
meant fulfilling some of his highest personal aspirations as well. But
there to thwart him stood the intransigent Andrew Johnson, whom
Phillips desperately wished to see impeached and driven from office.
Johnson's future hinged on a sweeping Republican victory in these crucial midterm elections while Phillips' hopes, as usual, depended on the
success of the same party he distrusted so greatly. In the spring of 1866,
it was not at all clear that Phillips and the Republicans were marching in
the same direction.

Never in American history had there been a more important midterm
campaign. On what terms should the southern states be readmitted?
What branches of government were empowered to define these terms?
What rights, if any, should the freedmen be accorded? These issues had
driven Johnson and the Congress into bitterest deadlock beginning in
January, 1866, when Edward McPherson had made good his promise to
send the southern delegations away. Although divided, the Republicans
had been forced into action when Johnson's vetoes thwarted their legislative initiatives. Moderates like Maine's William Pitt Fessenden and
Lyman Trumbull of Illinois had gingerly sought consensus with radicals
like Thaddeus Stevens, Julian, Butler, and Charles Sumner. Johnson,
meanwhile, had openly turned against the party that had elected him,
allying with the hated Democrats even before the election campaign
had begun. In response, Republicans in Congress developed a plan of Reconstruction to take to the voters, embodied in a proposed Fourteenth
Amendment.

Drawn up on the reasonable assumption that most public opinion did

2. Montgomery, *Beyond Equality*, 269–70; *National Anti-Slavery Standard*, October 13, 1866; Powell to Phillips, October 20, 1866, Blagden Papers.

not support black suffrage, the amendment guaranteed for all citizens, including former slaves, equal protection and due process under the law. It indirectly encouraged black enfranchisement by reducing the congressional representation of any state that denied voting privileges to parts of its non-Indian male population. When it had first been proposed in March, 1866, however, Phillips had reacted sharply, warning congressional radicals that he would oppose the amendment vigorously. "We do not see how it is not a substantial surrender of the negro into white hands and permission for *unrepublican* governments," he had admonished Sumner. To Stevens he had complained that the amendment was a "fatal and total surrender. The South carried off enough of the victory to mould its policy and shape its legislation for a dozen years to come. . . . The country is ready for its duty. It only needs leaders," he had said. "Do not let the Republican party desert its post." Congress passed the amendment, however, over both Phillips' protests and Johnson's veto, sending it to the states for ratification. Then the legislators gave Phillips' confidence one final jolt. Just before adjourning for the elections, they readmitted Tennessee, on the sole basis of its ratification of the Fourteenth Amendment. The Republicans had begun their own Reconstruction program without insisting on black enfranchisement. Phillips feared that they might never require it of the South. "Tennessee is now *a white man's government*," he had lamented. "What shall prevent a similar admission of other states?"[3]

So as elections began, Phillips found himself in the same frustrating position that had so bedeviled him in 1864. Once again, he felt driven to seek influence in the Republican party as he pressed for his own more radical ends. Yet that party, once more, seemed to be pursuing policies that negated all he was hoping to achieve. In 1864 Phillips had turned to Fremont, had accused Garrison of servility to the Republicans, and had encountered disaster. Now, he nearly repeated the same feckless experiment, but this time without even an alternative candidate to back. Plainly, there would be no more radicalism put into Reconstruction without a prior Republican landslide. Yet Phillips could not bring himself to play the role that he had found so objectionable in Garrison just two years before. The moment the amendment passed Congress, therefore, Phillips called on the public to reject it by repudiating the Republi-

3. Phillips to Thaddeus Stevens, March 30, 1866, Thaddeus Stevens Papers, LC; Phillips to Sumner, March 17, 24 (quotation), April 30, 1866, Sumner Papers; *National Anti-Slavery Standard*, August 4, 1866.

cans at the polls. "Let that party be broken that sacrifices principle to preserve its existence," he announced. In June at the New England Anti-Slavery Society annual meeting he offered resolutions calling on abolitionists to work for the party's overthrow. "If the party can be defeated," Phillips asserted, "the North will finally unite for liberty."[4]

Charles C. Burleigh, Aaron Powell, and others firmly reminded Phillips that they had heard such predictions before—in 1864 to be exact—and after arguing some, Phillips withdrew his resolutions. Then after further reflection, he stood before the Massachusetts Anti-Slavery Society annual meeting the following month to reverse his position. When Stephen S. Foster reiterated Phillips' original hope for Republican defeat, Phillips replied that such a policy stood little chance of success. Instead, he urged abolitionists to support only those candidates "who do maintain, and promise to support, the true idea of freedom. We are now in a transition state," he said and then spoke even more bluntly. Thoroughgoing Reconstruction was impossible, he now emphasized, unless the Republicans garnered an enormous majority in this election. "I know of no other channel, this summer, in which to work," he declared. "I cannot tell you to desert the Republican Party; I know no where else for you to go."[5] Phillips' long transition into the Republican party's radical wing was now apparent to all, though, unlike Garrison, he had hardly become complacent. Instead, as elections headed into their final months, Phillips fashioned a platform that moderate and conservative Republicans could only decry.

To the masthead of the *Standard*, he affixed a new slogan: *"Defeat the Amendment—Impeach the President."* He rejected the Fourteenth Amendment as a fraud, a new version of the three-fifths compromise that would actually reward southern states with extra representatives if they refused to grant the vote to the freedmen. Hurrying to the Massachusetts legislature, he testified against ratification, and the slogan he had chosen for the *Standard* furnished the title for his remarks. "The Constitutional Amendment, so far as the Negro is concerned, is a swindle," he charged. "The abused, the unheard, the disenfranchised race is sacrificed between the upper and nether millstone[s] of Rebeldom, while the Republican party, knowingly, systematically and persistently sacrifices it to preserve their political supremacy." There should be "no more

4. *National Anti-Slavery Standard*, June 9, 1866.
5. *Ibid.*, and see July 28, August 4, 11, 18, 1866.

compromise under the Constitution, no more surrender of the omnipotence of the war power until Louisiana and South Carolina are made over into the likeness of New England," he said. "The war," he concluded, "has given me the right to annihilate."[6]

Moderate and Conservative Republicans, obviously, filled his list of those fit for annihilation, but the most eligible of all was Andrew Johnson. In September, Phillips had first demanded his impeachment and immediate suspension from office, causing a great stir in the northern press. By now, campaigning was in its final stages, accompanied by terrible incidents of violence against blacks reported from the South. In late July, mobs swept through New Orleans, avenging themselves by murdering dozens of black and white radicals who had peacefully assembled in a constitutional convention to consider Negro suffrage. Johnson, however, excused the rioters as high-minded patriots, using reasoning that echoed James A. Austin's defense of Elijah Lovejoy's killers so many years before. Johnson blamed the abolitionists and Radical Republicans for the violence. "Every drop that was shed is upon their skirts, and they are responsible," he charged, specifying Sumner, Stevens, and Wendell Phillips as the principal culprits. Dismayed by the violence and incensed at the slander, Phillips responded by denouncing "the President's riot in New Orleans" and declaring: "Left to himself, the President begins a career which, if left unchecked, will drive the present Congress from the Capitol unless . . . they receive the blood-stained rioters of New Orleans as their co-members. What New Orleans is today," Phillips warned, "Washington will be in December, ruled by the President and his mob—unless the people prevent it." Meanwhile, a black man named John Oliver confirmed Phillips' worst fears that Johnson was permitting bloodlust to overcome the white South. Oliver, who had been Phillips' protégé at Oberlin College and who was now a Freedmen's Bureau official in Richmond, Virginia, wrote to tell Phillips of how whites were starving their former slaves and subjecting them to other tortures such as scalding and maiming. Such, Oliver reported, was "the barbarism of slavery as it now exists in King William County, Virginia, in 1866."[7]

6. *Ibid.*, July 4, November 3.
7. *Ibid.*, September 9, 1866; Ann Phillips to Phillips, September 27, 1866, Oliver to Phillips, July 6, 1866, both in Blagden Papers; Johnson quoted in Donald O. Reynolds, The New Orleans Riot Reconsidered," *Louisiana History*, XXV (December, 1964), 10–11; *National Anti-Slavery Standard*, August 18, 1866.

Supplement to the National Anti Slavery Standard.

American Anti-Slavery Society.

Wendell Phillips, *Boston, Mass.*,
PRESIDENT.

CHARLES K. WHIPPLE, *Boston, Mass.*,
AARON M. POWELL, *New York,*
SECRETARIES.

RICHARD P. HALLOWELL,
90 Federal Street, Boston, Mass.,
TREASURER.

National Anti-Slavery Standard.

A. M. Powell, *Editor.*

Wendell Phillips,
Special Editorial Contributor.

A THOROUGHLY RADICAL JOURNAL.
PUBLISHED EVERY SATURDAY.

Three dollars per year; Six Cents per copy.

39 Nassau St., New York.

PETITION

To the Fortieth Congress of the United States:

The undersigned, citizens of
earnestly pray your honorable body without unnecessary delay to
impeach Andrew Johnson and to depose him from the office of
President of the United States.

NAMES: NAMES:

You Black Son of a Bitch

Kiss my ass, you Black Bastard

Part of the campaign to impeach Andrew Johnson, petitions such as this
one sometimes came back bearing nothing but racist abuse.
By permission of the Houghton Library, Harvard University

Two weeks after the New Orleans riot, Phillips began filling columns with calls for Congress to "impeach the rebel . . . *Rebel!* Too dignified a designation! The great *mobocrat* of the White House . . . and the second step is—depose him." Johnson, Phillips insisted, must be suspended from office while an impeachment trial went forward, for next in line as chief executive, as Phillips obviously knew, was the very radical Benjamin F. Wade, president pro tempore of the Senate. "The moment that rebel hand leaves the helm," Phillips declared, "New Orleans is safe for New York capital and New York men." The nation, which now stood at a crisis much like the one the English had faced in 1688, needed great leaders to fuse "such popular enthusiasm as the Civil War has left" into a bold policy that would stop the abuse of blacks and deliver them to full citizenship. In these extraordinary times, the nation could not bear Johnson's "treachery, his resistance to the laws of Congress, the blood of New Orleans upon his conscience, his sins against the whole spirit and essence of the hour," nor could it condone "waiting two years while a rebel in the White House builds up the Southern aristocracy, gives it strength, cohesion, property, capital." There were political reasons and constitutional precedents aplenty for impeachment, Phillips maintained. The Republicans must achieve a great triumph at the polls, thereby obtaining a clear mandate to remove the president and begin Reconstruction anew, this time on the basis of "*LAND, SUFFRAGE AND EDUCATION . . . under the guarantee of the Federal Government.*"[8]

Most Republicans certainly were not prepared to support so massive and egalitarian a use of state power as Phillips demanded. Nevertheless, as the elections went into their final weeks, northern voters and Wendell Phillips suddenly seemed to be headed in much the same direction. More disturbing news from the rebel states accounted for some of this trend. Southern legislatures began rejecting the Fourteenth Amendment, passing resolutions in praise of Johnson's policies, and practicing widespread legal discrimination. Former slaves, Republican leaders admitted, clearly needed some further guarantees of political freedom, and Phillips now appeared to be a prophet vindicated, for his warnings that Johnson sought to make the south victorious began to seem disturbingly well grounded. Many Republicans had also developed a keen awareness that Johnson's Reconstruction plans meant leaving the ballot in white southerners' hands, thereby jeopardizing their own party's ma-

8. *National Anti-Slavery Standard*, November 23, June 16, 1866.

jority status in the electorate. Slowly they too began to see the logic of freedmen's suffrage, for blacks would surely vote Republican.

All these factors, and Johnson's own ineptitude as a campaigner, led to his party's crushing defeat in the elections. The new Congress was overwhelmingly Republican, by a full two-thirds in both houses. The party also possessed a clear mandate to enact black suffrage in the South and possessed all the power it needed to legislate over Johnson's veto. Phillips rejoiced over the outcome, a far cry from his original call for Republican defeat. "The people have spoken and uttered their *veto* on Johnson, his policy and its adherents." Now, he declared, the voters had made it "a declaration of national purpose" that "oligarchy . . . with all its roots, branches, suckers, parasites and dependents shall utterly die forever." The new Congress must impeach, suspend, try, and convict the president, he declared, and it must also "throw out the chaff" of existing Reconstruction policies, treating the South like a conquered and occupied territory. It must bolster the Fourteenth Amendment with others securing the franchise and compulsory education, and pass confiscation laws that would provide each freedman with land sufficient to insure the power of his ballot.[9]

As we have seen, a rich counterpoint between order and freedom had always provided Phillips with many levels of personal meaning. Now, as Radical Reconstruction took shape late in 1866, these two great forces finally achieved a national conjunction in Phillips' rhetorical explanation of the goals of Reconstruction. In November he projected his vision to an audience of Republicans, speaking panoramically of the social inspiration that had always informed his abolitionism and rejoicing at the prospect that his social ideals and Republican party policy were possibly to unite:

> It has been said I wish to make everything over into the likeness of New England. Far from it. I detest monotony. I hate a street full of black coats and pipe-stove hats, where men all look as if they had been taken out of one band-box. I like variety, but would have a likeness and homogeneity that makes nationality. I would have a loyalty to one central idea, which, as Coleridge says, makes nationality. . . . In America, that idea is the Constitution . . . representing the Declaration of Independence, the equality of man-

9. *Ibid.*, November 17, December 15, 22, 29, 1866, January 5, 1867.

hood as the basis of the State. . . . I want for Massachusetts and South Carolina what God already decrees for Massachusetts and Illinois. They cohere by the school house, a common lineage, a common language, common books, common associations, common habits of labor, invention and ingenuity. At ten thousand points they touch, and at every point they adhere. The reason why it was possible for the South to secede from the North, was that they touched at only one point, and that was a sham—the parchment of 1789. What we need to do is create a society that shall touch our own at every point. [10]

Lincoln and many other Republican leaders had also spoken many times of creating "a more perfect union." Now many northern voters demonstrated their wish for the national triumph of their culture, as well as their army, and began to demand a stringent southern Reconstruction policy. Though no less radical than ever, Phillips' compelling formulations reinforced the North's deepest free-labor predispositions, which were, thanks especially to southern white intransigence, rapidly growing stronger within the electorate.

The Republican Congress acted quickly on its mandate. Overriding Johnson's vetoes, it passed Reconstruction acts that divided the South into five military districts and sent in twenty thousand troops to oversee elections and supervise the formation of new state governments. To obtain readmission, rebel states were now required to ratify the Fourteenth Amendment, disenfranchise leading Confederates, and adopt new constitutions that provided for black suffrage. Congress also attempted to prevent Andrew Johnson from thwarting their programs. It weakened his control over army appointments and passed the Tenure of Office Act, making it illegal for him to appoint executive officers or military commanders without the Senate's approval. It was not impeachment, but it was an unmistakably serious challenge to Johnson's power.

By the summer of 1867, as Congress pushed Radical Reconstruction forward, some began to suspect that Phillips had written a script which the Republican majority was now enacting into law. Few, to be sure, spoke as he did for land confiscation or compulsory education. Nevertheless, as Congress moved ahead, friends of the embattled Andrew Johnson lamented that "where Mr. Phillips stood a few months ago, the Radicals stand to-day; where he stands to-day, they will doubtless be a

10. *Ibid.*, December 8, 1866.

few months hence." By mid-1867, after Congress had passed the Reconstruction and Tenure of Office acts, the pro-Johnson New York *World* observed dejectedly that as Phillips pressed forward, he pulled along an army of powerful editors and politicians. Here, from one of the North's most hostile journals, was evidence to confirm every one of Phillips' exalted claims for the power of the republican agitator. "Mr. Weed lags in the rear; Mr. Raymond is only six months behind Mr. Greeley and Mr. Greeley is only six weeks behind Thad Stevens, and Thad Stevens is only six days behind Wendell Phillips, and Wendell Phillips is not more than six inches from the tail and shining pitchfork of the master of them all." Republicans were no less aware of Phillips' commanding position, as they showed when the conservative Republican New York *Herald* encouraged Phillips to "keep up his hue and cry. It will only serve to rally the great mass of the Republican party, and the Southern states in their work of reconstruction." Two months later, that same paper devoted six long columns to an interview with Phillips, wherein the orator endorsed Thaddeus Stevens for president in 1868, demanded Johnson's ouster, and insisted that Congress pass constitutional amendments guaranteeing universal male suffrage, compulsory public education, and national citizenship. Such proposals certainly kept Phillips far beyond acceptable limits of Republican policy. Yet the interview itself confirmed the more significant fact that Phillips, the radical pundit, had also become an influential symbol of Republican party conscience. The Rochester, New York, *Morning Express* captured his image aptly, declaring early in 1867, "Probably no other man in the country has been generally so right in the past quarter century as Wendell Phillips."[11] That summer, with Johnson hamstrung and Radical Reconstruction in the South about to begin, Phillips believed that he had actually caught a glimpse of the new America he had so long wished to create, even as he stood at the apex of his career. His lifelong desire to determine the direction of national politics without risking the corruption of holding office actually seemed close to fulfillment.

It all happened at a peculiarly compelling personal moment. By 1867 three decades had passed since Elijah Lovejoy had been slain and Wendell Phillips had been reborn an abolitionist. Phillips now sensed a dramatic conjunction between his present moment of clear triumph and his sharp memories of that transforming event. The terrible anarchy of slavery,

11. *Ibid.*, November 24, 1866, May 25, June 1, September 1, March 28, 1867.

which had put Lovejoy in his grave while bringing himself to life, was about to be crushed forever. In March, 1867, therefore, he announced in the *Standard* that the American Anti-Slavery Society would convene the following month, so that "members and friends" could "gird their armor for a final struggle" against slavery. "The great strides which the nation has made towards a right settlement within the last year, and the marvelous readiness of the masses for thorough measures, encourage us to persevere," he wrote. "The day dawns. May we be worthy to rejoice at its noon." As he penned this exultant announcement, he was again on tour in the Midwest, triumphantly addressing thousands as he headed for Elijah Lovejoy's gravesite in Alton, Illinois.[12] Approaching the summit of his aspirations, Phillips had now undertaken a reflective pilgrimage to that special place, intending to examine as fully as he could the meaning of his abolitionist career.

Alton inspired retrospection. There, on a "beautiful spring day," Phillips stood on a wooded bluff overlooking the Mississippi and surveyed the broad river valley below him. He recalled that hearing the name of the town had always brought about in him an "involuntary shudder," but this visit had "broken that spell," he wrote, "and I trust hereafter to think of it as the home of brave and true men." Phillips, in other words, felt that he had finally found reconciliation with the people who had killed his great hero, for the war had purged them at last of slavery's murderous anarchy. In recognition of this redemption, Phillips mused, the citizens of Alton would do well to place a monument to Lovejoy at the top of this scenic bluff, where it could overlook a beautiful panorama that so perfectly symbolized the social synthesis of order with freedom that Phillips saw emerging from Civil War. "The grand valley spreads," Phillips wrote, "North, East, South and West, holding great states bound together by the golden ribbons of the Mississippi." Steamboat passengers, he thought, "the millions of busy and prosperous men," ought to be able to look up as they traveled past and see on the bluff a monument to "him who consecrated this great valley to liberty."[13]

Such a monument would also hold a deeper personal meaning, Phillips acknowledged as he closed his meditation. It would testify not only to Lovejoy's example, but also to the heroism of all the great figures who had endowed the orator's life with direction and inspiration. "What

12. *Ibid.*, March 23, 30 (quotation), April 29, 1867.
13. *Ibid.*, April 29, 1867.

world-wide benefactors these 'impudent' men are," Phillips exclaimed, "the Browns, the Lovejoys, the saints and the martyrs. How 'prudently' most men creep into nameless graves, while now and then one or two of them forget themselves into immortality."[14] Many years of agitation still lay ahead for Phillips, but now he wished to believe that he, like these other powerful figures, was being vindicated and sanctified in the nation's memory. For the moment, he was savoring the feeling of impending triumph and wanted to share his sense of its implications with his co-workers. Upon returning from his trip, he accordingly assured his fellow abolitionists that "we seem to be on the very eve of all that the friends of freedom have ever asked of this nation . . . That is, the absolute civil and political equality of the colored man under our institutions of government."[15]

Phillips, however, unlike Garrison, could never transform moments of fulfillment into a belief in permanent victory. For three decades his double vision had led him to claim one political success after another for his crusade while at the same time condemning party leaders as corrupt and their constituents as pawns. In 1867 these old suspicions remained just as strong, prompting him to declare, even as he spoke so optimistically, that "five or six years" of military rule were hardly sufficient to eradicate the disease of slavery, which "still convulses the body politic." As he knew, "Old prejudices revive, bitter party strife reappears . . . , cunningly weaving up old errors and appealing to old prejudices. . . . the best minds of the masses grope their way, childlike."[16] Government, as always, seemed to be sliding into corruption, and no matter how satisfied he felt for the moment, there could be no permanent respite for so politically ambivalent an abolitionist as Wendell Phillips.

From a different direction, meantime, Susan B. Anthony, Elizabeth Cady Stanton, Lucy Stone, and others added to Phillips' uneasiness. At the end of the war, these feminist abolitionists had begun insisting that the American Anti-Slavery Society support impartial suffrage, not just universal male suffrage, and had turned to Phillips for support. Ever since the 1830s, of course, Phillips had often spoken warmly for women's right to political and economic equality, and those who knew anything

14. *Ibid.*
15. *Ibid.*, May 18, 1867.
16. *Ibid.*, October 5, 1867.

of Ann Phillips appreciated both her feminist convictions and her powerful influence with her husband. Stanton, Anthony, and their colleagues, moreover, had been Phillips' loyal supporters during the split with Garrison. For all these reasons, feminists had expected him to endorse ballots for women as part of his Reconstruction program and thus had been deeply hurt when Phillips had announced in 1865 that women's suffrage had no place in the American Anti-Slavery Society's platform. The issue, he had declared, must be deferred until racial discrimination had been obliterated from the Constitution. "One question at a time," he had declared. "This hour belongs to the negro."[17]

By 1866 the ensuing conflict between Phillips and the feminists was being widely aired. Elizabeth Cady Stanton inquired sharply of him, "My question is this, Do you believe the African race is composed entirely of males?" When Phillips spoke before the National Woman's Rights Convention in 1866, he explained bluntly that he did not find the female suffrage issue sufficiently pressing to include it in an amendment to the Constitution. Women already possessed enormous social influence, he asserted, through the home, the church, and the benevolent association. He therefore supported their right to vote as a way not to augment but to check their pervasive social authority by involving them in the heavy responsibilities of political decision making. In short, Phillips did not believe that society actually oppressed women, despite his recognition that it curtailed their political activities and economic self-determination. Women already possessed power, in his view, while blacks most clearly did not. Phillips' bias no doubt derived from his lifelong deference to his wife and mother. Moreover, Ann also believed Reconstruction to be exclusively the "Negro's hour." Women's claims, Wendell Phillips declared, must wait and be pressed as a separate movement. "I do not feel by any means that keen agony of interest in this question that I did in the slavery question," he admitted, for "here is woman, educated, influential, walking down the highway of society, wielding all her power."[18]

Phillips' adversary relationship with the feminists became clear when they tried several times to introduce resolutions committing the

17. *Ibid.*, June 13, 1865.
18. Stanton quoted in Ellen DuBois, *Feminism and Suffrage: The Emergence of an Independent Woman's Rights Movement in America* (Ithaca, 1978), 60; Ann Phillips to Henry C. Wright, December 7, 1868, Henry C. Wright Papers, BPL; Phillips, "Woman's Rights and Woman's Duties," 136–38; *The National Anti-Slavery Standard*, June 4, 1868.

American Anti-Slavery Society to women's suffrage. In defeating their efforts, he took the correct historical position that abolitionists had never made an extraneous issue like pacifism, temperance, or women's suffrage "tests of membership." All such causes, he vowed, "are equally able to fight their own battles." Phillips angered Stanton and Anthony by ceasing to print women's suffrage announcements in the *Standard* without charge, by vetoing the use of American Anti-Slavery Society funds for suffragist purposes, and by refusing to support wholeheartedly a campaign to achieve women's suffrage in Kansas. Now was the Negro's hour, Phillips announced, as well as his own moment of political triumph.[19]

Yet Phillips had not personally forsaken women's rights, as he made clear on May 7, 1867, just a week after his return from his visit to Alton, when he delivered a candidly autobiographical speech before the American Anti-Slavery Society. Extending the meditation begun at Lovejoy's grave, Phillips spelled out the tasks remaining for abolitionists in southern Reconstruction, linking them explicitly to the causes of feminism, temperance, and labor reform. At fifty-six years of age, he was attempting to reconcile his recent reflections on his abolitionist past with the social struggles he envisioned in the decades ahead. What he said little reassured any serious abolitionist. He began his speech by recalling how Lovejoy's murder had awakened him to oppose slavery and how, during the ensuing "ten, twenty, thirty years in the thick of the fight," events had revealed to him slavery's absolute influence in American life. "There was no inch of ground, moral, intellectual or political," he recalled, "where slavery had not dominated." Whenever the abolitionists had "torn off the masks" of religion, history, politics, or fashion, "the same hideous features were behind it—the sneering, gibbering spectre—this was America," and it was a memory that now seemed to present a frightening legacy.[20]

For the moment, because of the war, northerners were supporting black political equality, but only out of a desire to secure their victory over the South, Phillips declared. "The only lines today running among the masses of the people is loyal and rebel," he asserted. Yet the potent influence of the slave power in race relations and politics that Phillips remembered so vividly could not be overcome that easily, he feared. Its

19. *National Anti-Slavery Standard*, June 15, February 3, 1866; DuBois, *Feminism and Suffrage*, 82–93.

20. *National Anti-Slavery Standard*, May 25, 1867.

influence, as his memories strongly suggested, made the idea of "absolute equality of blacks" an alien concept, which still in 1867 "does not belong in American life," according to most Americans. "It does not fit anywhere," Phillips continued, "it does not belong to us." Whites invariably seemed to "throw it off the moment we are left alone, as something we picked up and do not wish to retain." It was hardly a self-congratulatory thought, the idea that three decades of tireless abolitionist effort and an enormous war had left the nation no less mired in bigotry than before.[21]

Phillips had only begun his chilling meditation. Race equality, he next observed, could never be achieved in America by means of "cunningly devised parchments set up in Washington" by political compromisers like the Republicans. "I know as well as Henry Wilson does that there is no hope for the people, politically, . . . [other] than the triumph of the Republican party. There is no other boat. A man might as well have attempted in Noah's day to build another ark," he admitted. What then must abolitionists do, he asked, with the problem of race so indelibly ingrained in the nation and its political remedies so weak and uncertain? In the end, they could only continue to agitate in the hope that their words made some enduring difference, just as they had done thirty years before, "when riot and bloodshed ruled the seacoast from Philadelphia to Portland . . . and the devil showed all his proportions because the nation called him a saint. . . . It is time to talk as we did in 1850."[22]

Time was now precious, he warned, and abolitionists must get all that they could from the Republican party while it retained its fleeting mandate for Radical Reconstruction. "I only want that if we sell out, we sell in the dearest market and get the best price. If I cannot get the whole that I ask for, then I want to get as much as I can." Congress must be made, at all costs, to remove Andrew Johnson. By the very act of purging him, Phillips hoped, Republicans would naturally commit themselves to "plant the seeds of New England"—the ballot box, the forty-acre plot, the schoolhouse, the mercantile exchange—in the defeated South. These, not the "cunningly devised parchments," would slowly dissolve the terrible legacy of the slave power.[23] Clearly, impeachment had become Phillips' desperate *sine qua non*, were America to evolve into a racially free society in the decades ahead. Just as clearly, Phillips pos-

21. *Ibid.*
22. *Ibid.*
23. *Ibid.*

sessed at this late hour no resources for developing some original, more effective means for influencing Radical Reconstruction or for preserving his sense of political fulfillment. Unchangeable circumstances and his own thirty years as a republican agitator had left him able only to appeal to his recently sharpened memory of his antebellum role.

These same decades of struggle, however, had also left him "an American" as well as an abolitionist, Phillips emphasized, continuing his meditation. Therefore he naturally wished to shape one "broad fate of humanity" by addressing "all the great questions which concern the people to whom the continent belongs." As he understood it, Radical Reconstruction in the South was inextricably linked to the abolitionists' struggles to achieve temperance, women's rights, and labor reform, the other pressing issues that challenged the republican nation. In confronting them all, he declared, abolitionists must retain their historically unique roles as independent agitators, acting as "the balance wheel, the safety valve, the great check on republican institutions." Even as they had struggled to "take forever and entirely out of politics the question of race," so abolitionists must also, for example, purge politics of alcohol. "You cannot have a ballot box resting on a drunken people," he insisted. "It is impossible to trust republican institutions to men who have no control over themselves." Abolitionists must likewise prepare to make politics transcend gender. Women must mount "the last protest against the injustice of the one half of the human race" who denied them full equality. They must gain the franchise in order to assist temperance, using their votes to prevent the corruption of politics by the liquor vendors. Finally, "of still more immediate and disastrous moment" was the "relationship between capital and labor, consolidating their seeming feud." By enrolling in labor's cause, abolitionists must strive to make politics obliterate class antagonism and destroy industrial poverty. Workers must be rallied to vote their own interests, thereby "putting the American laborer where he belongs . . . where labor is his only capital, lifted to a man intellectually, with leisure for full development of all of his nature."[24] In Phillips' mind at least, the stakes in the struggle for nationality had never been so comprehensive or clearly defined. The nation's ability to meet future challenges depended most of all on the abolitionists and the success of their efforts to secure unqualified freedom for the emancipated slaves. When he was forced—as he believed he soon

24. *Ibid.*

would be—to sell out to the Republicans, he must exact from them the largest possible concessions. Above all else, the abolitionists' decades of struggle would be justified and their place in the nation's future properly defined only if Andrew Johnson were driven from the White House.

Although Phillips could not have known it in 1867, land redistribution and compulsory public education for freedmen could never be serious currency in his transactions with the Republicans. Starting in 1865, Johnson returned to their former owners nearly all abandoned or confiscated lands. Congress passed a Southern Homestead Act, but the land set aside was poor, the freedmen lacked venture capital to buy it, and fewer than a thousand actually filed for title. Republicans had little taste for land redistribution, as Thaddeus Stevens discovered when Congress crushed his confiscation bill in 1867. At the time, Phillips declared Stevens a great legislator, but Republicans who wished to cultivate southern white voters could not easily hand over rebel lands to the freedmen. Except for Stevens, few Republicans were willing to support Phillips' most extreme formulations of the free-labor ideology, that former slaves had already "earned their right to this land." They certainly did not believe Phillips' assertion that "suffrage is nothing but a name because the voter has not . . . an acre from which he could retire from the persecution of landlordism."[25] For the most part, Republicans believed instead that free labor required the freedmen to gain political independence by rising unassisted in the economic world. Grants of land, they argued, would only undermine the blacks' incentive to work, save money, and learn upright habits. When most Republicans spoke of equal rights, they meant in essence the granting of citizenship to men of both races. To protect that citizenship, they were willing to venture far beyond antebellum conceptions of state power, social justice, and the law by passing constitutional amendments, civil rights acts, and enforcement bills, and by deploying federal troops; but land redistribution (not to mention compulsory primary education) went far beyond equal rights into the realm of special privileges, as far as they were concerned.

Early in 1867, however, Phillips could hardly foresee such limits on his demands while the Republicans' struggles with Andrew Johnson escalated. As presidential elections drew closer, Johnson defied the Tenure of Office Act by suspending his secretary of war, Edwin M. Stanton, and replacing him with Ulysses S. Grant. Republican congressmen reacted

25. *Ibid.*, June 8, 1867.

by introducing impeachment resolutions, and Phillips began to anticipate a truly radical turn in Reconstruction policy. "We demand, then . . . an impeachment of Johnson as a necessary preliminary step . . . to guarding for the negro his right in the land," he editorialized. "Inscribing 'Impeachment, Revocation of Pardons, Pre-Emption of Surrendered Lands' on our flag . . . , the Negro will be able to defend himself and his ballot, standing on his own acres." In February, 1867, after Phillips had excoriated them for three months as the "Dawdling Congress" and the "Swindling Congress," Republicans finally mustered sufficient votes to impcach the president and to bring him to trial.[26] Meantime, they also began to regard Grant as their most attractive candidate for president.

Suddenly, as Phillips saw it, the critical moment for Radical Reconstruction, the future of the abolitionist movement, and his own political vindication were finally at hand. Johnson's impeachment, and the Republican party's position on southern policy in the upcoming presidential election would surely determine if the freedmen would receive land and education to go with the ballot. If Congress actually purged Johnson, Phillips believed, the Republicans would proceed to conduct social revolution in the South. They would be disposed toward nominating a true radical for president and would spurn Grant, whom he had already excoriated as a drunkard and a political cipher. "The Radical Standard cannot be lowered," Phillips declared. "It remains the duty of Congress both to dispose of Johnson and to dispossess the rebellious occupants of the large landed estates. . . . as to the question of land and education in the South, as connected with the ballot for the negro, the Republican National Convention will also have to meet. So will the standard bearer to be chosen by that Convention."[27] Phillips now rested all his hopes for achieving nationality on Johnson's conviction and the radical impact that action would have upon the Republican party. The moment to sell, or to declare victory, was not far off.

Phillips called together what remained of the American Anti-Slavery Society, which now had neither paid agents nor funds to maintain the *Standard*. By now many feminists had turned in their memberships, and budgets had eroded further once Quincy, Garrison, and others tied up in litigation a bequest intended for the society. Nevertheless, special meetings still generated impressive turnouts, so Phillips arranged a subscription festival, which was held late in January in Boston's Horticultural

26. *Ibid.*, November 16, 30, December 28, 1867.
27. *Ibid.*, July 21, October 26, 1867.

Hall. He hoped to raise funds sufficient to sustain one large petition and speaking campaign "in this last critical hour." When the proceedings had finished and the hat had been passed, it did seem for a moment as if some of the old abolitionist spirit had returned. "It melted folks together," Phillips wrote Henry C. Wright; "all the old friends were there but you."[28] But the fact was that the old supportive community had long ago passed into oblivion. When the meeting had ended, Phillips headed westward alone, once again hoping to inspire public opinion to force a purging of Andrew Johnson and a rejection of Ulysses S. Grant.

His tour took him through the familiar succession of midwestern cities, from Pittsburgh to St. Paul and back with a dozen major stops along the way. At night, after his lectures, he wrote letters to the *Standard*, hailing Johnson's impending trial and praising the high tone of public opinion. "Over timid parties, scheming politicians and reluctant Presidential candidates, the people have at last made this way and carried out their purposes," he rejoiced. Abolitionists were finally assuming direct, even complete command over the politics of Reconstruction. "We can, as to the negro question, shape the party platform exactly as we wish it," he wrote. Phillips followed the congressional proceedings against Johnson with great care, interpreting them to Ann in his letters. She, in turn, exhorted him to be "rousing up the people with all the fire that you can, that they have got to *keep up* the Senate to impeachment." Wendell, she hoped, would "excuse so much preaching, but you know the whole civilized world and 'millions yet to be' are hanging upon the verdict with regard to this man." Phillips, by return mail, assured Ann, "I speak as warmly as I can, talk to everybody. . . . Grant and impeachment are my topics all day, and [in] the evenings I try to fling the people at the senate *just* as you suggest." A month later, back in Boston with Johnson's trial now underway, Phillips wrote a hopeful editorial for the *Standard* that opened with this thought: "Everything looks bright in Washington." He sent advance copies of his blasts against Johnson and Grant through Aaron Powell to all the New York dailies, which reprinted them eagerly. "I feel pretty sure Johnson will go out, which will clear the field for action," he rejoiced privately, daring to hope that selling abolitionists cheaply to the Republicans might not be necessary

28. Grew to Phillips, January 1, 1868, Blagden Papers; Phillips to Gerrit Smith, January 19, 1867, Smith-Miller Papers; *National Anti-Slavery Standard*, February 2, 1867—all give information on the declining state of the American Anti-Slavery Society. Phillips to Henry C. Wright, February 16, 1868, Wright Papers.

after all. Perhaps nationality, the abolitionist historical mission, and he himself would be victorious in the end.[29]

Finally, of course, Andrew Johnson did not "go out"; the votes of seven Republican moderates, led by William Pitt Fessenden and Lyman Trumbull, saved him from conviction. A few days later, the Republicans selected for president Ulysses S. Grant, a candidate "whose private habits and public training," according to Phillips, "both unfitted him for the post." Phillips had lost, as he knew full well. In his first public response in the *Standard*, he angrily predicted that race violence and political intimidation would engulf the South, and he feared for the "unsheltered heads of southern loyalists, white and black." In his next editorial, he wrote even more bitterly. "Money Kings," he charged, had connived to acquit Johnson, and "Money Kings can hit back. The Negro has no friends. Let him go to the wall, starve, or be shot. Who cares?" As for Grant and the Republican party, his angry analysis was accurate and succinct: "The two elements of the party, the Radical and the Conservative, have grappled, and out of this struggle the conservative element has come forth victorious." When the American Anti-Slavery Society met in New York's Steinway Hall ten days after Grant's nomination, Phillips offered a resolution that condemned both parties as "essentially indifferent to the rights and the welfare of the colored race," and urged abolitionists "either to abstain altogether from voting, or to scatter votes for candidates of their own selection."[30] The disturbing but challenging meditation that Phillips had developed since visiting Lovejoy's gravesite had ended in agonizing frustration and terrible personal defeat.

Most galling of all, as Phillips painfully realized, he still remained completely dependent on the same Republican party that had just blasted all his hopes. His bitter resolution proposing an election boycott made no sense, he knew, when Grant's Democratic opponent was Horatio Seymour, bigot, peace-Democrat, and political ally of Andrew Johnson. That much, at least, he had learned from past elections. Therefore, in August, as the campaign rolled on, Phillips nearly admitted publicly that his Reconstruction program of "land, education and the ballot" were politically impossibile. "At present, it is not to be hoped for," he

29. *National Anti-Slavery Standard*, March 7, 1868; Phillips to Henry C. Wright, February 16, May 20 (quotation), 1868, both in Wright Papers; Ann Phillips to Phillips, March 1, 1868, Phillips to Ann Phillips, March 8, 1868, Powell to Phillips, May 20, 1868, all in Blagden Papers.
30. *National Anti-Slavery Standard*, May 23, 30, June 6, July 15, 1868.

declared, for the Republican party was "shuffling, evasive, unprincipled, corrupt, cowardly, and mean, almost beyond the power of words to describe." Yet the fact was also clear, he wrote, that "a vote for Grant means the negro's suffrage recognized; a vote for Seymour means the negro disenfranchised. . . . Yes, on the whole, all things considered, we prefer Trumbull and Fessenden to Forrest and Toombs" (two arch-secessionists who campaigned for Horatio Seymour).[31] Phillips' endorsement of Grant for president in 1868 was perhaps the single most humiliating public act of his career. He had tried to sell out for the highest possible price, but by his own reckoning, the Republican party had returned him only a pittance.

Phillips, in essence, settled for the Fifteenth Amendment, a constitutional guarantee of the franchise to all adult American males, Indians excepted, which the Republican-dominated Congress passed soon after Grant took office. Phillips worked hard over the next two years to secure its ratification. All the while, he warned of a bloody South, where freedmen's rights remained in jeopardy from vengeful whites, and he demanded confiscation in order to protect them. Phillips had no choice but to move forward, for at least his vision of nationality had remained unblurred by Johnson's exoneration. His ultimate means of adjusting emotionally to this terrible defeat was finally to declare that the proposed franchise amendment itself represented the last and most necessary of all the abolitionists' victories and the key to solving all the other social issues to which he had become so heavily committed.

Speaking out in favor of the amendment, Phillips therefore contended that the axiom that justified black voting—that the "poor and ignorant masses" were the "great strength" of the nation—must be applied universally if Americans were to redress the many class inequities of industrialization. Nothing else, in his opinion, would guarantee "the justice, wisdom and safety of our Republican theory." In the North, he admonished, "our peril lies on the side of Capital. What are party lines in the presence of a Vanderbilt and Drew united? Of what value is the United States Senate when its votes are dictated in Wall Street?" Phillips' remedy for such capitalist dictation in politics lay in vastly multiplying the frequency of balloting. Representation in state legislatures, he declared, must be expanded significantly to undercut the power of the rich. Legislatures must be made up not just of "editors, lawyers and adventurers,"

31. *Ibid.*, August 29, 1868.

whom Phillips regarded as "particularly purchasable" but of "every class, one thousand strong"; legislators should be mixed "as promiscuously as a lecture audience." Moreover, the same principle should be applied to the control of private corporations, he declared; their governing organizations should be reconstructed to include the working class as voting stockholders and as members of boards of directors. "Inaugurate co-operative industry," he urged. "Let the operative own the mill. Make the interest of Capital and the community identical. In no other way shall we have free self-government in this country."[32]

Phillips' proposals certainly reflected his lifelong republican beliefs about power and representation, revised to meet the postwar era, but they also anticipated some of the social thought of the decades ahead. In the 1880s and 1890s, utopian theorists like Henry George and Edward Bellamy would attempt, as Phillips did now, to subdue concentrated wealth and end warfare between classes by insisting that the state promote economic and political cooperation. Like Phillips, both attempted to speak as moralists who attacked laissez-faire economics while trying to lead the nation toward new vistas of prosperity, technological progress, and social harmony. For Phillips, the franchise supplied the means to such ends, but for Henry George, America's salvation would lie in the single tax, and Edward Bellamy would find it in the growth of industrial monopoly itself. Henry Demarest Lloyd and Eugene V. Debs, by contrast, would find compelling precedents in Phillips' republicanism for their socialistic commitments to class struggle. Thus, even as republican antislavery traditions were fast losing their political vitality, Phillips was already adapting these principles to a new world of industrial capitalism and, in so doing, would directly inspire some of the most influential social critics and activists of the coming decades.[33]

As 1868 drew to a close, Phillips filled in the last elements of this expanding design for nationality. With congressional proposals for a Fifteenth Amendment before him and Grant's election nearly inevitable, he felt compelled to make "a fresh statement of principles" for reforming the nation, an absolute necessity for all Americans, in his view, "if the republican government" was going to be able to "outride the storms

32. Ibid.
33. For an excellent development of these trends of the 1880s and 1890s, see John L. Thomas, *Alternative America: Henry George, Edward Bellamy, Henry Demarest Lloyd and the Adversary Tradition* (Cambridge, Mass., 1983); Nick Salvatore, *Eugene V. Debs: Citizen and Socialist* (Champaign, 1983).

of the coming half century." He had already begun convincing himself that the successes of southern Reconstruction were demonstrating how best to establish "the true relation between capital and labor." He now argued further that the same approaches must be applied wherever new forms of injustice appeared. As Phillips now rationalized, Reconstruction had not been derailed by Johnson's exoneration after all, but stood instead as a model for all other reforms. On the West Coast, for example, Chinese immigrants who were now being reduced to a system of peonage run by white overseers must be granted full voting citizenship at once. Otherwise, Phillips declared, they would fall victim to a new class of masters, who would exploit them to undercut the wages of free laborers. Native Americans, Phillips likewise urged, needed the protection of the ballot, and desperately so, for they lived in a nation where "every ten miles from Massachusetts Bay to Omaha is marked by an Indian massacre." Finally, in New York City, where fifty thousand Irish immigrants were "made . . . the tools of a few knaves," municipal reform and temperance must be used to mobilize voters against the Tammany Hall machine. "The moment our laws take note of Negro, Indian, Chinese or Irishmen and forget the *man* . . . ," Phillips summarized, "they plant seeds of discord and weakness." Abolitionists must use the Fifteenth Amendment to inspire Americans to apply the victorious solutions of southern Reconstruction to gain equality for every other disadvantaged group. "Every community," he was convinced, "shall hasten to educate in order to avoid the ignorant ballot," and to prevent the social disruption that would surely follow were millions of voters to act as "the tools of knaves" instead of becoming intelligent citizens.[34]

As Phillips revised his understanding of Reconstruction to make it increasingly positive, he gave himself compelling motives for expanding his own spheres of activity and for justifying his struggles of the past. In 1869, for example, he appeared twice before Massachusetts legislative committees. The first time, he spoke for women's suffrage in state elections and for laws making gender discrimination illegal in public and private institutions. On the second occasion he explained why he thought the commonwealth must create an independent labor commission to investigate exploitation in Massachusetts factories. Once the state learned how terrible the workers' lot had become, he argued, and reported their findings to the public, voters would surely demand an

34. *National Anti-Slavery Standard*, December 5, 1868.

eight-hour day. In the *Standard*, meantime, he wrote editorials that classified the exploitation of blacks, Chinese, Indians, and the working class as a single problem of labor and capital, which the ballot box must solve. He renewed his call for land and education for the freedman. He lectured widely on prohibition, too, urging it as the most vital prerequisite of all for perpetuating an intelligent electorate, whatever its class or color.[35]

Soon Phillips was to discover the great frustrations of so completely equating social harmony, political equality, and a moral economy with the ballot box, for despite his pleas to the contrary, industrializing America was entering a period of deepening conflict between races, classes, and genders. Nevertheless, as Phillips pressed for ratification of the Fifteenth Amendment, he was still able to challenge middle-class Americans to look far beyond corporate balance sheets, stock quotations, and the value of expanding factory capacities. His faith in the franchise did reflect antique republican traditions, utopian expectations, and his need for self-justification, but it also furnished him with a deeply moralistic, egalitarian standard by which to judge political culture in the "Gilded Age." In this way, Phillips was able to retain a genuinely radical role, even as the country moved on and his career slowly drew to a close.

Phillips was lecturing in upstate New York when he learned that the Fifteenth Amendment had finally been ratified. "Our long work is sealed at last," he wrote in triumph to his friend John T. Sargent. "The Nation proclaims equal liberty. Today is its real 'Birthday' . . . Thank God." A few days later, however, when the American Anti-Slavery Society convened for one last time in New York's Apollo Hall, his old misgivings returned, and predictably enough, his own assurances of victory again sounded hollow to him. From early 1869 onward, Phillips had made clear his intention to dissolve the society once the Fifteenth Amendment had been ratified, but some of his oldest and dearest supporters— led, of course, by the Fosters and Pillsbury—believed that the amendment itself was not enough. Using language and logic that was once Phillips' own, they argued that the franchise meant nothing to freedmen in the face of planter intimidation unless they had been granted land as well. Abolitionists, therefore, must not disband until they had forced the government into adopting a substantial program of land confiscation

35. *Ibid.*, April 10, 17, 28, May 29, June 17, July 30, September 11, 25, November 3, 1869.

and distribution. Phillips, however, was by this time convinced that the franchise constituted the most that abolitionists could expect to extract from the Republican party and that land redistribution, though laudable, was no longer politically feasible. Besides, since Phillips now relied so completely on the ballot box in his many reform commitments, he could hardly concur when Stephen S. Foster argued that the vote by itself counted for nothing.[36] At this final gathering, when Foster moved that the society remain united until land redistribution had been secured, Phillips could only disagree.

Some of his reasoning might have reminded listeners of Garrison's in 1865. "The American Anti-Slavery Society, for thirty years, with straining oars . . . has at last reached the level of the nation's frigate," he announced. "We don't disband; she takes us on board. We have no constitution under which to exist. The Constitution of the United States has absorbed it all." The federal government had now "put the mighty arm of the nation" in support of black citizenship and abolitionists should be satisfied and should turn their attention to the "crusades of the future," temperance, labor, women's rights, and municipal reform. Foster's resolutions were then gently defeated, when Phillips offered an endorsement of land redistribution as part of a larger motion to disband the American Anti-Slavery Society, which passed easily. Phillips bade farewell to a movement that, as he said in conclusion, had allowed him to "know the noblest men and women of my day" and that for thirty years had sustained his "faith in human nature."[37]

This final parting was neither easy nor gratifying, however, for up to the very last, Phillips felt nagging reservations about the actual success of the crusade. The Fosters' last obstreperous motion forced him to remember that their sentiments about land reform had been his too, just two years before, when Johnson's impeachment had been at issue. Perhaps the Fosters were right this time as well. Phillips, after all, had joined them for nearly fifteen years in warning of the Republican party as an unreliable custodian of black people's rights. Phillips voiced these troubling doubts several times in his last remarks, even as he tried to persuade his colleagues, as well as himself, to feel satisfied with the victory of the Fifteenth Amendment. "I am no longer proud, as I once was,

36. Phillips to John T. Sargent, March 30, 1870, quoted in Martyn, *Phillips*, 371; *National Anti-Slavery Standard*, May 12, June 5, 1869, April 16, 1870.
37. *National Anti-Slavery Standard*, April 16, 1870.

of the flag or of the name of an American," he confessed at one point. "I am no longer proud of the Declaration of Independence. . . . I still do not read it with any national pride." At another juncture, he cautioned his colleagues that "our long crusade for [the slaves] is not therefore really and fully ended." Though the "ranks are to break up," abolitionists must "not yet dismiss our care or lessen our interest. While this generation lasts," he warned, "the negro will need the special sympathy of his friends. The victim of cruel prejudice, of long disenfranchisement, of accumulated wrongs, he struggles under a heavy disadvantage."[38]

Shortly after this final meeting of the society, Henry Wilson wrote to Charles Sumner that it was to "Wendell Phillips, more than to any other, more than to all others," that credit must be given for the fact that "colored people were not cheated out of their citizenship after Emancipation."[39] Wilson's was indeed a true evaluation of Phillips' greatest significance for Reconstruction and for the Civil War era as a whole. It was Phillips' personal tragedy that he could never fully accept this more just and balanced view than his own of his magnificent abolitionist career.

38. *Ibid.*
39. Wilson to Sumner, April 19, 1870, Sumner Papers.

THIRTEEN

The Eclipse of Republicanism

"I am happy to tell you that Wendell Phillips has been handsomely snubbed at the election last week," Edmund Quincy gossiped to Richard D. Webb in November, 1870. Quincy, retired, had come to scorn Phillips, who he felt had degraded himself and thrown aside the last vestiges of his vaunted independence by running for governor as a labor and temperance candidate. According to Quincy, if Phillips "had acted with ordinary common sense and good temper when slavery was abolished," it would have been "very likely that he might have been the next Senator" from Massachusetts and a respected leader of the Republican party. Instead, Phillips was now "'played out,' as we say," fated to be "merely a popular lecturer and small demagogue for the rest of his life."[1] Value judgments aside, Quincy's forecast of Phillips' future proved all too accurate. After this one attempt at running for office, his public stature slowly began to decline.

During the late 1860s, working people had been organizing to achieve results that heartened Phillips and greatly complicated Massachusetts politics. By 1869 they had developed the Labor Reform party into an extension of their own industrial unions and had endorsed some principles that Phillips could firmly support. Capital and labor, mutually dependent, needed to be restored to parity, they had declared, calling for an

1. Quincy to Webb, November 30, 1870, Quincy-Webb Papers.

eight-hour day and for laws requiring cooperative investments by workers in the incorporation of new companies. By 1869, moreover, Massachusetts Republicans were divided between radical Benjamin Butler and
all who despised him. Seeing an opportunity to hold a balance of power,
the labor reformers ran as a third party and reduced the Republican margin of victory to only 8,000 out of 138,000 votes cast.[2] Here, Phillips believed, was just the situation in which an aroused citizenry could confirm his sweeping theory about the social power of the franchise.

The upcoming 1870 election for governor certainly seemed to address
every aspect of Phillips' reform programs, and with its new amendments,
the United States Constitution no longer presented moral barriers
against his engaging in electoral politics. Once temperance advocates,
suffragists, and working-class politicians had all promised support, he
took the unprecedented step of declaring himself a candidate. At the
same time, a Massachusetts factory owner added greatly to Phillips' interest in the campaign by inflaming the issue of Chinese "coolie labor."
Announcing that he would no longer tolerate union-organized workers
in his plant, this employer openly negotiated with a coolie importer in
San Francisco to the applause of his fellow entrepreneurs. In protest, the
Weekly American Workman, Massachusetts' leading labor newspaper,
published an orientalized cartoon of Simon Legree, over the caption
"Coolie Slavery in Massachusetts!" Phillips added his own statement in
praise of the Chinese as an "industrious, thrifty, inventive and self-
respectful" people. They could be naturally absorbed into the work force
as political equals without lowering wages, he argued, so long as they
immigrated voluntarily and had not been lured by the false inducements
of grasping factory owners.[3] Finally, as Phillips weighed the merits of
seeking the governorship, there were also the intriguing political prospects of Benjamin F. Butler to contemplate.

Butler, of course, had always been one of Phillips' favorites—the
battlefield liberator of the slaves in 1861, the guardian of black freedom
in New Orleans in 1863, the manager of traitorous Johnson's impeachment trial in 1868. Now Butler had succeeded Thaddeus Stevens as the
most powerful radical in Congress and had built an impressive political
organization in Massachusetts. Whenever Phillips sought a place in government for a deserving friend, Butler was able to accommodate him,

2. Montgomery, *Beyond Equality*, 369–70.
3. *Weekly American Workman*, July 2, 28, 1870; *National Standard*, July 30,
1870.

and when Phillips was lobbying in the state legislature for the creation of a bureau of labor statistics, Butler helped out. Butler, moreover, in 1868 had become a "greenbacker," declaring his support for basing the nation's currency on an inflated medium of exchange, a proposal that Phillips and many working-class politicians and labor leaders also favored. That same year Butler had marshaled working-class voters to survive a purge attempted by conservative Massachusetts Republicans, led by former Cotton Whigs like Amos A. Lawrence, whom Phillips, of course, had always despised. Thus, by deciding to run for governor in 1870, Phillips clearly hoped to develop enough power to secure Butler's election the following year, thus avenging himself once more on the Republican conservatives and putting himself in position to help direct Butler's policies once he took office.[4] Even in deciding to transform himself into a candidate, Phillips continued as always to search for power by the "purer" means of amassing indirect influence.

Although sometimes inept as a politician, Phillips had never before misled himself so thoroughly. This time, he had attached himself to one of postwar America's most controversial figures, for Butler represented a bewildering mixture of blatant opportunism and egalitarian appeal. Some labor historians now consider Butler a perfect embodiment of the Republican party's postwar moral decline, even though few in Congress could match his consistency as a defender of black people's rights and workers' interests. In Massachusetts, in fact, Butler had pursued his own political fortunes by manipulating class feelings. A maverick unfettered by party rules, he either appealed directly to labor's interests or ignored them, as personal interest dictated. Phillips, like so many of his contemporaries, could not clearly distinguish between principle and expedience in Butler's supportive gestures.[5] In October, 1870, Phillips headed into a wilderness of electioneering from which he was not to emerge until late 1871, when Butler himself finally failed to secure the governorship.

Phillips declared that he "had no wish to become Governor," so instructing the Labor Reform and Temperance parties even as he accepted

4. Phillips to Butler, April 20, 1869, April 5, 1870, Benjamin Butler Papers, SCL; Montgomery, *Beyond Equality*, 365–67; Hans L. Trefousse, *Ben Butler: The South Called Him "Beast"* (New York, 1957), 222–23.

5. For these judgments on Butler, see Dawley, *Class and Community*, 198–99; Montgomery, *Beyond Equality*, 160–61; Trefousse, *Ben Butler*, 56–59.

their separate nominations. Expressing great "dislike" at seeing his "name drawn into party politics," he nevertheless informed his backers that they were welcome to endorse him, but only because he wished to "enlighten the public mind" on the great questions of the campaign. It was certainly one of Phillips' most antipolitical moments—and one of his most naïve, as Samuel J. May appreciated from his vantage point in retirement. "Our labor reform party is one of follies and inconsistencies," he wrote to Richard D. Webb, "and Wendell Phillips is stirring them up to measures wholly at variance with his earlier principles." Similarly convinced, Mary Grew, a dear personal friend, refused to let Phillips rest easy in self-deceiving declarations of political independence. "To me," she wrote, "it seems like a deplorable descent from the high moral vantage ground, for you to step into such a post." People were beginning to assume "that personal political advancement is one of your aims."[6]

Since Phillips did clearly seek to promote himself by influencing Butler, Grew's strictures had considerable merit. Yet Phillips' style of campaigning also made it clear that he cared little about actually achieving office. His father would have appreciated his approach, for he campaigned much as an old Federalist might have, making no attempt to organize his supporters and relying on his good name alone to get him a hearing. In every speech, moreover, Phillips stood forthrightly by all his principles, ignoring the complications he created by inextricably linking labor, temperance, and other reform questions. By making prohibition, industrial cooperation, female suffrage, greenbackism, and the eight-hour day into one self-reinforcing program, he lessened his appeal in several important respects. Workers, on the one hand, felt ambivalent about supporting temperance, while socially proper temperance supporters felt reluctant to stand up for working-class issues. Garrison noted these problems with a wry accuracy: "This attempting to sit on two streets at the same time is a dangerous matter, or at least a very difficult one." Worse still, Phillips' constant attacks on anti-Butler Republicans such as Henry Wilson, F. W. Bird, and Amos Lawrence only made it all too obvious that he was directing his efforts towards Butler's eventual triumph. Those not enamored of this widely distrusted figure were unlikely to vote for Phillips either. Finally, no abolitionist-minded voter wished to hand Massachusetts over to the Democrats, and voting

6. *National Standard*, August 8, 1870; May, Jr., to Webb, August 24, 1870, Quincy-Webb Papers; Grew to Phillips, August 12, 1870, Blagden Papers.

for Phillips instead of the Republican candidate meant jeopardizing the future of Senator Henry Wilson who was up for reelection by the state legislature. For many reasons, Phillips' protest that "I do not give a chip which party places its nominees in the gubernatorial chair" was guaranteed to repel voters in large numbers.[7]

Yet Phillips' campaign efforts were not wasted. He was still a magnificent speaker, who at sixty could make a lecture hall shiver as if an earthquake were passing through it, according to the *Standard*. If nothing else, he endowed working-class politics with some of its richest language and clarified the ideas of such serious labor theoreticians as Ira Steward. Steward, whose justifications for the eight-hour day were sophisticated and difficult to follow, was often misunderstood to be proposing reductions in wages along with a shorter work week. Phillips corrected such errors. "Give me a million of men in Massachusetts working eight hours and studying three," he would declare, "adult schools, open libraries, free lectures, a larger interest in politics," and workers would never "take four-fifths of their old wages. . . . They will demand more money for their eight hours than they had for ten." Phillips also presented a provocative campaign promise of his own, a plan for a graduated tax on real estate income, which Tom Paine would have understood far better than Franklin Roosevelt might have. Phillips illustrated his thinking by proposing that a man owning a single house ought to pay a tax of one hundred dollars, but "if he owns ten houses, . . . we won't tax him one thousand dollars, but two thousand dollars. The richer a man grows, the bigger his tax, so that when he is worth forty million dollars he will not have more than twenty thousand to live on. . . . We'll crumble up wealth by making it unprofitable to be rich." Such ideas were not a legacy for New Deal economic planners but reflected Phillips' traditional republican preoccupation with preserving a society where all classes owned real property, could rise at will, and blended together "like the colors on a dove's neck."[8]

Despite these appeals for harmony between workers and industrialists, Phillips' powerful characterization of labor's plight could only heighten his listeners' class awareness and social resentment. Once, for example, he decried collusion among factory owners in forcing layoffs and blacklisting union organizers, asking:

7. William L. Garrison to Francis Jackson Garrison, September 15, 1870, Garrison Papers, BPL; *National Standard*, October 29, November 3, 12 (quotation), 1870.
8. *National Standard*, November 18, 3, October 29, November 12, 1870.

What does "get out" mean? Take your wife out of the corporation tenement. Perhaps your babe is one day old. . . . put your wife and children into the street. Fall River answers to Lowell and Lowell cries out to Lawrence and Lawrence, from her misty prosperity thunders out to Valley Falls. "There is a victim of capital. See to it that you starve him wherever he treads." Wealthy men combine until there is not a spot for the hunted victim to earn his bread this side of the Connecticut River, and this is God-like civilization. [But] let poverty combine [and the owner exclaims] "did you ever see such nasty Crispins?" That is the strand in the cable by which angry, selfish capital is dragging down a certain class to practical slavery, creating a permanent laboring class so that there is not one chance in ten, compared with what it was, that the children of those men shall lift themselves. [9]

Such provocative statements, made at working-class gatherings, must have seemed incongruous, coming from a man dressed in gentleman's waistcoat, starched shirt, and soft woolen trousers. One Jennie Collins certainly thought so and attacked him as "nothing but a great baby" who lived among imported luxuries and was really "the representative of men and women who lived upon interest without producing anything." Yet Phillips' democratic style of rhetoric erased some of these suspicions even as his denunciatory language enriched his listeners' vocabularies of protest against the oppressive clichés of Gilded Age capitalism. It could hardly have been otherwise when, for example, Phillips assailed the "babble and chaff of supply and demand" as a "political economy that forgets God, abolishes hearts, stomachs and hot blood, and builds its world as children do, out of tin soldiers and blocks of wood." [10]

In November, however, the vote totals revealed that Phillips' rhetoric had done little to advance the Labor Reform and Temperance parties. His rigid adherence to principles, his whiggish campaign, the hostility of the Republican party press, and the specter of Benjamin F. Butler all kept his total to a meager 12 percent. Neither party that endorsed him gained any legislative seats. One of Phillips' supporters afterward claimed, "Today our strength shows. . . . 13,000 men with an idea behind them are not

9. *Ibid.*, November 12, 1870.
10. *Weekly American Workman*, July 24, 1869; Phillips, "The Outlook," *North American Review* (July, 1879).

easily winked at. We have the same metal that went into making the Liberty Party."[11] Yet for all Phillips' efforts and his supporters' justifications, Massachusetts was no closer to enacting an effective eight-hour law in 1870 than it had been in 1865. Women's suffrage, mandatory cooperative business charters, and temperance enforcement likewise remained arid campaign slogans, for the ballot had indeed demonstrated its power, but in ways that gave Phillips little cause for cheer.

The next year, when Butler openly bid for the governorship, the validity of any analogy between Phillips' campaign and the old Liberty party was also disproven. Phillips worked hard for Butler's nomination, declaring in the *Standard* that "we must concentrate, and if we cannot get saints, just put up with sinners who will do our bidding."[12] Butler's multitude of enemies united to deny him the endorsement, however, and to tear apart Phillips' last justifications for having run the year before. During the nomination struggle, Phillips hardly helped Butler's cause by endorsing with phrases and logic reminiscent of John Brown's time the violence that accompanied the Paris Commune in revolutionary France. "I have not a word to utter . . . against the grand declaration of popular indignation which Paris wrote on the pages of history in fire and blood," he declared. Few noted his recommendation, which immediately followed, that American workers ought to secure "orderly majorities at the ballot box" instead of emulating the French example.[13]

In the aftermath, as Phillips commiserated with his defeated champion Butler, the futility of it all was very clear at least to Ann Phillips. Learning in early 1872 that her husband had attended yet another gathering of the Labor Reform party, she told him he must stop. "I have received a dreadful blow. I find that the convention you told me of as a labor one is really a *political one*," she exploded. "Why did you not tell me?" Politics, she lectured, "are awfully wicked. Do not meddle with them." Why, she demanded, "cannot labor be a moral question?" The fact was, however, that from the mid-1870s onward, labor was neither a moral nor a political question, as Ann Phillips understood such terms. The cause most of all demanded the organization of local communities against lockouts and scabs. There was no role for a gentleman agitator

11. *Weekly American Workman*, November 19, December 8, 24, 1870; *National Standard*, November 19, 1870 (quotation).
12. Wendell Phillips, *"The Foundation of the Labor Movement": A Speech Delivered . . . October 13, 1871* (Boston, 1871); Phillips, *Address at the Salisbury Beach Gathering. . . .* (Boston, 1871); *National Standard*, October 20, 1871 (quotation).
13. *National Standard*, May 31, July 8, August 19 (quotation), 1871.

whose republicanism denied the need for militant unions or strikes. Although Phillips was to continue speaking out on labor issues for several years, he submitted to Ann's demands. In 1872 he repudiated Ira Steward as a self-serving politician and thereafter campaigned no more for working-class candidates.[14]

While Phillips was fighting for Butler's candidacy in Massachusetts, Butler himself had been active in Washington battling the Ku Klux Klan. Whatever else Butler may have stood for, his posture on Reconstruction was as radical as Phillips could expect from any politician. This fact, perhaps more than any other, explains the orator's enduring loyalty to the general. Decrying the "prevalent terrorism and anarchy against landless freed people" that swept through parts of the South during the early 1870s, he applauded Butler all the more for his outspoken leadership as Congress passed two so-called Ku Klux Klan acts.[15] This legislation made political terrorism a felony, set up machinery for federal prosecution, and provided the army with authority over registration, voting, and southern civil rights enforcement. But the efficacy of these laws, as Phillips knew, depended solely on the Republican party's willingness to uphold them vigorously. Hence he warned its "party managers . . . that unless something can be done, there is little hope of the Republicans carrying the next Presidential election." Klan violence, unless checked, would keep blacks from the polls and deliver "all the Southern states into the Democratic Party." Until the Republicans guaranteed the safety of "these united loyalists, black and white," moreover, the party had "no right to ask them to vote for their candidates." Instead, as Phillips emphasized, "every humane man must allow them to make peace with their enemies by any submission required." "NOTHING," he editorialized, "SHORT OF SHOOTING HALF A DOZEN SOUTHERN MILLIONAIRES AT THE DRUMHEAD WILL AWE THE KU KLUX KLAN INTO SUBMISSION." Such a violent-sounding demand for law and order indicates the depth of Phillips' fear. Perhaps it was actually proving true that the idea of black equality was no more palatable to most Americans than it had been forty years before. "We have not yet outsailed the possibility of a 'South victorious,'" he wrote.[16]

Though Grant enforced the Ku Klux Klan Acts with circumspection,

14. Phillips to Butler, n.d. [1871], May [?], 18, 1872, all in Butler Papers, SCL; Ann Phillips to Phillips, January 11, 1872, Blagden Papers.
15. *National Standard*, April 17, 1870, March 4, 1871.
16. *Ibid.*, March 4, 18, 1871.

Republicans were clearly divided over the wisdom of continuing to support southern military rule. Phillips' distress therefore mounted as party splits developed between disaffected liberal Republicans and the supporters of Ulysses S. Grant. Liberals found Grant's political style distasteful and despised the patronage machines (like Butler's) that inspired it. They also disliked Grant's commitment to high tariffs and wished to reform his corrupt administration of the civil service. Most of all, however, when liberals looked South, they sniffed the taint of "Negro misrule." Hence, when some leading Democrats endorsed the Fourteenth and Fifteenth Amendments, these liberals saw a chance to develop a political alliance with which to drive Grant from office and terminate southern Reconstruction. Together with "reformed" Democrats they began speaking of a new departure in southern policy, a healing of sectional wounds, general amnesty for former rebels, and the return of "honest government" in the old Confederate states. Complicating matters further for Republicans loyal to Grant was Charles Sumner's bitter opposition to the president's proposal to annex Santo Domingo. In May, 1872, all these issues came to a head when liberal Republicans convened in Cincinnati; pledged themselves to tariff reductions, civil service reform, and sectional reconciliation; nominated Horace Greeley for president; and sought Sumner's support. Soon after, the Democrats, too, endorsed Greeley's candidacy, and after agonizing greatly, Sumner finally decided to avenge himself on Grant by doing likewise.[17] The politician Phillips had always loved best now seemed willing to remand the freedman to the care of Democrats and Klansmen.

Sick, aging prematurely, and devastated by misfortune, Sumner had remained close to Phillips, receiving his firm support in the dispute with Grant over Santo Domingo. But even before the Liberals endorsed Greeley in Cincinnati, Phillips had warned Sumner that he was planning to support Grant's reelection. When Sumner declared his support for Greeley anyway, the orator carefully admonished him to prepare for political attack. "Whatever criticism I make of your position will be made with the sharpest regret and wrung from me by the gravest conviction of duty to the negro race, which your mistake exposes to such horrible peril," he wrote. Lydia Maria Child, Frederick Douglass, Gerrit Smith, and Garrison also feared that Greeley's candidacy threatened

17. James M. McPherson, *The Abolitionist Legacy: From Reconstruction to the NAACP* (Princeton, 1975), 24–34; David H. Donald, *Charles Sumner and the Rights of Man* (New York, 1970), 374–555.

black freedom, and they joined Phillips in this one last crusade, hoping to keep the distracted Republicans fixed on the tasks of nationality. Such veterans as Franklin B. Sanborn, Elizur Wright, Jr., and several others spurned this final call, however. They condemned Grant's corrupt rule, and supported Greeley as the best person to end the hopeless task of Reconstruction.[18] They thus contributed to the distractions that were leading the North toward "reunion and reaction."

Believing sincerely that he had no other choice, Phillips endorsed Grant with a desperate enthusiasm in sharp contrast to his hostility toward the same candidate in 1868. Greeley's supporters immediately dredged up his old attacks on the president for drunkenness and political ineptitude, and Phillips naturally became all the more eager to justify his position. In August a committee of Boston's black leaders asked Phillips whether they should follow his advice or Sumner's regarding Grant and Greeley in the upcoming election. Phillips' blunt reply conveyed his realization that the Republican party's commitments to Radical Reconstruction were flagging rapidly. Declaring his judgment as "exactly opposite" of Sumner's, Phillips insisted that "every loyal man, and especially every colored man should vote for General Grant." The nation and the black race "are only safe in the hands of the old, regular Republican party," for Greeley was "a trimmer by nature." Moreover, he asserted, "President Grant means peace, and an opportunity to agitate the great industrial questions of the day." Greeley in the White House, however, "means the scandal and wrangle of Andy Johnson's years over again." He warned that blacks would have to "arm, concentrate, conceal your property, . . . organize for defense" if Greeley were elected. White working-class voters, too, should "rally now, to save your great questions from being crowded out," and native Americans must hope for Greeley's defeat, since Grant, Phillips claimed, had developed an "original and Christian policy toward the Indian," which marked him "as a statesman." For Phillips, if for few other whites, the 1872 elections had thus become a national referendum not just on southern Reconstruction, but on his entire agenda for creating a republican America.[19] That Grant was swept back into office, however, did not signify the end of that popular

18. *National Standard*, March 4, 1871; Phillips to Sumner, April 11, August 4 (quotation), 1872, both in Sumner Papers; McPherson, *Abolitionist Legacy*, 24–34.

19. Boston *Advertiser* reprinted in Martyn, *Phillips*, 480–82. See also Phillips to A. F. Spinc, Iowa Republican State Central Committee, December 17, 1872, Blagden Papers.

disillusionment with Reconstruction. During Grant's second term it continued to grow, fed by economic depression, government scandal, and deepening white revulsion against the carpetbaggers' misrule.

With the election over, Phillips made amends to Charles Sumner, his last link, save Butler, to what remained of the old Radical Republicans. Sumner needed this reassurance badly, for he had now been censured by the Massachusetts Republican party for his rebellion against Grant, and his influence in the Senate had been reduced to almost nothing. "The *real* old friends never waver a hair in their love and trust," Phillips attempted to reassure him, before calling on Sumner at home, where he found his old friend ill and despondent. As they reminisced, a servant interrupted to remind the senator that he must take a prescribed foot-bath. Phillips rose to leave, but Sumner implored him to remain. The two continued their talk until well after midnight around a tub of water into which the senator dipped his feet.[20]

This generous act on Phillips' part was also a gesture of gratitude, for ever since 1870, Sumner had been sponsoring a national civil rights act that would have outlawed racial discrimination in all public conveyances, public schools, juries, restaurants, theaters, hotels, incorporated churches, and cemetery associations. His efforts had been thwarted by ambiguous Supreme Court rulings, by fears that integration would make chaos of southern education, and by political apathy and hostility. When Grant's reelection gave the Republicans another large majority in Congress, however, abolitionists and southern blacks began demanding the passage of Sumner's bill. Still no action was forthcoming, even after Sumner died in March, 1874, soon after his late-night conversation with Phillips. On his deathbed, he implored, "My bill . . . , don't let it fail," but Congress once again adjourned without passing the legislation.[21]

By this time, Phillips had become familiar with bereavement, for he was now presiding with increasing frequency at the funerals of abolitionist comrades. Nevertheless, Sumner's death came as a devastating blow, especially in light of congressional indifference to his friend's unfinished work. "Poor Sumner—Dear Fellow," he lamented to Ann. "It seems as if a part of me is gone—I can't get it out of my mind, day or night." To Lydia Maria Child he sent "a cup and saucer once owned by Sumner" as a memento of the friendship the three of them had shared,

20. Phillips to Sumner, December 20, 1872, Sumner Papers; Donald, *Sumner and the Rights of Man*, 584.
21. McPherson, *Abolitionist Legacy*, 16–23.

and to the people of Boston he wrote that there had been no "political name" in Massachusetts since the Revolution "worthy to stand by the side of Charles Sumner." Yet in this eulogy he also worried revealingly about Sumner's unfinished work, "the completion of which many of us, I fear, will not live to see." Phillips had now begun to experience the consequences of his inability to convince himself of victory or to regard his great career with untroubled satisfaction. Perhaps he, like Sumner, was soon to die, he now feared, leaving the struggle of a lifetime not only unresolved but slowly being won by his enemies. In a last gesture of mourning, Phillips sent George William Curtis, editor of *Harper's Weekly*, the most flattering photograph of Sumner he could find, hoping that Curtis would have it lithographed for publication in his magazine.[22]

Curtis and Phillips were old acquaintances, and *Harper's*, a widely read periodical, had staunchly supported Sumner's Civil Rights Bill. In sending the picture, therefore, Phillips did not distinguish between personal and political motives. As he set forth to finish his dead friend's last crusade, he also sought to redeem his own. The 1874 congressional election complicated his task, however, by producing fierce violence against black voters in the South and giving the Democrats a majority in the next House of Representatives. Freedmen might experience increasing repression, but the new Congress would certainly be ill-disposed to pass protective legislation. Aware of this likelihood, those sponsoring Sumner's bill decided that compromise was essential and proposed deleting the section prohibiting segregated schools and cemeteries. As soon as Phillips heard of this plan, he sent off an angry scrawl to Butler. "It is not only *useless*, but a *fatal* concession to the South," he protested. "It is a weak and timid surrender to mere bluster. . . . The insertion of a principle of *caste* and race superiority in our laws [is] as disastrous as the slave compromise of '89." Phillips might as well have invoked the year 1846, when he had assailed Horace Mann for condoning segregated schools. What had been gained in the thirty-year interval? he wondered, as he posted two additional protests to Butler, demanding that Congress "crush all bills but Sumner's." Phillips' long public letter supporting the Civil Rights Bill echoed his denunciation of caste in Massachusetts so many years before: "The Negro child loses if you shut

22. Phillips to Ann Phillips, March [?], 1874, Blagden Papers; Phillips to Child, June 11, 1874, in Lewis (ed.), "Letters of Phillips," 734; Phillips to "Mr. Mayor & Fellow Citizens," Garrison Papers, BPL; Phillips to George William Curtis, July 16, 1874, George William Curtis Papers, HL.

him up in separate schools, no matter how accomplished his teachers or how perfect the apparatus." What had the war been fought for? Phillips asked. Why had the Fourteenth and Fifteenth Amendments been passed at all, if not to settle the principle "that neither Law nor Constitution here can *recognize race* in any way or circumstance? I protest against the national disgrace and crime of putting caste in the statute books."[23]

As Phillips worked desperately to salvage Sumner's bill, mobs in Louisiana committed racial murder, and Boston politicians rallied to support them. He suddenly found himself thrust into grotesquely familiar circumstances that recalled to him most painfully his very first moments as a self-proclaimed abolitionist. The 1874 election marked only the latest phase of racial violence in Louisiana, a state worse afflicted than any other in the South. White Leaguers there resorted to lynch mobs against politically active blacks and radical whites, and Military Commander Philip Sheridan used his troops decisively to restore order. The president approved his commander's action, as did Phillips, who sent a supportive note to the secretary of war. Garrison was also among the loudest in hailing this display of federal power. But in Boston, "new departure" Democrats and liberal Republicans viewed these same events very differently, and they booked Faneuil Hall for a meeting to protest Grant's "usurpation." In St. Louis and New York City there were similar gatherings, and in Boston some even talked of establishing a White League of their own.[24]

Phillips suddenly found himself awash in memories of Elijah Lovejoy, as past and present collapsed into each other one final time. Just as they had forty years earlier, Boston's citizens were again assembling in Faneuil Hall. Again a hero had fallen, his work uncompleted, his reputation needing vindication, but instead of Lovejoy, it was now Sumner, battling to the last against segregationists like the White Leaguers who terrorized the black South. Phillips could not do otherwise than sit conspicuously near the podium, knowing that people would see him and demand that he speak. "These fellows who are getting up the Faneuil Hall meeting to protest Grant . . . are *floundering* in a quagmire of prejudice and ignorance as they always *have been*," he assured Butler.[25]

23. Phillips to Butler, January 6, 13, 24, 1875, Butler Papers, SCL; "A Letter from Wendell Phillips," Boston *Advertiser*, January 11, 1875.
24. McPherson, *Abolitionist Legacy*, 46–48; Jesse H. Jones (ed.), *Wendell Phillips' Last Battle and One of His Greatest Victories, Being the Speech of Wendell Phillips in Faneuil Hall on the Louisiana Difficulties* (Boston, 1897), 14.
25. Phillips to Butler, January 13, 1875, Butler Papers, SCL.

At this late hour, Phillips had determined to act once more as he had so long ago. By recapitulating the first moments of his abolitionist career, he now hoped to save his city, a hero's memory, the black race, and his own standing in posterity from a final defeat by the resurgent slave power.

The meeting opened with resolutions expressing "the citizens of Boston's deep indignation" at Sheridan's action and calling on Grant to relieve him of his post. Louisiana's White Leaguers, it was also moved, should be commended for their patriotic emulation of "the colonies before the American Revolution" in using force to defend their republican governments. Phillips, of course, understood such words as the same perversions of history that James T. Austin had once fabricated to defend Lovejoy's killers. Then a series of speakers denounced Grant's southern policies and showered praise on Louisiana's white insurgents. Phillips continued to sit quietly until the motion was made for a vote on the resolutions. Then loud cries began to ring out, calling for him to speak, and pandemonium rose in the hall as Phillips, hat in hand, made his way to the podium.[26]

Though stoop shouldered and heavy of frame, Phillips at sixty-six still commanded the platform as few could. It was with strong voice and energetic gestures that he began his defense of Sheridan, and it was clear from the first that the orator needed both. As he began speaking, loud remarks and catcalls ("That's a lie! . . . Smoke a.cigar!") mingled with hisses and cheers. Exasperated, Phillips pleaded at one point, "Now gentlemen, be patient. You are American citizens. You have grave questions to discuss." As raucous cries and applause continued, Phillips attempted, in spite of the noise, to show that the violent train of events in Louisiana had justified Sheridan's intervention. All the while, the stenographic reporter seated near the podium recorded the developing scene of humiliation:

> Men of Boston, I am not here to defend the administration. (Voices, "You are!" "You are!" "You are paid for it!") If these resolutions are passed—(Great uproar.) Men of Boston, men of Boston, if these resolutions are passed, they will carry consternation and terror into the house of every Negro in Louisiana. (A voice, "We will pass them all!" Applause, hisses, groans, laughter, cheers and cries, loud and long.) They will carry comfort to every assassin (a

26. Jones (ed.), *Wendell Phillips' Last Battle, passim.*

voice, "Not a bit of it!") in New Orleans. ("Oh!" and loud hisses and applause.) My anxiety is not for Washington. I don't care who is President. My anxiety is for the hunted, tortured, robbed, murdered population, white and black, of the Southern States (a voice, "That's played out!") whom you are going to consign to the hands of their oppressors. (Hisses.) If you pass these resolutions—(Cries of "We will!" "We will!") If you pass these resolutions—(Renewed cries of "We will!" "We will!") If you pass these resolutions, gentlemen (loud cries of "We will!" "We will!")—I say it in the presence of God Almighty (cries of "Sh!" "Sh!" "Oh, ho!" "Oh, ho!" hisses and voices, "He don't know you!" "Whom you don't believe in!")—the blood of hundreds of blacks, and hundreds of whites, will be on your skirts before the first day of January next. (Loud laughter and hisses.)[27]

So it continued while Phillips introduced counterresolutions supporting Grant and then sat down.

Phillips had failed to still the hostile crowd, and after he concluded people became even more boisterous. A "man who was so unknown that the president of the meeting had to ask his name" came forward next and "poured out a bitter diatribe against Mr. Phillips." The chairman then put Phillips' substitute resolutions to the vote, and they were defeated. Finally, the motion applauding the White Leagues and condemning Grant passed on a divided vote, and the meeting broke up.[28]

Then and since, Phillips' sympathizers have claimed that Phillips actually triumphed in this encounter, despite what had happened.[29] He had, of course, been shouted down many times before, but this time it was different. There were no post mortems about freedom of expression, no further discussion of the specific issues raised in the meeting. Instead, people went on about their daily lives, unaffected by controversies involving Wendell Phillips' views on the South. An editorialist from the New York *Times* put the outcome in its proper perspective, observing that "Wendell Phillips and William Lloyd Garrison are not exactly extinct from American politics, but they represent ideas in regard to the South which the majority of the Republican Party have outgrown."[30]

27. *Ibid.*, 29–30.
28. *Ibid.*, 31.
29. *Ibid.*; Boston *Advertiser*, January 16, 1875; Korngold, *Two Friends of Man*, 379.
30. New York *Times*, quoted in McPherson, *Abolitionist Legacy*, 49.

Three weeks after the Faneuil Hall meeting, Congress confirmed this judgment, passing a civil rights bill shorn of its provisions covering schools and burial grounds. In so doing, it marked the end of Wendell Phillips' career as an active participant in racial struggles. He would, to be sure, protest in 1877 when the Republicans withdrew the last federal troops from the South, and occasionally thereafter he spoke out when whites grossly abused the freedman's political rights.[31] Yet by weakening Sumner's bill, Congress had confirmed that the abolitionist commitment that Phillips embodied had now outlived its age. The crowd that had hooted Phillips down in Faneuil Hall had likewise demonstrated that he could not force history to repeat itself.

As the 1870s wore on, Phillips could still draw appreciative audiences to lectures on temperance, women's rights, and labor questions. "Daniel O'Connell" became a great favorite among Boston's Irish and on the lyceum circuit, and "The Lost Arts" still drew well. But as he reached his later sixties, Phillips began to find touring increasingly difficult. From Chicago he complained of "being shaken in omnibuses and hacks to a terrible degree," and of "no privacy—hotels all of one crowd. I rejoice that dear old Boston (how I love those streets) has no such infliction." He also grew weary of "horrid trains and telegraphs and wild distances," as Ann's health became ever more delicate and her pain more constant. She began needing large doses of laudanum to relieve the neuralgia that sent pains "all over her body," and all too often, when he was traveling, Phillips would receive letters from her that read: "I am very sick this m[ornin]g, awake till mg and then had to get, in utter despair, Mrs. Fletcher in bed with me. . . . Hope I shall be able to hold out the week." By spring 1875 Phillips had begun refusing invitations even to local meetings, except "to talk 5–10 minutes *provided* Mrs. Phillips' state of health allowed. . . . This is *all*." Early that same year he wrote to William Lloyd Garrison in nearby Roxbury, expressing hope "some time to get out and see you—But I never leave without anxiety and hate to go more than a stone's throw off." Ann, he confided, now had "only memories to live on—weakness and pain and weariness make up the days now, so old memories are the pleasantest and she lives in the past."[32]

31. *Ibid.*, 83, 89, 90.
32. Phillips' letter quoted in Martyn, *Phillips*, 442–43; Phillips to Elizabeth N. Gay, January 30, [1875], Gay Papers; Phillips to Helen B. Garrison, [1875], Garrison Papers, BPL; Ann Phillips to Phillips, [1874], Blagden Papers; Phillips to Butler, April 8, 1875, Butler Papers, SCL; Phillips to William L. Garrison, February [?], 1875, Phillips to Helen B. Garrison, December [?], 1875, both in Garrison Papers, BPL.

At sixty-five, Phillips was still speaking regularly on the lyceum circuit. This photograph by Conly of Boston is from a cabinet card, a four-by-
two-inch rectangle of pasteboard sold to lecture goers as a keepsake. Often
Phillips was asked to autograph such mementos.

Chicago Historical Society, ICHi-18541

Occasionally, Phillips tried to revive his optimism concerning Ann's health by forecasting "the possibility . . . of blue sky," but he also wrote more realistically (and much more frequently) of days with Ann that "have been dark indeed, very dark." He and Ann had now begun to prepare for death, discussing the subject openly in their correspondence. "Dear Char," he wrote her in March, 1874, "I must love her more as time grows shorter." Their summer vacations also grew longer, beginning in the spring and extending well into October. Phillips' desire to mix in public diminished in proportion, and Ann Phillips, despite her increased discomfort, worried about his growing reclusiveness. When he declined an invitation to join a New York City literary society, she wrote, "I was sorry you did not accept the Lotus Club. I wanted you to see a new circle in New York. . . . Do find some new society to be with." His own public reversals and Ann's declining health were rapidly driving Phillips toward retirement.[33]

He did, however, try to heed Ann's advice about remaining socially active by joining a literary society in Boston known as the Radical Club. Occasionally, he participated when Emerson, Higginson, Longfellow, Louisa Alcott, and other members convened at John T. Sargent's house to discuss theology, aesthetics, and history. Phillips enjoyed the company of these transcendentalists and perfectionists, as well as the chance to argue for the concept of original sin and the idea that Jesus had been an agitator, not a contemplative philosopher.[34] While seeking some new acquaintances in this way, however, Phillips actually became far more anxious to reestablish one very special old friendship. William Lloyd Garrison had missed Phillips for a long time, at least since the early 1870s. In 1871, for example, he had asked Wendell Phillips Garrison to help begin a reconciliation. Send Phillips some Garrison family pictures, the older man had urged, and at the same time "incidentally state that you had been presented by me with Allen's large and excellent likeness of himself." When Phillips in turn encountered Garrison at social gatherings during this period, he always left feeling sad and a bit anxious. "It was very pleasant," Phillips remarked after one such meeting. "I saw

33. Phillips to Helen B. Garrison, December [?], 1875, Garrison Papers, BPL; Phillips to Abby K. Foster, December 21, 1874, Foster Papers; Phillips to Ann Phillips, March [?], 1874, Ann Phillips to Phillips, February 8, 1874, both in Blagden Papers.
34. Mary Sargent, *Sketches and Reminiscences of the Radical Club of Chestnut Street* (Boston, 1880), *passim*.

Garrison in the hall as he came in. I am very glad his life is ending so happily and so full of honor. He seems wholly at rest."[35]

They kept meeting at the gravesides of co-workers, sharing responsibilities for the conduct of Samuel J. May's funeral in 1871, and Henry C. Wright's in 1875. Even before Wright's death, however, Phillips began to commiserate openly with Garrison over such losses, writing him in January, 1875, "What a year of death in our ranks. I had not thought of it until your article in the Independent brought up the long list. . . . They die," Phillips lamented, "but how much work seems to be impending. . . . How keenly the South watches for our hour of weakness." Garrison's emphatic support for Sumner's Civil Rights Bill, moreover, must have drawn them closer together by convincing Phillips that his old friend had finally conceded the necessity of political vigilance. Phillips, in turn, clearly yearned for some of the peace of mind that he believed Garrison enjoyed. Hence, by February, 1875, Garrison had begun sending Ann Phillips his homemade jam as old bonds tightened and angry memories faded. When Helen Benson Garrison died in 1876, Phillips officiated at the funeral. Her husband was too devastated to attend, and Phillips designed his short eulogy to give comfort to his grief-stricken friend. "She is not dead—she has gone before," Phillips said. "She has joined the old band that worked life-long for the true and the good."[36]

Soon after the funeral, as a token of appreciation, Garrison sent Phillips a memoir he had written in honor of his departed wife. As soon as Phillips began reading it, whatever remained of his resentments toward Garrison were swept aside. In gratitude, Phillips replied that the gift "takes me back so many years—and brings back to memory so many dear names—the memories of our toilsome, triumphant day." As he thumbed through the pages, he told Garrison, "Cambridgeport, Pine St., and that somewhat bleak south end house come back to me, where so many happy and well-freighted hours passed—the plans—the hopes—the hurry—the crowds—the eagerness—the sorrows—the oddities mixed with the saints. . . . Your recollections go straight to one's heart."[37] Thus did he and Garrison renew their friendship, and Phillips found his thoughts

35. William L. Garrison to Wendell P. Garrison, August 1, 1871, Garrison Papers, BPL; Phillips quoted in Lillie Buffum Chase Wyman, *American Chivalry*, 12.

36. Phillips to William L. Garrison, January [?], 1875 (quotation), February [?], 1875, Phillips to Helen B. Garrison, October 18, 1875, all in Garrison Papers, BPL; Phillips to William L. Garrison, Jr., January 2, 1876, Garrison Papers, SCL; Phillips, "Helen Benson Garrison," in his *Speeches, Second Series*, 454–57.

37. Phillips to William L. Garrison, May 6, 1876, Garrison Papers, BPL.

turning ever more frequently to memories that gave a richness to his declining years.

There were, fortunately, moments of recognition when Phillips could confirm these recollections. Once in 1878 he found himself seated next to Garrison as a guest of honor at a commemorative dinner hosted by Boston's black leaders. Until late in the evening, "reminiscences of the anti-slavery struggle were given with zest," one participant recalled; "the words of wisdom and hope which fell from the lips of Garrison and Phillips that night will . . . never be effaced from the memory of those present." Later that same year, Phillips, Garrison, and a few others met to commemorate the forty-third anniversary of the 1835 Boston mob. In this last public appearance with his dear liberator, Phillips had the satisfaction of hearing Garrison claim that the mob's dangers had been worth the risk, for they had drawn his friend Wendell Phillips into the cause.[38] In settings like these, Phillips could indeed feel that history was being brought to life once more, despite the finality of his reversal in Faneuil Hall.

Phillips enjoyed these satisfying perspectives on the past, but he also saw multiplying signs that the events of the antebellum decades were now turning into dying memories. Soon, he knew, all those possessing personal knowledge of the Civil War would be dead, and perhaps, he feared, no one in the rising generation would even remember the anti-slavery struggle and his own great claim to a place in history. In July, 1878, an obscure abolitionist named Calvin Fairbanks gave such fears sad plausibility when he came to Phillips and "begged me to help him and his dying wife." Turning to others for assistance, Phillips "could only think of WLG and [Samuel] Sewall who *knew who he was* if I approached them." That same year, Phillips wrote a troubled article for the *North American Review*, in which he lamented the passing of the old generation of politicians, the Giddingses, Wades, and Stevenses, "who had created the Republican party." These had been men of conviction, he asserted. Their successors, however, the Blaines and the Conklings, "seek only to use for personal ends the power they have inherited." They had lost all personal contact with the moral drama of antislavery and were therefore incapable of inspiring "the active young men of today [who] were in their cradles" in the 1850s. A whole generation would

---

38. Archibald F. Grimke, *Wendell Phillips: A Memorial* (Boston, 1884), 9–16, Bartlett, *Phillips*, 388.

soon take up the nation's tasks, knowing, he feared, "nothing of . . . the events of the ten years before the war." Worse still, there was no convenient source from which they could learn, for the history of that era was not yet written. Phillips recalled that he had already heard "more than one man, twenty-five years old," ask in all innocence, "Was there a mob in Boston and what was it about?"[39] In his own college days, Phillips' immersion in history had yielded him axioms and dreams that had served him for half a century. Now, as an old man, he began working to preserve the record of his own life and times, hoping to perpetuate a heritage that would powerfully inspire generations to come.

Everywhere, he believed, he saw evidence of historical illiteracy and indifference; he complained that Gilded Age culture was completely disrespectful of America's heritage. Only a people who cared nothing for their past would cheat and slaughter the Plains Indians and dismantle historical buildings. In Chicago, for example, he had noticed a log cabin erected by the city's earliest white settlers, now surrounded by warehouses and long forgotten. At the time, he had imagined that it should be covered with a glass dome and preserved as a shrine, for the building had once served as "the cradle of the great city of the great lakes." Instead, wreckers had torn it down. Another time, an out-of-town friend had been greatly moved when Phillips had shown him the old Hancock House on Beacon Street. When the city decided to tear it down in 1875, Phillips was heartsick. He did not report his feelings when the once-bucolic Common was "improved" by the erection of a huge brass fountain in the "frog pond," or when the Back Bay, in which he had waded as a boy, was filled in to accommodate the elaborate Public Garden, but it is hard to imagine that he entirely approved.[40]

He did register vehement protests when the city threatened to tear down the Old South Meeting House to make room for new commercial buildings. "What does *Boston* mean?" he demanded, speaking at a rally protesting the city's plan. "Since 1630, the living fibre running through history which owns that name means jealousy of power, unfiltered speech, keen sense of justice, readiness to champion any good cause.

39. Phillips to Elizabeth N. Gay, July 23, 1878, Gay Papers; Phillips, "The Outlook," *North American Review* (July–August, 1878).
40. *National Anti-Slavery Standard*, June 12, 1869; *National Standard*, July 17, 1871; Bartlett, *Phillips*. For a brilliant analysis of the transformation of republicanism in elite American political culture into a pervasive rationale for class, sexual, and racial exploitation, see Slotkin, *The Fatal Environment*, 301–70.

That is the Boston Laud suspected, North hated and the negro loved."
The meetinghouse stood for all the enduring qualities of republican history that Phillips had always associated with his city and that had so
enriched his lifetime of crusading. Every generation, Phillips insisted,
needed instruction from the monuments left by its fathers. "Gentlemen, these walls are the college for such training. . . . The influence of
these old walls will prevent men, if anything can, from becoming tools
of corruption and tyranny." Afterward, Garrison marveled that Phillips,
"as a reformer and iconoclast," should plead "for the preservation of
so much brick and mortar" and denounce the proposed removal "as
something almost sacrilegious."[41] Despite his renewed closeness with
Phillips, the religious perfectionist would go to his grave puzzled by his
friend's fierce dedication to the past. Phillips, by contrast, prepared for
death by attempting to secure his place in history, by preserving the
records of the abolitionists themselves.

Samuel J. May set Phillips a good example, writing his memoirs and
bequeathing his personal papers to the Cornell University Library.
Phillips took up May's project in 1874, organizing a fund drive so that
Cornell might hire an archivist to preside over this "largest and best collection on the subject [of antislavery] in America." From this time forward, Phillips took every opportunity to recover antislavery sources and
insure their accessibility. When Charles L. Remond died in 1878, for example, Phillips launched an exhaustive search for his scrapbooks. Two
years later, he superintended the acquisition of Henry C. Wright's papers
by the Boston Public Library and then campaigned to secure the appointment of Charlotte Forten, a black abolitionist, as curator of this
collection. When Phillips learned that Francis Jackson's grandson had inherited a "very extensive" antislavery library, he sent the young man to
see John Jay, Jr., who was sorting his own father's extensive papers.
"Having heard that your father had gathered the most complete anti-
slavery library on the continent, I thought you . . . might like to add to
it," Phillips explained. "Such a collection ought finally to rest in some
public asylum."[42] Garrison was not responsive when Phillips urged him

41. Phillips, "The Old South Meeting House," 236–43; William L. Garrison to
Wendell Phillips Garrison, July 6, 1876, Garrison Papers, BPL.
42. Phillips, William L. Garrison, Gerrit Smith, and May, Jr., form letter, October 1,
1874, Garrison Papers, BPL; Phillips to Sidney H. Gay, July 10, 1878, Gay Papers;
Phillips to Francis J. Garrison, September 15, 1880, William Lloyd Garrison Papers,
LC; Phillips to John Jay, Jr., July 25, [1870s], Jay Family Papers.

to write his memoirs and to place his files of the *Liberator* in the Boston Public Library. Those tasks finally fell to Garrison's sons, who began a multivolume biography of their father even before his death. Phillips, meanwhile, began taking measures "to get rid of twenty-five hundred volumes" of his own library, donating complete runs of the *Standard* to the Library of Congress and the Boston Public Library. He also gave the latter repository "all my reports, pamphlets, surplus numbers of newspapers, bound and unbound, *Emancipators* and *Heralds of Freedom*." Phillips' father had once bequeathed a large sum to improve the Boston Public Library. His son, however, acting, he said, as his "own executor," left it the richer legacy of history itself.[43]

In May, 1879, William Lloyd Garrison died, and the family asked Phillips to deliver the funeral oration. His remarks about the man who had both inspired him and claimed his deepest friendship eloquently reflected his preoccupation with the abolitionists' place in history. That William Lloyd Garrison, Jr., took offense at Phillips' statements seemed to confirm the orator's misgivings about the values of the rising generation. "We do not come here to weep," Phillips assured those gathered at the First Church in Roxbury, but to remember the "grand lesson" of Garrison's life, his fearless discovery of the sin of slaveholding. As a "mere boy," Garrison, by himself, had challenged "church, commerce and college" to announce a "miracle of insight," the "complete solution" to the problem of American slavery. Acting with "unerring sagacity," Phillips claimed, Garrison had "made every single home, press, pulpit and senate a debating society" on the proposition of immediate emancipation. It was, Phillips insisted, an achievement future generations could understand only by comparing it historically to "the age of Vane and Cromwell, Luther's Reformation and the establishment of Christianity." Phillips also remarked that the same Roxbury pulpit from which he was speaking had never given "one word of approval or sympathy" to Garrison during the early struggles against slavery. He meant the comment as a graphic illustration of the adversity Garrison had once encountered, but Garrison's sons were furious. Phillips had insulted their family's church, they declared, protesting the remark as "a violation of good taste that father never would have approved." William Lloyd Garrison, Jr., demanded that Phillips delete the offending remarks in the published

43. Bartlett, *Phillips*, 338; Phillips to Powell, August 16, 1882 reprinted in Martyn, *Phillips*, 472.

version of the eulogy, but Phillips, far more concerned about posterity's judgments than about the younger Garrison's, refused.[44]

Soon after the funeral, Phillips observed that "most of our public men take the precaution to strengthen and vindicate themselves by studied explanations of what they did and careful explanations of all they said." Garrison, however, "'the most abused man of his day,' had stooped to no vindication." Instead, he had left his words "to be gathered up, or not, as neglect or loving reverence should choose."[45] In just such a loving and reverential way, Phillips had taken up the task that Garrison had spurned, enquiring after his deceased colleague's correspondence and preparing his own files for public inspection. Only long after, in the 1960s, would the influence of the Civil Rights movement finally repay Phillips for his careful efforts. While freedom riders defied southern segregation, historians calling themselves neoabolitionists were to claim Garrison and Phillips as the most important white egalitarians of the Civil War era. As these scholars successfully challenged the then-prevailing view that abolitionists were misguided fanatics, they would mine, as had no scholars before them, the rich collections of documents assembled by Phillips and his friends.[46] For the long-departed pessimistic republican, historical vindication awaited after all.

44. Phillips, "William Lloyd Garrison," in his *Speeches, Second Series*, 459–72; William L. Garrison, Jr., to Wendell P. Garrison, June 2, 5, 1879, Robert Walcutt to May, Jr., June 4, 1879, all in Garrison Papers, BPL.
45. Phillips, "William Lloyd Garrison," *North American Review* (August, 1879).
46. This very large body of scholarship is well exemplified by the essays collected in Martin L. Duberman (ed.), *The Antislavery Vanguard: New Essays on the Abolitionists* (Princeton, 1965), and best of all by Kraditor, *Means and Ends*.

FOURTEEN

The Travail and Solace of History

In July, 1878, Wendell Phillips sent apologies to Elizabeth Gay, informing her that he could not comply with her request to help underwrite a new temperance journal. "Crippled by the times so as to be struggling to pay debts, I have no right to send you anything," he told her. "If I could, I would. . . . But we just live nowadays and what we undertook years ago would appall me now." Actually, the Phillipses had been living precariously for some time. Six years before, Phillips had been forced to refuse when Franklin Sanborn asked him to contribute for a monument to John Brown. "I have done so much within the last ten years for the associates of J. B.," Phillips explained, "that I have no more left to do with." By the late 1870s, Phillips' fabled fortune had totally vanished, depleted in part by four decades of charitable giving. In one memorandum book alone he listed donations that added up to over sixty-five thousand dollars. He had also invested poorly, losing over eighty thousand dollars in just one stock transaction.[1] Poverty, not persistence, explains the intermittent lecturing of Phillips' last years. Money became a dominating preoccupation as he and Ann reached old age.

For Ann's sake, Phillips tried to pretend that he did not mind touring. "I never felt or looked better," he assured her, and "really I think nobody

1. Phillips to Elizabeth N. Gay, July 23, 1878, Gay Papers; Bartlett, *Phillips*, 394–95, 43 n. 20; Martyn, *Phillips*, 510.

would fancy me more than seventy—I have grown younger and thrown off five or ten years." To others, however, he complained that he was "not well enough even to lecture, and it is not right that I should," for Ann was no longer strong enough even to walk to the window of her room. His own stamina had begun to wane, and he confided in 1877 that he had been so "worn down . . . by the hard winter" that he was too weak to lecture at all. People began to notice his frayed gloves and scuffed travel bag, and one day, Henry Ingersoll Bowditch, an old acquaintance, spied Phillips leaning against a bank building on crowded State Street, a vacant stare on his face. "Wendell," he remarked jokingly, "if you want these people to give you money, you must take off your hat and hold it in your hand." The attempt at humor, too perfect a reminder of Phillips' financial difficulties and fatigue, must have hurt him deeply. Friends began to see a "bitter and malign" look in Phillips' features, a sign that his temper had "become sharp and his mind melancholic."[2] If so, there were good reasons, for the Phillipses' last years together were never easy and sometimes heartbreaking.

Fortunately for Ann, Wendell reached seventy enjoying reasonably good health and able to nurse her. On vacation in Princeton, Massachusetts, in the summer of 1880, he still took rides on horseback and was able to report proudly, "I weigh one hundred and seventy-five pounds and don't feel as old as I am." He used some of his remaining vigor and charitable nature to help infirm friends such as Lydia Maria Child and the Fosters with legal matters as they, like the Phillipses, prepared for death. "Tell Stephen to take courage and we'll agree if he survives me that he shall say a good word for me and if I outlive him, I'll testify to the truth on his behalf," Phillips wrote Abby K. Foster in mid-1880.[3] Nearly as important as good health for Phillips' peace of mind were his occasional opportunities to remind the world that he still considered himself an active reformer. For most of these he had the *North American Review* to thank.

The *Review* spoke for Brahmin gentility and looked distastefully on greenbackers, black Republicans, and working-class anarchists. Phillips' contributions therefore gave this proper journal an appealing voice of

2. Phillips to Ann Phillips, February 28, [1870s–1881], Blagden Papers; Wyman, "Reminiscence of Phillips," 734, 738–39; Korngold, *Two Friends of Man*, 392–94.
3. Martyn, *Phillips*, 454–55; Phillips to Abby K. Foster, July 26, 1880, Foster Papers; Child to Phillips, June 14, 1880, Blagden Papers; Phillips to Mrs. Parson, November 8, 1881, May-McKim Papers.

dissent, attracting the notice of those curious to sample the opinions of a legendary radical. Almost to the end, Phillips succeeded in remaining somewhat the pundit. From 1878 to 1881, he used the *Review* to address public issues that still concerned him vitally. In 1878, for example, he decried the Republicans' new policy of southern home rule. Early the following year, Phillips published a vigorous argument that black enfranchisement was proving successful in the old Confederacy. Though it would have been far better had the freedmen been given land, even in the face of rising white repression, "there is no need even now of bating one jot of hope," he wrote. "The United States government is amply able to protect its own citizens," and meanwhile, southern blacks continued to gain education and amass property. "Right is stronger than wrong," he wrote. "Barbarianism melts before civilization."[4] Predictably, Phillips had now delivered his final assessment of the conflict over slavery, declaring nationality and himself the indisputable victors. At this late hour he could no longer afford his old skepticism.

Phillips offended few of the *Review*'s genteel readers when he defended women's suffrage or attacked clerical figures for their support of capital punishment and liquor licensing, but his admonition that workers should vote, not strike, hardly reassured them when in the next line he defended greenbackers or, far worse, the violence of some European Communists. Such workers' uprisings, in Phillips' view, were the moral equivalents of slave insurrections, "the righteous and honorable resistance of a heart-broken and poverty-stricken people to a despotism which flaunts its insolence and cruel rule. Of all the cants that are canted in this canting world, the cant of our American hypocrites bewailing European communism is the most disgusting." He doubly insured his fanatic's reputation by next encouraging Fenian insurgents in their struggles against "an England that has planned that Ireland shall starve, hoping that she would be too weak to resist."[5]

Harvard's overseers, therefore, had a clear idea of what to expect in the spring of 1881 when they invited Phillips to address the centennial anniversary meeting of the college's Phi Beta Kappa chapter. They also

4. John G. Sproat, *"The Best Men": Liberal Reformers in the Gilded Age* (New York, 1969), 8, 17–18, 23, 101; Phillips, "The Outlook," *North American Review* (July–August, 1878, March, 1879).

5. Phillips, "The Other Side of the Woman Question," *North American Review* (November, 1879); "A Review of Dr. Crosby's 'Calm View of Temperance,'" *North American Review* (June, 1879); "The Outlook," *North American Review* (September, 1879); Phillips to Patrick Ford, November 2, 1881, reprinted in Martyn, *Phillips*, 468.

knew that June, 1881, marked the passage of exactly five decades since Phillips had last spoken at Harvard, at his own commencement exercises. In the interim, Harvard had chosen to ignore its greatest living orator. Phillips, to be fair, had continually supplied them with reasons for snubbing him. He had showered Harvard's leading men with abuse, assailing them first as pawns of the slave power, then as labor-oppressing money kings. Every spring, he had once declared, Harvard was "taken up bodily, and put away [in] the vaults of the State Street banks," where it was preserved over the summer, to be taken out again like a bar of gold, "glittering and exceedingly cold," in time for fall classes.[6]

Now, however, the overseers realized that Phillips' return to the Yard would turn their celebration into a moment of unusual interest, and for this reason, they were willing to overlook his abuse. They deplored his views on communism, labor, and currency questions, but they agreed that Phillips embodied traditions that "correct" Bostonians could claim with pride. His name, after all, called forth memories of epochal antislavery struggles, when high ideals and manly courage had counted for so much. "Wendell Phillips" also meant Faneuil Hall, Boston's great tradition of patriotic oratory, and an expression of the city's conscience that extended back to Revolutionary days. A speech by Wendell Phillips would treat Harvard to a sample of living history, which was precisely how Phillips now regarded himself. When a copy of the invitation reached him through the mail, he immediately readdressed it to Tom Appleton, his boyhood playmate and classmate of 1831. Do attend, he urged Appleton, for "one more meeting for auld lang syne."[7]

Before the Civil War, Phillips had addressed academic audiences at Brown, Yale, Dartmouth, and Williams. Each time he had criticized collegians for avoiding social conflict and had urged them "to leave the heights of contemplations [and] come down to the everyday life of the people . . . , utter truth and labor for right and God."[8] Such remarks reflected his abiding belief in the idea of the agitator as a republican combination of scholar and statesman, the self-conception that had supported him for a lifetime. Now the overseers had offered him the rare chance to return with his inspiration to the place where he had first encountered it in his historical studies. By lifting their ban, they had conceded him a terribly satisfying victory, but far more important, they had

6. *Liberator*, August 14, 1857.
7. Phi Beta Kappa Centennial Anniversary Invitation, Garrison Papers, BPL.
8. Editor's Introduction to Phillips, "The Scholar in a Republic," 331.

furnished him one last opportunity to examine his past for the instruction of others and to assert his own vindication. In the audience would be precisely those whom Phillips believed most needed to learn from his example, that rising generation that he found so ignorant of history. Had he designed the occasion himself, Phillips could hardly have improved it.

Once the overseers had announced their choice, people began to wonder what Phillips would say. Would he "regard the amenities of the occasion" and address some "purely literary theme"? Or would he use the occasion to attack complacent authorities and his personal enemies, "seize his mother by the hair and gracefully twist it out with a smile"? James Freeman Clarke, an acquaintance, observed that if Phillips had "been bitter before, he can be ten times more bitter now," turning the Phi Beta Kappa celebration into "the day of judgment for the sins of a half century." Clarke felt sure it would be a unique moment for Phillips that would "never come again." Keenly appreciating this fact, Phillips decided for once to depart from his usual procedures and write out his speech in advance.[9] He was taking no chances.

When the day arrived on June 30, 1881, however, Phillips carried no script as he followed the long procession into Harvard's Sanders Theatre. In front of him, decked in academic regalia, marched delegations from seventeen of the twenty existing chapters of Phi Beta Kappa, the president of the society, President Charles W. Eliot of Harvard, President Daniel Coit Gilman of Johns Hopkins University, Justice Oliver Wendell Holmes (Phillips' kinsman), George William Curtis, James Freeman Clarke, Edward Everett Hale, Phillips Brooks, and Professor Andrew Peabody, chairman of the proceedings. Thomas Wentworth Higginson sat in the audience of notables and listened as his old friend began his speech. "Never," Higginson recalled, had Phillips "seemed more at ease, more colloquial and more extemporaneous." For one last time, he set out to hold "an unwilling audience spellbound."[10]

Phillips titled his address "The Scholar in a Republic," and predictably he opened it with a history lesson, choosing the revealing subject of Harry Vane. Discerning striking parallels between the life of this great Puritan revolutionary and his own career, Phillips felt the subject a perfect vehicle for affirming his view of himself in history. After a wayward

9. Korngold, *Two Friends of Man*, 390; Martyn, *Phillips*, 464.
10. Higginson, "*Phillips*," 14–15.

adolescence, Vane, a wealthy English aristocrat, had converted to Puritanism, moving to America to become the governor of the Massachusetts Bay Colony. There, he had upheld the rights of religious dissenters before returning to England to fight in Cromwell's army. After the Restoration, Charles II had ordered Vane beheaded for treason. Standing before the chopping block, this handsome noble had spoken eloquently in defense of his decision to enroll as Christ's soldier in the struggle against kingly despotism. Like Phillips' other heroes—Lovejoy, Brown, Toussaint, and the rest—Vane had maintained his convictions with his final breath. Phillips clearly believed himself to be following this example as he stood before this august gathering to deliver his last major address.

He gestured toward Boston, speaking as he did so of Harry Vane as "the noblest human being who ever walked the streets of yonder city. I do not forget Franklin or Sam Adams, Washington or [La]Fayette, Garrison or John Brown. Vane dwells an arrow's flight above them all, and his touch consecrated the continent to measureless toleration of opinion and entire equality of rights." Vane, according to Phillips, was the original founding father, whose life and death had set in motion a historical process of ever-expanding freedom. Phillips described it as "the seed bursting with flower, infancy becoming manhood. It was life, in its omnipotence, rending whatever dead matter may have confined it." Traveling from England, "that grand wave" had "struck our shores" and shaped a democratic republic, and "when the veil was withdrawn, what stood revealed astonished the world."[11] With this rhapsodic meditation on America's beginnings, Phillips prepared his listeners for his final justification for his life as a republican agitator.

"When I was a student here, my favorite study was history," Phillips recalled. The subject was burdened with "loose conjecture," valueless minutiae, and "the day dreams of pedants and triflers." Nevertheless, he emphasized, people must read history and "hope to discover the great currents and massive forces that have shaped our lives." Those currents, Phillips declared, were precisely what Harry Vane had loosed upon the world when he had gone so bravely to the block. He had sent the "massive forces" rolling forward through Sam Adams, Jefferson, and Garrison, leading America to destroy slavery and achieve "what no race, no nation, no age had ever dared even try." The United States, he declared

11. Phillips, "Scholar in a Republic," 330–62.

triumphantly, had now become a fully republican nation, the first of its kind, governed by "the unlimited suffrage of the millions. We have actually worked out the problem," Phillips insisted, "that man, as God created him, may be trusted with self-government." The America of 1881 displayed the grand results, "with a territory that joins ocean to ocean, with fifty millions of people, two wars behind her. . . . The great Republic, stronger than ever, launches into its second century," he enthused. "The history of the world has no such chapter in its breadth, its depth, its significance or its bearing on [the] future."[12] For one last time, Phillips had asserted his democratic nationalism by celebrating a republican past, placing himself, by every implication, directly in the forefront of these grand developments.

He next shifted from historical meditation to issue a present-minded challenge, telling his audience of scholars to put aside their pedantry and elitism, their "parrot note [sic] and cold moonlight reflection of older civilizations." In America, he said, public opinion accounted for all true education, and university scholarship for none, as history confirmed at every turn. John Brown, for instance, had edified the entire country as he had gone to the gallows. "God lifted a million hearts to his gibbet, as the Roman cross lifted the world to itself in that divine sacrifice of two thousand years ago." Meanwhile, "the first of American scholars," powerless before Brown's magnificent act, had only been able to pour out a "rich vocabulary of Saxon scorn words. . . . How little, brothers, can we claim for bookmen in that uprising." The record, Phillips claimed, confirmed at every point that "timid scholarship either shrinks from sharing in these agitations, or denounces them as vulgar and dangerous interference by incompetent hands." The "book-educated class of the North" had ever betrayed a "chronic distrust of the people" and a desire to stifle their free expression. To become university educated, Phillips told his scholarly listeners, was to become an enemy of popular rights.

This fact was crucial, Phillips warned, for undemocratic forces that sought the scholar's assistance were currently at work in America. "The White South hates universal suffrage. The so-called cultivated North distrusts it. . . . Timid scholars tell their dread of it." Meanwhile, in the great cities, spurious reformers recommended "taking away the ballots of the poor citizens" in order to stem corruption in politics. As in all

12. *Ibid.*

other ages, aristocrats were again grasping for control, claiming the enlightened power to rule the lower orders in the name of social peace; and their efforts, as always, threatened tyranny and anarchy. "Corruption does not so much rot the masses," he declared. "It poisons Congress. . . . As usual, in Chemistry, the scum floats uppermost. . . . It is not the masses who have most disgraced our annals," Phillips insisted. "I never saw or heard of any but well-dressed mobs, assembled and countenanced . . . by respectability and what called itself education." Scholars therefore faced the choice of abetting tyranny or opposing it, Phillips declared. "I urge on college-bred men that . . . they fail in republican duty when they allow others to lead in the great social questions which stir and educate the age."[13]

Phillips used his remaining remarks to reinforce this challenge by repeating the justification for radical abolitionism he had first developed in the 1840s. "The freer a nation becomes," he argued, and "the more utterly democratic in form, the greater the need of outside agitation." Politicians and clerics, "laden with the burden of securing their own success," inevitably succumbed to inertia and corruption. The moral critic, alone, had the power to reverse this degeneration by "standing outside of organization with . . . no object but truth—to tear a question open and riddle it with light." His old examples of Burke and Sam Adams still seemed as pertinent as ever. "These 'agitators,'" he declared, "are . . . the means God offers us to refine the taste, mould the character, lift the purpose, and educate the moral sense of the masses on whose intelligence and self-respect rests the State." America now needed a new generation of scholar-patriots, young men like the one he had been when Elijah Lovejoy had called him to make noble use of his Harvard education.[14]

The republican scholar faced many challenges, Phillips concluded, beginning his final demonstration of the agitator's rhetorical art. There was the spreading poison of alcohol. "Neither an incapable civil service, nor an ambitious soldier, nor Southern vandals, nor venal legislators, nor the greed of wealth . . . will put universal suffrage into eclipse," he prophesied. "It will be rum entrenched in great cities, commanding every ground." There was also the forty-year-old controversy over "the equal recognition of women," a "weary and thankless though successful

13. *Ibid.*
14. *Ibid.*, 362.

struggle" to secure equality, which would free women to combat "that ghastly curse [liquor]—the vice of the great cities, before which social science stands palsied and dumb." There was, above all, the battle to secure labor's right to organize peacefully, for "when the easy class conspires to steal, what wonder that the humbler class draws together to defend itself." If indeed American workers found their peaceful organizing efforts thwarted by repression, he warned, they would have perfect justification to emulate Russia's violent nihilists. "I honor Nihilism," he maintained, "since it redeems human nature from being utterly vile, made up only of heartless oppression and contented slaves." Whenever oppression secured dominion, Phillips declared, "dynamite and daggers are necessary and proper substitutes for Faneuil Hall and the *Daily Advertiser*." The republican scholar must accept the obligation to make the nation measure itself by the highest standards of its own history:

> To be as good as our fathers we must be better. They silenced their fears and subdued their prejudices, inaugurating free speech and equality with no precedent on the file. Europe shouted "Madmen!" and gave us forty years for the shipwreck. With serene faith they persevered. Let us rise to their level. Crush appetite, and prohibit temptation if it rots great cities. Entrench labor in sufficient bulwarks against that wealth which, without the tenfold strength of modern incorporation, wrecked the Grecian and Roman States; and with a sterner effort still, summon women into civil life as reinforcement to our laboring ranks in the effort to make our civilization a success.[15]

From earliest recollection, Phillips had felt compelled to redeem the legacies of his Revolutionary forebears. Now, as he ended his address and sat down, he hoped he had inspired his young audience to feel likewise and to look upon him, too, as one of their own founding fathers.

In the aftermath, then, it probably mattered little to him that some critics, including Higginson, applauded his speech as "in some respects, the most remarkable of his career" or that others, like Henry Wadsworth Longfellow, praised only his forensic style. "Yes," Longfellow remarked, "it was marvelous and delightful, but preposterous from beginning to end." It certainly did not surprise him that the religious press scourged him for defending nihilism. What mattered most this time was not the

15. *Ibid.*

public's range of opinions but simply that he had been able to state his final explanation and bequest. "Well," Phillips commented soon afterward, "I suppose they wanted me to bring *myself*."[16] Except for a very brief appearance in 1883, he never again addressed the public. He sensed now that he too was fast becoming a fact of history, and therefore, he had nothing more that he wished to say.

There was another reason for Phillips' retreat to silence, the desperate effort he had begun to maintain ownership of his single most important possession, 26 Essex Street. It was a nightmarish struggle, begun in 1880 when city officials informed Phillips that they had condemned his home. Harrison Street, a block away, was to be extended to accommodate heavy industrial traffic, and 26 Essex Street stood in the way. Ann, partially paralyzed and bedridden, faced the terrifying prospect of being uprooted from her only place of security for the past forty years. Neither she nor Wendell could conceive of life together outside the haven in which they had for so long nurtured their special relationship. They appealed to city authorities and filed motions in the courts—all without success. Early in May, 1882, an ambulance pulled up in front of the condemned structure, and Wendell helped the attendants carry Ann down the stairs. In dread of this terrible day, she had spent the previous eight weeks nearly sleepless and in pain, "unable to stand alone or to turn her head or to use [a] pillow." Wendell had "never seen her so ill," he reported to Abby Foster.[17]

The ambulance deposited Ann and Wendell at 37 Common Street, far from their familiar neighborhood. They salvaged the mantel and grate from the fireplace in Ann's old room, installed them in her new chamber, and arranged the furniture to look as it had before, but such cosmetics only heightened their grief and sense of victimization. Bitterly condemning the "tyrannous and mad city," Wendell lamented that Ann could "never, ever" call the new arrangement home. Once, a few weeks later, Phillips and a friend visited the old Essex Street location, and gazing at the vacant lot, he remarked how unfair it was "that the city would not let me stay 'till the end." Then he turned away, muttering, "It is no matter. I am almost through with it all." There are transparent ironies to note—that the great apostle of progress had been uprooted by capi-

16. Higginson, *Phillips*, 13–14; Bartlett, *Phillips*, 392; Martyn, *Phillips*, 465.
17. Child to Phillips, July 14, 1880, Blagden Papers; Phillips to Abby K. Foster, June 7, 1882, Foster Papers.

talist expansion, that the eloquent preserver of landmarks had been unable to save his own home, that the city he loved so deeply had spurned his most urgent pleas, that the republican enemy of unregulated power had been crushed by nameless urban planners. Even together they do not begin to measure the depths of the Phillipses' agony. "May you never learn what uprooting is," Wendell Phillips wrote to Wendell Phillips Garrison, and even a full year after moving, he told Abbey Foster, "Ann and I can't bear to have the old home spoken of."[18]

Poverty, obscurity, and loneliness filled the Phillipses' last three years together. Wendell, by his own account "not very strong," reported soon after the move that he was now "a house-keeping youth" who did little but take care of Ann. "I am a good boy," he assured a friend, "and stay home—cleaning up and giving away my books and pamphlets—acting as my own executor and getting ready to go." Hoping to save enough to maintain Ann in case she outlived him, Phillips became ever more strapped for cash. In 1883, desperate, he wrote to his abolitionist colleague Samuel Sewall, asking to be informed about work "for a person who has been flung out of business by one of those movements that the city calls 'improvement' but that I call public plunder. Do you have an opening for him to earn a living?" Clearly, Phillips was referring to himself. There were, unfortunately, no close relatives to assist them, for Wendell had outlived all his brothers and sisters, and Ann, of course, had no surviving kin from her own generation either. They were thrown on their own resources, and day-to-day life demanded more of the Phillipses and rewarded them less. Young Lillie Wyman, descended from two generations of abolitionists, once spied Phillips on the street, stopped her carriage, and gave him a ride. As they chatted, Phillips spoke "mournfully . . . of his wife's condition . . . and of their life. . . . 'We sit and grumble together,'" he said. Wyman, sensing his defeated spirit, "impulsively begged him not to let sadness be the dominant feeling of his life." He smiled, but said nothing.[19]

Phoebe Garnaut, their adopted daughter, still wrote the Phillipses often, but she had left Boston years before when her husband became a

18. Phillips to Elizabeth N. Gay, December 20, 1882, Gay Papers; Korngold, *Two Friends of Man*, 393; Phillips to Wendell P. Garrison, August 13, 1882, Garrison Papers, BPL; Phillips to Abby K. Foster, August 10, 1883, Foster Papers.
19. Phillips to Abby K. Foster, January 15, 1882, Foster Papers; Phillips to Caroline Dall, May 15, 1883, Caroline Dall Papers, MHS; Phillips to Samuel Sewall, March 1, 1883, Sewall-Robie Collection, HL; Wyman, "Reminiscence of Phillips," 735.

European correspondent for the New York *Tribune*. Wendell's only local family consisted of cousins and nephews, who found it awkward to associate with this ill, unhappy couple. Phillips clumsily tried to reach out to them, sending them family relics that he hoped would unite them in common memories and traditions. One Christmas, for example, he presented Oliver Wendell Holmes with two decorative tiles that had been salvaged from "the old Wendell House which stood where now stands the Parker House." He also gave a wooden panel from the home of his beloved grandparents the Walleys to his nephew John C. Phillips, but when he learned that his gift had ended up on its recipient's back kitchen wall, he upbraided his relatives at length. His own kin, he sorrowfully believed, were proving to be just as uncaring about history as the rest. "When I offered you that fragment of your great-grandfather's home, I thought I was giving you something of special value to anyone who shared his blood," Phillips stated. "It is more than a hundred years old. It saw my father and mother married, looked down on the faces of the dead and witnessed the joys and sorrows of two generations very dear to us. Proud men," Phillips maintained, "would give a thousand for such an inheritance, and thoughtful men would enshrine it. . . . I ask, therefore, that you will return it to me."[20] John Phillips no doubt dismissed the angry letter as evidence of an old man's growing irascibility, and limited his contact with his uncle thereafter.

The only relatives who successfully expressed their concern for Wendell and Ann Phillips were the Samuel Blagdens, generous people who lived in New York City. In 1882 when Wendell's nephew Samuel and his wife, Julia, named their son Wendell Phillips Blagden, the orator was deeply touched. It gave him the assurance, despite his childlessness, that his name would be perpetuated in one branch of his family. Much in contrast to the John Phillipses of Boston, the Blagdens understood their relative's concern for posterity and were happy to honor him in this way. "Ann was much pleased with your tribute," Phillips wrote them in gratitude, "and says she has no fear but that the little fellow will inherit brains enough and only hopes that he will be as good as his namesake— So you can see she still lives with honeymoon dreams of my perfection." Warmly he assured the Blagdens, "You will have to be seventy years old before you know how grateful such an affectionate remembrance is."

20. Phillips quoted in Bartlett, *Phillips*, 375–76.

Soon he began sending the Blagdens genealogical information on the earliest American Phillipses so they could teach the boy the significance of his name.[21]

Sometime early in 1884, Phillips decided that once Ann had died, the Samuel Blagden family must inherit his estate and his personal correspondence. It was the best gesture of gratitude and trust remaining to him, for his papers contained intimate records of life with Ann, of lifelong friendships, and of the many struggles against social injustice. In the end, his faith in the Blagdens proved well placed. The papers would remain safe in family hands for nearly a century until another generous, historically minded descendant, Crawford Blagden, would deposit them in Harvard's Houghton Library, an inestimable gift to scholars of the Civil War era and a final disproof of Wendell Phillips' fear that all his descendants had grown callous to history.[22]

Samuel and Julia Blagden knew, too, that the lonely Phillipses needed immediate comfort, not understanding decades hence. So they sent the couple pictures of their children and then decided to pay them a visit. When the first photograph of Wendell Phillips Blagden arrived, Phillips sent thanks by the next mail. Describing Ann's reaction, he reported, "I have not seen her so charmed and thoroughly delighted for years at the sight of 'her baby.'" In deep gratitude, he continued: "I thank you most sincerely for many happy hours in that weary room where she lies in patient helplessness—she never parts with the picture, keeps it near her and exhibits it to every body. I cannot say I blame her much!" Ann even began to insist that Phillips leave her to attend the baby's christening, but he "crushed that madness before it came to a head."

Late in 1883, when the Blagden family arrived at 37 Common Street, the Phillipses could hardly contain their excitement. Wendell felt the occasion demanded special notice, declaring "If I were only Gov[erno]r (as I ought to be) I'd order 100 guns fired when W[endell] P[hillips] B[lagden] lands at the station and have him met by my staff in blue and gold." After the visitors had left, he composed a letter to his small namesake, telling the boy that he must come again, "as soon as you can. Now be as sweet and bright as your mother," he advised, "and you will prove yourself as wonderful a fellow as your [great] aunt already thinks of you." Phillips never indicated whether the visit relieved his and Ann's

21. Phillips to Samuel Blagden, September 24, 20, 1882, Garrison Papers, BPL.
22. Phillips, Last Will and Testament, Garrison Papers, BPL. For the immediate background of this bequest, see Bartlett, "New Light on Phillips," 1–5.

loneliness more than its aftermath deepened it, but the whole interlude, including the impromptu "sweet comical farce" that young Crawford Blagden put on in Ann's sickroom, brought them much-needed respite.[23]

Phillips, by this time, had prepared as fully as he could for death. He was confident of his spiritual standing, seeing his life as conforming to Jesus' example of agitating against moral wickedness and social injustice. Heaven, as he conceived it, contained all his reformer colleagues, and he anticipated "no fearful change" as death carried him across its threshold. "All my world—with a dozen exceptions—is over there—I sometimes feel impatient to see the great and the good again." Peaceful thoughts about eternity never removed his fears about being misunderstood by earthbound people who read history, however. In 1883, for example, he corrected James Freeman Clarke at length for misstatements in a published account of the abolitionist movement. A similar concern inspired the note he wrote to Robert Purvis, who had invited him to the fiftieth anniversary celebration of the founding of the American Anti-Slavery Society. "Let it not be said," Phillips emphasized, "that the old Abolitionist stopped with the negro and was never able to see that the same principle he had advocated at such cost claimed his utmost attention to protect all labor, white and black, and to further the discussion of every claim of downtrodden humanity."[24] This statement, though patently inaccurate for the antislavery movement as a whole, perfectly described Phillips' last and most satisfying conception of his own career.

Death alone could relieve his terrible fears for Ann, should she happen to survive him. As he told Susan B. Anthony when she paid a visit early in 1884, he remembered his grandfather's words just after his grandmother's funeral: "Thank God I have lived to see her go first." Phillips recalled that he had not understood his grandfather's meaning when he was young, "but now I know what it was. I have lived to have every hope and wish merge itself and be lost in the one wish that I may outlive Ann."[25] Later that month, violent chest pains brought the realization that his hopes had been in vain. Heart attack had begun to claim him, much as it had his father.

23. Phillips to Julia Blagden, January [?], 1883, Phillips to Samuel L. Blagden, November [?], 1883, and n.d., all in Garrison Papers, BPL.
24. Phillips to Miss Thayer, November 29, 1880, David Thayer Papers, Miscellaneous Collections, LC; Phillips to Clarke, April 1, 1883, Clarke Papers; Phillips to Robert Purvis, December 4, 1883, quoted in Martyn, *Phillips*, 473–74.
25. Bartlett, *Phillips*, 395.

The seizures struck, subsided, and struck again for nearly a week. By February 3, Phillips lay on his deathbed battling great pain. When nurses brought Ann to his room on a cot, he assured her that he felt "no fear of death" and confessed his belief in the saving power of Christ. Ann, people remembered, kept herself "in strong control and did not groan," for as she said, "that would have made it so much harder for poor Wendell to die." As always, Ann Phillips was helping her husband as no one else could to manage a difficult moment. Still, his last spoken thoughts were troubled and centered on her. "What will become of Ann?" he asked.[26] Relatives and friends saw to Ann's care, and she lived on for fourteen months, until April 23, 1885.

In 1912, the successful black poet and activist James Weldon Johnson recalled the ceremony that had marked his graduation from his Jacksonville, Florida, grammar school in 1887.

The real enthusiasm was aroused by "Shiny." He was the principal speaker of the day, and well did he measure up to the honour. He made a striking picture, that thin little black boy standing on the platform, dressed in clothes that did not fit him any too well, his eyes burning with excitement, his shrill, musical voice vibrating with such great intelligence and earnestness as to be positively handsome. What were his thoughts when he stepped forward and looked into that crowd of faces, all white with the exception of a score or so, lost to view? I do not know, but I fancy he felt his loneliness. I think there must have rushed over him a feeling akin to that of a gladiator tossed into the arena and bade to fight for his life. I think that solitary little black figure standing there felt that for the particular time and place he bore the weight and responsibility of his race; that for him to fail meant general defeat; but he won, and nobly. His oration was Wendell Phillips' "Toussaint L'Ouverture," a speech which may now be classed as rhetorical— even, perhaps, bombastic; but as the words fell from "Shiny's" lips their effect was magical. How so young an orator could stir so great

26. Recollection of Mrs. E. F. Crosby and Dr. David Thayer, reprinted in Martyn, *Phillips*, 480–81; Mary Livermore, "Does the Ideal Husband Exist?," *North American Review* (February, 1896); Bartlett, *Phillips*, 395; Korngold, *Two Friends of Man*, 396; Francis Jackson Garrison, *Ann Phillips, Wife of Wendell Phillips: A Memorial Sketch* (Boston, 1886).

enthusiasm was to be wondered at. When, in the famous perora-tion, his voice, trembling with suppressed emotion, rose higher and higher and then rested on the name "Toussaint L'Ouverture," it was like touching an electric button which loosed the pent-up feelings of his listeners. They actually rose up to him.[27]

27. James Weldon Johnson, *The Autobiography of an Ex-Colored Man*, reprinted in John Hope Franklin (ed.), *The Negro Classics* (New York, 1965), 416.

Bibliography

MANUSCRIPTS

American Antiquarian Society. Worcester, Massachusetts.
    Foster, Stephen S., and Abby K. Papers.
Boston Public Library, Antislavery Collection. Boston, Massachusetts.
    Chapman, Maria Weston. Papers.
    Garrison, William Lloyd. Papers.
    May, Samuel J. Papers.
    Phelps, Amos. Papers.
    Phillips, Wendell. Commonplace Books.
    Quincy, Edmund D.–Richard D. Webb. Papers.
    Spooner, Lysander. Papers.
    Vigilance Committee. Records.
    Weston, Ann Warren. Papers.
    Wright, Henry C. Papers.
Columbia University Library. New York.
    Conway, Moncure. Papers.
    Gay, Sidney Howard. Papers.
    Jay Family. Papers.
Cornell University Library. Ithaca, New York.
    May, Samuel J.–J. Miller McKim. Papers.
Harvard University Archives. Cambridge, Massachusetts.
    Buckingham, Edgar. Papers.
    Holland, Frederick. Papers.

Library Records.
    Phillips, Wendell. Composition Books.
Historical Society of Pennsylvania. Philadelphia.
    Chase, Salmon P. Papers.
Houghton Library. Harvard University, Cambridge, Massachusetts.
    Blagden, Crawford. Papers.
    Clarke, James Freeman. Papers.
    Curtis, George William. Papers.
    Emerson, Ralph Waldo. Papers.
    Higginson, Thomas Wentworth. Papers.
    Norton, Charles Eliot. Papers.
    Palfrey, John Gorham. Papers.
    Sewall-Robie Collection.
    Sumner, Charles. Papers.
    Villard, Oswald Garrison. Papers.
Henry E. Huntington Library. San Marino, California.
    Phillips, Wendell. Miscellaneous Letters.
Library of Congress. Washington, D.C.
    Butler, Benjamin. Papers.
    Garrison, William Lloyd. Papers.
    Giddings, Joshua R.–George W. Julian. Papers.
    Stanton, Elizabeth Cady. Papers.
    Stevens, Thaddeus. Papers.
    Thayer, David. Papers.
Massachusetts Historical Society. Boston.
    Dall, Caroline. Papers.
    Dana, Richard H. Papers.
    Lawrence, Amos. Papers.
    Quincy, Edmund. Papers.
    Washburn Family. Correspondence.
New Hampshire Historical Society. Concord.
    Phillips, Wendell. Miscellaneous Letters.
New York Historical Society. New York.
    Spooner, Lysander. Papers.
Ohio State Historical Society. Columbus.
    Giddings, Joshua R. Papers.
Smith College Library, Sophia Smith Collection. Northampton,
    Massachusetts.
    Butler, Benjamin. Papers.
    Garrison, William Lloyd. Papers.
Syracuse University Library. Syracuse, New York.
    Smith-Miller, Gerrit. Family Papers.

NEWSPAPERS AND PERIODICALS

Boston *Advertiser.*
Boston *Herald.*
Concord (N.H.) *Herald of Freedom.* 1843–45.
Liberator. Boston. 1837–65.
National Anti-Slavery Standard. New York City. 1841–70.
National Standard. New York City. 1870–71.
New York Home Evangelist.
Non-Resistant. Boston. 1839–40.
Weekly American Workman. Boston. 1869–70.

BOOKS AND PAMPHLETS

Abzug, Robert. *Passionate Liberator: The Life of Theodore D. Weld.* New York, 1978.
Austin, George. *The Life and Times of Wendell Phillips.* Boston, 1884.
Bailyn, Bernard. *The Ideological Origins of the American Revolution.* Cambridge, Mass., 1969.
———. *The Origins of American Politics.* New York, 1968.
Bartlett, Irving. *Wendell Phillips: Brahmin Radical.* Boston, 1961.
Bearse, Austin. *Reminiscences of Fugitive Slave Days in Boston.* Boston, 1880.
Bender, Thomas. *Toward an Urban Vision: Ideas and Institutions in Nineteenth-Century America.* Lexington, 1975.
Benedict, Michael Les. *A Compromise of Principle: Congressional Republicans and Reconstruction, 1863–1869.* New York, 1973.
Blackett, R. J. M. *Building an Antislavery Wall: Black Americans in the Atlantic Abolitionist Movement, 1830–1860.* Baton Rouge, 1983.
Bode, Carl. *The American Lyceum: Town Meetings of the Mind.* New York, 1956.
Boyer, Paul. *The Urban Masses and Moral Order in America.* Cambridge, Mass., 1978.
Brauer, Kinley. *Cotton Versus Conscience: Massachusetts Whig Politics and Southern Expansion, 1843–1848.* Lexington, 1967.
Cochran, Paul E. *Political Language and Rhetoric.* Austin, 1979.
Conway, Moncure. *Autobiography,* 2 vols. London, 1914.
Cover, Robert M. *Justice Accused: Antislavery and the Judicial Process.* New Haven, 1975.
Cox, John H. and LaWanda Cox. *Politics, Principles, and Prejudice, 1865–1866: The Dilemma of Reconstruction America.* New York, 1963.
Crawford, Mary C. *Romantic Days in Old Boston.* Boston, 1922.

Curtis, George W. *A Memorial of Wendell Phillips from the City of Boston.* Boston, 1884.

Daniels, John. *In Freedom's Birthplace.* Boston, 1914.

Davis, David B. *The Problem of Slavery in the Age of Revolution, 1770–1823.* New Haven, 1974.

Dawley, Alan. *Class and Community: The Industrial Revolution in Lynn, Massachusetts.* Cambridge, Mass., 1976.

Dillon, Merton. *The Abolitionists: The Growth of a Dissenting Minority.* De Kalb, Ill., 1974.

———. *Elijah Lovejoy, Abolitionist Editor.* Urbana, 1961.

Donald, David. *Charles Sumner and the Coming of the Civil War.* New York, 1960.

———. *Charles Sumner and the Rights of Man.* New York, 1970.

Duberman, Martin L. *The Antislavery Vanguard: New Essays on the Abolitionists.* Princeton, 1965.

DuBois, Ellen. *Feminism and Suffrage: The Emergence of an Independent Woman's Rights Movement in America.* Ithaca, 1978.

Edelstein, Tilden. *Strange Enthusiasm: A Life of Thomas Wentworth Higginson.* New York, 1970.

Faler, Paul. *Mechanics and Manufacturers in the Early Industrial Revolution: Lynn, Massachusetts, 1780–1860.* Albany, 1981.

Fisher, David Hackett. *The Revolution in American Conservatism.* New York, 1965.

Foner, Eric. *Free Soil, Free Labor, Free Men: The Ideology of the Republican Party Before the Civil War.* New York, 1970.

———. *Tom Paine and Revolutionary America.* New York, 1976.

Forgie, George B. *Patricide in the House Divided: A Psychoanalytic Interpretation of Lincoln and His Age.* New York, 1980.

Fredrickson, George M. *The Black Image in the White Mind: The Debate on Afro-American Character and Destiny.* New York, 1971.

Friedman, Lawrence J. *Gregarious Saints: Self and Community in American Abolitionism, 1830–1870.* New York, 1982.

———. *Inventors of the Promised Land.* New York, 1975.

Garrison, Francis Jackson. *Ann Phillips, Wife of Wendell Phillips: A Memorial Sketch.* Boston, 1886.

Garrison, Francis Jackson, and Wendell Phillips Garrison. *William Lloyd Garrison, 1805–1879.* 4 vols. New York, 1885–89.

Gatell, Frank D. *John Gorham Palfrey and the New England Conscience.* Cambridge, Mass., 1965.

Goffman, Erving. *Forms of Talk.* Glencoe, Ill., 1981.

Gouldner, Alvin W. *The Dialectic of Ideology and Technology: The Origins, Grammar and Future of Ideology.* New York, 1976.

Greven, Phillip. *The Protestant Temperament: Patterns of Childrearing, Religious Experience, and the Self in Early America.* New York, 1977.

Grimke, Archibald F. *Wendell Phillips: A Memorial.* Boston, 1884.

Handlin, Oscar. *Boston's Immigrants.* Boston, 1959.

Hersh, Blanche G. *The Slavery of Sex: Feminist Abolitionists in America.* Urbana, 1978.

Hewitt, Nancy. *Women's Activism and Social Change: Rochester, New York, 1822–1872.* Ithaca, 1984.

Higginson, Thomas Wentworth. *Cheerful Yesterdays.* Boston, 1896.

———. *Wendell Phillips.* Boston, 1884.

Holt, Michael F. *The Political Crisis of the 1850s.* New York, 1978.

Horton, James Oliver, and Lois E. Horton. *Black Bostonians: Black Life and Community Struggle in the Antebellum North.* New York, 1979.

Howe, Daniel Walker. *The Political Culture of the American Whigs.* New York, 1978.

Jameson, J. Franklin, ed. *The Correspondence of John C. Calhoun.* Vol. II of the *Annual Report of the American Historical Association, 1899.* Washington, D.C., 1900.

Johnson, Paul. *Shopkeepers' Millennium: Society and Revivals in Rochester, New York.* New York, 1978.

Jones, Jesse H., ed. *Wendell Phillips' Last Battle and One of His Greatest Victories, Being the Speech of Wendell Phillips in Faneuil Hall on the Louisiana Difficulties.* Boston, 1897.

Kirker, Harold, and James Kirker. *Bulfinch's Boston, 1787–1817.* Boston, 1964.

Korngold, Ralph. *Two Friends of Man: The Story of William Lloyd Garrison and Wendell Phillips and Their Relationship with Abraham Lincoln.* Boston, 1950.

Kraditor, Aileen. *Means and Ends in American Abolition: Garrison and His Critics on Strategy and Tactics, 1834–1850.* New York, 1969.

Lane, Roger. *Policing the City: Boston, 1822–1885.* Boston, 1967.

Lynd, Staughton. *The Intellectual Origins of American Radicalism.* New York, 1968.

Mabee, Carleton. *Black Freedom: The Nonviolent Abolitionists from 1830 Through the Civil War.* New York, 1970.

McKivigan, John R. *The War Against Proslavery Religion: Abolitionism and the Northern Churches, 1830–1865.* Ithaca, 1984.

McPherson, James M. *The Abolitionist Legacy: From Reconstruction to the NAACP.* Princeton, 1975.

———. *The Struggle for Equality: The Abolitionists and the Negro During the Civil War and Reconstruction.* Princeton, 1964.

Maier, Pauline. *From Resistance to Revolution.* New York, 1972.

Marshall, Jessie A., ed. *The Private and Official Correspondence of General Benjamin F. Butler During the Period of the Civil War.* 5 vols. Norwood, Mass., 1917.

Martyn, Carlos. *Wendell Phillips: The Agitator.* New York, 1890.

May, Samuel J. *Some Recollections of Our Antislavery Conflict.* Boston, 1869.

Mayfield, John. *The New Nation.* New York, 1982.

Merrill, Walter, ed. *I Will Be Heard! 1822–1835.* Cambridge, Mass., 1970. Vol. 1 of *The Letters of William Lloyd Garrison.* 5 vols.

Montgomery, David. *Beyond Equality: Labor and the Radical Republicans, 1862–1872.* New York, 1967.

Morison, Eliot. *Harrison Gray Otis, 1765–1848: Urbane Federalist.* Boston, 1969.

Morris, Thomas D. *Free Men All: The Personal Liberty Laws of the North, 1780–1861.* Baltimore, 1974.

Nye, Russel B. *Fettered Freedom: Civil Liberties and the Slavery Controversy.* Ann Arbor, 1949.

———. *Society and Culture in America, 1800–1860.* New York, 1974.

O'Connor, Thomas. *Lords of the Loom: The Cotton Whigs and the Coming of the Civil War.* New York, 1968.

Palfrey, John Gorham. *A Sermon Preached . . . on the Late Hon. John Phillips.* Boston, 1823.

Pease, William H., and Jane H. Pease. *Bound with Them in Chains: A Biographical History of the Antislavery Movement.* Westport, Conn., 1972.

———. *They Who Would Be Free: The Black Search for Freedom, 1830–1861.* New York, 1974.

Perry, Lewis. *Childhood, Marriage, and Reform: Henry C. Wright.* Chicago, 1980.

———. *Radical Abolitionism: Anarchy and the Government of God in Antislavery Thought.* Ithaca, 1973.

Perry, Lewis, and Michael Fellman, eds. *Antislavery Reconsidered: New Perspectives on the Abolitionists.* Baton Rouge, 1979.

Phillips, Wendell. *Address at the Salisbury Beach Gathering. . . .* Boston, 1871.

———. *Address to the Mass Meeting of Working Men in Faneuil Hall, November 2, 1865.* Boston, 1865.

———. *Can an Abolitionist Vote or Hold Office Under the United States Constitution?* New York, 1845.

———. *The Constitution, a Proslavery Document; or, Selections from the Madison Papers.* New York, 1844.

———. *"The Foundation of the Labor Movement": A Speech Delivered . . . October 13, 1871.* Boston, 1871.

————. *"The Immediate Issue": A Speech Delivered at the Annual Meeting of the Massachusetts Anti-Slavery Society*. Boston, 1865.

————. *"The Laws of the Commonwealth: Shall They Be Enforced?" A Speech Before the Massachusetts Legislative Committee*. Boston, 1865.

————. *No Slave-Hunting in the Old Bay State*. Boston, 1859.

————. *Review of Lysander Spooner's Essay on the Unconstitutionality of Slavery*. . . . Boston, 1847.

————. *Speeches, Lectures, and Letters*. Boston, 1863.

————. *Speeches, Lectures, and Letters: Second Series*. Boston, 1891.

————. *Who Shall Rule Us? Money or the People?* Boston, 1878.

Phillips, William P. *The Freedom Speech of Wendell Phillips*. Boston, 1890.

Pillsbury, Parker. *Acts of the Anti-Slavery Apostles*. Boston, 1869.

Powell, Aaron. *Personal Reminiscences of the Anti-Slavery and Other Reforms and Reformers*. Plainfield, N.J., 1899.

Proceedings of the American Anti-Slavery Society at Its Third Decade Meeting. . . . New York, 1864.

Proceedings of the Seventh Annual Meeting of the Massachusetts Anti-Slavery Society. Boston, 1838.

Quarles, Benjamin, ed. *Blacks on John Brown*. Champaign-Urbana, 1972.

Rogin, Michael. *Fathers and Children: Andrew Jackson and the Subjugation of the American Indian*. New York, 1975.

Rossbach, Jeffrey. *John Brown, the Secret Six, and a Theory of Slave Violence*. Philadelphia, 1982.

Ruchames, Louis, ed. *A House Dividing Against Itself, 1836–1840*. Cambridge, 1971. Vol. II of *The Letters of William Lloyd Garrison*. 5 vols.

Salvatore, Nick. *Eugene V. Debs: Citizen and Socialist*. Champaign, 1983.

Sargent, Mary. *Sketches and Reminiscences of the Radical Club of Chestnut Street*. Boston, 1880.

Sears, Lorenzo. *Wendell Phillips: Orator and Agitator*. New York, 1909.

Sewell, Richard H. *Ballots for Freedom: Antislavery Politics, 1837–1861*. New York, 1976.

Slotkin, Richard. *The Fatal Environment: The Myth of the Frontier in the Age of Industrialization, 1800–1890*. New York, 1985.

Smalley, George W. *Anglo-American Memories*. London, 1911.

Sproat, John G. *"The Best Men": Liberal Reformers in the Gilded Age*. New York, 1969.

Stearns, Frank P. *The Life and Public Services of George Luther Stearns*. Philadelphia, 1907.

Stewart, James Brewer. *Holy Warriors: The Abolitionists and American Slavery*. New York, 1976.

————. *Joshua R. Giddings and the Tactics of Radical Politics*. Cleveland, 1970.

Story, Roland. *The Forging of an Aristocracy: Harvard and the Boston Upper Class, 1800–1870.* Middletown, Conn., 1980.

Sutherland, Arthur E. *The Law at Harvard: A History of Men and Ideas, 1817–1967.* Cambridge, Mass., 1967.

Taylor, Claire, ed. *British and American Abolitionists: An Episode in Transatlantic Understanding.* Edinburgh, 1974.

Thomas, John L. *Alternative America: Henry George, Edward Bellamy, Henry Demarest Lloyd and the Adversary Tradition.* Cambridge, Mass., 1983.

————. *The Liberator, William Lloyd Garrison: A Biography.* Boston, 1963.

Trefousse, Hans L. *Ben Butler: The South Called Him "Beast".* New York, 1957.

————. *The Radical Republicans: Lincoln's Vanguard for Radical Justice.* New York, 1974.

Walker, Peter. *Moral Choices: Memory and Desire in Nineteenth-Century American Abolition.* Baton Rouge, 1978.

Walters, Ronald. *The Antislavery Appeal: American Abolitionism After 1830.* Baltimore, 1976.

Wiecek, William. *Sources of Antislavery Constitutionalism in America.* Ithaca, 1977.

Wilentz, Sean. *Chants Democratic: New York City and the Rise of the American Working Class, 1788–1850* New York, 1984.

Wilson, Major L. *Space, Time, and Freedom: The Quest For Nationality and the Irrepressible Conflict, 1815–1861.* Westport, Conn., 1974.

Wood, Gordon. *The Creation of the American Republic, 1776–1787.* Chapel Hill, 1969.

Woodward, C. Vann. *The Burden of Southern History.* Baton Rouge, 1960.

Wyatt-Brown, Bertram. *Lewis Tappan and the Evangelical War Against Slavery.* Cleveland, 1969.

————. *Southern Honor: Ethics and Behavior in the Antebellum South.* New York, 1982.

Wyman, Lillie Buffum Chace. *American Chivalry.* Boston, 1913.

Wyman, Lillie Buffum Chace, and Arthur Wyman. *Elizabeth Buffum Chace.* 2 vols. Boston, 1914.

ARTICLES AND DISSERTATIONS

Appleton, Thomas. "Old Boston." In his *A Sheaf of Papers.* Boston, 1875, pp. 143–67.

Bartlett, Irving. "New Light on Wendell Phillips and the Community of Reform, 1840–1880." *Perspectives in American History,* XII (Cambridge, 1979), 3–251.

Bruce, Roscoe Conkling. "The College Career of Wendell Phillips." *Harvard Illustrated Magazine*, XVII (April, 1901), 170–86.

Cayton, Andrew R. L. "The Fragmentation of 'A Great Family': The Panic of 1819 and the Rise of the Middling Interest in Boston." *Journal of the Early Republic*, IV (June, 1982), 143–67.

Curry, Richard D. "The Abolitionists and Reconstruction: A Critical Appraisal." *Journal of Southern History*, XXXIV (November, 1968), 516–37.

Demos, John P. "The Antislavery Movement and the Problem of 'Violent Means.'" *New England Quarterly*, XXXVI (December, 1964), 501–26.

Foner, Eric. "Abolitionists and the Labor Movement in Antebellum America." In *Antislavery, Religion, and Reform: Essays in Memory of Roger Anstey*, edited by Christine Bolt and Seymour Dresher. Folkstone, Eng., 1980.

Gamble, Douglas A. "Joshua Giddings and the Ohio Abolitionists: A Study in Radical Politics." *Ohio History*, XXIX (November, 1979), 36–56.

Haskell, Thomas L. "Capitalism and the Origins of Humanitarian Sensibility: Part 1." *American Historical Review*, XC (April, 1985), 339–61.

Hinton, Richard J. "Wendell Phillips: A Reminiscent Study." *Arena* (July, 1895), 220–35.

Hofstadter, Richard. "Wendell Phillips: The Patrician as Agitator." In his *The American Political Tradition and the Men Who Made It*. New York, 1948.

Huston, James L. "Facing Angry Labor: The American Public Interprets the Shoemakers' Strike of 1860." *Civil War History*, XXVII (September, 1982), 198–212.

Jenz, John B. "The Antislavery Constituency in New York City." *Civil War History*, XXVII (June, 1981), 101–22.

Johnson, Reinhard D. "The Liberty Party in Massachusetts, 1840–1848: Antislavery Third Party Politics in the Bay State." *Civil War History*, XXVII (September, 1982), 236–65.

Kenyon, Cecelia. "Radicalism and Republicanism in the American Revolution; An Old-Fashioned Interpretation." *William and Mary Quarterly*, 3rd ser., XIX (Aril, 1962), 153–82.

Lewis, Eleanor, ed. "Letters of Wendell Phillips to Lydia Maria Child." *New England Quarterly*, V (June, 1892), 115–40.

Livermore, Mary. "Does the Ideal Husband Exist?" *North American Review* (February, 1896).

Marcus, Robert D. "Wendell Phillips and American Institutions." *Journal of American History*. LVI (June, 1969), 39–56.

"Memoir of John Phillips." *Boston Monthly Magazine* (November, 1825), 281–92.

Osofsky, Gilbert. "Abolitionists, Irish Immigrants, and the Dilemma of Romantic Nationalism." *American Historical Review*, LXXIX (June, 1975), 889–912.

Pease, Jane H., and William H. Pease. "Confrontation and Abolition in the 1850's." *Journal of American History*, LVII (March, 1972), 923–37.

Phillips, Wendell. "The Other Side of the Woman Question." *North American Review* (November, 1879).

———. "The Outlook." *North American Review* (July-August, 1878).

———. "The Outlook." *North American Review* (March, 1879).

———. "The Outlook." *North American Review* (July, 1879).

———. "The Outlook." *North American Review* (September, 1879).

———. "A Review of Dr. Crosby's 'Calm View of Temperance.'" *North American Review* (June, 1879).

———. "William Lloyd Garrison." *North American Review* (August, 1879).

Reynolds, Donald O. "The New Orleans Riot Reconsidered." *Louisiana History*, XXV (December, 1964), 3–18.

Scott, Donald M. "The Popular Lecture and the Creation of a Public in Mid-Nineteenth Century America." *Journal of American History*, LXVI (March, 1980), 791–809.

———. "Print and the Public Lecture." *Printing and Society in Early America*, edited by William L. Joyce *et al.* Worcester, Mass., 1983, pp. 278–99.

Shalhope, Robert. "Republicanism in Early American History." *William and Mary Quarterly*, 3rd ser., XXXIX (February, 1982), 334–56.

Smalley, George. "Memoir of Wendell Phillips." *Harper's Magazine* (June, 1894), 133–41.

Sparks, Robert V. "Abolition in Silver Slippers: A Biography of Edmund Quincy." Ph.D. dissertation, Boston University, 1978.

Stewart, James Brewer. "The Aims and Impact of Garrisonian Abolitionism, 1840–1860." *Civil War History*, XV (September, 1969), 198–209.

———. "Garrison Again and Again and Again," *Reviews in American History*, IV (December, 1976), 539–45.

———. "Young Turks and Old Turkeys: Abolitionists, Historians, and Aging Processes." *Reviews in American History*, XI (June, 1983), 226–32.

Takaki, Ronald. "The Black Child-Savage in Antebellum America." In *The Great Fear: Race and the Mind in America*, edited by Gary B. Nash and Richard Weiss. New York, 1970.

Thomas, John L. "Antislavery and Utopia." In *The Antislavery Vanguard: New Essays on the Abolitionists*, edited by Martin Duberman. Princeton, 1965.

Villard, Oswald Garrison. "Wendell Phillips After Fifty Years." *American Mercury* (January, 1935), 89–99.

Willentz, Sean. "On Class and Power in Jacksonian America." *Reviews in American History*, X (December, 1982), 45–63.

Wyatt-Brown, Bertram. "William Lloyd Garrison and Antislavery Unity: A Reappraisal." *Civil War History*, XIII (March, 1967), 5–24.

Wyman, Lillie Buffum Chace. "Reminiscence of Wendell Phillips." *New England Magazine* (February, 1903), 715–36.

Index